E-Governance

A Comprehensive Framework

E-Governance

A Comprehensive Framework

- *Business Process Reengineering (BPR)*
- *Change Management*
- *Organisational Development*

By
D.N. Gupta

Institute of Social Sciences
New Delhi

in association with

NEW CENTURY PUBLICATIONS
NEW DELHI, INDIA

NEW CENTURY PUBLICATIONS
4800/24, Bharat Ram Road,
Ansari Road, Daryaganj,
New Delhi - 110 002 (India)

Tel.: 011 – 2324 7798, 4358 7398, 6539 6605
Fax: 011 – 4101 7798
E-mail: indiatax@vsnl.com
www.newcenturypublications.com

Editorial office:
34, Gujranwala Town, Part-2,
Delhi - 110 009

Tel.: 27247805, 27464774

First Published – **2008**

Reprint: **2022**

ISBN: **978-81-7708-169-5**

Published by New Century Publications and printed at Salasar Imaging Systems, New Delhi

Cover Design: W & P Graphics Pvt. Ltd., New Delhi

PRINTED IN INDIA

To my son Amit

About the Book

The book draws on the diagnostic study of E-Governance projects in India, carried out with an objective to capture the inter-dependence of technology (IT), people (functionaries), processes and systems. The study employed a combination of participatory and management tools and techniques. Through in-depth analysis and academic rigour, the book covers the following vital aspects of E-Governance:

- Business Process Reengineering (BPR) and change management,
- Strategy formulation, and
- Citizen-centric E-Governance system design.

The book emphasises that the success of E-Governance initiatives hinges on institutional changes and not only on introduction of IT, and it requires a coherent integration of IT, people and the processes.

The National e-Governance Plan (NeGP) in India has provided a big platform for scaling up initiatives under E-Governance across the country. It offers big opportunity for the Government to transform its functioning. Though there have been a number of successful pilot projects under E-Governance in the country, a complete roll out will require successful handling of complex issues of system design – process reengineering, work culture management, capabilities, organisational development, citizens' aspirations and so on.

The book provides invaluable insights about E-Governance system design and management, and will contribute significantly for operationalising NeGP.

About the Author

D.N. Gupta, B.E. (Mechanical Engineering) joined the Indian Administrative Service (IAS) in 1989. He has been closely associated with development, planning and implementation of various social and rural development programmes.

He has worked in various capacities in the Departments of Revenue, Textiles and Tribal Welfare, Government of Orissa. He was also Deputy Secretary, Ministry of Rural Development, Government of India (1999-2002). He specialises in development administration, E-Governance and quality in public services. He has written numerous books and articles on development issues and more specifically on rural development system, integrated development planning and decentralisation.

He is a Fellow, Institute of Social Sciences (ISS), New Delhi, handling areas of e-Governance, GIS and decentralised planning.

Institute of Social Sciences

8, Nelson Mandela Road, New Delhi - 110 070

www.issin.org

Institute of Social Sciences (ISS) is dedicated to systematic study of social issues and problems that confront India, in trans-disciplinary perspective. Its objectives are to study contemporary social, political and economic issues and problems with an inter-disciplinary perspective and to make its findings and recommendations available to the government bodies, civil society organizations, policy makers, social scientists and all concerned citizens, so as to widen their options for action. The evolution of an informed and action-oriented public opinion is its primary aim.

Foreword

E-governance offers vast opportunity for transforming governance in general and improving capacities of government in particular in empowering citizens and providing services efficiently. The National e-Governance Programme in India has provided an important platform for scaling up initiatives under e-Governance across the country. It offers an opportunity for the government to re-engineer processes. Though there have been a number of successful initiatives in different States in e-Governance in the country, a complete roll out will require successful handling of several complex issues.

The book draws on the diagnostic study undertaken to capture the inter-dependencies of technology (IT), people, processes and systems. For this purpose, the study of performance of some e-Governance projects viz., *Janmitra*, *e-Bhoomi* and *RDS* in Karnataka, *Gyandoot* in Madhya Pradesh and OLTP in Andhra Pradesh, was undertaken. The study has specifically looked at the measures that are necessary to strengthen E-Governance systems and to provide good governance to citizens.

Some very critical findings have been reflected in the study. It expresses concerns about the poor service standards and lack of usage of e-Kiosks for e-Governance services. As e-Governance projects are usually complex, people-oriented and have long gestation period, the book stresses that along with technology, what is required is to align human resource skills, competencies and work culture with the transformation process. It calls for a calibrated shift from discussions on systems and processes to that of leadership. team building, incentives, civil service reforms, and creation of a citizen-oriented organisation.

The study has also emphasised the factors that affect the ability of an E-Governance project to perform and grow in a sustained way. It highlights the need to take strategic decisions by integrating internal and external factors in the solution matrix, and to design systems by anticipating citizens' requirements that will lead to improved preparedness for meeting unexpected internal and external demands.

The book will lend balance to the e-Governance debate. It strongly emphasises that the success of e-Governance initiatives hinges, apart from introduction of IT, on efficient institutions. Good governance means that the processes and institutions produce results that are consistent, reliable and meet the desired standards. In the context of delivery of services, the quality of services has to be the touchstone of good governance which includes information sharing with citizens and their empowerment and participation in the decision-making process. It also calls for a paradigm shift from the traditional way. Successful e-Governance initiatives require coherent integration of IT and delivery institutions. The behavioural issues like leadership, work culture, attitudes, motivation, commitment and teamwork play vital role in building organisations, and developing effective delivery systems.

This is a very valuable addition to the growing literature on e-Governance in India. I congratulate the author for having done an excellent job.

(B.K. Chaturvedi)
former Cabinet Secretary,
Member, Planning Commission
Government of India

PREFACE

"For the e-Governance initiatives to be successful, it requires coherent integration of IT and delivery institutions - the scale of success is immense".

E-Governance is a fast emerging area in India. By bringing government closer to citizens, it offers large opportunities to citizens in the villages to avail various services. It can be immensely helpful in online monitoring, transparency, accountability, people's participation in governance and bridging geographical divide.

A diagnostic study was undertaken to capture the inter-dependence of technology (IT), people (functionaries), processes and systems. For this purpose, the performance of one e-Governance project in Jaipur, Rajasthan in particular and case studies of *Janmitra* and *Lokmitra* projects in Rajasthan, *e-Bhoomi* and RDS in Karnataka, *Gyandoot* in Madhya Pradesh and OLTP in Andhra Pradesh were undertaken. The study had a specific focus on the following:

- How E-Governance has helped citizens in accessing the services?
- Whether the delivery system has adequate capacity to deliver services efficiently?
- Measures that are necessary to strengthen e-Governance system and to provide good governance to citizens.

The study has covered four aspects viz. (a) services delivery, (b) performance of e-Kiosk owner, (c) performance of service provider (e-Governance) and (d) delivery system (tehsil, primary education, health, agriculture, animal husbandry etc.).

The study applied combination of participatory and management tools and techniques. The models and frameworks developed by the study, if applied appropriately, can facilitate effective system design for e-Governance projects.

The present book covers issues concerning policies, strategies, and management of implementation of e-Governance projects.

Significant findings of the study are as under:

1. E-governance has limitations, and the real benefit to citizens can be realised when the delivery system for various services is rightly placed. While going for E-Governance, efforts were made to provide hardware, software and network, but little consideration was given to improve the capacity of existing delivery system to deliver efficiently. Though IT is vital and a big enabler, the

inputs for delivering services have to come from the delivery system (concerned service department).

2. Behavioural dimension is as important as process of service delivery or technological intervention. The neglect of this dimension has been impacting and will continue to impact adversely on the efforts under e-Governance.

3. The study has brought to the fore that the issues of good governance like efficiency of service delivery, empowerment of citizens, transparency, accountability have not been addressed. It is mainly due to two factors: *first*, lack of emphasis on 'good governance' at the system design stage, and *second*, lack of appreciation about quality issues in service delivery.

4. Some of the vital performance indicators listed below do not speak good about the service delivery under e-Governance projects:
   - Poor service standards
     - Quantitative indicators like cost and time for availing services through e-Kiosk have not been to the satisfaction of citizens
     - Qualitative indicators like responsiveness and reliability have not improved
   - Lack of usage
     - Less than 2 per cent of Tehsil services are accessed in a year through E-Kiosk
     - Less than 1 per cent of families have accessed e-Governance services
   - Grievances redressal has been unsatisfactory
   - Information sharing with citizens on government programmes, panchayat plans etc. has been insignificant

5. In the backdrop of poor standards of service delivery and imperfect system design and preparation, there is an apprehension that e-Governance projects may end up as being beneficial only in a limited way: in creating IT infrastructure and in providing a few services like collection of utility bills or information on land certificate.

Way Ahead

- The book strongly emphasises that the success of e-Governance initiatives hinges more on making institutions efficient and subsequent introduction of IT. Good governance means that the processes and institutions produce results that are consistent, reliable and meet the desired standards. Regarding the delivery of services, quality has to be the touchstone of good governance.

- Specifically, the study stresses that improving performance of service delivery should be top priority. It will require business process reengineering (BPR) and backend computerization. Along side these efforts, the reliable and efficient network should be laid for connectivity between e-Kiosk and service departments.
- Also, it calls for a paradigm shift from a traditional way of working to a new mode of working with IT. The behavioural issues like leadership, work culture, attitudes, motivation, commitment and teamwork play vital role in building organisations and developing an effective delivery system.

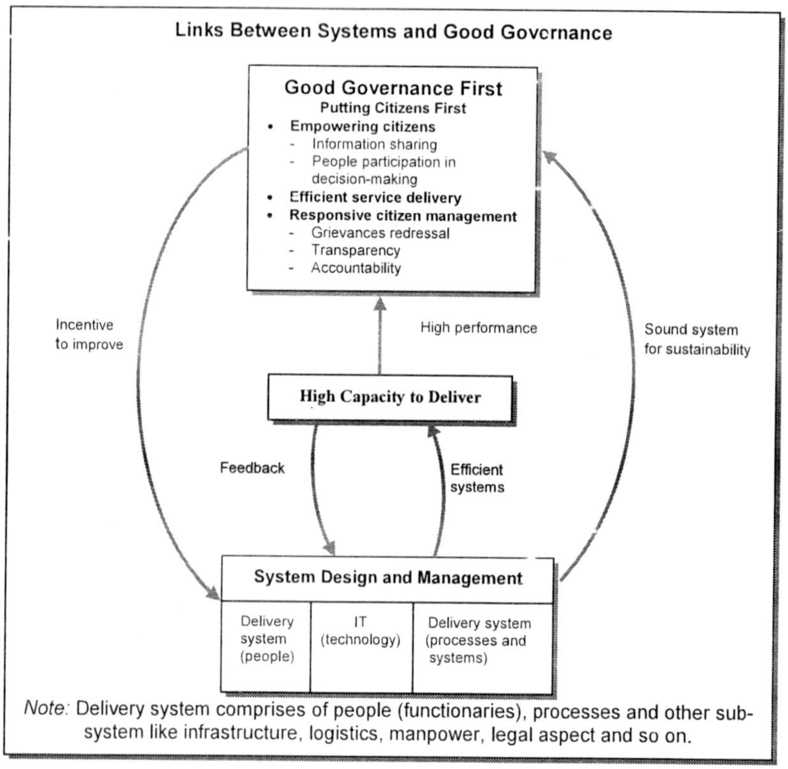

Finally, for good governance, the top priority has to be accorded to healthy work culture, developing capabilities, redesigning processes and systems to improve efficiency.

April 15, 2008
New Delhi

D.N. Gupta

ACKNOWLEDGEMENTS

The book is a product of in-depth research work. For conducting the research study, the ideas were shaped during consultations with administrators and professionals engaged in e-Governance projects. During the course of the work, the help and support was received from a good number of officials, experts, academicians, field officers and colleagues.

First and foremost, I am grateful to Shri. R. Chandrashekhar, IAS, Additional Secretary, Government of India, Ministry of Communications and Information Technology (MCIT), for providing inspirations for carrying out the study. I am thankful to Shri. S.R. Das, Senior Director, Mrs. Renu Budhiraja, Director, Mr. Ashis Sanyal, Director, and Ms. Kavita Bhatia, Joint Director, all of Ministry of Communications and Information Technology (MCIT), and Ms. Indu Gupta, State Director, NIC, Jaipur.

Special thanks are due to Shri Y.L. Agarwal, Managing Director, Aksh Broadband Limited, Shri Sanjay Gaden, RajComp and Shri R.K. Sharma, DOIT, Government of Rajasthan.

I thank Shri Sudhansh Pant, IAS, formerly District Collector, Jaipur, Shri Rajeshwar Singh, IAS, District Collector, Jaipur, Shri Rohit Singh, IAS, formerly Secretary, IT, Government of Rajasthan; and Shri Akhil Arora, IAS, Director, DOIT, Government of Rajasthan for their help and support during the study. I also thank NIC, Jaipur, RIPA, Jaipur, BGVS, Jaipur, and IIQM, Jaipur for their help and support.

I especially thank Professor Rajendra Prasad, Professor Sushil, Dr. V.K. Vijay, and Dr. M.P Gupta of IIT (Delhi); Professor Udai Pareek, formerly Professor IIM (Ahmedabad); Dr. Purnima Mathur, formerly Professor IIT (Delhi); Major General V.K. Khanna, Mr K.P. Thomas, Mr. S.S. Yadav and Dr. B.S. Nagi for their valuable inputs. I am indeed grateful to Dr. George Mathew, Director, ISS and Shri Sanker Sen, Senior Fellow, ISS for their support and inspiration.

I thank researchers Mr. Manish Kaduskar, Mr. Chintan Shivani, Mr. Sandip Chandak, Mr. Rajesh Kumar, Mr. Subhash Negi, Mr. Aloke Deb, Ms. Rakhsita Bhatala and Mr. Vimal Kumar who all contributed their best.

I would also like to thank Mr. Sandeep Sury of New Century Publications, New Delhi for meticulous planning and patience in bringing out this book.

D.N. Gupta

CONTENTS

LIST OF TABLES IN THE TEXT

LIST OF FIGURES IN THE TEXT

LIST OF BOXES IN THE TEXT

LIST OF STATISTICAL TABLES

LIST OF STATISTICAL FIGURES

LIST OF STATISTICAL BOXES

LIST OF ANNEXURES

LIST OF APPENDICES

ABBREVIATIONS

AF	Application Form
BEP	Breakeven Point
BPR	Business Process Reengineering
C&E	Cause and Effect
CTQs	Critical to Quality Characteristics
DEMAIC	Define, Measure, Analyse, Innovative Improvement, and Control
DF	Delivery Form
DOIT	Department of Information Technology
FMEA	Failure Modes and Effects Analysis
G to C	Government to Consumer
ICDS	Integrated Child Development Scheme
ICT	Information Communication Technology
ISS	Institute of Social Sciences
IT	Information Technology
MCIT	Ministry of Communication and Information Technology
MIS	Management Information System
MOC	Matrix of Change
NISG	National Institute of Smart Government
OD	Organisational Development
OK	Office Kanungo
PHED	Public Health & Engineering Department
Rajcomp	Rajasthan Computers
ROR	Records of Rights
RPN	Risk Priority Number
SDM	Sub Divisional Magistrate
SERVQUAL	Service Quality

1

E-Governance: An Introduction

"...the best businesses in the world have given top priority to having healthy work culture, developing capabilities, redesigning processes and systems to improve efficiency. Only, after that they have successfully deployed technology to further enhance efficiency." (Collins, 2005)

1.1 Introduction

E-governance refers to the use of information and communication technologies (ICTs) to improve the efficiency, effectiveness, transparency and accountability of government. Traditionally, the interaction between a citizen or business and a government agency took place in a government office. With the emergence of ICTs, it is possible to locate service centres closer to the citizens (clients).

In India, e-Governance is an application area, where IT has made considerable progress and it offers vast potential to provide good governance. Under ICTs there are several projects (http://www.egovdatabase.gov.in) being run across the states in the country by various agencies in both public and private sectors. These projects are in the area of land management, transport, grievance handling, education, health and so on. IT can be immensely helpful in on-line monitoring, transparency, accountability, direct peoples' participation in governance, and contribution to bridging geographical divide. With the setting up of Kiosks at the village level, citizens can utilise them as *One Stop Shop* for availing basic services at the village level. The village level Kiosks provide scope for timely availability of services and access to vital information as may be needed on a routine basis.

1.1.1 What is e-Governance? E-governance is a use of information and communication technologies with the aim of improving information and service delivery (of government sector), encouraging citizen's participation in the decision-making process and making government more accountable, transparent and effective. Among others, e-Governance offers the advantages such as:

- empowerment through information sharing,
- involving people in decision-making,
- providing better service delivery,

- increasing transparency and
- reinforcing government credibility and accountability.

E-governance offers opportunities to transform both the mechanics of government and the nature of governance itself. It affects all government functions and agencies, the private sector, and the society in general. Needless to emphasize the application of IT in information and knowledge area, there is a great deal of possibility of its usage in providing good governance to people in remote places in rural areas.

It will change: the *style* – by electronic way of approaching, interacting with, and delivering services to citizens; the *stance* – by being more efficient, transparent, and accountable; and the *substance* – the information (and knowledge) that can be shared or the feedback that can be taken from citizens.

1.1.2 What is Good Governance? It means achieving the desired goals and delivering through a system of adequate capacity to perform with sound norms and values. Good governance is in essence about being able to provide equal socio-economic and political opportunities to people, being responsive to people's needs, being able to provide basic services to people, and being fair and accountable in dealings.

1.1.3 How to Judge Good Governance? In the context of present state of socio-economic development at the grassroots level, among others, the good governance will be determined by:

- when the citizens have access to information and their grievances are attended to by the local institutions,
- when the citizens have access to basic services in their local area, and
- when the citizens have opportunities for social, political and economic activities in the village?

According to OECD (2003), the prominent ingredients of good governance are effectiveness, efficiency and responsiveness. Good governance means that the processes and institutions produce results that are consistent, reliable and meet the desired standards. Also, it requires that institutions and processes are sensitive to the problems of people and try to serve all stakeholders within a reasonable timeframe.

1.1.4 What Should e-Governance Result into?

- *Better Information Sharing:* Information about local resources, guidelines of schemes, funds, on-going projects, etc. should be available to citizens in order to facilitate them to give their views to the government departments. It would be a first step towards *citizens'* participation in development process.

- *Quality Service Delivery:* The delivery of services to citizens' should conform to set standards.
- *Grievance Redressal:* The grievances should be redressed within a time limit.
- *Feedback:* Citizens should be in a position to give feedback to government departments / service provider about the services / information provided to them.
- *Involving People in Decision-making for Local Development:* Citizens should get the opportunities to participate in the decision-making processes of local development.
- *Transparency:* It should provide transparency in decision-making, and the citizens should have access to the reasons for the decisions taken.
- *Accountability:* It is essential for maintaining public confidence in governance, justifying and ensuring the overall legitimacy of the e-Governance system.

1.2 E-governance in India: Need of Comprehensive Study

The available literature has brought out categorically the limitations of technology and the importance of addressing other system issues like work culture, capabilities, process re-design and so on. Sometimes projects acquire technology without modifying their human resource practices, mistakenly assuming *technological determinism* – that technology's effects are independent of the organisational structure in which it is embedded. In several cases, the technology upgrade provided no significant productivity or quality improvements (Osterman, 1991). Despite investment of US$ 800 billion in the service sector in USA, there was a productivity loss of 6 per cent (Joe Peppard and Phillip Rowland, 2002). One of the many reasons why IT had failed to deliver its potential was that it had been applied to *old and existing ways of doing things*.

One of the key value eroding issues in using technologies is the assumption that technology is best managed by the technologists with an engineering perspective. There is little emphasis or even an appreciation of another perspective that technologies add value when managed better. A software application is not something created by a programmer. A programmer contributes to it by writing the codes. But it is in the overall conceptualising, designing, looking for the customer's perspective, rather than the doers and finally implementing in a way that the benefits are realised the way initially intended or along those lines that a software application becomes valuable.

Similarly, Collins (2005) has laid emphasis on people, values and system, and expressed that great companies first build a culture of discipline – disciplined people who engage in disciplined thought and who take disciplined action – and create a business model that fits squarely at the intersection of three circles: what they can be the best in the world at, a deep understanding of their system and the core values they hold with deep passion. They then use technology to enhance these pre-existing variables, never as a replacement.

The studies on e-Governance (Gupta, M P, *et al* 2004a, EPW, 2003, Gupta, 2002 and Girija, 2002) have expressed concern about lack of awareness and knowledge of the government processes with the IT professionals, and emphasised that most governments have not changed their processes in any way, and instead have automated the existing processes. Basically, a government web-site (with some information database, and a small facility to send application form for accessing a few services) has been provided at the e-Kiosk level. And there is a big gulf between a pretty web-site (at e-Kiosk in a village) and integrated service delivery. Also, there is a lack of system ownership and there are occasional problems of accountability due to involvement of many stakeholders (*see Box 1.1*).

In the delivery of services, there are other important issues that need to be understood and analysed. For instance the processes involved. Among others, the processes may involve indexing of application, verification, making enquiries, recording, etc. before the services are provided or grievances are redressed. Besides this, of importance are institutional factors involved in the delivery of services. For example, the capabilities (competence level) of personnel, work-culture – responsiveness, transparency in functioning, accountability of decision-makers, etc. are going to determine the efficiency and effectiveness of delivery of services.

The study was undertaken in the backdrop of critical issues related to people's needs, processes and institutions (of delivery of service). The brief description is made below:

- From the *people's perspective*, more often, the citizens lack access to information about government programmes. Even if they have, they do not have adequate knowledge of the guidelines and procedures for accessing services. Lack of access to information deprives them from availing various socio-economic opportunities. For example, people may not be aware about social security schemes, say, *personal insurance scheme* or *maternity benefit scheme*, which may benefit them significantly. In some other cases the guidelines for getting ration card or for availing loan are not within the reach of people. Similarly, information about immunisation, which may be critical for children or about current prices of various agricultural commodities that may be useful for disposing the surplus (from crops) and getting adequate returns, is not available with citizens. All these have far reaching consequence on their socio-economic life. Also, poor people's participation in development process and the inadequacy of feedback system to know the satisfaction level of people, add to the problems of meeting the desired standards of services.

Box 1.1: Some Important Observations about e-Governance

- An important area of concern is the gap of understanding about the government processes at the IT professionals level
- What is lacking is the induction of government process training to the IT professionals
- Lack of understanding of the software development cycle at the government functionary level
- There is a lack of system ownership and the IT professionals become the system owner
- Most e-Governance projects have not changed their processes in any way, and instead have automated flawed processes
- There is a big gulf between a pretty web site (at internet Kiosk in a village) and integrated service delivery
- Too much attention to *citizen portals* has taken attention away from internal government functioning
- Even in the best IT States (Andhra Pradesh, Karnataka), local e-Government solutions have not gained widespread adoption
- The most difficult issue is the change in mindset, from a traditional department-centric thinking to a customer-centric and user-friendly approach
- Citizen and business portals are organized around government departments and agencies, and not around citizen needs and goals

Source: Gupta, M P, et al 2004a; EPW, 2003; Gupta, 2002 and Girija, 2002

- *Process part*: Studies (EPW, 2003, Gupta, 2002 and Girija, 2002) have indicated that while making efforts under e-Governance, the processes have not been changed, and instead the existing processes – which have several deficiencies (*see Box 1.2*) – have been automated. The internal government functioning has not been adequately studied. There is a lack of awareness and knowledge of the government processes with the IT system managers. Mostly the departments have been computerising the processes, core or secondary as it is, without doing a careful process re-design to meet IT requirements. The processes are un-structured and non-standardised, and are not institutionalised. There is a wide gap between a web site (at internet Kiosk in a village) and integrated service delivery. Due to inefficient processes in delivery of services, quite often, the lead time in making services available to people remains high.

Box 1.2: Factors Affecting and Questions Concerning e-Governance

Important Factors

A. Process-oriented

Processes are:

- Long and cumbersome
- Unstructured
- Non-standard
- Not institutionalised

B. Work Culture

It is marked with:

- Lack of responsiveness
- Inability to work with people
- Lack of appreciation for quality work
- Insensitivity to timeliness of delivery of services

C. Other Factors

- Lack of capabilities in functionaries
- Inadequacy of information system
- Inadequate networking among departments and institutions
- Lack of monitoring and feedback system

Important Questions

- How do the personnel in the departments respond to people's problems?
- Whether they have adequate capabilities?
- What is their efficiency level?
- Whether the processes are user-friendly?
- Whether the processes need changes due to change of time?
- Whether the processes are IT compatible?
- Whether people have access to information?
- Whether people can participate in the decision-making process?

Source: EPW, 2003; Gupta 2002 and Girija, 2002.

- From the *institutional* point of view, the available literature (EPW, 2003 and Gupta, 2002) has brought out evidently the problems such as: personnel are not sensitised about responsiveness to people's grievances and timeliness of providing services. They also lack adequate knowledge and skills to perform their duties efficiently. Also of importance is teamwork that is often missing, which hampers coordination and delays the processing of applications. The monitoring system is not rightly placed in order to take corrective measures from time to time. Finally, the work culture is not tuned to meeting the demands of people in time and with quality.

Finally, the above discussion prompts us to ask two questions like: *first*, whether the processes are simplified and synchronised with IT. And, *second*, whether the delivery departments have enough institutional capacity to meet the challenge of good governance?

1.2.1 Hype Cycle Model: Studies have indicated that there has been initial enthusiasm due to high expectations (Linden and Finn, 2002), but soon it evaporates with the problems that start surfacing. It leads to disillusionment, and with increasing realisation, appropriate actions are required. It is explained by *hype cycle model* (Figure 1.1). The purpose of this cycle is to caution the managers and administrators to take prior care while designing the new system (in this case e-Governance).

Figure: 1.1: Hype Cycle Model

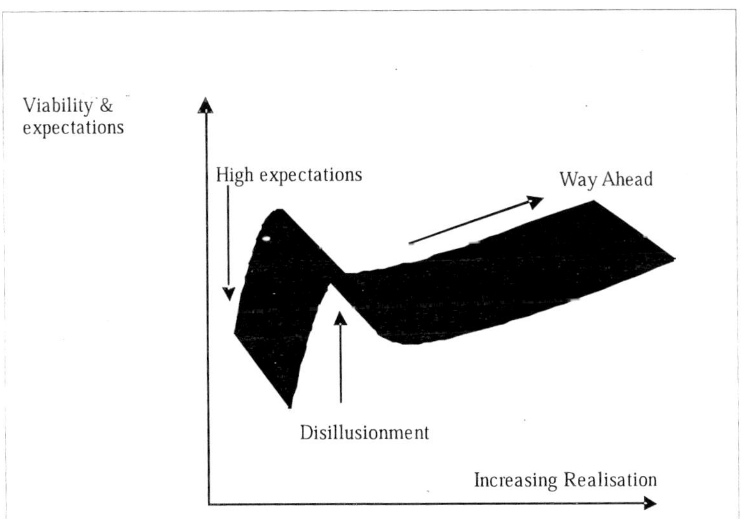

1.2.2 Framework for Innovations: The design of new system should follow certain steps in order to have clear roadmap ahead. It requires having a framework for innovations (Figure 1.2). It begins analysing the problems and learning from there (e.g. about service delivery requirements, system problems, etc.), then generating possible alternatives and selecting that are possible, experimenting with new ideas (incubating) (e.g. BPR, backend computerisation, etc.) and validating them, and finally replicating and scaling up (successful interventions). This cycle helps in sequencing the interventions and making corrections, and finally coming out with the right system design.

Figure 1.2: Framework for Innovations

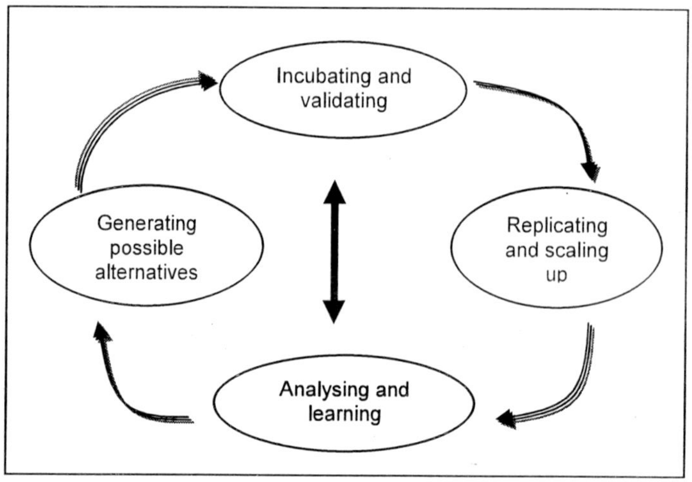

2

E-Governance: Evaluation Framework

"The potential of IT is not so much in question, but: first, whether the delivery systems engaged in service delivery have enough institutional capacity to meet the challenge of good governance; and second, whether the processes are simplified and synchronised with IT. The relevant issues require to be diagnosed with appropriate tools and techniques to come to definite conclusions"

2.1 Objectives

In all the states in the country, several good attempts have been made to start e-Governance projects. These have made significant contribution for providing interface to citizens sitting in their locality or villages and get a few services from e-Kiosks. In the process, a few successful models have emerged, especially in the areas of land records management in tehsil and collection of utility bills in the urban areas. In spite of such efforts, still, there remain areas of concerns (EPW, 2003; Gupta, 2002 and Girija, 2002) affecting the performance of e-Governance. Among others, prominent areas are: long & cumbersome processes to provide services, lack of citizen-centric approach, inadequate capacity of delivery system to deliver, and lack of responsive work culture.

In the study the attempt was made to diagnose the performance of one e-Governance project in Jaipur district of Rajasthan in particular {and to develop case studies of Janmitra and Lokmitra projects (in Rajasthan), e-Bhoomi (in Karnataka), Gyandoot (in Madhya Pradesh) and OLTP (in Andhra Pradesh), with a specific focus on the following:

- How e-Governance has helped citizens in accessing the services? The specific issues examined included:
  - Processes involved in the delivery of services
  - Whether processes are IT compatible
- Whether the delivery system has adequate capacity to deliver services efficiently? The specific issues examined included:
  - Infrastructure, manpower and logistics under delivery mechanism
  - Work culture
  - Transparency and accountability
  - Customer (citizen) management

- Measures those are necessary to strengthen e-Governance system and to provide good governance to citizens

The objectives of the study are outlined below:

2.1.1 Long-term Objectives

- Integration of 'Information Technology' with 'Service Processes', 'Organisational Development', 'Information Database', and 'Network of development agencies'
- To improve the Organisational Effectiveness for efficient Delivery of Services in order to improve the Quality of Governance

2.1.2 Specific Objectives: Diagnostic / System Study

- Identification of grievances and their redressal mechanism
- To diagnose the delivery system engaged in basic services
- To identify the information needs of citizens
- To identify the MIS requirement for enabling people to access the information for business, learning and participation in the development process (planning and implementation)
- To provide framework for process reengineering and organisational development (OD), and for introducing interventions for effective and efficient delivery of services

2.2 Methodology

2.2.1 Process Approach: The methodology of research followed process approach. This approach involves a cyclic process of assessment, analysis, interventions, feedback and modifications. Under the study, DMAIC (Define, Measure, Analyse, Innovative improvement, Control) tool has been applied for the diagnostic study, and later it would be applied for improvements of system. It has five stages. *First*, define, it includes identifying the customer (citizen) and defining the problem; *second*, measure, it includes study of organisation, and measuring the processes and organisational behaviour; *third*, to analyse the system; *fourth*, innovative improvement, introducing interventions for improving organisational effectiveness; and, *finally*, control, it includes developing feedback and control system, and taking corrective action.

2.2.2 Diagnostic Study:

Study for Delivery of Services: It included the study of, *first*, processes (for the services given); and, *second*, components of organisation – organisational behaviour, support system (infrastructure, logistics, etc.), and rules and legal system.

Steps in Diagnostic Study: It included the following steps:

Step 1: Define: Identification of departments and the services to be provided by each department; and identification of information, services and grievances requirements of citizens.

Step 2: Measure: Studying the delivery system. Salient methods are as follows:

- Process mapping of delivery of services (certificates issued by Tehsil) and grievances handling. Identification of measurable qualitative and quantitative indicators
- Data collection: Data collection was done through primary as well as secondary sources. The primary data collection was attempted through focused group discussions (FGDs), field survey at the village level, and interviews with personnel of service delivery departments. For this, questionnaires were also developed (specific details given below in field survey). The secondary data was taken from the available records of the departments. Together with this, case studies were prepared to illustrate some specific shortcomings.
- Study of organisational behaviour: It included organisational culture, roles and responsibilities, motivation, capabilities, leadership and teamwork. The management tools, non-participant observations and focused group discussions were the tools utilised for the purpose of study.
- Study of delivery system: Study of delivery of system viz., Tehsil, Primary Education, Health, Agriculture, Animal Husbandry, Drinking Water, ICDS, Panchayat. Specific issues related to infrastructure, manpower, logistics, work culture, etc. were studied.

Step 3: Analysis: It included process analysis and working out cause-effect (CE) matrix. Also, it would identify the areas where maximum improvement is needed.

Finally, diagnostic study would result into the development of framework for grievance handling, process reengineering, organisational development and networking.

2.3 Participatory Approach to Governance Evaluation

The participatory approach to evaluation is still relatively new, and hence its application to governance is newer still (OECD, 1997). But while the practice of participatory governance evaluation is still in its formative years, the international development community appears to have adopted, or to be adopting, many of its theoretical and methodological underpinnings. An important feature of a participatory approach is that, because it focuses on the *process* of evaluation, its methodology is easily adaptable to programming across the various components of governance. The following is a summary of what are seen to be the main features and strengths of a participatory approach to evaluating a range of governance activities (IDRC, 1999):

Participation expands the project / programme information base for governance evaluation. Identifying, defining and measuring results hinges on comprehensive information collection. Bringing together all project / programme stakeholders can help ensure that:

- a full and wide variety of information and knowledge held by stakeholders is identified, coordinated / linked;
- information on, and interests of, a diverse range of social groups, including disadvantaged or marginalized social groups (women, children, disabled people, aboriginal peoples, religious / cultural minorities, etc.), are integrated;
- quantitative information is complemented by qualitative information and descriptive statements, based on stakeholders' perceptions and judgements; the use of stakeholders / clients subjective assessment of change before, through and after the programme can help do away with the need to commission 'baseline studies'; and
- local knowledge and creativity, including 'home grown' cultural and socio-political practices and institutions, are incorporated.

- It is in the context of above, under the project participatory methods were utilised to reach out to stakeholders – service provider, functionaries, citizens and panchayat members. The methods included FGDs, case studies, interviews and field survey.

2.3.1 Touchstone for Good Governance: In the context of service delivery, the *quality* of services should be the touchstone. *Quality* reflects how close the output is with respect to the benchmarks / standards fixed. In the study, the identified quality parameters for service delivery are:

- Time
- Cost
- Reliability
- Behaviour
- Responsiveness
- Transparency

- Accountability

2.4 People, Process and Technology Model

The organizations are required to be built on three main pillars viz., processes (systems), people and technology (Box 2.1) (Peppard and Rowland Philip, 2002). In designing a set of processes these three elements must be aligned to the needs of the market (society) and the customers (citizens) within it, and with each other. It is imperative that each of these three pillars is considered in turn. To begin, we should start with the processes of the organization (system), which must be identified and designed. We should then consider the people who will operate the processes. This stage is iterative: having considered the people it will be necessary to go back and review the processes and then return to the people. People can only perform, if they have desired level of skills, knowledge, attitude and motivation, and these are to be rightly placed. The third element to consider is the technology to be used to support the processes and people. In technology, in the context of e-Governance, we should include network, hardware and software, and it needs to be correctly chosen. In considering technology it will also be important to revisit the process and people designs as technological opportunities or constraints become apparent. In a way, under this e-Governance study all three, processes (process of giving certificates), people (functionaries) and technology (IT), were studied to design the system suitably. The specific issues were:

Processes

- Process reengineering
- Quality of services

People

- Work culture
- Change Management
- Citizens' satisfaction

Technology

How the service delivery is affected by:

- Hardware
- Software
- Network

Box: 2.1
People, Processes and Technology (PPT) Model

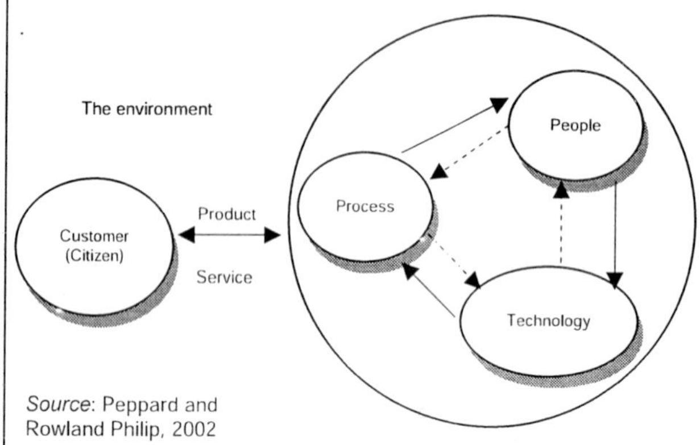

Source: Peppard and Rowland Philip, 2002

People: It refers to personnel / functionaries of service department
Process: It refers to process of service delivery
Technology: It refers to IT

2.4.1 Workshops: The workshops were organised at the district, block and gram panchayat levels to elicit views from different stakeholders about the e-Governance project in Jaipur. Also, the field workshops were organised for FGDs in four gram panchayats viz., Shivdaspura, Chandlai, Kumhariyawas, and Teetriya, to elicit information about delivery system, citizens' requirements (information, services and grievances), and problems in service delivery through e-Kiosk.

2.4.2 Field Survey: The field survey was organised for the identification of requirements of information, services and grievances by the citizens; and quality of services. For identification of requirements, questionnaires were developed for a variety of information, services and grievances (under different sectors) availed by citizens in rural areas (Annexure 2.1). Among others, questionnaires included frequency of visits by customers (citizens) to departments, time and cost of availing services, usage of e-Kiosk, performance of service delivery, satisfaction level and so on. The questionnaires also included the profile of the citizens in terms of gender, caste, education, income and age, in order to make analysis under different sub-categories (e.g. male / female, etc.).

2.4.3 Training Programmes

The following training programmes were organised for project staff and officials and functionaries of Chaksu Tehsil:

- Quality in Govt. Services & Process reengineering

- Training for understanding delivery system
- Training for organisational development
- Field Data Collection for Process Mapping and Analysis'
- Process reengineering and Process Mapping

The purpose of these programmes was to sensitise the participants about different issues under e-Governance, research study, how to do process mapping and data collection and analysis, and business process reengineering (BPR) (see Appendix 2.1 for training inputs).

2.4.4 Study of Organisational Behaviour: To study the organisational behaviour, the schedules were designed. For this purpose, the service delivery departments covered were: Tehsil, Primary Education, Health and Drinking Water. The issues studied were:

- Organisational culture
- Role clarity
- Motivation
- Leadership
- Teamwork

For the purpose of FGDs, the following workshops were organised:

- Roles and responsibilities of functionaries (For understanding roles and responsibilities of officers and field staff engaged in delivery of services)
- Work culture assessment in the services delivery departments (For Identifying work culture / value system)
- Motivation level (For assessing the motivation level)
- Leadership and teamwork (For assessing the leadership of the head of the department, and team work)
- Training needs assessment of functionaries (For identification of training needs)
- Focused groups discussions in villages (For identification of requirements for information, services and grievances; and quality of services)

2.4.5 Process Mapping: The process mapping was done for the key processes viz., Income certificate, Caste certificate, Domicile certificate, Jamabandi, Seema gyan, Mutation, Allotment of govt. land, Encroachment, Division of land, Sale deed, No dues, Solvency, Birth certificate, Death certificate, and Ration card.

For the purpose of mapping various stakeholders viz., Citizens, and SDO, Tehsildar, and field and office functionaries of Chaksu Tehsil were consulted. But detailed study of four processes viz., i. Income certificate; ii. Caste certificate; iii. Domicile, and iv. Jamabandi was done, as these services were provided by project through e-Kiosk.

Note: The purpose of covering 15 processes was two fold, *first*, to cover processes involved in basic services, and *second*, to study the processes related to certificates by Tehsil, so that in future, these processes may be attached to e-Governance project in Jaipur.

2.4.6 Case Studies: Case studies of Janmitra and Lokmitra projects in Jhalawar and Jaipur were prepared. Also, case studies of three e-Governance projects viz., e-Bhoomi (in Karnataka), Gyandoot (in Madhya Pradesh) and OLTP (in Andhra Pradesh), and e-Business project e-Chaupal (in Rajasthan) were prepared in order to understand the trends in other projects and the performance level of service delivery. Besides, a few other case studies about performance of e-Governance project in Jaipur and delivery system were documented.

2.5 Issues under Study

The study covered four aspects viz., i. service delivery, ii. performance of e-Kiosk owner, iii. performance of service provider (e-Governance), and iv. delivery system (Tehsil, Primary Education, Health, Agriculture, Animal Husbandry, etc.) (see Table 2.1). A brief description about the issues covered is given below:

Service Delivery

- Process mapping & BPR: The process mapping of important processes involved in service delivery was done to study about: i. number of activities, ii. sequence of activities, iii. time and cost incurred by citizens (customers), iv. citizen's satisfaction, etc.
- Quality of services: The parameters considered for study are: time, cost, reliability, behaviour, responsiveness, transparency and accountability

Performance of e-Kiosk Owner

- Kiosk owner role: How the Kiosk owner has taken his role in terms of becoming facilitator for providing services to citizens?
- Relationship with citizens: Behaviour, responsiveness and rapport building with citizens were the issues covered.
- Revenue generation: The revenue earned by the Kiosks is an important indicator for evaluating the financial viability.

Performance of Service Provider

- System design: How the service provider has taken various factors into account, while designing the system?

- Sustainability: Whether the financial and technical viability has been addressed?

Delivery System[1] (Tehsil, Primary Education, Health, Agriculture, Animal Husbandry, Drinking Water)

- Whether delivery system has capacity to meet citizens' requirement: The delivery of services can be done only by a sound delivery system. The issues covered include: infrastructure, manpower and logistics for Tehsil, primary education, health, agriculture, animal husbandry, drinking water and PDS.
- Organisational behaviour: It included issues like role clarity, motivation, leadership, teamwork, and work culture. (It is an important dimension for building any organization). The values included for the study were: punctuality, time consciousness, responsiveness, behaviour, etc.
- Change management: Issues included change in work culture, coordination between Tehsil and services provider and whether there has been improvement in efficiency.

Under the above categories, the issues covered, parameters for evaluation, methodology utilised, and models/tools for analysis are listed in Table 2.1.

2.6 Study Framework and Area

The study framework is depicted in Figure 2.1. It shows sequentially the following:

- Study of existing System
- Process Mapping
- Analysis
- System redesign: Process reengineering and organisational development
- Output: Framework for 'e-Governance' for delivering quality services

The study was conducted in Chaksu block of Jaipur district. In this block four gram panchayats viz., Shivdaspura, Chandlai, Kumhariyawas, and Teetriya were chosen for the purpose of field survey, workshops and FGDs.

2.7 Factors Affecting Usage of e-Governance Services

Based on the discussions with citizens and the service provider, following were identified as the important factors that influenced the usage of e-Governance services by the citizens (see Figure S2.1):

Table: 2.1: Issues Under Study

S.No.	Categories / Aspects	Issues Covered	Parameters for evaluation	Methodology	Models / Tools for Analysis
1.	Services Delivery	• Process Mapping & BPR	• Process (Throughput) efficiency	• Process mapping • FGDs • Field survey	• FMEA • Fishbone diagram
		• Quality of services	• Time • Cost • Reliability • Behaviour • Responsiveness • Transparency • Accountability		
2.	Performance of e-Kiosk owner	• Kiosk owner role • Relationship with citizens • Revenue generation	• Usage of services by citizens from e-Kiosk • Revenue by the e-Kiosk	• FGDs • Field survey	• FMEA • Fishbone diagram • Strategic analysis •
3.	Performance of Service provider (e-Governance)	• System design • Sustainability	Existing status of: • Technology network • Management systems	• FGDs • Field survey	• SWOT • Growth model • SERVQUAL model • Strategic analysis

Contd...

S.No.	Categories / Aspects	Issues Covered	Parameters for evaluation	Methodology	Models / Tools for Analysis
1.	Delivery System (Tehsil, Primary Education, Health, Agriculture, Animal Husbandry, Drinking Water)	• Whether delivery system has capacity to meet citizens' requirement	• Existing status of: • Infrastructure • Manpower • Logistic requirement	• FGDs • Field survey	• System approach • SERVQUAL model
		• Organisational Behaviour	• Role clarity, motivation. leadership and teamwork • Work culture (punctuality. timeliness consciousness. • responsiveness, behaviour)	• FGDs • Field survey	-
		• Change management	• Change in work culture • Coordination • Improvement in efficiency	• FGDs • Field survey	-

Figure: 2.1: E-governance Study Framework

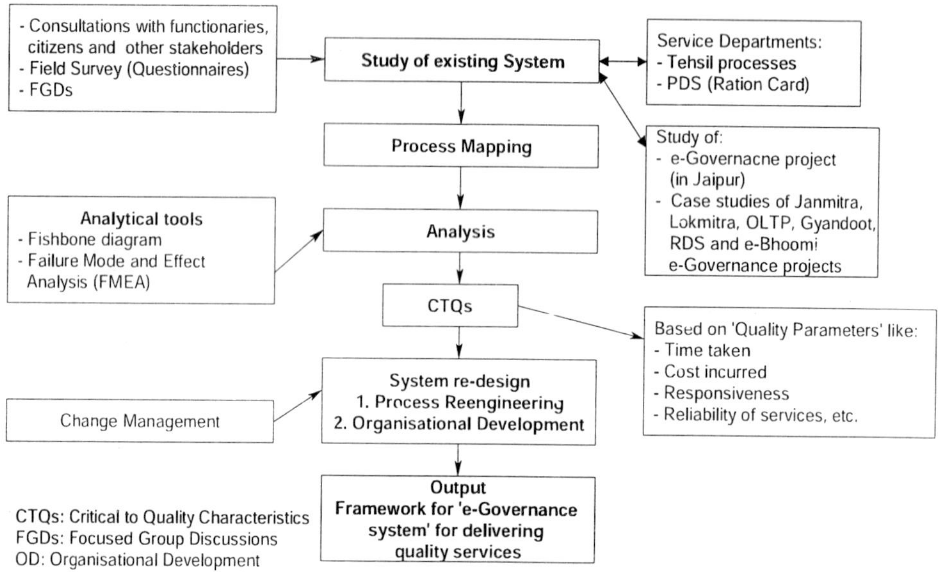

- *Awareness:* It indicates about the awareness of e-Kiosk functioning and the services provided by it.
- *Access (availability of e-Kiosk):* The distance of Kiosk from the house is an important factor.
- *Ease of use:* How easy it is to use a computer.
- *Opportunity cost* (or performance of delivery of services, especially in terms of time and cost savings): It is important to assess how much would be the savings in terms of time and cost to avail services, that would encourage the citizens to avail services from the e-Kiosk.
- *Security of data:* It is important, as the user must feel that his documents will not be lost and will be accepted by concerned offices; and also that data and information would be secured and not be tampered and lost.
- *Number of services:* The usage of e-Kiosk depends upon the number of services provided by the Kiosk. If the number of services is going to be large and provided successfully, citizens would like to use it more.
- *Reliability:* How reliable is the system, when a citizen attempts to use. It is measured in terms of how sure a citizen is that the system would be functional when he would go to the e-Kiosk to avail services and that he

would get services of desired standards.

2.8 Factors Affecting Quality of Services (Performance of Delivery of Services)

During FGDs in workshops in different gram panchayats, citizens expressed their concern about the delivery of services by e-Kiosk under e-Governance project in Jaipur. They expressed that they did not get certificates in time from e-Kiosk due to a number of problems. Similarly, the discussions were held with managers of service provider and the officials of Tehsil to know their views. Based on consultations, five factors that were identified, affecting the quality of delivery of services are (see Figure S2.2):

- *IT infrastructure:* It includes hardware, software and network.
- *Business process reengineering (BPR) and backend computerisation:* Whether the processes are simplified and based on that backend computerisation has been carried out. It is important for efficient processing of application for any service.
- *Delivery system (DS):* The system that would provide services to citizens. It would include infrastructure, manpower, and logistics support; coordination with other departments; and transparency and accountability of functioning. For example, in case of providing certificates for land, caste, income, etc., 'Tehsil' is a delivery system.
- *Electricity:* The supply of electricity to e-Kiosks for a given number of hours in a day.
- *Citizen Relationship Management (CRM):* How citizens' concerns are taken into account, efforts have been made to provide services efficiently, their grievances are redressed, and they are retained by the e-Kiosks for future usage.

2.9 Models and Tools employed for Analysis

2.9.1 Models: The study has applied two models viz., SERVQUAL Model and Growth model. These are explained below:

A. SERVQUAL Model: This model indicates that customers form their perception of quality from different elements of the service (Mohanty and Lakhe, 2002) (see Figure S2.3).

It shows the vital activities of a service organisation that influence the perception of quality. In addition, the model shows the interactions between these activities and identifies the links among them, which are pertinent to the delivery of a satisfactory level of service quality. The links are considered as gaps or discrepancies, a gap representing a significant hurdle to achieving a satisfactory level of service quality. Gap 5 is a service quality shortfall as seen by the customer, and gaps 1-4 are shortfalls within the service organisation. Thus, gaps 1-4 contribute to gap 5. The gaps are outlined below:

- Gap 1 is between expected service by consumers (citizens) and management perception of citizen expectations.
- Gap 2 is between management perception of consumers (citizens) expectations and translation of perceptions into service quality specifications.
- Gap 3 is between service quality specifications (of service provider) and service delivery.
- Gap 4 is between service delivery and external communications to consumers (citizens).
- Gap 5 is between perceived service and expected service by consumers (citizens).

B. Growth Model: The study has used a 5 stage growth model. This model indicates how the growth in the e-Governance system should take place. It has 5 stages having the following salient features:

- **Stage I:** Interface: To provide interface to citizens with government departments, and sharing information and redressing grievances.
- **Stage II:** Transactional: This stage involves providing a few services in the beginning, to citizens by a few departments. Then, add on more services together with BPR and backend computerisation, in order to provide services in the form of a package.
- **Stage III:** Vertical Integration: In this stage, vertical integration of service delivery department is required for quicker processing of applications. For example, in the case of 'revenue department' (dealing with land records, certificates, etc.), the offices at district (Collectorate), Tehsil and *Patwarghar*[2] (field office of tehsil at group of villages) need to be integrated.
- **Stage IV:** Horizontal Integration: Here, the services of a number of line departments at every level viz., district, block / tehsil and gram panchayat need to be integrated. In this stage, citizens can avail a large number of services from e-Kiosk
- **Stage V:** Networking: This stage would facilitate having linkages with other development agencies with education, banks, insurance companies and so on.

The salient features of these stages are given in Table 2.2 and depicted in Figure S2.4.

2.9.2 Tools for Analysis: For the purpose of analysis, the following tools have been utilized:

- Failure Mode and Effect Analysis (FMEA): To identify the failure modes and the causes for failure and prioritising the causes (see Appendix 2.2 for details)
- Pareto diagram: It is a special type of histogram that helps to determine which problems to solve and in what order. The bars in Pareto diagram are rearranged in descending order of their heights, showing the individual contribution of each factor as well as the cumulative contribution (see Appendix 2.3 for details).
- Cause and Effect Analysis (C&E) (or fishbone diagram): It is utilised for displaying pictorially the relationship of causes and their effects (see Appendix 2.4 for details), and to identify the root causes.
- Matrix of Change (MOC): It is applied for identifying strategy for change from manual system to IT system in an organisation (see Appendix 2.5 for details)
- SWOT Analysis: To evaluate the system in terms of its strength, weakness, opportunity and threat (see Appendix 2.6 for details).
- Analytic Hierarchy Process (AHP): It is for determining the weightage of different independent factors affecting dependent variable (see Appendix 2.8 for details)
- Process (Throughput) efficiency: Throughput efficiency is a key indicator of an organisation's value adding efficiency. It tells us how much of the time is definitely not contributing to the goals of the process (see Appendix 2.9).
- Why-why analysis: To understand the relationship of causes and their effects
- Statistical package for the Social Sciences (SPSS): Under this, t-test and correlation analysis have been utilised for data analysis of field survey of the citizens' requirements

Notes

[1]The term delivery system refers to agencies or organisations through which development programmes are implemented to ensure availability of inputs and / or services such as delivery of certificates through Tehsil, agriculture inputs, marketing of agricultural produce, health services, primary education, drinking water and so on. In the report various decrements like Tehsil, Education, Health, PHED are referred as Delivery Systems, for their respective service provisioning.

The ineffectiveness of the present delivery system has raised the question of sustainability of service delivery / programme outputs and has also resulted into sub-optimal performance. The ineffectiveness is due to a whole range of problems viz., lack of infrastructure, logistics and manpower support, ineffective planning, weak monitoring & evaluation system and so on.

S. No.	Delivery System / Department	Services delivered (a select list)
1.	Tehsil	Delivery of certificates, disaster management
2.	Agriculture	Agriculture inputs
3.	Education	Primary education
4.	Health	Health services like immunisation, family planning
5.	PHED	Drinking water

[2]Office where Patwari works

Table: 2.2: Growth Model

S.N.	Type	Features	Remarks
1.	Stage I: Interface	1. Web-site	• Preparing web-site
		2. List of services	• Providing list of services
		3. List of information	• Providing information about various programmes, guidelines, etc.
		4. Sending letters / grievances	• Citizens can send their grievances
2.	Stage II: Transactional	i. Providing a few services	• Beginning with a few services
		ii. BPR for a few services	• Process reengineering of important processes
		iii. Backend computerization (BC)	• To provide database to facilitate on-line processing
		iv. BPR for all services in a Department	• In order to provide services in the form of a package, all the necessary services
		v. System integration	• Integrated databases of various sections (of a service department) and processes so as to have integrated service delivery package, through IT
		vi. Grievance redressal and Feedback	• Feedback to departments about their performance
3.	Stage III: Vertical Integration	i. Linking systems vertically with similar functionalities	• Linking departments vertically (different levels) e.g. Patwarghar to Tehsil to Collectorate)
		ii. Linking other services vertically	• Services requiring multi-level interaction, can be integrated
		iii. System integration	• Integrated databases of different levels
		iv. Paperless transaction	• Among different levels, file processing electronically
		v. e-participation	• Participation by citizens

Contd...

S.N.	Type	Features	Remarks
1.	Stage IV: Horizontal Integration	i. Integrated systems horizontally (across departments)	• Different service deliver departments are to be inter-linked to provide services through e-Kiosk
		ii. System integration integrated database	• Integrated databases of different service deliver departments
		iii. Value added services	• Services like deed writing, bank credit, insurance, etc.
		iv. One-stop shop for online services	• Integrated service delivery through e-Kiosk
2.	Stage V: Networking	i. Government agencies	• Linking different government agencies
		ii. Banks and insurance	• Linking for credit and insurance coverage
		iii. Health (check-up) online	• Health check-up at e-Kiosk
		iv. Education (comp. courses)	• Computer educational courses
		v. Participation by citizens in decision-making	• Participation in government policy and programme formulation
		vi. Other agencies	• Universities, banks, etc.

Figure: S2.1
Factors affecting usage of e-Governance Services

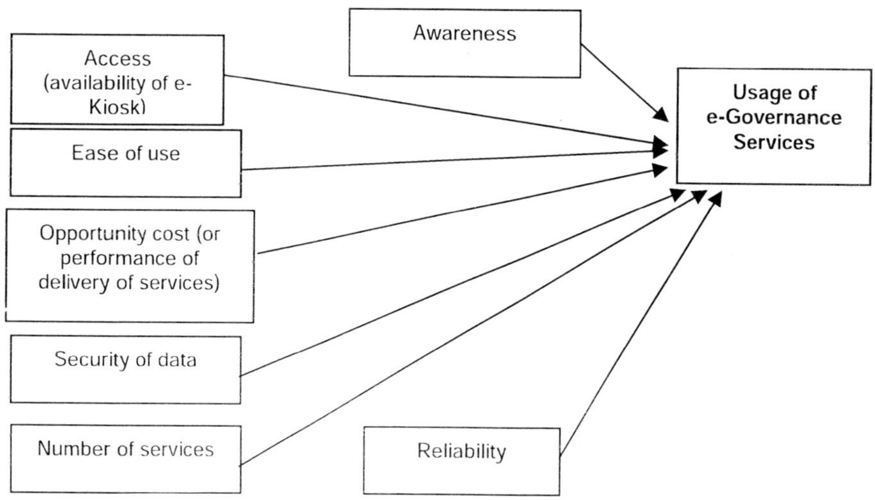

Figure: S2.2
Factors affecting Quality of Services

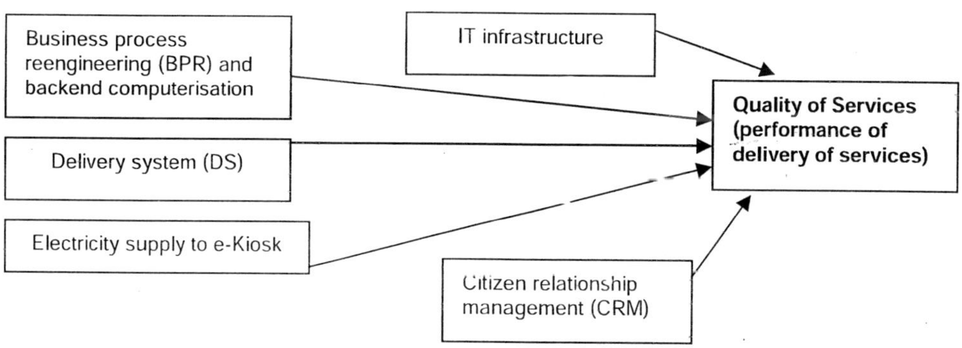

Figure: S2.3
SERVQUAL Model

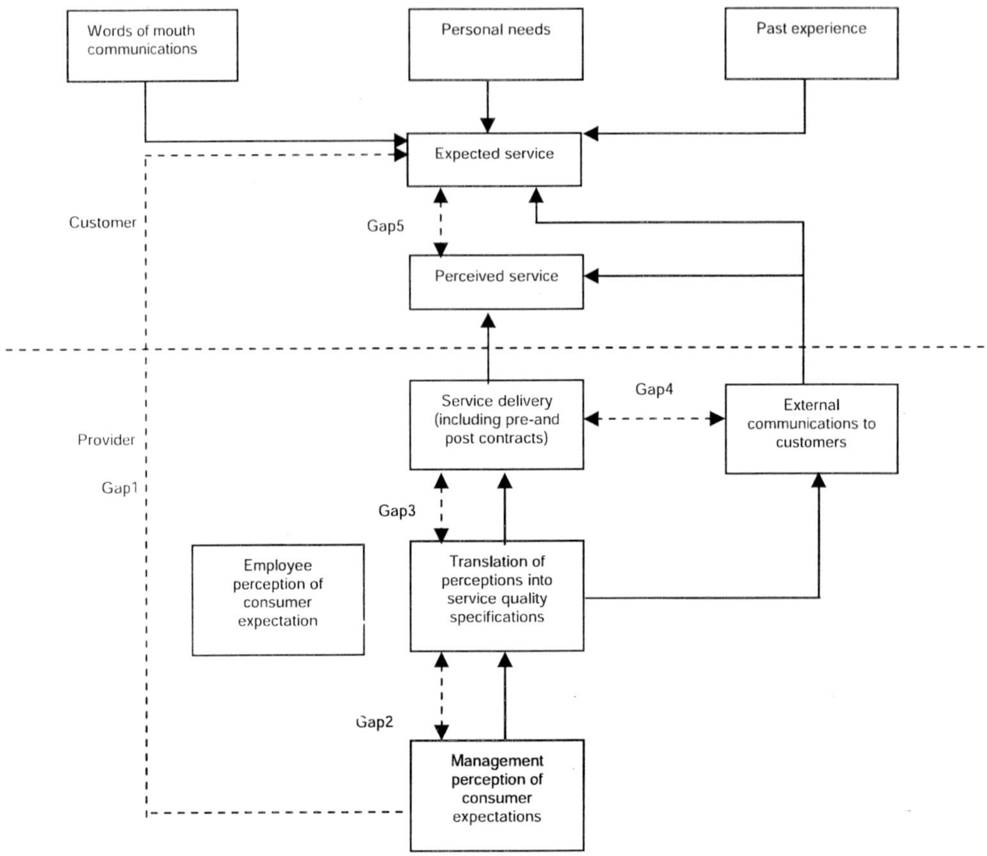

Figure: S2.4
Five stage e-Governance Growth Model

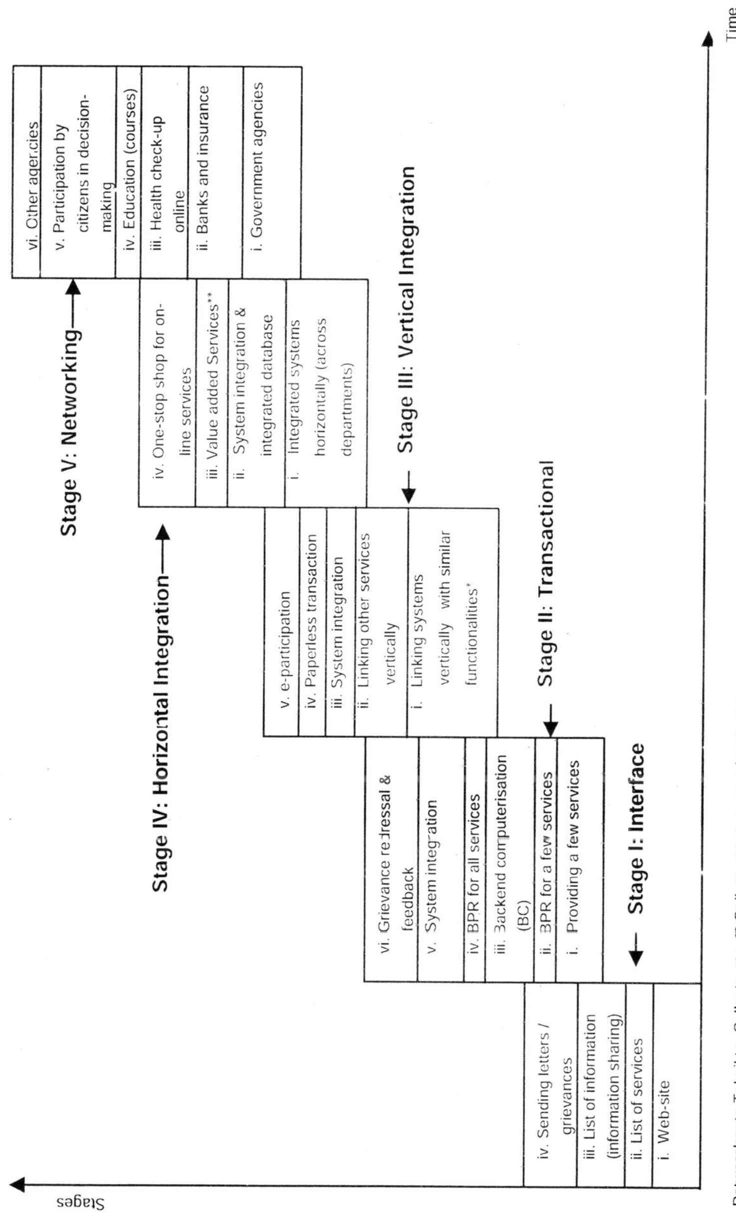

*e.g. Patwarghar to Tehsil to Collectorate. ** Online payment, crop insurance
Note: Information sharing, service delivery, grievance redressal and feedback will be an on going and continuous process

3

E-Governance Projects in India: An Evaluation

"There is a need to recognise and study the critical role that interdependencies of technology (IT), delivery mechanism, processes, peoples' (functionaries') behaviour, work culture and citizen's requirement, ignoring such interdependencies may be counterproductive."

3.1 Field Study

The main focus of the study was Janmitra e-Governance project in Jhalawar district of Rajasthan. Along with this, the study of Gramdoot project in Jaipur district and Lokmitra project in Jaipur district was also made to draw comparison. Also, the case studies of three other e-Governance projects viz., Gyandoot, e-Bhoomi and OLTP were prepared (see Table 3.1).

Table: 3.1: Names of Projects under Study

S. N.	Location	Projects	Remarks
1.	Jaipur district (rural), Rajasthan	Gramdoot	Detailed study (along with study of service processes of Tehsil) also study of delivery system
2.	Jhalawar district, Rajasthan	Janmitra	Case study
3.	Jaipur district (urban), Rajasthan	Lokmitra	Case study
4.	Dhar district, Madhya Pradesh	Gyandoot	Case study
5.	Bangalore urban district, Karnataka	e-Bhoomi	Case study
6.	Mandia district, Karnataka	RDS (including e-Bhoomi)	Case study
7.	Jhalawar district, Rajasthan	e-Chaupal	Case study

3.1.1 Study of Tehsil Processes: The process mapping (in the light of guidelines for process mapping in Annexure 2.3) was done for the following Tehsil processes:

i. Caste certificate

ii. Income certificate

iii. Domicile certificate
iv. Jamabandi
v. Seema gyan
vi. Mutation
vii. Allotment of government land
viii. Encroachment
ix. Division of land
x. Sale deed
xi. No dues
xii. Solvency
xiii. Birth certificate
xiv. Death certificate
xv. Ration card

The purpose of covering these 15 processes was two fold, *first*, to cover processes involved in basic services, and *second*, to study the processes related to certificates by Tehsil, so that in future, these processes may be attached to e-Governance project. Also, the services are inter-connected, so for backend computerisation, integrated database can be prepared.

But study of four processes viz., i. caste certificate, ii income certificate, iii. domicile certificate, and iv. Jamabandi was done in detail, as these services were provided by Janmitra project through e-Kiosk.

3.1.2 Study of e-Governance Service Processes: Janmitra and Gramdoot project provided a number of services in the areas of e-Governance, e-business, and e-rural convergence as shown in Table 3.2.

Table: 3.2: Services Offered by e-Governance Project

S. N.	Type of services	Items
1.	e-Governance	Certificates, single window, complaints redressal etc.
2.	e Business	Photograph, *mandi bhav*, computer games, horoscope, matrimonial etc.
3.	e-Rural convergence	Cable TV, computer education, video conferencing etc..

The process mapping of i. caste certificate, ii. income certificate, iii. domicile certificate, and iv. Jamabandi processes is reflected by Figures 3.1, S3.1, S3.2 and S3.3. For the purpose of mapping various stakeholders viz., citizens, Kiosk owners, manager of project; and SDO, Tehsildar, field and office functionaries of Tehsil were consulted.

Figure: 3.1: Flow Diagram of Caste Certificate given by e-Governance Project (in Jaipur)

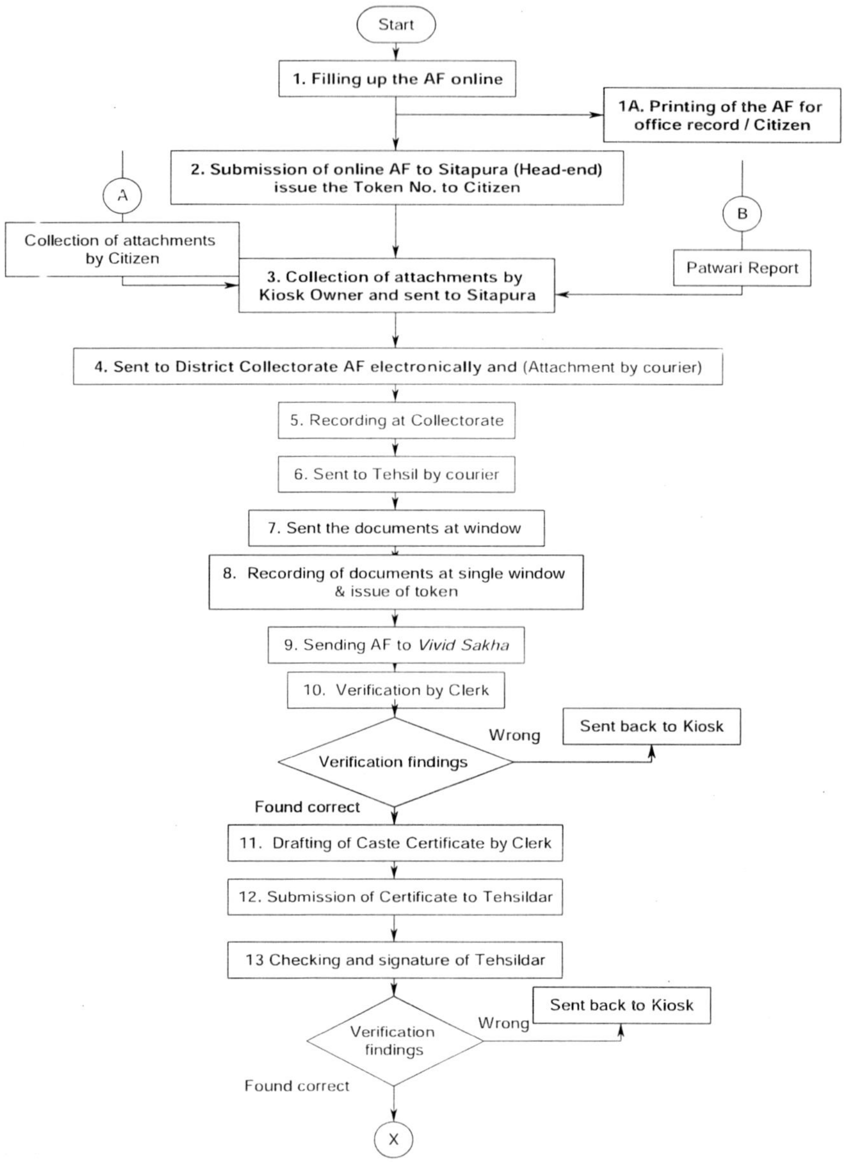

Note: Bold activities are electronic activities.

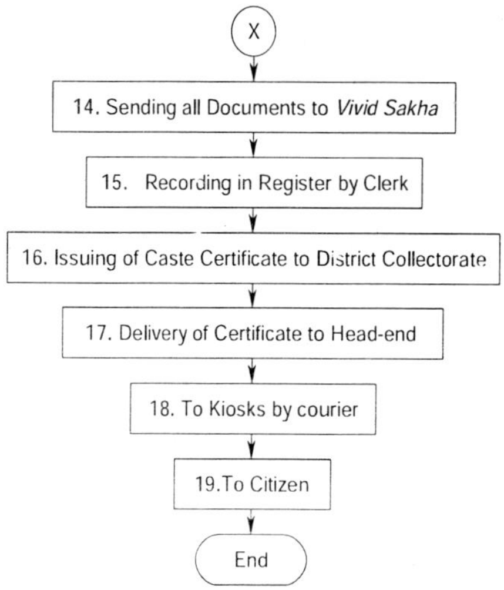

Collection of attachment by Citizen

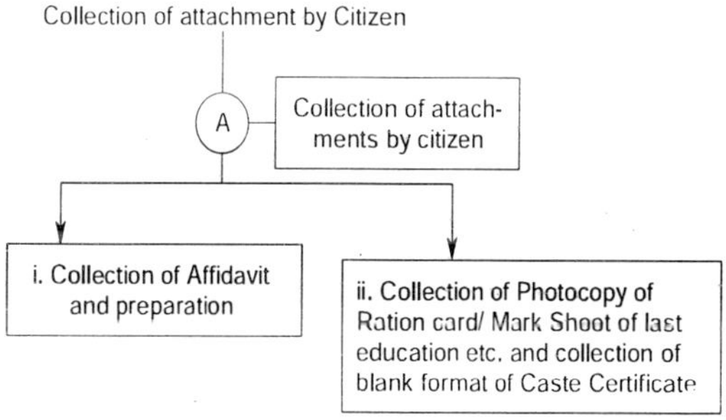

Patwari Report

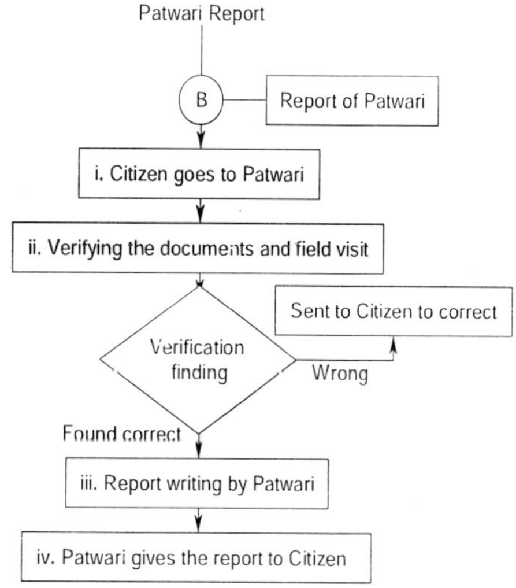

3.2 Analysis

3.2.1 Critical to Quality Characteristics (CTQs): Based on the flow diagrams (FDs), the critical to quality characteristics (CTQs) were identified. The CTQs are:

A. Quantitative Indicators

Process-related:

- Number of activities in a process
- Number of activities online (through computer)
- Touch points
  - For citizens
  - For application
- Number of decision making level
- Number of visits by citizens
- Number of attachments

Citizens' satisfaction related:

- Time (total time to provide service to citizens by Kiosk)
- Cost (total expenditure by citizens in availing the service)

The quantitative CTQs of four services viz., caste certificate, income certificate, domicile certificate and Jamabandi availed through manual system and project are indicated in Table 3.3.

B. Qualitative Indicators

Service-related (regarding citizens' satisfaction):

- Behaviour
- Responsiveness
- Reliability
- Transparency
- Accountability

Note: e-Governance (e-gov.) services: Services, these are availed from the government departments, through e-Kiosk.

3.2.2 Critical Observations: The Table 3.3 reflects that the number of activities in the process of delivery of caste certificate has increased from 19 in manual processing to 26 in e-Governance project. Similar has been the case with regard to other certificates viz., domicile and income.

Through e-Kiosk, for caste, domicile and income certificates, the number of online (through computer) activities is 4 and it is 14.8 per cent of total activities. It shows that most of the activities are done manually. It is important to mention that two major activities collection of attachments (required to be attached with application form) and Patwari report, which take 50 per cent of the time (see Table 3.4) remain manual. Besides, the dispatch of application form (with attachments) from e-Kiosk to Tehsil (via Collectorate) through courier to Tehsil has added more number of days (consuming about 39 per cent of the total time) (see Table 3.4) (thus off setting the gains made by some reduction in time of travel by citizens to Tehsil).

And with regard to visits by citizens, these have remained more or less same, as they have to go to Patwari, e-Kiosk and Tehsil for necessary follow-up, besides for collection of attachments. Due to above reasons, the time required in availing the services and the cost incurred by the citizens is not much different (before and after introducing e-Kiosks), rather there is an increase in time in e-Governance project due to significantly more time taken by courier (as explained above).

Tables 3.3 and S3.1A reflect about the touch points and the number of visits made by citizens. Though there is a reduction in touch points for citizens in the project, but for application, there has been an increase due to routing of the application via head-end and Collectorate through courier. While, there is no reduction in the number of visits to be made by citizens to different offices before he gets the certificate. The Box 3.1 reflects about the touch points by citizens and application, and visits by citizens before availing the services in manual system as well as the project.

Table S3.1B reflects the number of attachments to be attached with the application form. The numbers are quite large in case of caste (9) and income (8) certificates.

Table 3.4 shows that the time for collection of attachments (required to be attached with application form) and Patwari report together is maximum and it is about 50 per cent (16.66 + 33.33) of total time. Another activity where the time consumed in the processing of application is quite large, is sending application by courier (to Tehsil and from there getting certificate to e-Kiosk); and the such time is about 39 per cent of total time. While the time in filling of application form (AF) and processing in Tehsil is mere 11 per cent (approx.).

From Tables 3.3 and S3.1A, it is evident that for the following process-related quantitative indicators, the performance under e-Governance project has been less

Table: 3.3: Critical Indicators for Different Services by Manual and e-Governance Project (in Jaipur)

S. N.	CTQs		Caste certificateΨ				Domicile certificate				Income certificate				Jamabandi			
			Manual		e-Governance		Manual		e-Governance		Manual		e-Governance		Manual		e-Governance	
1	Number of activities		19		26		16		28		18		27		17		12	
2	Activities on-line (through computer)	Number	0		4		0		4		0		4		0		10	
		%age	-		15.38		0		14.81		0		14.81		0		83	
3	Touch points$	For citizen	Min	Max	Min	Max	Min	Max	Min	Max	Min	Max	Min	Max	Min		Max	
			7	13	6	12	8	9	7	8	6	12	5	11	3		2	
		For application	7		13		8		14		7		13		9		3	
4	Number of decision-making levels		3		3		4		4		3		3		1		2	
5	Number of visits by citizens		Min	Max	Min	Max	Min	Max	Min	Max	Min	Max	Min	Max	Min	Max	Min	Max
			7	15	6	14	8	11	7	10	5	14	5	13	3	5	2	4
6	Number of attachments		9		9		4		4		8		8		0		0	
7	Total time spent by citizens to avail service*		10-15 days		20-25 days		10-15 days		15-20 days		10-15 days		15-10 days		2-3 days		2-10 days	
8	Total expenditure by citizens in availing the service**		Rs 200-300		Rs. 200-250		Rs. 200-300		Rs. 200-250		Rs. 200-300		Rs. 200-250		Rs. 30-80		Rs. 20-25	
9	Process (throughput) efficiency (%age)		2.51		1.88		-		-		-		-		-		-	

Note1: Touch points for visits, time and cost for availing the certificates by citizens, vary depending upon the availability of attachments with citizens and follow-up to be made.

Note 2: Touch points: It refers to the points where either 'citizen' or 'application form' has to touch during the entire process of delivery of service.

* It includes time of collection of AF, visits to Patwari, travel to e-Kiosk, Tehsil, etc.

** It includes cost of collection of AF, traveling cost, wages lost and other miscellaneous experses.

$ Number of touch points has two categories viz. minimum (min) and maximum (max.); the first one is when the citizen has got attachments and second one is when the citizen has to collect all the attachments (number of attachments as per Table: S3.1B). , ΨOBC caste certificate

than that of Manual system or not better:

- Number of activities
- Touch points (for citizen and for application)
- Number of decision-making levels
- Number of visits by citizens
- Total time in availing service

Table: 3.4: Time Taken in Giving Certificate for Different Items in Caste Certificate through e-Governance Project (in Jaipur)

<table>
<tr><th>S.N.</th><th colspan="2">Items</th><th>Time
(no. of days)</th><th>%age</th></tr>
<tr><td>1.</td><td colspan="2">Collecting attachments</td><td>3</td><td>16.66</td></tr>
<tr><td rowspan="2">2.</td><td rowspan="2">Patwari report</td><td>i. Locating the Patwari</td><td rowspan="2">2 + 4</td><td rowspan="2">11.11 + 22.22 = 33.33</td></tr>
<tr><td>ii Report of Patwari</td></tr>
<tr><td>3.</td><td colspan="2">Collection of application form (AF) and filling of form</td><td>1</td><td>5.55</td></tr>
<tr><td>4.</td><td colspan="2">Time taken by 'courier' (for sending application to Tehsil and back)</td><td>7</td><td>38.88</td></tr>
<tr><td>5.</td><td colspan="2">Processing time in Tehsil</td><td>1</td><td>5.55</td></tr>
<tr><td></td><td colspan="2">Total</td><td>18</td><td>100.00</td></tr>
</table>

Also, with the increase of 'non-value adding' activities in the project due to movement of application form by courier, the process efficiency (throughput) has rather decreased from 2.51 per cent in manual system to 1.88 per cent in e-Governance project (see Table 3.3).

A. Qualitative Indicators: As regards service-related qualitative indicators viz., behaviour, responsiveness, reliability, transparency and accountability, the status is reflected in Table 3.5. It shows that there is a wide gap between what is delivered and what is expected. For example, the reliability of providing services has been poor, while it was stated at the time of starting of project that the citizens would get services all six days in a week. But, it did not happen so. Similarly in case of other indicators, promises did not match with the actual delivery of services. Out of these five indicators, two of them viz., reliability and accountability have fared poorly. It is due to this the system lost credibility and the citizens withdrew from going to e-Kiosks.

Box 3.1: Touch Points and the Number of Visits

Items		Manual Processing	e-Governance Project
Touch points	a. For citizens	**Minimum** 1. Collection of AF 2. Preparation of affidavit 3. Photocopy of income certificate (for creamy-layer) 4. Goes to Patwari for Patwari report 5. For taking the report from Patwari 6. To submit at single window 7. For collecting the certificate **Maximum** 1 to 7 of minimum and 8. Ration card 9. copy of ROR 10. Voter list 11. Two copies of parent's caste certificate, if candidate is a student 12. Mark sheet of last degree achieved 13. Identification from two Govt. employee (gazetted officers)	**Minimum** 1. Preparation of affidavit 2. Photocopy of income certificate (for creamy-layer) 3. Goes to Patwari for Patwari report 4. For taking the report from Patwari 5. To submit at e-Kiosk 6. To collecting the certificate **Maximum** 1 to 6 of minimum and 7. Ration card 8. copy of ROR 9. Voter list 10. Two copies of parent's caste certificate, if candidate is a student 11. Mark sheet of last degree achieved 12. Identification from two Govt. employee (gazetted officers)
	b. For application	1. Citizen 2. Patwari 3. Single window 4. Vivid Shakha 5. Tehsildar 6. Vivid Shakha 7. Single window	1. Citizen 2. Patwari 3. e-Kiosk 4. Head-end 5. Single window (Collectorate) 6. Single window (Tehsil) *7. Vivid Shakha* 8. Tehsildar *9. Vivid Shakha* 10. Single window (Tehsil) 11. Single window (Collectorate) 12. Head-end 13. e-Kiosk

Number of visits by citizens		**Minimum** 1. To Patwari (for giving the documents) 2. Goes to Patwari for taking the report 3. For submission of AF at single window 4. For issuing the certificate from Tehsil **Maximum** 1 to 4 and 5th & 6th visits for follow-up	**Minimum** 1. To Patwari (for giving the documents) 2. To Patwari for taking the report 3. For submission of AF at e-Kiosk 4. For issuing the certificate from e-Kiosk **Maximum** 1 to 4 and 5th & 6th visits for follow-up

Note: The above indicates that there is no improvement in e-Governance project in comparison to manual system, rather the touch points for application form have increased.

Table: 3.5: Qualitative Indicators for Availing e-Governance Services from e-Governance Project (in Jaipur)

S.N.	Indicators	Expected quality	Status	Average value of response	Interpretation of value of response
1.	Behaviour	Friendly	Passive	2.6	Above average
2.	Responsiveness	Timely redressal of problems	Lack of responsiveness	2.2	Average
3.	Reliability	Full reliability	Less reliable than manual	1.6	Poor to average
4.	Transparency	Complete transparency	Status is not known	2.5	Above average
5.	Accountability	Accountable to citizens	No accountability in case of delay	1.5	Poor to average

Note: It is based on likert's scale from 1 to 5.
Source: Based on field survey (N: 50). 5: Outstanding; 4: Very good; 3: Good; 2: Average; 1: Poor.

> *"For example, the reliability of providing services has been poor, while it was stated at the time of starting of project that the citizens would get services all six days in a week. But, it did not happen so. Similarly in case of other indicators, promises did not match with the actual delivery of services. Out of these five indicators, two of them viz., reliability and accountability have fared poorly. It is due to this the system lost credibility and the citizens withdrew from going to e-Kiosks"*

B. Failure Modes and Effects Analysis (FMEA): FMEA is a set of guidelines, a process, and a form to identify and prioritise potential causes (leading to failures) (see Appendix 2.2 about FMEA). Based on FGDs and field survey, FMEA has been prepared in Table S3.2 for the delivery of caste certificate. It indicates risk priority number (RPN) for various causes.

Table: 3.6: RPN for Different Causes under Different Activity-head

S. N.	Activity-head	Code of causes	RPN	%age of total RPN
1.	A1	C1	294	9.54
		C2	280	9.09
2.	A2	C3	196	6.36
		C4	96	3.12
		C5	8	0.26
3.	A3	C6	24	0.78
		C7	320	10.39
4.	A4	C8	210	6.82
		C9	200	6.49
		C10	280	9.09
5.	A5	C11	200	6.49
		C12	105	3.41
		C13	24	0.78
		C14	30	0.97
		C15	196	6.36
		C16	60	1.95
		C17	30	0.97
		C18	60	1.95
		C19	18	0.58
		C20	63	2.04
		C21	50	1.62
		C22	30	0.97
		C23	27	0.88
6.	A6	C24	105	3.41
7.	A7	C25	175	5.68

For the purpose of convenience in analysis, the causes (see Table 3.6) have been classified in seven activity-heads. If we look at the cumulative RPN of causes under a particular activity-head, the maximum value comes under the following three activity-heads (see Tables 3.6 and 3.7):

Table: 3.7: RPN for Causes under Different Activity-head

Activity head	Description of activity- head	Total of RPN activity-head		Critical causes of failure
		RPN	%age of total RPN	
A1	Collection of attachments and report of Patwari	574	18.63	• Delay in collection of attachments and getting report from Patwari
A2	Accessing and filling of AF	300	9.74	• Electricity failure, connectivity problem
A3	Submission of AF	344	11.17	• Electricity failure, connectivity problem
A4	At Kiosk, collection of attachments from citizen and submission to head-end	690	22.40	• Problem in managing/ sorting attachments • Delay in courier
A5	Processing (after submission of AF till certificate preparation in Tehsil)	893	28.97	• Delay in courier • Manual processing
A6	Dispatching of delivery certificate to Kiosk	105	3.41	• Delay in courier
A7	Delivery of certificate to citizen	175	5.68	• e-Kiosk remains closed
Total		3081	100.00	

(see Table S3.2 for details)

- A1: Collection of attachments and report of Patwari
- A4: At Kiosk, collection of attachments from citizen and submission to head-end
- A5: Processing (after submission of AF till certificate preparation in Tehsil)

The individual causes that have maximum RPN are (see Table 3.6):

- C7: UPS / electricity problem at head-end and connectivity problem
- C1: Lack of Information about attachments and attachments not available in time (to citizens)
- C2: Patwari's absenteeism and his work style (lack of responsiveness)
- C10: Courier misplaced

Based on the FMEA, the Pareto chart is drawn as shown by Figure 3.2. The chart differentiates (causes) between 'vital few' and 'trivial many'. As per this chart, the 'vital few' causes of failures are (in descending order of RPN):

- C7: UPS/electricity problem at head-end and connectivity problem (large down time)
- C1: Lack of Information about attachments and attachments not available in time (to citizen)
- C2: Patwari's absenteeism and his work style (lack of responsiveness)
- C10: Courier misplaced
- C8: Attachments not given by citizen (at Kiosk)
- C9: The Kiosk owner incognizant about which attachments are required
- C11: Delay in courier
- C3: Kiosk owner absent
- C15: Documents missing in Tehsil (due to courier)

(*Note:* In above, the overlapping causes, which are shown in Table 3.8, have been removed)

The above causes (numbering 9 out of total 25 i.e. 36 per cent of total) contribute about 79.71 per cent (approx. 80 per cent) of the total RPN, so the main focus should be on them in order to improve the performance of service delivery.

We further validated our findings through discussions with citizens. Finally, based on above, the 'most critical failure modes' as emerged from the analysis (FMEA and Pareto chart) and FGDs are:

- Delay in collection of attachments by citizens
- Delay in getting report from Patwari
- Delay in processing mainly due to courier

The critical observation, under different activity-head are shown in Table S3.4

C. Fishbone Diagrams: The purpose of drawing fishbone diagrams was to identify the root causes. Based on FGDs with citizens, service provider and officials, the diagrams are prepared for the following:

- Usage of e-Governance services through e-Governance project (in Jaipur) (see Figure 3.3)
- Performance of delivery of services (through e-Governance) in terms of time and cost incurred (see Figure S3.4).

D: Root Causes: From Table S3.5, for poor usage of e-Governance services two factors are crucial. These are 'poor performance (of delivery of services)' and 'very less number of services (available from e-Governance project)'. The root causes are:

- No programme of awareness building

Figure: 3.2: Pareto Analysis of Caste Certificate delivered by e-Governance Project (in Jaipur)

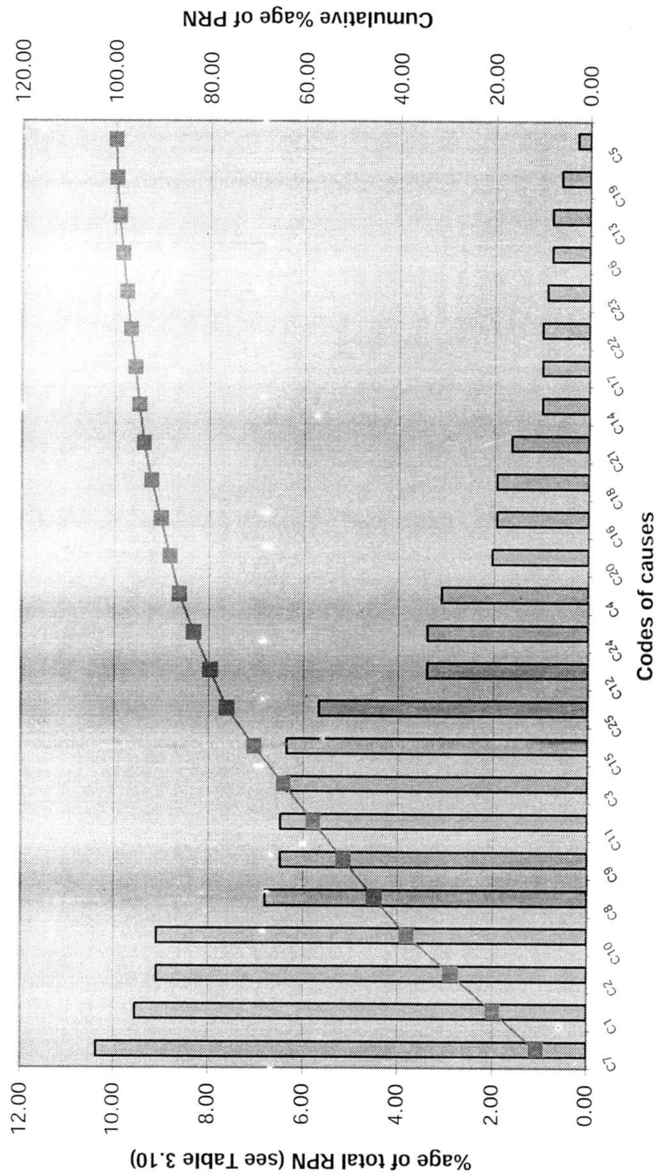

Figure: 3.3: Cause-effect Diagram (Fishbone Diagram) Usage of e-Governance Services (through e-Governance Project)

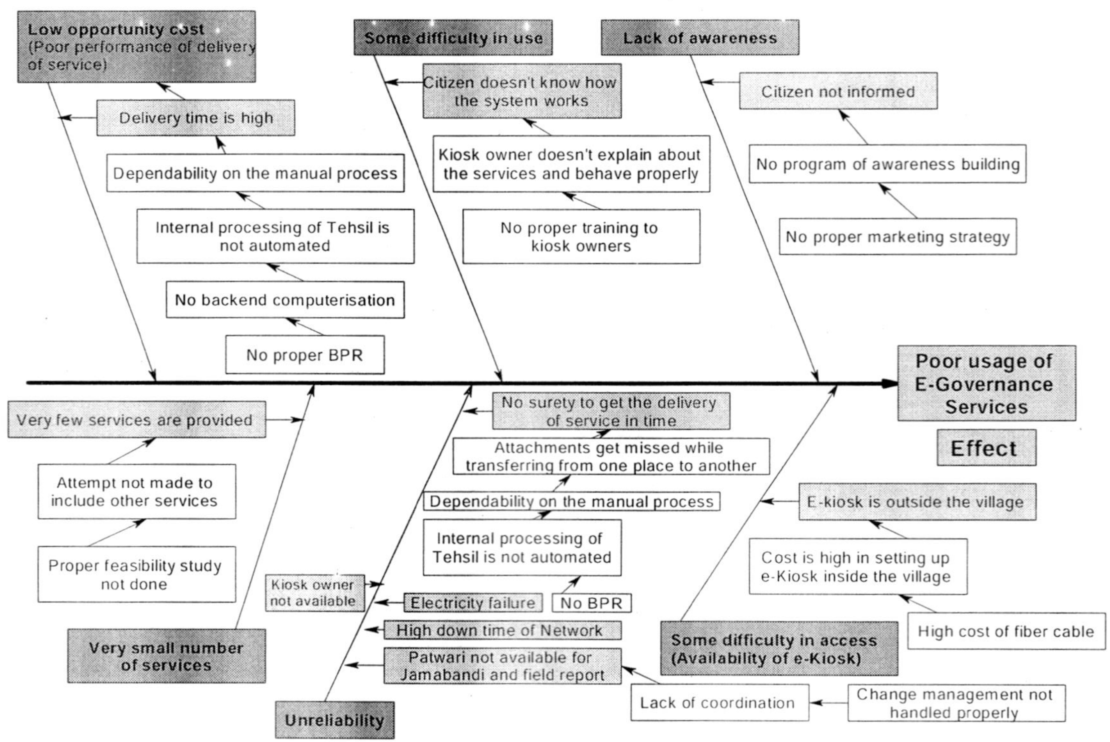

Table: 3.8: Cumulative %age of RPN of main Causes (from Pareto Chart)

S. N.	Code of causes	Causes	%age of total RPN	Commutative %age of RPN
1.	C7	• UPS/electricity problem at head-end and connectivity problem (large down time)	10.39	10.39
2.	C1	• Lack of information about attachments • Attachments not available in time (to citizens)	9.54	19.93
3.	C2	• Patwari's absenteeism and his work style (lack of responsiveness)	9.09	29.02
4.	C10	• Courier misplaced	9.09	38.10
5.	C8	• Attachments not given by citizen (at Kiosk)	6.82	44.92
6.	C9	• The Kiosk owner incognizant about which attachments are required	6.49	51.41
7.	C11	• Delay in courier	6.49	57.90
8.	C3	• Equipments/ technology / electricity problem Kiosk owner absent	6.36	64.26
9.	C15	• Documents missing in Tehsil (due to courier)	6.36	70.63
10.	C25	• Kiosk owner not present	5.68	76.31
11.	C12	• Connectivity problem (large down time)	3.41	79.71

- Cost is high in setting up e-Kiosk inside the village
- No proper training to Kiosk owners
- No backend computerisation
- No BPR done
- Proper feasibility study not done
- Electricity failure
- Network not working
- Kiosk closed
- Patwari not available
- No BPR done

For poor performance (large time and cost) of delivery of services, the main root causes are (see Table S3.6):

- No BPR
- No backend computerisation
- Frequent visits to offices (no feedback available to citizens / MIS)
- No citizen focus
- No fixed time of Patwari at e-Kiosk
- Change management not handled properly
- Long distance from e-Kiosks to Tehsil
- No prior experience of this type of project
- Electricity problem

3.2.3 Factors Affecting Usage of e-Governance Services from e-Governance Project (in Jaipur):

Weightage to Factors for usage of e-Governance Services: During the focussed group discussions (FGDs) with citizens, attempt was made to ascertain the weightage of different factors for usage of e-Governance services. Based on the importance given to the factors by the citizens, the values were given to these factors in the scale of 1 to 10 (by the researchers). Analytic Hierarchy Process (AHP) tool was applied to calculate the weightage of these factors. The purpose of calculating the weightage was to know which factor affects the usage the most. Based on that, the initiatives are to be taken for improving the usage of e-Governance services. The weightage to these factors are given in Table 3.9.

It shows that 'opportunity cost' of availing services is the most important consideration (factor) for citizens for accessing services through e-Kiosk and this factor has got weightage of 41.72 per cent (see Table 3.9). The second most important factor is 'number of services' provided by the e-Kiosk, and has weightage of 26.65 per cent. It evidently shows that the citizens would like to use e-Governance services when, *first*, there is an opportunity cost (or performance in terms of time and cost savings is substantial) and, *second*, a good number of services are provided by e-Kiosk. Otherwise, they would prefer to go to Tehsil office to get certificates, as one citizen expressed about the present performance, 'we can get the certificates from Tehsil (by going there) earlier than from e-Kiosk, so why we should go to e-Kiosk'.

3.2.4 Factors Affecting Quality of Services (Performance of Delivery of Services) from e-Governance Project (in Jaipur):

Weightage to Factors affecting Quality of Services: Through FGDs, similarly attempt was made to ascertain the weightage of factors affecting quality of services. Based on the importance given to the factors, the values were given to these factors in the scale of 1 to 10 (by the researchers). AHP tool was applied to calculate the weightage of these factors (see Table 3.10). The weightage can help in knowing which factor requires the maximum attention to improve the performance of delivery of services.

Table: 3.9: Weightage of Different Factors for Usage of e-Governance Services from e-Governance Project

S.N.	Factors	Value (of importance for usage) of factors *	Weightage (%age)**	Present status***
1.	Awareness	86	8.95 (Low to Medium)	Medium
2.	Access (availability of e-Kiosk)	83	3.66 (Low)	Medium
3.	Ease of use	84	4.12 (Low)	Medium
4.	Opportunity cost (or performance of delivery of services)	92	41.72 (High)	Low
5.	Security of data	83	3.66 (Low)	Medium
6.	Number of services at e-Kiosk	90	26.65 (Medium)	Low
7.	Reliability	87	11.21 (Low to Medium)	Low

* Based on focused group discussions (FGDs) with the users (about 50). The values were given by research staff based on feedback from citizens.
** Weightage has been calculated by AHP tool
*** Based on FGDs

Based on focused group discussions (FGDs), the reasons for lack of usage of e-Governance services (also e-Kiosk) are listed in Table S3.7.

Based on the weightage given in Table 3.10, BPR is the most important factor affecting quality of services (performance of delivery of services) and has got weightage of 46.31 per cent. It has been so as the existing processes were used without re-design, also backend computerisation was not carried out.

In a way, the process remained same and almost entire process was manually handled, and there was no improvement in efficiency. All this resulted into almost same time for delivery of certificates as that was before introducing e-Governance.

Table: 3.10: Weightage of Different Factors Affecting Quality of Services (Performance of Delivery of Services)

S.N	Factors	Value (of importance for performance) of factors *	Weightage (%age)**	Present status***
1.	IT infrastructure	86	7.22 (Low)	High
2.	Business process reengineering (BPR)	92	46.31 (High)	Low
3.	Delivery system (DS)	90	25.49 (Medium)	Low to Medium
4.	Electricity supply to e-Kiosk	87	9.12(Low)	Low
5.	Citizen relationship management (CRM)	88	11.83(Low to Medium)	Low

* Based on focused group discussions (FGDs) with the users (about 50). The values were given by research staff based on feedback from citizens.
** Weightage has been calculated by AHP tool.
*** Based on FGDs

The second most important factor affecting performance of delivery of services is 'delivery system'. While delivering e-Governance services through e-Kiosks, how the capacity of delivery system in the case of Tehsil services was lacking is briefly explained (see Tables S3.33 and S3.34 for details). In the present context, infrastructure (at Tehsil and Patwarghar) and working conditions remained unchanged (which were not satisfactory); and similarly manpower in terms of number and work culture in terms of attending citizens with care remained same. The shortcoming in these areas continued to affect service delivery adversely. Likewise, logistics support especially to Patwaris (field staff at the GP/village level) did not change, while he was supposed to do a lot of field work. In the new set-up of e-Governance, it was envisaged that Patwaris would come to e-Kiosk on two fixed days, but they were not able to do so, due to other engagements and lack of support for mobility to them to go to e-Kiosks. Due to above reasons, the organisational effectiveness of Tehsil (as delivery system) did not improve. And, so the delivery of certificates to citizens through e-Kiosks suffered.

To further substantiate how delivery system has been ineffective, a few more points are added. In the beginning, a number of grievances were sent through the e-Kiosks to Collectorate and different departments (see case study: Annexure 3.2), but most of them remained unresolved as the departments did not have wherewithal (delivery mechanism) to redress the grievances. For example, in the case of complaint regarding 'poor quality of education' in Teetriya GP, the block education officer explained that due to lack of teachers' strength and poor infrastructure and other facilities, it has been difficult to impart good teaching to children. Similarly in the cases of: i. fluoride content in drinking water; ii. non-supply of electricity to farmers; and iii. poor quality of mid-day meal (in primary school), the grievances could not be resolved satisfactorily, as the concerned departments did not have enough resources to provide fluoride removal plant (for providing safe drinking water); to procure transformer and have steady supply of electricity (for providing electricity); and to purchase better quality of food stuff and have proper means (utensils and fuel) of preparation of mid-day meal, respectively. Though, e-Kiosk provides scope for sending grievances, but due to unsatisfactory redressal, due to poor capacity of delivery system to deliver in time and effectively, e-Kiosk lost its credibility and citizens lost interest in using the e-Kiosk (see Figures 3.4 and 3.5 about the decline in the number for certificates availed and grievances received respectively).

Thus the above goes on to explain that 'e' (IT) under e-Governance has limitations, and the real benefit to citizens can be realised when the delivery system for various services is rightly placed. While going for e-Governance, efforts were made to provide hardware, software and network, but little consideration was given to improve the capacity of delivery system to deliver efficiently. Though IT is vital and a big enabler, but the inputs for delivering services or grievance management have to come from the delivery system (concerned department).

The above discussion evidently shows that for improving performance, business process reengineering (BPR) and backend computerisation are to be attended to as a priority and the efficacy of delivery system needs to be enhanced. Only then, are citizens going to use the e-Governance services and seek grievance redressal.

Figure: 3.4: Month-wise Certificates (under e-Governance) Issued by e-Governance Project in Jaipur District

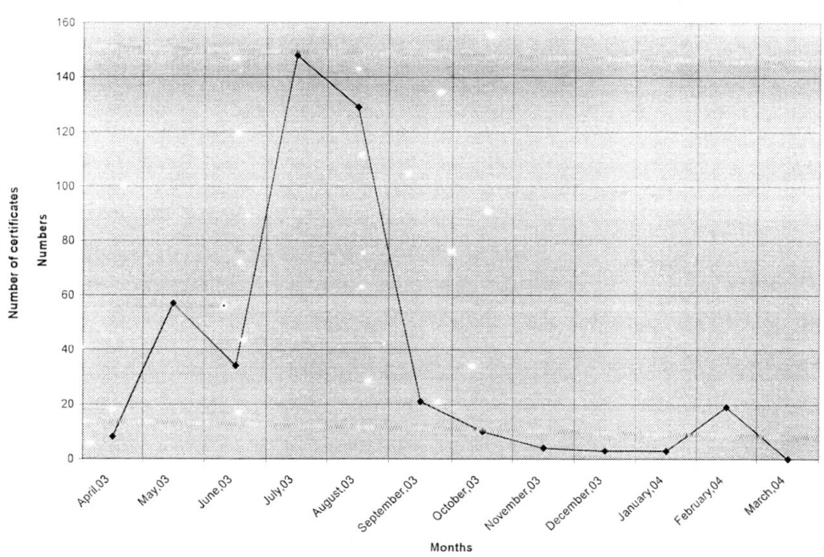

Figure: 3.5: Month-wise Grievances (under e-Governance) Issued by e-Governance Project in Jaipur District

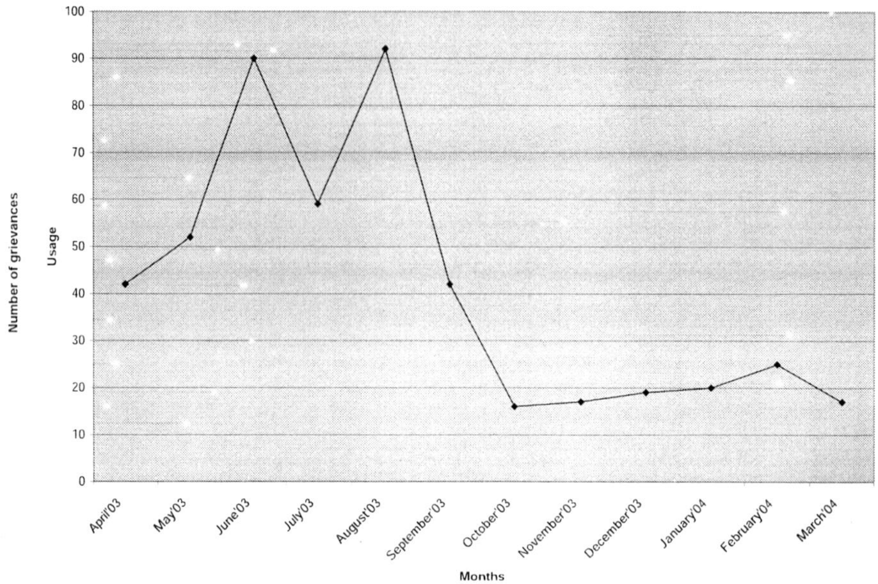

"Above goes on to explain that 'e' (IT) under e-Governance has limitations, and the real benefit to citizens can be realised when the delivery system for various services is rightly placed. While going for e-Governance, efforts were made to provide hardware, software and network, but little consideration was given to improve the capacity of delivery system to deliver efficiently. Though IT is vital and a big enabler, but the inputs for delivering services or grievance management have to come from the delivery system (concerned line department).

The above discussion evidently shows that for improving performance, business process reengineering (BPR) and backend computerisation are to be attended to as a priority and the efficacy of delivery system needs to be enhanced. Only then, are citizens going to use the e-Governance services and seek grievance redressal."

3.2.5 Analysis of Performance Indicators of e-Governance Project (in Jaipur): The Tables 3.11 and S3.10 indicate the performance of e-Governance Tehsil services through the project vis-à-vis manual system in Tehsil and district levels respectively. In Chaksu Tehsil, in 02-03, through e-Kiosk, a mere 1.74 per cent of Tehsil services were accessed and 0.15 per cent of citizens availed them; and these figures for Jaipur, District are 1.91 per cent and 0.057 per cent (see Table

Table: 3.11: E-governance Project Performance vis-à-vis Manual System in Chaksu Tehsil

(02-03)

S. N.	Services		Gramdoot (in Chaksu Tehsil)	In Chaksu Tehsil (by manual system)		%age of services provided by e-Governance w.r.t. manual system
1.	Jamabandi		251	6500		3.86%
2.	Certificates	Caste	40	3858	6129	0.65%
		Income		630		
		Domicile		1641		
3.	Other Tehsil Services	Mutation	0	1318	4017	0%
		No dues		1720		
		Seema Gyan		123		
		Wealth		60		
		Allotment of govt. land for public purpose		10		
		Division of land		9		
		Deed (For sale of land)		237		
		Deed (Release)		30		
		Deed (Lease)		120		
		Deed (Power of Attorney)		18		
		Deed (Mortgage)		372		
	Total		291		16,646	1.74%

Source: e-Governance project, Tehsil office, and own analysis

3.12) respectively. Or, 0.75 per cent of total families accessed (assuming a family of 5) the services in Chaksu and 0.285 per cent in the entire Jaipur district. Thus, in Chaksu Tehsil, indicating that less than 1 per cent of families have accessed less than 2 per cent of Tehsil services in one year, which are minuscule numbers. It evidently indicates about the heavy dependence of citizens on manual system, in spite of e-Kiosks.

The Tables S3.8 and S3.9 reflect about the month-wise certificates delivered and grievances received. It is evident that there has been sharp decline in services in the one year. The reasons attributed to this decline are discussed in preceding section. Similarly, the Figures 3.4 and 3.5 also depict the decline in the numbers for certificates availed and grievances received respectively. These show that the number of certificates availed reached 148 in July, 2003 and then declined to zero in March, 2004. Likewise, the number of grievances reached 92 in August, 2003 and then it slipped to 17 in March, 2004, as grievances redressal has been unsatisfactory (leas than 1 per cent satisfactory disposal) due to poor capacity of service departments to meet citizens' needs.

The comparison of performance during 02-03 and 2003-04 shows sharp decline in all the services viz., certificates, Jamabandi, *mandi* rates and *gram dak*, except for Grievances, which picked up momentum after January 2003 (see Table S3.11 and Figure S3.5).

Table: 3.12: e-Governance Services accessed and Citizens accessing as Percentage of Total Tehsil Services

S.N.	Items	Chaksu Tehsil	Jaipur district
1.	e-Governance Tehsil services accessed through e-Governance project as %age of total services	1.74	1.91
2.	%age of total citizens accessed e-Governance Tehsil services	0.15	0.057
3.	%age of total families accessed e-Governance Tehsil services (assuming a family of 5)	0.75	0.285

Source: Own analysis

3.2.6 Gap Analysis of Services by e-Governance Project: The gap analysis for IT system design is reflected in Table S3.12. Similarly, gap analysis for delivery of different services by the project is presented in Table S3.13. It shows that in almost all the parameters, there is a gap between the expected value by citizens and existing value of service provided.

A. Why-Why Analysis: Why-Why analysis has been carried out for factors affecting usage of e-Governance services (see Table S3.14) and for factors affecting the quality of services (performance of delivery of services) (see Table S3.15). Broadly, it reflects that the main causes relate to inadequate system design, which include no BPR, lack of network planning, and lack of marketing (of services) and change management.

3.2.7 Citizens Requirement Study: The field survey was conducted to elicit requirements for information, services and grievances. For this purpose hundred citizens were interviewed in four gram panchayats viz., Shivdaspura, Chandlai, Kumahariyawas and Teetriya in Chaksu block.

The citizens were classified in five categories as indicated below:

- Gender
- Age
- Caste
- Education
- Income

The categories were further broken into groups as indicated below. The purpose was to understand the requirement of different groups and their preferences for a variety of information, services and grievances under different sectors (see Annexure 2.1 for survey schedules), as also to utilise it for system design. The questionnaires were prepared based on the feedback collected from the citizens during FGDs.

Categories and Groups of Citizens

S.N.	Categories	Groups
1.	Gender	• Male • Female
2.	Age	• Young (18-30 yrs.) • Middle-aged group (31-40 yrs.) • Aged (> 40 years)
3.	Income	• Low income group (BPL) • Middle income group (>BPL but < Rs. 4000 pm) • High income group (income > Rs. 4000 pm)
4.	Education	• Low education group (illiterate to PE) • Medium education group (>PE but <HS) • High education group (>HS)
5.	Caste	• General • OBC • SC& ST

BPL: Below poverty line; PE: Primary education; HS: High school; pm. Per month

The different sectors covered for field survey are listed below:
- Education
- Drinking water
- Health
- Women and child welfare
- Social welfare
- Poverty alleviation
- PDS
- Agriculture
- Irrigation
- Animal husbandry
- Tehsil
- Electricity
- Road
- Others (miscellaneous)

The response was taken for 'scale of importance' and 'frequency of usage'

Scale of the importance: It shows about the importance given by citizens from 1 to 5 ('1' means least important and '5' means most important).

Note: The mean of the scale of importance has been calculated using SPSS package, which is used in the following tables.

Frequency of usage: under this category, the followings have been taken. These are: 'weekly', 'monthly', 'in three months', 'in six months to one year' and 'rarely'.

The details about the preferences of citizens of different groups are indicated in Appendix 3.1

Findings (Based on Scale of Importance)

A. Gender perspective:

- It is found that women in comparison to men are more interested in the subjects like health information, immunization, availability of medicines, non availability of doctors / health workers etc. as indicated in Table 3.13. It shows that they are more inclined towards social and welfare activities.
- The study revealed that unlike females, the males are more interested in computer education, prices of the commodities and its variation in the market, agricultural training centres, purchasing of seeds, marketing agricultural products, etc. as illustrated in Table 3.14. They are particularly

concerned about economic issues such as money spent on poverty alleviation programmes and vocational training.

Table: 3.13: Information, Services and Grievances preferred by Females over Males – A select list

S.N.	Sectors	I/S/G	Items	Mean	
				Male	Female
1.	Health	I	Health information	3.55	4.38
		S	Immunisation	3.85	4.55
		S	Making medicines available	3.87	4.31
		G	Non availability of doctors / health workers	3.27	3.86
		G	Non availability of medicines	3.70	4.14
2.	Education	S	Providing education to children	4.32	4.97
3.	Drinking water	S	Making water available	3.90	4.52
4.	Women and child welfare	G	Food is not given to children	0.90	1.55
5.	Social welfare	I	Schemes for BPL families	3.29	4.39
		S	Scholarship for SCs, STs	3.09	3.83
		G	Irregularities in running of hostels/ old age homes/ orphanages	1.96	2.67
6.	Animal husbandry	S	Supply of feed	4.07	4.75
		G	Street cattle	1.91	2.83

I: Information, S: Service, G: Grievance

B. Age Perspective

- The young citizens within the age group of 18-30 years have higher preference for the family planning, loan for self- employment, purchase of seed, fertilizer, pesticides, etc. as pointed out in Table 3.15. They are particularly inclined towards income generating activities and interested in internet browsing, driving license, etc.

- The middle-aged (31 to 40 years) group is more concerned about the non availability of ambulance, purchase of seeds, fertiliser, pesticide, land / caste and income certificate, conversion of agriculture land into non-agriculture land, non-availability of *Patwari,* supply of electricity, etc. that are highlighted in Table 3.16. They are especially interested in collecting various local and national news that have some bearing on their day to day life.

Table: 3.14
Information, Services and Grievances preferred by Males over Females – A select list

S.N.	Sectors	I/S/G	Items	Mean	
				Male	Female
1.	Education	S	Computer education	4.00	2.40
2.	PDS	G	Higher prices of essential commodities	2.62	1.33
3.	Agriculture	I	Daily mandi rates	3.51	2.22
		I	Agriculture training centres	2.95	1.89
		S	Purchase of seeds, fertiliser, pesticide, implements	4.23	3.33
		S	Marketing of agriculture produce	2.57	1.39
		G	Soil testing	2.99	1.61
		G	Crop loan	3.61	2.33
		G	Crop insurance	3.52	2.17
4.	Poverty alleviation	I	Amount spent on poverty alleviation programmes	2.30	1.00
5.	Others	S	Internet browsing	0.90	0.70
		S	e-mail	1.00	0.40

I: Information, S: Service, G: Grievance

Table: 3.15
Information, Services and Grievances preferred by Young Citizens – A select list

S.N.	Sectors	I/S/G	Items	Mean		
				A1	A2	A3
1.	Health	I	Family planning	3.28	2.42	2.86
2.	Poverty alleviation	S	Loan for Self-employment	4.38	3.93	3.59
		S	Training for Self-employment	4.38	3.90	3.19
3.	Agriculture	S	Purchase of seeds, fertiliser, pesticide, implements	4.35	4.38	3.57
		S	Training and demonstration	3.29	2.76	2.19
		S	Crop insurance	3.91	3.38	2.62
		S	Expert advice on agriculture	3.76	3.52	2.65
4.	Others	S	e-mail	1.96	0.94	0.36
		S	Internet browsing	1.56	0.90	0.48
		S	Driving license	3.19	2.58	1.79

I: Information, S: Service, G: Grievance,
A1: Young, A2: Middle-aged group, A3: Aged (above 40 years)

Table: 3.16
Information, Services and Grievances preferred by Middle-aged Groups Citizens – A select list

S.N.	Sectors	I/S/G	Items	Mean		
				A1	A2	A2
1.	Health	G	Non availability of ambulance	2.30	3.36	2.52
2.	Agriculture	S	Purchase of seeds, fertiliser, pesticide, implements	4.35	4.38	3.57
3.	Tehsil	S	Land certificate	3.37	4.32	3.02
		S	Caste certificate	2.81	4.06	3.33
		S	Income certificate	2.59	3.87	3.02
		S	Mutation	2.22	2.94	1.62
		S	Sale deed	1.15	2.26	0.93
		S	Conversion of agriculture land into non-agriculture land	1.63	1.65	0.69
		G	Non-availability of Patwari	2.19	3.81	3.12
		G	Complaint against Patwari	1.85	3.52	2.60
4.	Electricity	S	Electricity connection	3.74	4.42	3.10
		G	Electricity failure – for household	3.93	4.29	3.38
		G	Electricity failure – for agriculture pump sets	3.48	3.94	2.90
5.	Road	I	Timings of buses and bus routes	1.56	3.45	2.33
		G	Adding more buses	1.89	3.16	3.21
6.	Others	S	Local news	2.33	3.58	1.69
		S	National news	2.07	2.84	1.33
		G	Non-functioning of buses	2.59	3.45	2.14

I: Information, S: Service, G: Grievance
A1: Young, A2: Middle-aged group, A3: Aged (above 40 years)

C. Education Perspective

- The less educated citizens have given preference to availability of various schemes for BPL families as indicated in Table 3.17. It shows that they put special emphasis to fulfill their basic requirements.

Table: 3.17
Information, Services and Grievances preferred by Low Education Group – A select list

S.N.	Sectors	I/S/G	Items	Mean		
				E1	E2	E3
1.	Irrigation	I	Schemes for BPL families	2.81	2.53	2.00
2.	Animal husbandry	I	Schemes for BPL families	2.85	2.65	1.88
3.	Tehsil	I	Schemes for BPL families	2.23	2.23	1.29

I: Information,
E1: Low education group, E2: Medium education group, E3: High education group

- Higher educated citizens have given preference for the following (see Table 3.18):

Table: 3.18
Information, Services and Grievances preferred by High Education Group – A select list

S.N.	Sectors	I/S/G	Items	Mean		
				E1	E2	E3
1.	Education	I	Results for 10th and 12th classes	0.73	2.46	3.62
		S	Library activity	1.82	2.87	3.05
		S	Computer education	2.39	3.93	4.48
		G	Vacancies of teachers	1.18	2.61	3.86
		G	Late coming of teachers	1.27	1.91	2.95
2.	Drinking water	I	Village-wise drinking water resources	2.12	2.17	3.57
		I	Quality of water	3.06	3.57	4.52
		S	Making water available	4.48	3.74	4.19
		G	Poor quality of drinking water	2.94	3.67	4.71
3.	Women and child welfare	I	Facilities at Anganwadi centre	2.91	3.30	3.43
		S	Organising immunisation programme	3.85	3.57	4.57
		S	Nutritional programme for pre-school children and mothers	3.91	3.61	4.43
		S	Organising immunisation programme	3.85	3.57	4.57
4.	PDS	G	Complaint against retailer	2.62	1.98	3.29
5.	Agriculture	I	Agricultural implements used	2.52	2.65	3.82
		I	Daily mandi rates	2.62	3.72	3.00
		S	Purchase of seeds, fertiliser, pesticide, implements	3.52	4.24	4.47
		S	Training and demonstration	2.17	2.74	3.65
		S	Soil testing	2.24	2.70	3.71
		S	Crop loan	2.66	3.63	3.82
		S	Mandi rates	2.21	3.52	3.29
		S	Crop insurance	2.48	3.41	4.24
		S	Expert advice on agriculture	2.79	3.33	3.94
6.	Tehsil	I	Guidelines for accessing the certificates	2.46	3.60	4.18
		S	Income certificate	2.42	3.39	3.59
		S	Domicile certificate	2.96	4.14	3.82
7.	Electricity	I	Information about electricity cut	2.15	3.32	3.88
		S	Electricity connection	2.50	4.04	4.29
8.	Others	I	Employment notification	3.77	4.32	4.82
		I	For setting up rural industries	2.58	3.21	3.94

S.N.	Sectors	I/S/G	Items	Mean		
				E1	E2	E3
		I	Guidelines for schemes for all departments	1.50	2.25	3.18
		I	Telephone numbers of all departments	1.27	2.02	2.76
		S	e-mail	0.27	1.04	1.65
		S	Internet browsing	0.38	0.91	1.65
		S	Driving license	1.27	2.46	4.00
		S	Local news	1.65	2.82	2.41

I: Information, S: Service, G: Grievance
E1: Low education group; E2: Medium education group; E3: High education group

- Unlike the less educated, the more educated citizens and young are going to be prospective user for the educational results and computer education. Hence they are concerned about irregularities of teachers, training and demonstration on income generating activities, insurance, quality of drinking water, facility at anganwadi centre, etc. as pinpointed in Table 3.19. The educated citizens are much more action or result oriented.

D. Income Perspective

- The high income group has placed higher value with regard to all information, services and grievances. For example, computer education, organizing immunization programme, quality of water, loan schemes, marketing of agricultural produces, non-availability of quality seeds, sources of irrigation, cattle health care and availability of bus services as highlighted in Table 3.19. It shows that the high income groups are more concerned about availability of quality services. Also, as the income increases, the value also goes up as indicated in the Table 3.20.

E. Caste Perspective

Caste divide is clearly reflected in the scale of preference. The following remarks can be safely drawn:

- General caste & OBC have attached more preferences to those services which are economic in natural. Their preferences are on the availability of drinking water, education, women and child welfare, agriculture, requirement for veterinary doctors and electricity, etc. as illustrated in Table 3.21. As per their preferences, particularly general caste and OBC have given higher scale in comparison to ST&SC group.

Table: 3.19
Information, Services and Grievances preferred by High Education Group and Young – A select list

S. N.	Sectors	I/S/G	Items
1.	Education	I	Results for 10th and 12th classes
		S	Computer education
		G	Late coming of teachers
2.	Agriculture	S	Purchase of seeds, fertiliser, pesticide, implements
		S	Training and demonstration
		S	Crop insurance
		S	Expert advice on agriculture
3.	Drinking water	G	Poor quality of drinking water
4.	Women and child welfare	S	Facility at anganwadi centre
5.	Others	S	e-mail
		S	Internet browsing
		S	Driving license

I: Information, S: Service, G: Grievance

Table: 3.20
Information, Services and Grievances preferred by High Income Group – A select list

S.N.	Sectors	I/S/G	Items	Mean		
				I1	I2	I3
1.	Education	S	Computer education	2.10	3.82	4.16
2.	WCW	S	Organising immunisation programme	3.10	3.97	4.37
3.	Drinking water	I	Quality of water	3.05	3.61	4.16
4.	Agriculture	I	Loan schemes	4.03	3.24	4.25
		S	Mandi rates	2.89	2.94	4.42
		S	Marketing of agriculture produce	1.97	2.25	4.00
		G	Pest attack	3.22	3.47	4.33
		G	Non-availability of quality seeds, fertiliser, pesticides	3.30	3.84	4.33
5.	Road	S	Availability of buses	3.62	4.40	4.50
6.	Irrigation	I	Sources of irrigation	2.65	3.33	4.00
7.	Animal husbandry	I	Cattle health care and controls	3.92	3.64	4.38

I: Information, S: Service, G: Grievance, WCW: Women and child welfare
I1: Low income group; I2: Middle income group; I3: High income group

Table: 3.21
Information, Services and Grievances of Different Caste – A select list

S.N.	Sectors	I/S/G	Items	Mean		
				C1	C2	C3
1.	Drinking water	I	Village-wise drinking water resources	3.21	2.22	1.75
2.	Education	I	Number of schools	2.21	2.49	1.25
3.	WCW	I	Facilities at Anganwadi centre	3.41	3.29	2.25
4.	Social welfare	I	Schemes for handicaps	3.56	4.00	2.43
		S	Aids for handicaps	3.69	4.13	2.30
5.	Agriculture	S	Crop insurance	3.60	3.87	2.70
6.	Animal husbandry	S	Marketing of milk	3.09	2.95	2.00
		G	Requirement of veterinary Doctor in rural areas	4.52	4.70	3.92
7.	Electricity	G	Electricity failure – for household	4.23	4.02	2.92
		G	Electricity failure – for agriculture pump sets	3.84	3.55	2.52

I: Information, S: Service, G: Grievance, WCW: Women and child welfare
C1: General caste, C2: OBC, C3: SC & ST

- The marginalized groups, especially SC and ST attach higher preference for availability of scholarship, distribution of books, scheme for BPL beneficiaries, health related problems, social welfare measures like IAY, construction of village assets etc, as mentioned clearly in Table 3.22. It shows that SC / ST are more interested to obtain the caste and income certificates in order to avail various welfare schemes launched by government. Moreover, due to their lower economic conditions in the society, they are more interested in timely release of old age and widow pension, Antodaya cards, timely availability of essential commodities and special health camps, etc.

F. Some General Observations

- The study brings into sharp focus two different groups i.e. marginalized and privileged groups and the differences in their preferences for some selected services as illustrated in Table S3.19A. This reflects that the marginalized groups have overall higher value for the various sectors like health, social welfare, PDS, and poverty alleviation. Services like computer education, internet and e-mail are preferred by 'males, 'young', 'middle-aged group', 'high education group' and 'high income group' citizens.
- The vulnerable groups like 'Females', 'aged' (above 40 year), 'low education group', 'low income group' and 'SC&ST' citizens have

preferences for the schemes for BPL families, irregularities in mid-day meal, health information including immunization and availability of medicines, information about diseases, supply of fodder for cattle, social welfare programmes, old age / widow pension, fair availability of commodities, ration cards, caste/income and land certificate, the conditions of road for transportation and communication etc as pointed out in Table S3.19B. This reflects that they give importance to the need-based services.

Table: 3.22
Information, Services and Grievances preferred by SCs and STs – A select list

S.N.	Sectors	I/S/G	Items	Mean		
				C1	C2	C3
1.	Education	I	Type of scholarship	2.30	3.30	3.30
		I	Distribution of books	2.62	2.14	3.42
		I	Schemes for BPL families	1.45	2.39	3.50
2.	Drinking water	I	Schemes for BPL families	1.31	2.08	2.92
3.	Health	I	Type of diseases	3.59	3.56	4.42
		I	Special health camps	3.62	3.02	4.17
		S	Making medicines available	3.90	3.97	4.42
		I	Expert advice on health	4.07	4.14	4.67
		G	Non availability of ambulance	2.62	2.63	3.25
4.	Social welfare	S	Old age and widow pension	3.80	4.53	4.75
		S	Scholarship for SCs, STs	2.67	3.67	3.68
		G	Delay in pension	2.64	3.00	3.73
5.	Poverty alleviation	I	Construction of village assets	2.60	2.93	2.93
		S	Family-housing (IAY)	2.40	3.13	3.62
		G	Poor quality of implementation of work	2.60	3.93	3.98
		G	Name not included in BPL list	3.38	3.00	3.95
6.	PDS	S	Timely availability of essential commodities	3.47	4.00	4.28
		G	Complaints of BPL / antyodaya cards holder	2.76	2.27	3.13
		G	Non availability of commodity at fare price shop			
7.	Agriculture	S	Production	2.33	2.47	2.68
8.	Tehsil	S	Caste certificate	2.52	3.80	3.88
		S	Income certificate	2.58	3.36	3.56

I: Information, S: Service, G: Grievance
C1: General caste, C2: OBC, C3: SC & ST

- Citizens irrespective of gender, age, education, income and caste have the following preferences (see Table 3.23):

Table: 3.23
Information, Services and Grievances preferred Irrespective of Gender, Age, Education, Income and Caste – A select list

S. N.	Sectors	I/S/G	All groups
			High Scale & High Frequency
1.	Education	S	Computer education
		S	Providing education to children
2.	Health	S	Immunisation
		S	Making medicine available
		S	Expert advice on health
3.	PDS	S	Timely availability of essential commodities
4.	Agriculture	I	Daily mandi rates
5.	Electricity	G	Electricity failure for household
6.	Drinking water	S	Making water available
7.	Social welfare	S	Old age and widow pension
8.	Animal husbandry	G	Requirement of veterinary doctor in rural areas
		G	Non-availability of medicines
		S	Supply of feed
9.	Road	S	Availability of buses

- Citizens of all castes prefer the following three computer-based services:
  - Computer education
  - E-mail
  - Internet
- Citizens require more information, services and grievances for health, PDS and electricity. The ranks for different sectors are given in the following Table S3.20.
- Male citizens have given higher value in most of the cases (see Table S3.16).
- In service category, female citizens have given more value for health, social welfare and PDS sectors.
- Almost same preference by citizens of all the castes (see Table S3.17).
- 'Males', 'middle-aged group', 'OBC', 'high education group', and 'middle income group' citizens have given overall higher values (sum of mean of

all information, services and grievances in all sectors) than citizens of other groups (see Table S3.18) in their respective category.

- Marginalise groups ('female', 'SC & ST', 'low education group', and 'low income group' citizens) have overall higher (or the difference with other groups in the same category) values for the following sectors:
  - Health
  - Social welfare
  - PDS
  - Poverty alleviation

To sum up, findings of CRS reflect that different groups have different requirements, so we need to: position different services on portal as per requirements of different groups, and design the system accordingly. The findings provide value for the formulation of strategy and positioning of the products (information, services and grievances) on portal that may 'fulfill the requirements' of different groups of customers (citizens), and thus 'maximising the usage' of e-Kiosks. CRS can help in achieving the following specific objectives:

- Identifying the number of likely users in different groups
- Identifying right mix of information, services and grievances
- Revenue modeling
- Strategy formulation
- Positioning of information, services and grievances on portal at e-Kiosks, in the order of priority for different groups (like males, females, SCs / STs, etc.), as different groups have different priorities
- Identifying promotional activities for attracting citizens to utilise e-Kiosks
- Demand forecasting
- Designing system architecture, keeping in view the demand and usage in future

3.2.8 Study of Behavioural Issues:

The study of behavioural issues was undertaken to understand organisational culture, role clarity, motivation, leadership and teamwork, and how the officials and functionaries respond to the new requirements of e-Governance. Also, to identify the areas that would require interventions in order to tap potential of personnel; and improve the organisational effectiveness to implement e-Governance projects better. The study was based on the focussed group discussions (FGDs) with officials, functionaries and citizens during the workshops; and on survey through structured questionnaires. The specific issues covered under the study are listed in Table 3.24.

Table: 3.24: Issues Covered under Behavioural Issues

S.N.	Items	Issues
1.	Organisational culture	• Responsiveness to people's grievances • Concern for timeliness of work • Work climate
2.	Role clarity	• How do employees relate their role vis-à- vis the organisation • Role stress
3.	Motivation	• Level of motivation • Work environment and its impact on motivation
4.	Leadership	• Style / Type of leadership • Impact of leadership
5.	Team work	• Whether employees (like to) work in a team • Enabling and hindering factors for team work
6.	Organisational effectiveness	• How effective is organisation in meeting the grievances of people – or capacity of organisation

Note: Departments that were studied are: Tehsil, Health, Primary education, and PHED

Salient Findings of Field Survey

A. About Responsiveness: Table S3.21 elucidates that 63 per cent respondents agree and 25 per cent strongly agree that in their office priority was given to quality service in terms of timeliness, behaviour of employees and relationships whereas 5 per cent disagree and 4 per cent strongly disagree that priority was given to quality of services. 3 per cent neither agree nor disagree on this fact. Though the large sample believed that responsiveness was at top while dealing with citizens, but there are factors, which obstruct them to be responsive and they are to be studied in detail.

Survey shows that 71 per cent of the functionaries agree that they were responsible for the services delivered to the public while 17 per cent of the respondents strongly agree on this point, 2 per cent strongly disagree, 9 per cent disagree and 1 per cent neither agree nor disagree that they were responsible for the services delivered to the public.

It is evident from Table S3.21 that 65 per cent of the respondents consider that their work was a mere routine work however 23 per cent disagree that their work was a mere routine work. 3 per cent strongly disagree with this notion and on the other hand 6 per cent strongly adhere to this view.

It is observed that 68 per cent of the employees agreed that the citizens were given the exact status of their applications; on the other hand 14 per cent strongly disagree that exact status was given to the citizens of their applications. 15 per cent of the workers strongly agree with the opinion that the citizens were given the exact status of their applications.

With regard to above, the present value system (work culture) in the delivery system is presented in Table 3.25.

Table: 3.25: Present Value System (Work Culture) in the Delivery System*

S. N.	Present values (important in the e-Governance context)		Impact on functioning
	Indicators	**Status**	
	For citizen management		Lack of citizen focus
1.	Punctuality	Inadequacy of these Values	
2.	Timeliness		
3.	Responsiveness		
4.	Efficiency		
	For functional level		
1.	Autonomy	Rule-bound approach	Lack of involvement of functionaries in the work
2.	Decision-making	Top-down approach	

* The delivery systems where the study was conducted are: Tehsil, Primary education, Health, Agriculture, Animal husbandry, Drinking water

Source: Field survey and FGDs

B. Citizen's Perspective: The stakeholders gave a different picture of the manner in which the services were offered to them. In Table S3.27, on overall satisfaction while dealing with government official, 52 per cent of the citizens feel somewhat dissatisfied, 36 per cent feel dissatisfied. Other 7 per cent feel somewhat satisfied and 5 per cent feel satisfied while dealing with the government officials.

In Table S3.28, 29 per cent of the citizens felt that the dealing officials sometimes gave status of their applications while 31 per cent of the citizens felt that administrators never gave them correct information about their applications. 21 per cent felt that they were provided with accurate information. 11 per cent were not sure and 7 per cent are not saying any thing.

According to Table S3.29, 38 per cent of the citizens' felt that the general behaviour of the officials towards them was hostile. 35 per cent felt that behaviour of the officials dealing with them was very hostile. 10 per cent feel that the dealing was performed in very cordial manner and 7 per cent felt that the behaviour was cordial.

83 per cent of the respondents of the total sample felt that the services provided by officials were not dependable while 17 per cent feel that the services were not dependable as shown in Table S3.30.

Table S3.31 shows that 60 per cent of the citizens held the view that officials did not take responsibility of the services provided by them and on the other hand 40 per cent of the respondents held the opinion those functionaries took the responsibility of services provided by them.

C. Panchayat Members' Perspective: In Table S3.32, 84 per cent of the members surveyed take up the stakeholders matter with the concerned officials. Only 4 per cent of the sample members felt that the officials were difficult to reach. 12 per cent of the sample members did not take up the matter to higher officials.

D. Work Climate: Table S3.22 showed that 69 per cent of the functionaries agreed and12 per cent strongly agreed that they were encouraged in the organisation for taking individual initiative. However, 14 per cent contradicted this view and 5 per cent were unable to decide whether their initiative was encouraged or not.

It is observed from Table S3.22, 68 per cent of the employees agreed that they are equipped with outdated equipments, which hamper their performance and 14 per cent strongly agree with this notion. On the other hand 11 per cent disagree and 2 per cent strongly disagree that they have outdated equipments for work.

E. On Interpersonal Relationship and Training: 60 per cent of the respondents' report that they have friendly relationship with their peer group, 29 per cent strongly agree, whereas 9 per cent disagree and 2 per cent strongly disagree. Similarly survey highlights that the seniors also maintain friendly relationship with their juniors, agreed by 70 per cent and strongly agreed by 17 per cent. Survey also shows that 9 per cent disagree and 3 per cent neither agree nor disagree with the idea (see Table S3.22).

Table S3.23, indicates that the employees have strong urge for *learning new techniques* to enhance their performance. 65 per cent respondents of the total sample agree that training of new techniques is very essential, 23 per cent strongly agree with the idea, whereas 11 per cent of the officials do not find it necessary and 2 per cent of the respondents neither agree nor disagree on the argument.

81 per cent of the officials reported in the survey agree that multimedia knowledge is very essential and 11 per cent strongly agree, while 8 per cent believe the other way.

Table S3.24 depicts that 52 per cent of the employees feel that there are circumstances when they do not need to maintain courtesy with the citizens. 66 per cent of the respondents feel that they should maintain extra courtesy while dealing with senior citizens and women.

Table S3.25 shows that more than 66 per cent of the functionaries agree that in their organisation, time limits are set to serve the citizens. 74 per cent of the employees agree that they are extra cautious to meet the deadlines. 76 per cent of the functionaries agree that in their organisation deadlines are realistic and are actually achieved.

Table S3.26 expounds the agreement of 79 per cent of the respondents and strong agreement of 20 per cent that in their organization, transparency is maintained in all dealings however 2 per cent disagree with this.

Table S3.26 depicts that they 58 per cent of the respondents agree and 30 per cent strongly agree that punctuality is maintained in their organisation. However 11 per cent disagree and 1 per cent strongly disagree that punctuality is maintained in their organisation

3.2.9 Salient Observations Based on FGDs

- The field observations clearly reflected that the organisational culture is not conducive for the functionaries to produce their optimal output in their delivery of services. The beneficiaries as per the findings remain unsatisfied with the delivery system. The findings also highlight that there is a lack of innovativeness in the job work. The monotony of the work probably leads to dissatisfaction among the functionaries (see Box 3.2).
- The officials are equipped with obsolete equipments, therefore they lack enthusiasm. A significant finding of the current research is that officials assigned great importance to learning organisation to enhance their performance which is contrary to popular belief that government officials lack interest in learning new techniques. The survey also points that officials are not always courteous towards the citizens. The officials felt that the citizens lacked knowledge of cumbersome processes therefore keep pestering them, which sometimes obstruct smooth functioning. The functionaries also explained that sometimes it is not possible to furnish details. It seems that the officials perhaps try to exhibit their supremacy over stakeholders. The right

intervention strategies can help in bringing citizen-centric culture.

- The timeliness is an important factor. Functionaries explained that the targets were assigned to them and they had to act as per the agenda set by higher-ups. The officials felt that in the absence of any medium of communication such as telephone, mobile phone, or computer related facilities, etc. at grassroots level, more time should be given to achieve the target. An important issue emerged from the present study is that the functionaries felt that transparency was maintained in their organisation, hence a way was set for successful adoption of e-Governance in their departments.

- Role clarity is an important step for implementing strategy, building learning organisations and competing successfully in today's environment. The findings of the research showed that functionaries are probably unaware of their goals, and they just perform mechanically whatever is assigned to them. The officials felt that if they have the accountability of any action, proper authority should be entrusted for reward and punishment. The findings showed that the functionaries suffer stress due to heavy workload and pressure of deadlines. They have become habitual of public dealings. The exogenous factors affect their actions. The officials felt that they need to be freed from the clutches of external pressures (political and frequent transfer). The study reflected that the officials were more often sent on deputation to different departments, which affects the loyalty, and they lack knowledge of the new department and there is always a fear of transfer to remote areas, which results into ineffectiveness of an employee.

- The survey sustains the theory (Herzberg's theory of motivation) that if the necessary environmental factors like cleanliness, drinking water, toilet facilities, etc are provided to an employee the level of motivation increases and performance of an employee is enhanced. It has been found that the tangible benefits like seating arrangement and status symbols such as size of the chair and nameplate outside the room, salary on time, uniform, etc definitely boost the motivation to perform better. Some of the respondents work hard in the field, therefore when they report to headquarters they prefer pleasant ambience. In this context, the factors dampening motivation in functionaries are reflected in Table 3.26.

- Respondents felt that their supervisor should be an effective manager (officer). They elaborated that the credentials of the leader should be impressive as well as he should have the complete knowledge of the whole process of working. The research shows that majority of leaders follow laissez-faire style. This style is best suited to make employees feel secure at the unavailability of an officer. However the respondents observed that more powers should be delegated to the leader (officer) to maximise his performance.

Table: 3.26: Factors Dampening Motivation in Functionaries

<table>
<tr><th>S. N.</th><th>Factors dampening motivation</th><th>Impact on motivation</th></tr>
<tr><td>1.</td><td>Roles and responsibility not defined, causing confusion</td><td rowspan="4">• Lack of morale
• Lack of involvement of functionaries
• Lack of efficiency in the work
• Lack of citizen management, during service delivery</td></tr>
<tr><td>2.</td><td>Poor working conditions
• Poor work environment
• Poor support system</td></tr>
<tr><td>3.</td><td>Functionaries not empowered with knowledge, skills and autonomy</td></tr>
<tr><td>4.</td><td>Directional leadership (lack of participation)</td></tr>
</table>

Source: Field survey and FGDs

- The results depicted that the effectiveness of the team can be achieved if there is a proper strategy of the team. The respondents were totally unaware of the goal orientation of the team. A significant finding of the research reveals that there is a lack of resources (human, financial) for proper functioning of a team. The probe showed that the human resource was not appropriate as there were no new recruitments done for more than a decade. It was brought to light that the equipments for the team were obsolete. The functionaries observed that the team should have proper communication for operation.
- Survey highlights that organisational effectiveness can be attained if the personal values of an employee match with the employee's value. The respondents stressed the importance of organisation's participation in the process. It was further highlighted that the calm and tolerant environment adds to effectiveness of the organisation. The functionaries showed that if there were a feeling of security and confidence due to the fair and encouraging policies of the department it would eventually lead to effective operation of an organisation.
- Research show that there is a smooth ground for the introduction of e-Governance. All the categories namely stakeholders, panchayat members, functionaries advocate the presence of e-Governance. The panchayat members feel that it would bring development in their areas as well as would reduce wrong practices and bring promptness in the delivery system. The

citizens felt that it would make their dealing with government departments easier, as it would be easy even to lodge complaints in their village without fear. The functionaries also advocated the practice of e-Governance but in a systematic form, where fundamentals issues (like networking, database, etc.) are addressed and all necessary equipments are made available.

3.2.10 Critical Findings

A. E-governance is More than IT Connectivity: e-Governance is not merely delivering the services through e-mail, computer, fax etc., but it requires efficient way of providing services and information to people. Through the deployment of IT, existing government processes can be re-engineered to transform into government services based on paperless electronic mail for simple transaction, but for more complex transaction the provision of fully interactive online services will give the citizens access to government services with faster response at places and at times that are more convenient.

B. Citizens Lack Awareness: The citizens are not aware about the services provided by the project (service provider). Those who were aware of the services got some advantage. The advantages narrated by them was that this is a solution which offers services which are available in the village itself and they do not have to abstain from their work every now and then. The main reason (for lack of awareness) given by the citizens is that they have not been informed about the services. However, the citizens were quite enthusiastic about the concept and felt that the future generation in the villages, which is aligned towards education and development, would be more interested in the concept of e-Governance.

The citizen's level of satisfaction is very low for the e-Governance services. As stated by them, the main reason for this is that there is a lack of synchronisation between government officials and the Kiosk owners. The facilities (connectivity) provided to Kiosks are not adequate which bring down the level of satisfaction of citizens. Also, they feel that the staff of Kiosks is not efficient and responsible.

C. Though Government Provides Security and Reasonably Good Salary to Functionaries but little is done to provide Enabling Environment: The prominent findings of the study reveal that it is evident that the government job brings little satisfaction for the employees as it provides security and reasonably good salary but it fails to provide good environment (good work culture, cleanliness) and working facilities to them, which affect the performance of the functionaries. Though, presently these issues are considered peripheral in the context of output but these are vital for improving performance.

D. Processes are so Cumbersome and there are Large Formats required to be filled to compile any Information: There is a lot of hue and cry raised by the general public over the non-performance of the employees in the government sector but there is a lack of realisation that the processes are cumbersome and there are large formats, which are to be filled to compile any information. On the top of it, the absence of database and the non-availability of computers affect the timeliness of the output.

E. Little Focus on HRD, while Functionaries are expected to deal with 'Human Problems': The findings reveal that there is a lack of focus on HRD problems of the employees. There is always a fear of transfer at the back of their mind. The salary sometimes gets delayed. The employees have no horizontal and vertical growth in their career in spite of possessing merit. The irony is that the human aspect of employees is ignored and the functionaries have to deal with human problems of citizens.

Besides above, assignment of the work is skewed. Some of the employees are assigned too much work; as a result they have to work over time. On the other hand the non-performers remain idle and no action is initiated against them and above all they enjoy salary and other perks like the over burdened employees.

F. Field Functionaries who Matter the Most at the Cutting Edge Level are not provided Proper Working Conditions: The conveyance and the means of communication are met by the field staff at their cost so they resort to corruption. The proper information database is not provided to them to take actions regarding the services to be provided to citizens. The other complaint by the field functionaries is that higher-ups do not respect their opinion. Local politics affects the decision-making as they get pressure from it. The functionaries are not provided with basic equipments like almirah, tables, chair etc., which bring dissatisfaction among field workers.

G. Change Management Issues are not Addressed: The observations of the research bring forth a point that the government organisation does not want to change to a proactive posture. The aim of change management is to make changes in a planned way and manage them in a systematic fashion. The purpose is to effectively implement new methods and systems in an ongoing organisation. The changes to be managed lie within and are to be controlled by the organisation. In the context of e-Governance, issues like training, change of attitude, technology transfer, service processes, etc. need to be addressed.

H. Capacity and Right Work Culture Need to be created for e-Governance: The functionaries feel that e-Governance is the future of our nation. They mentioned that the current system is viewed as inefficient so the only solution available is e-Governance. The functionaries are loaded with work, so it can relieve them of the excessive workload. It would eventually enhance their motivation. The capability of the office staff to accept e-Governance cannot be held in reserve, as they are the significant instruments of the current system. E-governance is just a water flow and staff members can lean with it. The prompt delivery of the services would satisfy the citizens. A farmer spends his whole working day to get his work done so it can save his time. The data cannot be tampered and this would convey sense of security among the officials and ultimately transparency can be enhanced. The staff members made observation that all data should be fed with e-Governance system and a parallel manual system should not interfere with the working of e-Governance system.

3.3 Summing Up

Behavioural dimension is important in any execution of plan, and more so in the implementation of new strategy (Cummings and Worley, 2002). As Collins (2005) says, "even the best business companies in the world have given top priority to having healthy work culture, developing capabilities to improve efficiency. Only, after that they have successfully deployed technology to further enhance efficiency. Behavioural capabilities are vital links."

The study of behavioural issues has brought out some important findings. It shows that the present way of organisational working of service delivery departments, marked with bureaucratic (directional) leadership, individual-oriented working without much regards to teamwork, de-motivated functionaries, lack of involvement of functionaries in the decision-making process, work culture characterised by irresponsiveness, can not provide an organisation, where the personnel should work for the 'citizen management' and 'quality of services', which are the touchstones of good governance (see Figure 3.6). The salient findings are listed in Box 3.2.

3.4 Other Survey Findings

- **Low Awareness Level:** The awareness about e-Governance project (in Jaipur) has been low among citizens and only 28 per cent of the people were aware about it (see Table 3.27A1). It seems to be due to lack of initiatives made by the service provider to inform citizens. Also, a large percentage (44.4 per cent) of them (those who were aware of the project) were not aware about the availability of e-Governance services from the project (see Table 3.27A2).

Figure: 3.6: How Behavioural Dimension is Lacking in Service Delivery Department

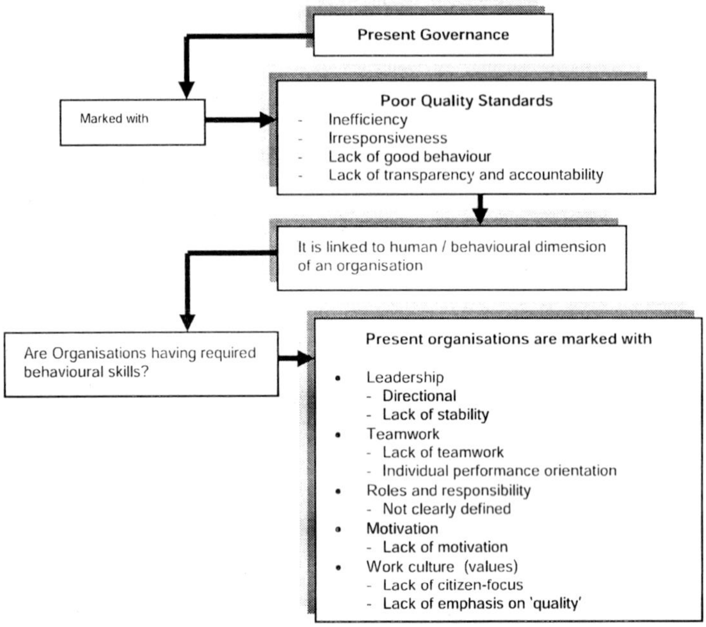

Box 3.2: Major Findings About Behavioural Issues Under e-Governance Projects

- Roles and responsibility of functionaries are not explicitly defined
- Low motivation level: The necessary environmental factors (like cleanliness, drinking water, toilet facilities, etc.) are not provided to functionaries that affect their motivation (It sustains the Herzberg's theory of motivation)
- The functionaries are unaware of the goals of 'good governance', they just perform mechanically whatever is assigned to them
- The officials work under external pressures (political and frequent transfer), which results into their ineffectiveness
- Little focus on HRD, while functionaries are expected to deal with 'human problems'
- Functionaries not empowered with knowledge, skills and autonomy
- Lack of involvement of functionaries in the decision-making process
- Field functionaries who matter the most at the cutting edge level are not provided proper working conditions to address problems (they are equipped with obsolete equipments, therefore they lack enthusiasm)

Table 3.27A1: Awareness about e-Governance Project (in Jaipur)

	Yes	No
%age	28	72

Table 3.27A2: Awareness about e-Governance Services

	Yes	No
%age	55.6	44.4

- **Both Functionaries and Citizens want e-Governance:** A large percentage of them want that the e-Governance should be introduced. The figure is as high as 90 per cent for functionaries and 92 per cent for the citizens (see Tables 3.27B and 3.27C). The probable reasons are: for citizens, it is convenience to get service at village level (if it is provided), and for functionaries, it is due to convenience and efficiency.

Table 3.27B: Citizens want e-Governance

	Yes	No
%age	92	8

Table 3.27C: Functionaries want e-Governance

	Yes	No
%age	90	10

- **Non-availability of Electricity at e-Kiosk:** The average availability of electricity is only for 20 per cent of total time (see Box S3.1) during daytime from 9 AM to 5 PM, due to unreliability of electricity supply.

- **Non-functioning of Network (at e-Kiosk):** Due to interrupted electricity supply and connectivity problem, the network does not work for 75 per cent of the time (even UPS is able to help partially) (see Box S3.2).

- **Different Users of e-Governance Services:** The field survey was carried out to know about: i. knowledge of e-Governance services offered by the project, and ii. usage of e-Governance services from the project. In both the cases, the young, high education group (above high school), high income group, OBC and males have more knowledge about and utilised more services from the project (see Tables 3.28A to 3.28C and Boxes S3.3 and S3.4). (in case of usage, general caste and OBC have equal percentage).

Table: 3.28A: Knowledge about the Services given by e-Governance Project (in Jaipur)

S.N.	Categories	Groups	Yes (%)
1.	Age	18-30 Years	66.67
		31-40 Years	33.33
		Above 40 Years	0
2.	Education	Low education group (illiterate to PE)	6.67
		Medium education group (>PE but <HS)	40
		High education group (>HS)	53.33
3.	Income	Low income group (BPL)	13.33
		Middle income group (>BPL but < Rs. 4000pm)	46.67
		High income group (income> Rs. 4000pm)	40
4.	Caste	General	26.67
		OBC	53.33
		SC/ST	20
5.	Gender	Male	86.67
		Female	13.33

Table 3.28B: Usage of e-Governance Services from e-Governance Project (in Jaipur)

S.N.	Categories	Groups	Yes (%)
1.	Age	18-30 Years	75
		31-40 Years	25
		Above 40 Years	0
2.	Education	Low education group (illiterate to PE)	0
		Medium education group (>PE but <HS)	0
		High education group (>HS)	100
3.	Income	Low income group (BPL)	0
		Middle income group (>BPL but < Rs. 4000pm)	50
		High income group (income> Rs. 4000pm)	50
4.	Caste	General	50
		OBC	50
		SC/ST	0
5.	Gender	Male	75
		Female	25

Table: 3.28C: Knowledge of e-Governance Services and Usage of Services from e-Governance Project (in Jaipur)

S.N.	Issues	Critical observations	Remarks
1.	Knowledge of e-Governance services given by e-Governance project	Young, high education group (above high school), high income group, OBC and males have more knowledge about and utilised more services from e-Governance. (in case of usage, general caste and OBC have equal %age).	Such findings may help in defining appropriate strategy and positioning services for different categories of users
2.	Usage of e-Governance services from e-Governance project		

3.4.1 Study of Delivery System: The study of delivery system[1] was attempted to understand whether it has the capacity to meet citizens' requirements or not. This is in the context of the fact that efficient delivery of services to citizens can be done only by a sound delivery system.

The service delivery departments studied for the purpose were Tehsil, primary education, health, agriculture, animal husbandry, drinking water and PDS, under the following heads (see Tables S3.33 and S3.34):

- Manpower
- Infrastructure
- Logistics
- Work culture
- Monitoring and supervision
- Autonomy
- Rules and procedures
- Internal and external environment

Salient Findings

- In all the service delivery departments as indicated by Table S3.33, the position of manpower, logistics and infrastructure is far below expectations. For example in case of primary schools there is a shortage of teachers, school rooms, adequate teaching-aids, etc.; and, in Tehsil the Patwari has to handle a large number of cases, and the shortage of storage space (for records and files) and lack of infrastructure only increase the difficulty of handling existing workload. Similar is the case in other delivery departments as well. Because of this the service delivery as well as grievances redressal are seriously affected.

- As regards work culture, it is marked with lack of responsiveness. The performance is affected by the fact that there is no monitoring and supervision done by the senior officials. They do not make adequate field visits to ensure good performance.
- Since major expenditure is never sanctioned at the village / Block level, lack of autonomy of the functionaries adversely affects their performance. For example, doctors cannot purchase medicines and even simple equipments. Delay in supply of these definitely hampers their efficiency.
- Rules and procedures for acquiring equipment are long and cumbersome and often beset with delays.
- There is a lack of training to all the field staff in all the service delivery departments which affects their ability to work.
- The field functionaries are de-motivated due to a number of reasons such as lack of incentive for good work, no scope of promotion and unsuitable working conditions. Also workload on the functionaries increases as they have to perform work related to those items, which are not the part of their primary job. For example, in case of teachers, they have to devote time to pulse polio or election or census counting etc. and 40-45 per cent of their time is consumed in such activities (see Table S3.34).
- Internal environment of all the service delivery departments is in a bad condition and invariably there is no cleanliness (see Table S3.34).

Similarly, in the context of above, if we look at the grievances redressal, four case studies (from 7 to 10 in Annexure 3.2) indicate that e-Kiosk was able to send the complaints to Collectorate, but these complaints were not resolved in time (less than 1 per cent satisfactory disposal) due to a variety of factors such as inadequacy of manpower and infrastructure, low capabilities, lack of commitment, lack of resources and equipments and so on. Due to this, citizens stopped sending grievances through e-Kiosk. Thus for good governance, IT is important for connectivity, but for efficient delivery of services, delivery system should be first strengthened.

3.4.2 Case Studies of Select e-Governance Projects: An attempt was made to prepare case studies of Janmitra, Gyandoot, e-Bhoomi, RDS and OLTP (see Table S3.35). The process of service delivery is given in Table S3.36. Based on FGDs, critical behavioural indicators; and strengths, weaknesses and challenges are reflected in Tables 3.1.1 and 3.1.2 in Annexure 3.1 respectively. Likewise, the indicative performance indicators such as time spent, cost incurred and visits by citizens, and their satisfaction are indicated in Table 3.1.3 in Annexure 3.1. Indicative number of applications and income from these projects are given by Tables 3.1.4 and 3.1.5 in Annexure 3.1.

The specific points about the field visits to some of the e-Kiosks are given below:

A. Visit to E-bhoomi: *Visit to Tehsil of South Taluk:* In this Tehsil the following services (under e-Bhoomi) are made available:

- RTC (record of rights, tenancy and crop)
- Mutation extract
- Khata detail
- RR-5 (ROR in the last 5-10 years)
- RR-6 (changes in RORs)

The above services were offered by the e-Kiosk at Tehsil. For this purpose, Patwaris are engaged after giving them adequate training. There was only one Kiosk in one Tehsil.

As regards the processing (of RTC, Khata detail, RR-5 and RR-6), there has been considerable improvement in giving these four services. But, the activities for giving mutation certificate have remained same (as existing process is automated). In a way, there was no process improvement for mutation. And the time taken by citizens, the cost involved in getting mutation certificates remained almost same. However the efforts made on a pilot basis deserve appreciations. Such efforts together with process re-engineering, if replicated in e-Kiosks at village, would bear good results.

As there were no other e-Kiosks in villages so people had to come from far off villages to Tehsil office.

No other services (like caste, income and domicile certificates) other than above mentioned were offered to citizens.

From above it is evident that the services provided by e-Kiosk (of e-Bhoomi at Tehsil) are mainly related to land records, for which computer records are available. In a way very limited services are made available. While challenge lies in process re-designing. As in case of mutation, where the process is involved for change of records, it (process) has not changed much. Similarly, in the cases of caste, income or domicile certificates, where processes need to be re-designed to give them through e-Kiosk, BPR would be required.

In the light of above it has to be carefully watched, as to how such efforts under e-Bhoomi and other services (where large processes are involved) would be replicated in other locations (villages) in the Tehsil.

B. Visit to Sathnum Village e-Kiosk (in Mandia District): In this Kiosk together with five services (under e-Bhoomi) as mentioned above, three more services viz., caste, domicile and income certificates were also provided as a part of rural digital service (RDS) programme.

In this Kiosk, while discussing with some citizens and Kiosk owner, the following problems were revealed:

- Electricity problem: There has been electricity cut for 10-12 hours per day and there was no certainty of timings for electricity supply.
- Connectivity problem: The connectivity has been provided through dial-up mode, but getting connectivity to server at head-end (at district hqs.) was a chronic problem, probably due to problem of lack of system management.
- Coordination problem: Though the application is sent through e-Kiosk, but the remaining process has remained manual. In this process the stakeholders involved are citizens, Kiosk owner, Tehsidar, dealing clerk and Patwari, and none have proper coordination with one another for trekking the application. As the process remains manual and without MIS, it is difficult to track the application and inform to Kiosk owner / citizen in time.

Due to above the impact has been as follows:

- Time and cost deduction is not significant, sometimes it takes more time to deliver certificates.
- Citizens stopped approaching e-Kiosk, preferred to go to Tehsil office.
- Income of e-Kiosk: The average income of e-Kiosk through e-Governance services is Rs. 585 and average income of e-Kiosk through total services is Rs. 1085. It shows 53 per cent of income is through e-Governance services and 47 per cent of income from non-e-Governance services (see Table 3.29).
- Kiosk becoming business centre: E-Kiosk is more engaged in business activities like typing, photocopying, and other job work.

C. Visit to OLTP: Regarding the study of OLTP, two Kiosks viz., Wadaparthy and Hanmanpur were visited. Services availed by the citizens through e-Kiosk are: grievance redressal, certificates (caste, income and domicile), ROR, *gram hat,* and e-mail.

It was revealed by Mandal Revenue Offices (MRO) that in the last one year

Table: 3.29: List of e-Kiosks: visited during Field Visits and their Performance

(Average per Kiosk per month)

S.N.	Projects	Name of e-Kiosk	Numbers			Income (in Rs.)				%age of BEP ****	Remarks
			E-gov. Servi-ces*	Other services**	Total	E-gov. Services*	Other services **	Total	%age *** of total		
1.	e-Gover-nance project	i Shivdaspura	5	8 (2 photographs + 1 horoscope + 2 computer educations + 3 *mandi* rates)	13	100	700	800	13%	22.85%	Unviable
		ii Chandlai	2	3 (1 photographs + 1 horoscope + 1 computer education)	5	40	70	100	40%	2.85%	Unviable
		iii Vatika	Nil	12 cable TV connections	12 Cable TV conne ction	Nil	1800	1800	0%	51.42%	Unviable
		iv Kadera	10	11 (5 photographs + 1 horoscope + 1 computer educations + 2 *mandi* rates + 2 cable TV connections	21	120	650	770	15 %	22.00 %	Unviable
				Average				867.5	17%		

Contd...

S.N.	Projects	Name of e-Kiosk	Numbers			Income (in Rs.)				%age of BEP ****	Remarks
			E-gov. Servi-ces*	Other services**	Total	E-gov. Services*	Other services **	Total	%age *** of total		
2.	Janmitra	i. Khanpur I	195	1300 (300 Salary bills+ 100 property rates+ 800 stamp papers+ 100 typing)	1495	3500	5500	9000	39%	257.14%	Viable (near Tehsil Hqs.)
		ii. Khanpur II	Nil	Nil	Nil	Nil	100	100	0%	2.85%	Unviable
		iii. Jhalara-patan	50	60 (15 salary bills+ 10 property rates+ 20 stamp paper+ 5 typing+ 10 result)	110	1000	1500	2500	40%	71.40%	Unviable
		iv. Sarola I	12	50(30 salary bills+ 10 property rates+ 8 stamp paper +2 typing)	62	500	850	1350	37%	38.57%	Unviable
		i Sarola II	Nil	35 (15 salary bills + 10 property rates+ 8 stamp paper+ 2 typing)	35	0	300	300	0%	8.57%	Unviable
				Average				2650	23.2%		
3.	Gyan-doot	i Sundarpur	150	200	350	1900	3000	4900	38%	140.0%	Viable (near to Tehsil Hqs.)
		ii Mangod	30	150	180	425	1800	2225	19%	63.57%	Unviable
		Average						3562.5	28.5%		

Contd...

S.N.	Projects	Name of e-Kiosk	Numbers			Income (in Rs.)				%age of BEP ****	Remarks
			E-gov. Services*	Other services**	Total	E-gov. Services*	Other services **	Total	%age *** of total		
4.	i. e-Bhoomi	South Taluk (Hqs)	NA								
	ii. RDS (including e-Bhoomi)	Sathnum village	45	25	70	585	500	1085	53%	31.00%	Unviable
		Average						1085	53%		
5.	OLTP	i Wadaparthy	20	7	27	250	150	400	62%	11.42%	Unviable
		ii Hanmanpur	25	10	35	375	220	595	63%	17.00%	Unviable
		Average						497.5	62.5%		

Note: Assuming breakeven point (BEP): Rs. 3,500

Source: Concerned e-Kiosks. *Caste, Income, Domicile certificates; RORs, and grievances.**Mandibhav, horoscope, computer education, Cable TV, photocopy, etc. ***Income from e-Governance services to total income **** Total income as % of BEP

(2004-05) about 8000 applications under different services were received. Or, it can be inferred that about 800 applications per Kiosk in a year, or 65 applications in a month or 2-3 applications in a day. It implies that the citizens have not been enthusiastic about availing services through e-Kiosk. MRO also informed that citizens preferred to come to Tehsil office than to go to e-Kiosk.

This project, as evident from field visit, has suffered due to following reasons:

- Interrupted supply of electricity and the problem of connectivity of e-Kiosk with mandal revenue office (MRO).
- As the number of activities (as process re-engineering not carried out) in the process of delivery of certificates has remained same, so the time and cost involved in availing certificates (caste, domicile, etc.) have remained same.
- Lack of initiative by the service provider and Kiosk owner to take citizens in confidence through better services delivery, personal contacts, awareness building, etc.
- It appeared though this project was launched with a lot of interest, but when the problems started surfacing, concerned stakeholders viz., MRO, Kiosk owner, and system manager (in this case it was outsourced to one company) started withdrawing and lost interest. It reflected the case of lack of system ownership.

D. Visit to Gyandoot: The main services provided by e-Governance Gyandoot project in Dhar district are: caste, income, domicile, ROR certificates and *mandi bhav*. The following Kiosks were visited during the field visit:

- Sundarpur (near to Tehsil)
- Mangod (about 20 Km from Tehsil)

In Sundarpur, e-Kiosk owner informed that there has been major problem of connectivity and electricity (it does not come for 12-14 hours). Besides this, due to connectivity problem, he is not able to inform head-end. Also, there is no functional MIS so it is difficult to keep track of application and liaison with Tehsil. Besides, entire process has remained manual. Due to these reasons, Kiosk owner or his nominee goes to Tehsil office with a bunch of applications. There he gets certificates made through a normal manual process. And thereafter he handovers the certificates to citizens in the afternoon. Thus, though he is a e-Kiosk owner but in a way he works as a mediator between Tehsil and citizens. Such a process of giving certificates through e-Kiosk is certainly not intended, and this is a serious matter.

The income of e-Kiosk: The average income (in 2004-05) of Kiosk was Rs.1162 from e-Governance services, and it varied from Rs. 425 (in remote village) to Rs.1,900 (see Table 3.29).

Also there was no MIS available through computer at e-Kiosk and it was not possible to know total number of applications received and pending. It was informed that the Kiosk owner was not feeding data regularly in order to inform head-end. Further, it was informed that there is no MIS developed for e-Kiosk.

At Mangod e-Kiosk, the performance has been much poorer. This Kiosk is about 20 km away from Tehsil. Here Kiosk owner has been facing acute problems of electricity cut and poor connectivity. He also visits Tehsil office for making certificates, but he faces more problems due to more distance from Tehsil, so he is not able to provide certificates to citizens in time. And thus, he is not able to attract citizens to his e-Kiosk.

Kiosk owner informed that initially there was good response but soon, when problems started arising, there has been delay in providing certificates to citizens, then people stopped coming to Kiosk, and started going to Tehsil directly.

Note: The problem was more acute in remote villages due to 'distance factor' (as Kiosk owner had to go to Tehsil for making certificates, covering large distance), besides frequent closer of Kiosk due to highly interrupted electricity supply.

The above shows that in the last 2-3 years, in-spite of initial big campaign and euphoria, e-Kiosk owners and service provider (district administration) could not instill confidence in citizens to avail services from e-Kiosk.

The major problem as stated by Kiosk owners, citizens and Tehsildar were similar to e-bhoomi and OLTP and are listed below:

- Electricity and connectivity problem (and no BPR)
- Manual processing
- Poor MIS
- Lack of citizen focus to attract citizens to e-Kiosks to avail services
- Lack of system ownership

E. Visit to Janmitra: *Visit to Khanpur Tehsil: Non-availability of Patwari at e-Kiosk and Non-functional MIS:* At Khanpur Tehsil, the Kiosk owner Yogesh Sharma informed that he was not able to get signature of Patwari on Jamabandi at e-Kiosk. So he had to visit the Tehsil for verification of Jamabandi and signature of Patwari.

Sometimes the Kiosk owner had to wait for 2-3 hours for Patwari, affecting the working of e-Kiosk. Besides this, there was no functional MIS so it was difficult to keep track of application and liaison with Tehsil.

Visit to Sarola I Kiosk, Khanpur Tehsil: Connectivity and electricity problem: In village Salora I, Kiosk owner Ansuman Singh informed that there is a major problem of connectivity, as electricity does not come for a long period (10-15 hours in a day). Besides, due to connectivity problem, Kiosk owner is not able to send application through network at head-end. As the remaining process is manual, so Kiosk owner or his nominee goes to Tehsil office with a bunch of applications. There he gets certificates made through a normal manual process, thereafter he handovers the certificates to citizens in the afternoon. Thus though he is a e-Kiosk owner but in a way he is working as a mediator between Tehsil and citizens. One can safely assume that e-Kiosks are turning into e-Business centres and e-Kiosk[2] owner into mediator as far as e-Governance is concerned.

"Besides, due to connectivity problem, Kiosk owner is not able to send application through network at head-end. As the remaining process is manual, so Kiosk owner or his nominee goes to Tehsil office with a bunch of applications. There he gets certificates made through a normal manual process, thereafter he handovers the certificates to citizens in the afternoon. Thus though he is a e-Kiosk owner but in a way he is working as a mediator between Tehsil and citizens."

Visit to Jhalarapatan Tehsil: MIS Problem: The e-Kiosk owner Nausad Ali of Jhalarapatan was asked to give the information about the number of applications received and pending. The Kiosk owner could not give details and informed to check it from the registers. On being asked, he informed that the MIS does not work either due to failure of server or non-maintenance of MIS at the head-end. Such incidents were also reported by the Kiosk owners of Salora I, Salora II and Khanpur I.

Due to inefficient MIS, citizens were not able to know the status, which created uncertainty in their mind and found process of submitting application form at e-Kiosk, an unreliable proposition.

Visit to Sarola II Kiosk, Khanpur Tehsil: Non-acceptability of Application Form of Janmitra: In the village Sarola II, Kiosk owner Jadhraj Nagar informed that there has been problem of non-acceptability of application form of different services of Janmitra in Tehsil. On enquiry, Tehsildar replied that the application form given by e-Kiosk is different from prescribed form. It has created confusion and uncertainty in the mind of citizens. So, the citizens did not like to avail services from e-Kiosk.

3.4.3 Upshot of Findings

A. Performance of Delivery of Services: As evident from Table 3.1.3 in Annexure 3.1, in all the projects under study, the performance of service delivery in terms of time spent and cost incurred in availing caste certificate has not been very different from manual system of getting certificate from Tehsil before introducing e-Kiosk. It is so, as no effort has been made to re-design the process of service (certificate) delivery, so the time and cost consuming activities (like collection of attachments, visits to Tehsil and *Patwarghar*, etc.) have not come down. Also, in e-Kiosk, an element of uncertainty remains regarding its functioning – whether it would be open, or, Kiosk owner would attend problems in time.

B. Withdrawal Syndrome among Citizens: In all the projects, in the beginning there has been a lot of enthusiasm by service provider and district administration. Citizens also showed a lot of interest when e-Kiosks were launched in their localities. But with the passage of time, when the performance of service delivery was not up to expected levels, citizens started withdrawing from going to e-Kiosks and preferred availing services from Tehsil office (see Figure 3.10).

Figure: 3.7: Average Monthly Income of e-Kiosks Under Different Projects

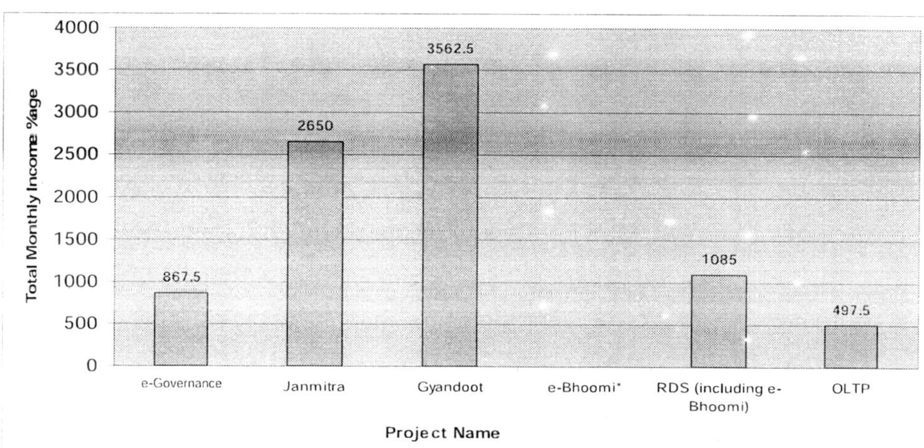

* Data not available

Source: Based on Table 3.29

C. Kiosks are not having Financial Viability: The total average monthly income of e-Kiosks has been less than Rs. 1711 and varies between Rs. 497 in OLTP project to Rs 3562 in Gyandoot project (see Figure 3.7 and Table 3.29). While on discussion with the Kiosk owners, it was revealed that the breakeven point (BEP) (per month) is between Rs. 3000 and 4000 (average Rs. 3500), thus indicating that the average monthly income of almost all Kiosks (twelve out of fourteen) in all the study projects is less than BEP (see Table 3.29). Rather it is far below by as much as 50 per cent of BEP in many Kiosks (see Figure 3.8), except in the cases of Khanpur I and Sundarpur e-Kiosks, which are in towns and near Tehsil office and major income is from business (or non-e-Governance) services. It is a cause of serious concern.

Figure: 3.8: Total Income of e-Kiosks to Breakeven Point

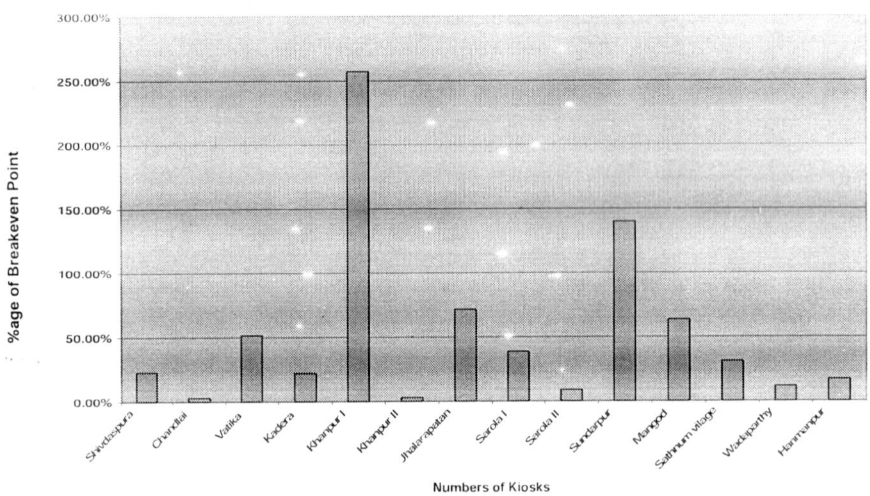

Source: Based on Table 3.29

Another important point to highlight is that only a few e-Kiosks (which would be less than 10 per cent of total number of Kiosks) mainly in towns or near Tehsil office, is functional, while in far-off / remote (15-20 Kms. away from Tehsil office) villages, these are almost non-functional. Further, it is worth noting that income of e-Kiosks near towns or Tehsil office is mainly due to non-e-Governance services (like typing, photocopying, etc.) and as for the income from e-Governance services, it is earned by Kiosk owners by manual effort (i.e. manual collection of application form, then visiting Tehsil, getting certificates made manually and finally giving them to citizens), not by electronic medium.

Figure: 3.9: Income from e-Governance Services to Total Income by e-Kiosks

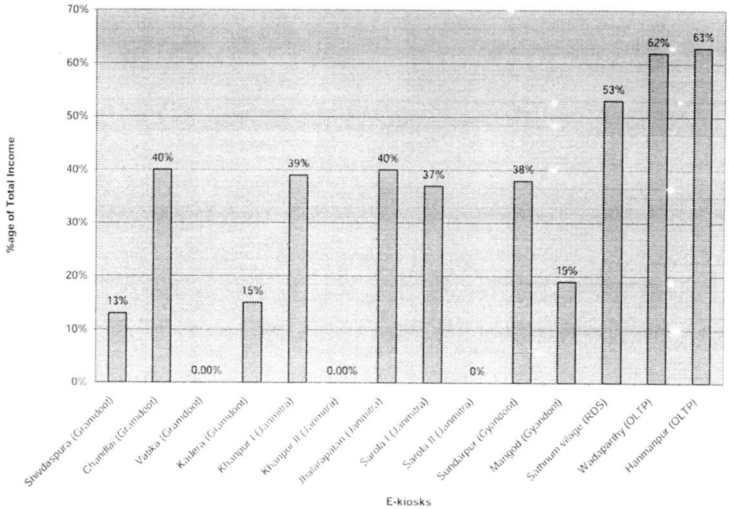

Source: Based on Table 3.29

If we examine the income from e-Governance services (see Table 3.29) it is much less. The average income from e-Governance services to total is between 17 per cent and 63 per cent (see Table 3.29 and Figure 3.9). It indicates that if e-Governance has to succeed it requires complete overhauling.

Figure: 3.10: Change in Citizens' Behaviour under e-Governance Projects

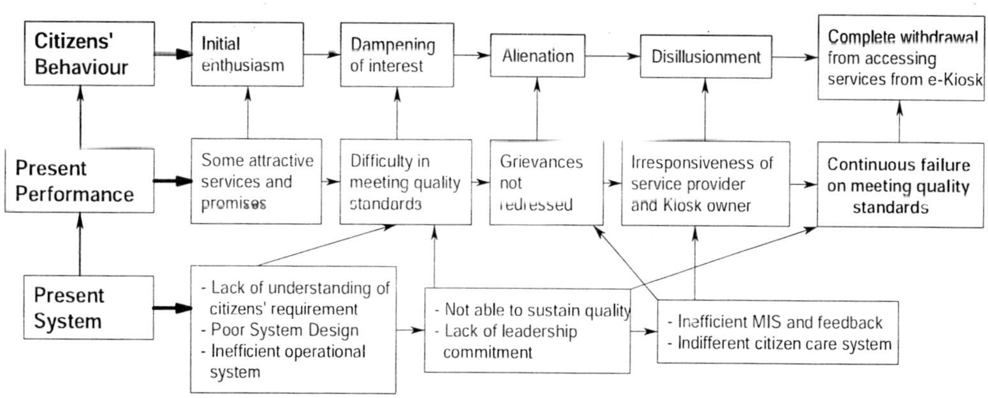

During the discussions in field visits, it was echoed by the stakeholders that in the beginning there was some income flow due to good initial response by citizens due to campaigning for awareness building in villages, but later income to Kiosks steadily came down.

D. Lack of Sustainability of e-Governance Projects: It is evident from Table 3.29, total income for e-Kiosks is very less and also it is much less than BEP. This income of e-Kiosk has been going down day-by-day due to difficulty in providing services efficiently to citizens. And citizens are disenchanted with e-Governance projects. It is affecting not only the viability of e-Kiosks but also of e-Governance projects.

3.4.4 Comparison between Lokmitra Project (for Payment of Utility Bills) in Jaipur and Other e-Governance Projects: The study of Lokmitra project in Jaipur district has been successful from the point of view of efficient handling of citizens and financial viability. It has provided win-win situation for all the stakeholders viz., citizens, service provider and concerned departments. The main reasons for such success are: *first,* high concentration of citizens near e-Kiosks; *second,* simplified and small process, which takes only a few minutes for completing the service transaction; *third,* backend computerisation; and *fourth,* sound MIS for monitoring, detection of problems, grievance redressal and so on. Besides, there is no dependency on network on a continuous basis, as transactions are settled at Kiosk / desk level, and also for MIS at e-Kiosk, high bandwidth is not required as data flow between e-Kiosk and head-end is not much.

While, e-Governance projects like Gramdoot, Janmitra, Gyandoot, OLTP in rural areas have faced difficulties like: *first,* low density (except near Tehsil headquarters) of citizens around e-Kiosks, *second,* long processing time (1-20 days, depending upon the service), *third,* dependency on network for sending application and attachments, which is slow and unreliable (due to dial-up mode and / or electricity failure), *fourth,* no process reengineering and backend computerisation, and *finally,* weak MIS. Besides, weak delivery system and lack of addressal of change management issues have not helped the cause of smooth functioning.

3.5 Summing up

- **Lack of Focus on Governance:** The field study reflects that the main focus has been to install IT infrastructure (network, e-Kiosks, software) rather than on good governance. The project documents do not categorically define governance. There is emphasis on listing services to be offered. The issues like citizen empowerment, improving work culture, quality of services, transparency and accountability find little mention (in some cases no mention).
- **Leadership:** Leadership of the e-Governance projects though enthusiastic,

but appears to be in hurry to demonstrate some results quickly. While doing so, vision and mission have not been defined in clear terms. The study of e-Governance projects gives an impression that the projects were started without clearly defined framework or road map. Also, leadership has been less participatory (local functionaries, though consulted, but were not involved in decision-making). It excluded the scope for taking field level problems into account.

- **Lack of System Design Study:** It is evident from field visits that adequate study about system has not been carried out. The system study should have looked more in-depth about efficacy of delivery system (which will deliver services). For example people (functionaries) involved, work culture, skills and knowledge required and processes involved in service delivery should have been studied more carefully. In the absence of detailed study, vital issues such as OD, process re-engineering, 'quality' issues, etc. have been overlooked.

- **Lack of System Ownership:** In providing services the main stakeholders involved are *first,* state IT department, *second,* district administration, *third,* local service provider (like IT company) and *fourth,* local service department (like Tehsil). All these have several important roles to play, but none is answerable to any single agency let alone to citizens. There is always a tendency to shift responsibility or pass the blame on others and in this process, service delivery continues to suffer.

- **Alignment of People, Process and Technology (PPT) not Addressed:** While designing new system, the main pillars are people, process and technology. Here the issues are: *first,* the required knowledge, skills, attitude and motivation have not been developed in the people (functionaries), who have to manage the system. *Second,* processes have not been aligned to the requirements of providing services at e-Kiosk level. The processes are not IT compatible and also not supported by adequate system support (under delivery system) to provide services efficiently. Or, in other words the processes are not re-engineered (re-designed) as per new requirements. *Third,* similarly the technology has not been aligned with new requirements of providing services at Kiosks in the villages. Necessary software design, backend computerisation, MIS and data security are not developed to the requirement of providing services at Kiosk level.

- **Inadequacy of Change Management:** The change management should have covered changes required in people who will manage system, changes required in processes, and changes required in technology in order to align people, processes, and technology perfectly to one another. For example, change management should have included strategy and programme for new skills or attitudes to be imparted to functionaries to adapt to new environment, or, how the citizens should be taken in confidence to use new system, or how field problems like electricity cut or unreliable connectivity can be handled. But, no such strategy for adapting to new system was suitably developed. It appears that new system was placed without adequate understanding of relevant issues and preparation.

- **Non-database-based Services not Delivered Satisfactorily (or Database-based Services Delivered Satisfactorily):** If we analyse the performance of e-Kiosks carefully, it has been evident during the visits to Kiosks and discussion with concerned stakeholders that services (like Jamabandi, ROR / RTC, payment of utility bills) that require information directly from computer database in backend, are delivered to citizens to their satisfaction. But services, which require long processing as in the case of caste, income, domicile and mutation certificates, and are not having backend computerisation, are not delivered to citizens to their satisfaction.

Box: 3.3: Critical Features of e-Governance Projects under Study

- Lack of focus on governance
- Enthusiastic top leadership, but less participatory, local / lower level officials / managers not involved fully
- Lack of system design study
- Lack of system ownership
- Alignment of people, process and technology (PPT)* not addressed
- Inadequacy of change management
- Non-database-based services not delivered satisfactorily

* People: It refers to personnel / functionaries of service department.
Process: It refers to process of service delivery.
Technology: It refers to IT

3.5.1 Concluding Remarks: There are many e-Governance initiatives taken up in the country today. But what is observed is that the focus in most of these cases is on computerisation and automation using IT (see Box 3.3). As a result, such projects do not sustain after the roll-out. Assessments and studies conducted indicate that for a successful e-Governance project implementation, government process change and organisational development (cultural & behavioral change) are very critical.

The problems such as lack of BPR and backend computerisation and poor capacity of delivery system, are common (in varying degrees) across the districts where study was made; and such problems have affected all the e-Governance projects, where study was made. Though there were definitely design problems, but service provider cannot be faulted so much, as BPR and backend computerisation and sound delivery system are to be provided by government. And without them, other e-Governance projects in rural areas in the field of service delivery would also find it hard to succeed.

3.6 SERVQUAL Analysis of e-Governance System

Analysis of SERVQUAL Model for e-Governance System is summarized in Table 3.30), which is as follows:

Gap 1: Gap between Expected Service by Consumers (Citizens) and Management Perception of Citizen Expectations: It is due to lack of proper assessment of the citizens' requirement. For example, a citizen expects a certificate (from Tehsil) to be delivered within 3-4 days with one visit to an office / e-Kiosk, reliability and convenience, and that the field functionaries and Kiosk owner should show good behaviour. And in case, there is any delay he would be appropriately informed. But it has been evident that such expectations of citizens were not captured by system designer or top management, who were designing the system. And it has resulted into this gap of perception vis-à-vis expectations. It could be due to lack of knowledge and prior experience and lack of appreciation of requirements of good governance by management.

Gap 2: Gap between Management Perception of Consumers' (Citizens) Expectations and Translation of Perceptions into Service Quality Specifications: It is on account of lack of focus on building delivery system based on 'quality parameters'. It has resulted into mismatch between capacity of delivery system to deliver and quality expected from it. The quality parameters (specifications) like timeliness, cost, reliability, behaviour, responsiveness, transparency, accountability are important determinants of 'good governance'. Such parameters have not been addressed while designing the e-Governance projects. In the case of e-Governance project (in Jaipur), there has been more focus on laying OFC & cable network (technology) and less on government service delivery.

Several available literature (Peppard and Rowland Philip, 2002) indicate that for utilising technology effectively, people and process are to be given first priority and the technology should be aligned to the requirement of business after re-designing the processes that meet the requirement of efficient delivery of services, and simultaneously, proper capabilities and values are developed in the organisation not only to delivery efficiently and but also to respect norms of providing service. But such an approach has been missing in all the e-Governance projects. And, before technology is brought, neither BPR is carried out nor capabilities and values in people (functionaries) were adequately developed to meet the changing requirements.

Gap 3: Gap between Service Quality Specifications (of Service Provider) and Service Delivery: When the design of the system is faulty, it leads to poor service delivery (see Tables 3.30 and 3.31). Under the project, the causes that can be attributed to this gap are:
- Tehsil office not connected with computers
- Poor output of services to citizens
- Poor coordination between Kiosks and field functionaries of departments
- Inadequate change management by service provider
- Inability of Kiosk owners to take citizens in confidence due to poor citizen (customer) focus.

Gap 4: Gap between Service Delivery and External Communication to Consumers (Citizens): Exaggerating the likely deliverables without commensurate system capacity. For example, expectations were raised that citizens would be provided certificates within 3 days, by telling citizens that they would get cable TV at reasonable price and with good quality of reception. But it did not happen so, due to various operational problems.

Gap 5: Gap between Perceived Service and Expected Service by Consumers (Citizens): Gap 5 is a service quality shortfall as seen by the customer, and gaps 1-4 are shortfalls within the service organisation. Thus, gaps 1-4 contribute to gap 5. The causes that can be attributed to this gap are:
- Poor service delivery
- Poor citizen relationship management (CRM)
    - Lack of interaction with citizens,
    - Lack of awareness building,
    - Lack of care of citizens' grievances,
    - Citizens not able to give feedback, etc.

3.6.1 SERVQUAL Analysis of Delivery System: Based on the study of delivery system of Tehsil, primary education, health, agriculture, animal husbandry, drinking water, and PDS, the salient points are given below (see Table S3.37).

Table 3.30: SERVQUAL Analysis of e-Governance System

S. N.	Gaps	Nature of gaps	Impact	Causes
1.	Gap 1	Gap between expected service by consumers (citizens) and management perception of citizen expectations	• Poor assessment of citizens' requirement and expectations	• Lack of appreciation of citizens' expectations and requirements of good governance • Lack of knowledge and experience
2.	Gap 2	Gap between management perception of consumers (citizens) expectations and translation of perceptions into service quality specifications	• Poor system design	• More focus on technology (laying OFC & cable network), less on service delivery – processes and people • Over ambitious approach
3.	Gap 3	Gap between service quality specifications (of service provider) and service delivery	• Poor service delivery	• Tehsils not connected with computers • Poor coordination between Kiosks and field functionaries of departments • Poor capacity of delivery system • Poor output of services • Inadequate change management by service provider • Cable cuts in the initial phase, so interrupted communication for both sending applications to offices and Cable TV. • Inability of Kiosk owners to take citizens in confidence due to poor citizen (customer) focus

Contd...

S. N.	Gaps	Nature of gaps	Impact	Causes
4.	Gap 4	Gap between service delivery and external communications to consumers (citizens)	• Wrong communication	• Exaggerating the likely deliverables without commensurate system capacity (raising expectations by telling citizens that they would get cable TV at reasonable price & services at one place with ease)
5.	Gap 5	Gap between perceived service and expected service by consumers (citizens)	• Citizens dissatisfaction • Lack of response of citizens to further avail services • Closure of e-Kiosks	• Poor service delivery • Poor citizen relationship management (CRM) i Lack of interaction with citizens, ii Lack of awareness building, iii Lack of care of citizens' grievances iv Citizens not able to give feedback, etc

Table 3.31: Comparison between Desired and Current Value of Quality Parameters – An Illustrative List

S.N.	Sectors (service name)	Parameter	Desired value	Current value
1.	Tehsil (caste certificate)	Time limit	3 days	10-15 days
		Cost to citizens	Rs. 12*	Rs.200-300**
		Number of visits by citizens	2	7-15
2.	Health (health check-up)	Access	Within village or GP	• Lack of infrastructure • Lack of manpower
		Cost	Free	Rs. 50-200**
		Facility	Free medicines	Inadequate / no supply of medicines
			Free tests	Lack of infrastructure / equipments for tests
			Free indoor facility	Indoor facilities are mostly non-functional
3.	Primary education (teaching, MDM, books)	Teaching	Free	Free but of poor quality
		MDM	Free	Bad quality of MDM
		Books	Free	Not all the books, copies and pencils are provided
4.	PHED (drinking water)	Quality	Quality up to standards	Contaminated water (like fluoride, salt, etc.)
		Access	Pipe water connection	Taps not provided in houses

Source: FGDs with citizens and officials

Note: The above is illustrative, not comprehensive. MDM: Mid day meal, GP: Gram Panchayat

*Fees decided by government. **Traveling cost + wages lost + other expenditure

Gap 1: Gap between expected Service by Consumers (Citizens) and Management Perception of Citizen Expectations: It is due to lack of proper assessment of the citizens' requirement. For example, a citizen expects a certificate to be delivered within 3-4 days with one visit to a office; or in the case of getting credit from the banks, he does not expect to be visiting different offices (for clearance) and should get within one month. But such expectations of citizens are not captured by planners at higher-ups, who are designing the system. And it results into this gap of management perception vis-à-vis citizen expectations.

Further to substantiate, if we look at the grievances redressal, four case studies (from 7 to 10 in Annexure 3.2) indicate that e-Kiosk was able to send the complaints to Collectorate, but these complaints were not resolved in time because of inability of delivery departments. Due to this, citizens stopped sending grievances through e-Kiosk. Thus for good governance, IT is important for connectivity, but for efficient delivery of services, delivery system should be first strengthened.

Gap 2: Gap between Management Perception of Consumers (Citizens) Expectations and Translation of Perceptions into Service Quality Specifications: It is because of lack of focus on building delivery system based on 'quality parameters'. It results into mismatch between capacity of delivery system to deliver and quality expected from it. For example, in order to provide quality education to children in schools, good class rooms and motivated teachers in desired number with teaching-aids are necessary; and similarly for quality water, water treatment plants may be required. But these are not provided, which result into mismatch between capacity of delivery system to deliver and quality expected by citizens.

Also, there is a lack of appreciation of system approach, and various components of delivery system are not attended to meet the 'quality requirements'. (e.g. in case of primary schools, infrastructure, playgrounds, teachers, teaching-aids, conducive school environment, etc.; or in case of health services, health centres, doctors, medicines, beds, ambulance, etc. are not attended to in totality. Only in bits and pieces, a few items are provided.)

In several cases, the focus remains on setting up delivery points / mechanisms up to Block / Tehsil, but less at gram panchayat / village level. For example, inputs delivery for agriculture, or, health facilities (which are mainly at CHC level, even at PHC level only check-up facilities are available).

Gap 3: Gap between Service Quality Specifications (of Service Provider) and Service Delivery: Due to poor delivery system design (see Tables S3.33 and S3.34), the poor service delivery (see Table 3.31) is the result of combination of various factors such as:

- Inadequate infrastructure, field staff and equipment support at the field level, resulting in poor output of the system (for example inadequate class rooms, lack of teachers and inadequacy of teaching-aids lead to poor output of teaching)
- Inadequate capabilities of staff to deliver
- Lack of coordination among field functionaries of departments
- Inadequate change management by the service provider
- Inability of field staff to take citizens in confidence due to poor citizen (customer) focus

Gap 4: Gap between Service Delivery and External Communications to consumers (citizens): It is due to exaggerating the likely deliverables without commensurate system capacity (raising expectations by telling citizens that they would get services at village level with ease, but it does not happen). For example, in the case of primary education, the message communicated to citizens is that the children would be provided with good education and mid-day meal free of cost, while schools do not have necessary wherewithal to do so.

Gap 5: Gap between Perceived Service and Expected Service by Consumers' Citizens): It is the sum of all the four gaps. In nutshell, it is due to: poor delivery system design and lack of citizen focus, for example:
- Lack of interaction with citizens,
- Lack of awareness building,
- Lack of care of citizens' grievances,
- Citizens not able to give feedback, etc.

To conclude, the ineffectiveness of the present delivery system has raised the question of sustainability of service delivery/programme outputs and has also resulted into sub-optimal performance. The ineffectiveness is due to a whole range of problems viz., lack of infrastructure, logistics and manpower support, ineffective planning, weak monitoring & evaluation system and so on.

The purpose of highlighting the above is to bring home one crucial point that without proper delivery mechanism, citizens would not get quality services, and IT would be of little significance. And, this is precisely the reason why the efforts under e-Governance are resulting into poor standards of service delivery.

3.6.2 Growth Model Analysis: Presently, the e-Governance project (in Jaipur) is able to provide partially inputs under stage I, a few services under stage II, and education (computer courses) under stage V, and specifically the following is achieved:

Stage I: Interface

- Web-site
- List of services (partially)
- List of information (partially)
- Sending letters / grievances (partially)

Stage II: Transactional

- Providing a few services

Stage III: Networking

- Education (computer courses) (partially)

In terms of percentage achievement of total score under e-Governance project (in Jaipur), it comes out to be 7.79 per cent [(6.0/77) * 100, see Table: 3. 32] and see Figure: S3.6.

Table 3.32: Ratings for different Inputs for Growth Model

S. N.	Stage	Inputs	Rating Assigned	Total	Evaluation Rating
1.	Interface	(i) Web-site	1		1
		(ii) List of services	1		.5
		(iii) List of information	1		.5
		(iv) Sending letters/grievances	1	4	.5
2.	Transactional	(i) Providing a few services	2		1
		(ii) BPR for a few services	2		0
		(iii) Backend computerisation (BC)	2		0
		(iv) BPR	2		0
		(v) System integration	2		0
		(vi) Grievance redressal and feedback	2	12	
3.	Vertical integration	(i) Linking systems vertically with similar functionalities (e.g. Patwari to Tehsil to Collectorate)	3		0
		(ii) Linking other services vertically	3		0

S. N.	Stage	Inputs	Rating Assigned	Total	Evaluation Rating
		(iii) Linking systems vertically with similar functionalities (e.g. Patwari to Tehsil to Collectorate)			0
		(iv) Linking other services vertically			0
		(v) e-Participation	3	15	0
4.	Horizontal integration	(i) Integrated systems and services horizontally (across departments)	4		0
		(ii) System integration horizontally	4		0
		(iii) Value added services*	4		0
		(iv) One-stop shop for online services	4	16	0
5.	Networking	(i) Government agencies	5		0
		(ii) Banks and insurance	5		0
		(iii) Health (check-up) Online	5		0
		(iv) Education (computer courses)	5		2.5
		(v) Participation by citizens in decision-making	5		
		(vi) Other agencies	5	30	0
	Total			77	6.0

Source. Given by research team, based on FGDs, %agc achieved=(6.0/77)*100-7.79%

3.7 SWOT Analysis

SWOT analysis of e-Governance project (in Jaipur) was carried out. The salient points are summarised below (see Table 3.33 and Figure S3.7).

- **Strength:** The project has OFC network and high bandwidth, enabling it to handle high-density data; and also, one Kiosk set-up in most of the villages (one Kiosk for about 8,000 populations) and government support in terms of access to land records data, coordination with line departments and recognising services provided by the project. All these have helped in providing good network in rural areas.
- **Weakness:** It includes lack of citizen-centric approach. Citizens' needs and their concerns have not been adequately addressed. Besides, lack of

awareness among people and lack of capabilities of Kiosk owners to take people in confidence have weakened further the system. More importantly, the service processes have not been simplified and re-designed to make them IT compatible. Only a few activities of the existing processes have been automated, mostly the processes are same as in manual system. That is why, the efficiency of process has not changed, rather due to delivery of application from e-Kiosk to Tehsil by courier has caused delay in most of the cases. Lack of sufficient hardware in the government departments is also a handicap. Of crucial concern is the poor capacity of delivery system to provide services to citizens. It is resulting into delay in providing services and handling grievances.

In sum, present e-Governance system is unable to address citizens' need as processes & systems are not reengineered to the requirement of citizens' convenience and there is low efficiency of service delivery.

- **Opportunity:** This system offers a number of opportunities such as : services at village level, revenue generation for service provider, partnership with government, helping citizens (serving the cause of corporate social responsibility) and to spread services and business in other areas (districts).
- **Threat:** It is beset with some problems like erratic supply of electricity and cable cutting in some cases (affecting connectivity). It is resulting into unreliable performance, which is leading to unacceptability by citizens (rejection syndrome).

The SWOT analyses of various services are reflected in Table S3.38.

3.7.1 Cause-effect Matrix: Based on above analyses and findings, cause-effect matrix is presented in Table 3.34.

3.8 System Requirement Study (SRS): A Critique

Based on the field study and consultations with various stakeholders of e-Governance projects under study, a few comments are placed below about the system requirement study and design:

During the consultations with IT professionals of State department of IT, it was quite evident that they have strong desire to do some thing innovative. But they are not able to fully design and implement due to a variety of reasons such as: *first*, lack of opportunity (including time) to understand the details of the government processes and the difficulties involved in them; *second*, hurry to deliver something and to start the project (and then sorting out details after the project has been launched); *third,* piece-meal approach, without detailed system requirement study (SRS); and, *fourth,* inadequate funding support.

Similarly in private sector, the IT professionals are quite enthusiastic, but, their efforts are limited due to: *first,* lack of understanding of the government processes and the difficulties involved in them; *second,* inadequate funding support; and, *third,* hurry to deliver something in order to cover the cost and make profit.

The focus of e-Governance projects under study has been more on laying network and installing hardware and designing and developing software (and, in some cases giving maintenance of these items to IT professionals / companies), though very vital, but 'good governance' and 'citizen focus' have taken backseat 'completely'.

In the context of above, an attempt was made to understand in detail about emergence of such a state of e-Governance system. Invariably, in all the projects, it was observed that the design of the system has suffered due to:

- *First,* 'what is good governance?', is not defined in explicit terms.
- *Second,* the specific and detailed requirement of citizens is not made (though listing of some services is made)
- *Third,* lack of appreciation of field problems and difficulties faced by functionaries (these are not properly listed and their solutions are not identified)
- *Fourth,* lack of participatory approach in the departments [only some consultations are held, which are not enough to give field functionaries and also lower level officials (Tehsildar, BDO, other block officials) a sense of involvement]
- *Fifth,* lack of focus on delivery of 'quality services' for system (e-Governance) design

The above issues are summarised in Table 3.35. It shows about some of the vital issues that were not adequately studied during 'system requirement study' and their impact on performance.

3.8.1 Critical Findings: Based on the field study and the analysis presented in section 3.2, the salient findings are listed below:

A. In-depth Market Research Study (MRS) not Carried out to Capture the Requirements of Citizens and their Expectations: The requirement for

Table 3.33: SWOT Analysis

Internal	External
Strength • OFC Network and high bandwidth • One Kiosk setup in most of the villages (one Kiosk for about 8,000 population) • Government support • No competitor *Finally*, **good network**	**Opportunity** • To provide services at village level • To generate revenue • Partnership with government • Helping citizens (serving the cause of corporate social responsibility) • To spread services and business in other areas (districts) • Building awareness through Cable TV ***Finally*, there is a scope for providing services at village level**
Weakness • Citizens-centric system not designed. Citizens' needs, their concerns not addressed • Lack of awareness among people • Women, poor, less educated and old are less willing • Lack of capabilities of Kiosk owner – inability to take people in confidence • Processes not simplified, only a few activities of the existing processes automated partially – mostly the processes are same as in manual system • Lack of sufficient hardware in the government departments • Capacity of delivery system to provide services is poor • Lack of coordination between services provider, Kiosk owner and government functionaries ***Finally*, present e-Governance system:** • Unable to address citizens needs • Processes & systems not reengineered to the requirement of citizens'	**Threat** • Erratic supply of electricity • Cable cutting in some cases (affecting connectivity) ***Finally*, the above leading to:** • Unreliable performance • Lack of acceptability by citizens (rejection syndrome)

Internal	External
• Low efficiency of service delivery	
Overall…. • Insufficient system study and design • Governance issues (like 'quality' of services w.r.t. timeliness, citizen satisfaction, empowerment, etc.) not adequately understood	

Table: 3.34: Cause-effect Matrix

S.N.	Causes	Effects	Impact
1.	• Inefficient network planning and management • Improper system design - issues of **operational and financial viability** are not addressed	• 75% down time: Network does not work	• Less than 1% citizens utilise e-Governance services
2.	• Governance issues not understood • Citizens not at 'central position' - **CRM not addressed**	• Citizens' grievances and concerns are not addressed (dissatisfaction)	• Less than 2% of Tehsil services availed by citizens from e-Kiosk
3.	• Processes not improved: Existing processes automated **(No process reengineering)**	• Inefficiency in delivery of services	• Low revenue
4.	• Work culture not improved • **Change management** not handled properly	• Lack of coordination among different functionaries and service provider • Work culture of 'time consciousness' and 'responsiveness' is missing	• No operational and financial viability **(Against the BEP of Rs. 3500, present income is Rs. 1000-2,500)** • Shift in focus from e-Governance to e-business / business • Poor quality of services • Citizen dissatisfaction
5.	• Inefficient system of delivery - **System integration** is lacking	• Inefficiency in delivery system	
	Most Critical • **Low / unreliable bandwidth** • **Poor electricity supply** • **Inefficient processes** • **Poor citizen management**		

Table 3.35: Issues not studied during System Requirement Study and their Impact on Performance

S.N.	Issues	Status	Impact on Performance
1.	Issues under good governance from citizens' perspective	• In-depth citizen requirement study not carried out	• Citizens' perspective and requirements not captured for providing good governance
2.	Field problems	• Not adequately studied	• Frequent disruption • Cable cut • Network failure • No connectivity between Tehsil and *Patwarghar*
3.	Difficulties of field officials and staff	• Not adequately studied • Lack of appreciation of field problems*	• No coordination between officials and service provider • Lack of training to functionaries regarding new set of knowledge and skills for e-Governance • Field functionaries do not go to e-Kiosks
4.	Quality of services	• Lack of appreciation of quality services	• Services not benchmarked to the citizens' satisfaction • System not designed and capable to provide quality services • Inconsistency in providing services *The above resulting into:* • Quality of services not up to the level of citizen's requirement • Citizens do not use e-Governance services

* For example, Patwari has a number of other works, logistics problem for field functionaries (for travel), lack of infrastructure at Tehsil and *Patwarghar*, etc.

different categories of users like male and female; different income groups (low, middle, high); caste groups (general, OBC, SC / ST); age-wise group (young, middle-aged and aged); and educational groups (low, medium, high), who have different requirements, were not identified. Also, it appears that the entire set of information, services and grievances as may be required by citizens were not taken into account.

B. *Parameters for 'Good Governance' not Defined Explicitly:* Though a few quality parameters for time and cost of availing services were reflected in the brochure of the project, yet many service quality parameters (like actual cost incurred by citizen), especially qualitative ones (like reliability, behaviour, responsiveness, transparency and accountability); information sharing of government programmes; and participation in decision-making, which would determine the good governance, were not defined in explicit term.

C. *Appropriate System Requirement Study (SRS) has been Lacking:* The study of existing delivery system (engaged in service delivery, for example for issuing certificates, or, grievance management, etc.) was not undertaken suitably to understand the processes, work culture and the support system (like manpower, infrastructure, logistics, etc.). No mapping of processes involved in service delivery, and the process analysis to identify the CTQs and support system required, were carried out. Also, the field level difficulties and the causes for delay in service delivery were not examined. These are important: *first,* to understand whether the service delivery department has requisite capacity to deliver, *second,* to assess the capabilities of people (functionaries) to handle present and future job, and *third,* to align the technology (IT) with processes.

D. *Missing Elements in System Design:* The following findings emerge from the analysis:

- Vision and mission of the e-Governance projects not defined
- Roadmap (time-bound programme for system development, which could have included services to be provided over a period of time) was not clearly defined
- PPT (People, Process and Technology) interaction not aligned properly
    - Processes not re-engineered
    - People (functionaries) not prepared for new system, and necessary capabilities not developed in officials and functionaries
    - Technology not aligned with new requirement of service delivery

[technology (backend, software and hardware) not implemented on the required lines of efficient service delivery]

- Many field problems were not appreciated due to lack of knowledge about government processes and systems, and quality issues
- Poor capacity of delivery system to provide services and redress the grievances

E. *Lack of Management of System:* Management of system is grouped in two categories – internal and external. The salient concerns are:

- **Leadership:** Leadership of the projects (at district and directorate levels) has been enthusiastic and wants to deliver innovative things, but been less participatory (local officials and functionaries, though consulted, but were not involved in decision-making). It excluded the scope for taking field level problems into account. Due to this, the problems like difficulties of Patwari in attending e-Kiosk, hesitation of citizens to use e-Kiosk, difficulties expressed by officials of Tehsil, etc. could not be addressed in time by the project management, while such difficulties were vital.

- **Teamwork:** In all the projects, an e-Governance team was constituted at the district level. But it had mainly members from existing set of officials (who had several other important works to attend) and there was no project leader exclusively looking after the project. At the operational level (i.e. at Tehsil level), no dedicated team was made to coordinate with service provider, officials, functionaries, different departments, etc. During the field study it was observed that many pressing operational problems like electricity cut, non-attendance of e-Kiosk by Patwaris, grievances of citizens, etc., could not be resolved.

- **Local Project Champion (Leader):** with exclusive responsibility to implement the project was not identified.

- **Work Culture:** Work culture has not been sensitive to timeliness, responsive to citizens' grievances, friendly in behaviour, and transparent and accountable in functioning.

- **Motivation**
  - Field functionaries do not feel much motivated, due to several difficulties (lack of transport, office infrastructure, record rooms, etc.) faced by them in the field for which they do not have answers
  - Working conditions (neat and clean working environment, facilities

like fans, coolers, chairs, tables, canteen, etc.) are not adequately provided in the office, which cause inconvenience to functionaries in discharging their duties
- Though under e-Governance projects, sophisticated equipments are installed at head-end and e-Kiosk, but operational level of functionaries, systems (like type-writers, record management, file-keeping, etc.) are still obsolete / old

Among others, due to above factors, the organisational effectiveness of departments (Tehsil, PHED, Education, Health, etc.) for delivery of services or grievance redressal has been low and is unable to meet the set deadlines and meet citizens' requirements.

The upshot of above is that behavioral dimension is as important as the process of service delivery or technological intervention, after all it is the people in the organisations who matter the most and it is they who have to implement the programmes/projects. Organisational effectiveness (of delivery system), which is determined by, among others, leadership, teamwork, work culture and motivation, is seriously undermined due to existing state of behavioural aspect of departments engaged in service delivery under e-Governance project. The neglect of this dimension has been impacting and will continue to impact adversely on the efforts under e-Governance.

External Issues: The following vital issues that affected the functioning of e-Kiosks were not addressed to the satisfaction of their smooth functioning:

- Electricity cut
- Network management (due to external cable cutting)

F. *Service Delivery:* From the analyses of CTQs and FMEA (see Tables 3.3 and S3.2), the following can be inferred about the service delivery of certificates under governance project:

- Quality of services in terms of time and cost of service delivery remains poor (rather it has deteriorated marginally)
- No functional MIS (for monitoring of service delivery)
- Lack of reliability (of providing services through e-Kiosk)

The problems in service delivery are rightly captured by SERVQUAL model depicted in Table 3.30.

Pilot Study not Carried Out: It appears proper feasibility study to test the soundness of the process of service delivery was not carried. And if pilot study was carried out, system was allowed to continue without making desired improvements. It is clear from the following example:

Under the project, the citizens came to e-Kiosks with applications. After receiving them, the applications were sent to Tehsil from e-Kiosk through a circuitous route (from e-Kiosk to head-end to Collectorate, and finally to Tehsil by courier). It rather increased the time for delivery of service. Likewise, Tehsils were not having the computers before starting of the project and they were not provided even after starting the project. It resulted into the problem of trekking of application between e-Kiosk and Tehsil, and caused uncertainty. Similar problems were also noticed in all the projects. These are some of the vital issues that were overlooked, and if there had been pilot study, the above shortcomings would have been identified and actions would have been taken for improvement.

G. *System Design not in Commensuration with Quality Parameters:* Let us take the case of service of issue of certificates (caste, income and domicile) through e-Kiosk. It was promised that citizens would get them within 3 days. But, quite often, it took more than 15 days to collect certificates. As regards the cost, service provider did not take into account the cost involved in making visits, collection of attachments, etc., which is normally significantly high, and with the result, citizens did not find much advantage in availing services from e-Kiosks.

Similarly, for example, it was expected that the grievances would be redressed in 21 days. But due to 'manual processing' and 'lack of capacity' of delivery system (see Table for SERVQUAL model for delivery system) engaged in various services provisioning like primary education, health, drinking water, etc., to provide services in time and of desired quality, the grievance redressal could not be done.

The above reflect that the e-Governance system was not designed to meet the time requirement of service delivery and grievance redressal.

H. *Factors Affecting Performance:* The performance of service delivery is mainly affected by five factors as shown in Table 3.10. But, among them two factors viz., *first*, 'BPR', and *second*, capacity of 'delivery system' is affecting the performance maximum. Their combined effect on performance is 71.80 per cent (46.31 per cent + 25.49 per cent) (see Table 3.10).

Process (throughput) Efficiency: With the increase of 'non-value adding' activities in the e-Governance project (in Jaipur) due to movement of application form by courier, the efficiency (throughput) has rather decreased from 2.51 per cent in manual system to 1.88 per cent in the project (see Tables 3.3).

BEP: The breakeven point (BEP), which reflects the ability of the business to recover its expenses through revenue generation, is lower in comparison to the income earned by the e-Kiosks in most of cases (12 out of 14) studied during field visits (see Table 3.29 and Figure 3.8). It reflects that most of the e-Kiosks are not able to recover their cost / expenses and are making losses. A careful examination of the Table 3.29 and Figure 3.8, reflects that that 9 out of 14 e-Kiosks under study were having earnings less than 50 per cent of or far below BEP. And, only those Kiosks that are near towns have better performance.

Number of e-Governance Services Availed by Citizens: Under e-Governance services through the project, a mere 1.74 per cent of Tehsil services were accessed and only 0.15 per cent of citizens availed them. Or, less than 1 per cent of families have accessed e-Governance services in one year, which is a minuscule number (see Table 3.12). It evidently indicates about the heavy dependence of citizens on manual system, in spite of a number of e-Kiosks in villages (in Chaksu).

Similarly, Figures 3.4 and 3.5 also depict the decline in the number of certificates availed and grievances received respectively. These show that the number of certificates availed reached 148 in July, 2003 and then declined to zero in March, 2004. Likewise, the number of grievances reached 92 in August, 2003 and then it slipped to 17 in March, 2004.

I. *Lack of System Ownership:* In service delivery, there are many stakeholders involved. These are officials of State IT department, district collector, other district officials, SDO, block officials, service provider, consultants and Kiosk owners. But, as regards performance, none of them is accountable for poor delivery of service, which affects the remedial measures for improvement to be taken. Each one tries to shift responsibility from one to another, and it has been evident that there is a lack of system ownership.

J. *Citizen Dissatisfaction:* There has been low satisfaction level among citizens as regards the time and cost of availing the services. Also, on qualitative indicators like reliability, behaviour, responsiveness, transparency and accountability, the performance was not satisfactory.

Though, e-Kiosk provided scope for sending grievances, but due to unsatisfactory redressal, due to poor capacity of delivery system to deliver in time and effectively, e-Kiosk lost its credibility and citizens lost interest in using the e-Kiosk.

Based on interaction among present system, performance of service delivery and citizens' behaviour, the change in behaviour of citizens regarding the service delivery from e-Governance projects is reflected by Figure 3.6. It shows how improper system design and then poor performance have turned citizens' behaviour from 'initial enthusiasm' to 'complete withdrawal' from accessing services from e-Kiosk. In summary, such a state has arisen due to:

- Lack of understanding about concept of good governance
- Lack of appreciation about 'quality' issues in service delivery
- Hurry in setting up system
- Focus on IT, without careful study and design of delivery system to deliver

K. *Stage of Growth in Governance:* Presently, the project is able to meet partial requirement of stage I, i.e. Interface and stage II i.e. Transactional, and it has yet to make large efforts to reach stage V (see Figure S3.6). In terms of achievement under the project, it comes out to be 7.79 per cent [(6.0/77) * 100, see Table: 3.32]. And it has to go a long way before meeting citizens' needs substantially

L. *Where are e-Governance Projects heading for?* From the study of e-Governance projects, it is quite evident that the delivery of services by the projects is not to the satisfaction of citizens. With the result, most of the e-Kiosks are not in sustainable conditions. And, due to this either are 'e-Governance Kiosks' closed or have they turned into 'business Kiosks' (see Figure 3.11). Based on above description, critical findings are summarised in Box 3.4.

Box: 3.4: Critical Findings

- Governance issues not defined explicitly by services provider
- System requirement study (SRS) not carried out properly
- System ownership is lacking (many stakeholders involved, but no accountability at the point of delivery of services, it leads to shifting of responsibility)
- Citizen perspective (i.e. citizens' requirements and expectations) not reflected in: i. services to be provided and ii. process of service delivery
- Citizen-centric work culture not evolved
- People, processes and technology not aligned and developed to provide services efficiently
- Poor capacity of delivery system to deliver services
- Change management issues not addressed
- Poor quality of service delivery
- Citizen dissatisfaction
- Number of e-Governance services availed by citizens came down drastically in one year (from 02-03 to 03-04)
- Less than 2 per cent of Tehsil services were accessed in a year (02-03)
- Less than 1 per cent of families have accessed e-Governance services (02-03)
- The revenue earned by most of the e-Kiosks is much less than breakeven point (BEP)
- Projects are at Interface and Transactional stages (as per growth model), and have to go a long way before they start meeting citizens' needs substantially
- e-Governance Kiosks becoming financially unviable, and turning into business centers

Note: Based on study of e-Governance project (in Jaipur), and Gyandoot, Janmitra, OLTP, e-Bhoomi and RDS projects.

Figure: 3.11: Summary Findings of Study of e-Governance Projects

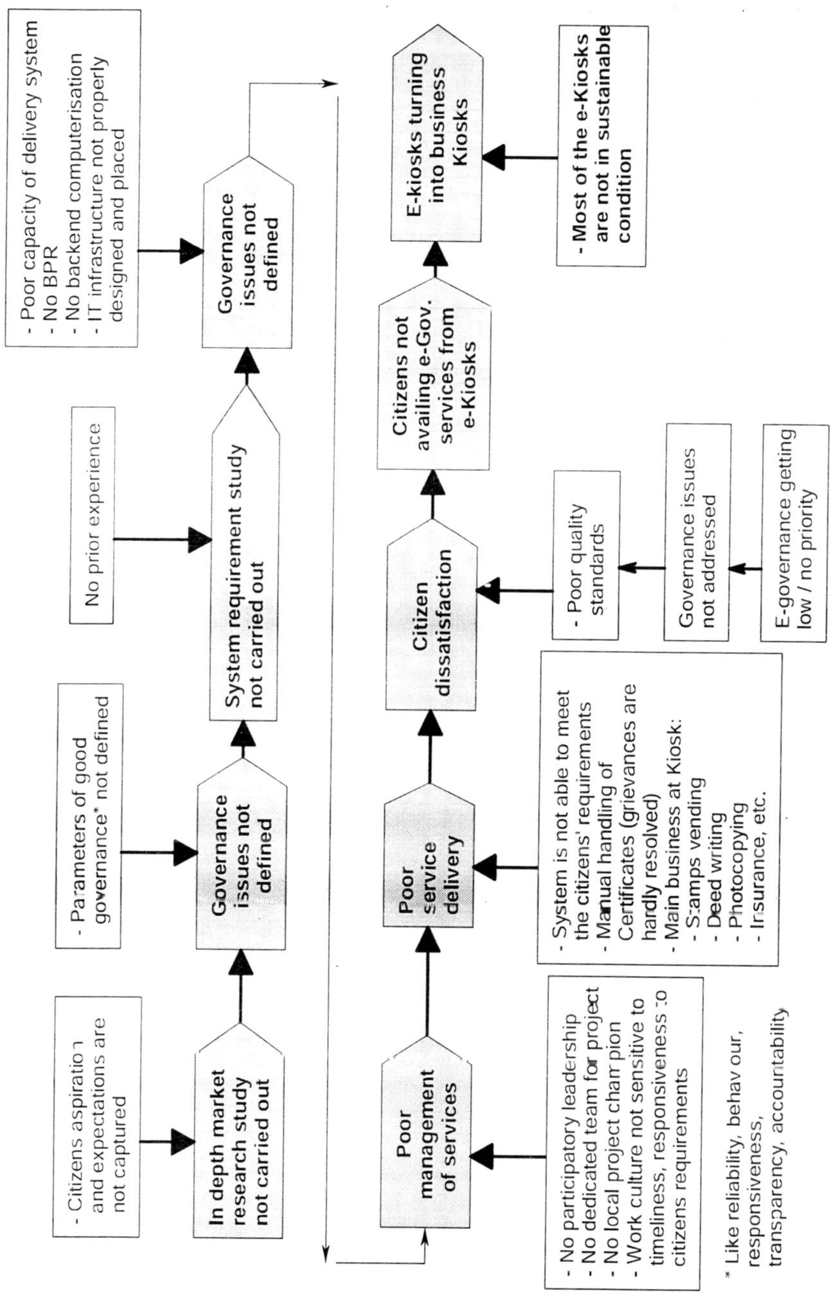

Notes

[1]The term delivery system refers to agencies or organisations through which development programmes are implemented to ensure availability of inputs and / or services such as delivery of certificates through Tehsil, agriculture inputs, marketing of agricultural produce, health services, primary education, drinking water and so on. In the book various service departments like Tehsil, Education, Health, PHED, etc. are referred as Delivery Systems, for their respective service provisioning.

S. N.	Delivery system / Department	Services delivered (a select list)
1.	Tehsil,	Delivery of certificates, disaster management
2.	Agriculture	Agriculture inputs
3.	Education	Primary education
4.	Health	Health services like immunisation, family planning
5.	PHED	Drinking water

[2]e-Kiosk is engaged in other business activities like typing, photocopy, etc. this is so in most of the e-Kiosks.

Box: S3.1
Non-availability of Electricity

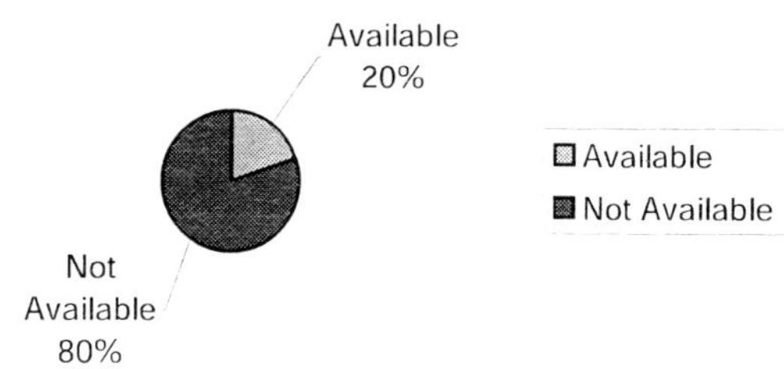

Box: S3.2
Non-functioning of Network (for e-Kiosk)

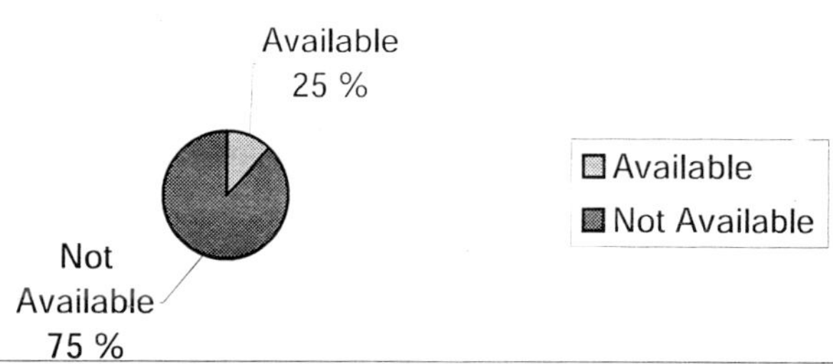

Box: S3.3 Knowledge about the Services given by e-Governance Project (in Jaipur)

Box: A
Age-wise: Young have more Knowledge about e-Governance Services

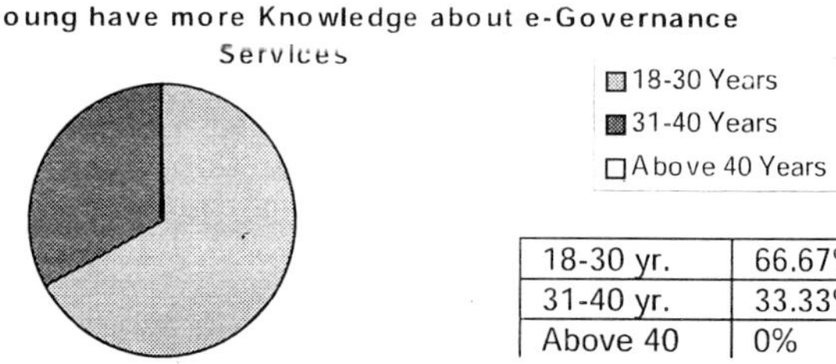

18-30 yr.	66.67%
31-40 yr.	33.33%
Above 40	0%

Box: B

Education-wise: High education has more Knowledge about e-Governance Services

Low education group	6.67%
Medium education group	40%
High education group	53.33%

Box: C

Income-wise: High Income group has more Knowledge about e-Governance Services

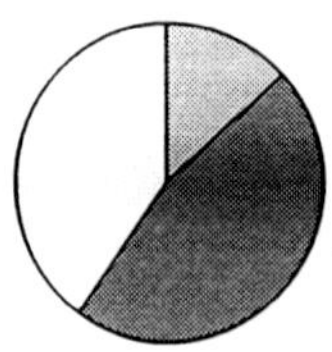

Low income group	13.33%
Middle income group	46.67%
High income group	40%

Box: D

Caste-wise: OBC have more Knowledge about e-Governance Services

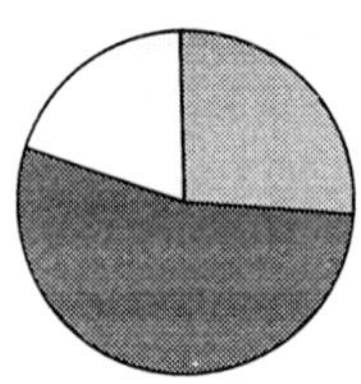

General	26.67%
OBC	53.33%
SC/ST	20.0%

Box: E

Sex-wise: Males have more Knowledge about e-Governance Services

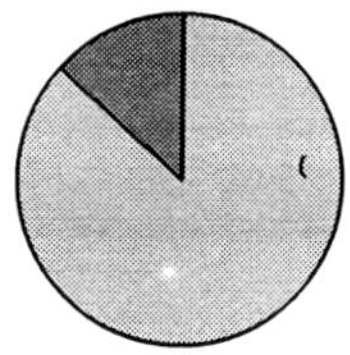

Male	86.67%
Female	13.33%

Box S3.4: Usage of e-Governance services from e-Governance Project (in Jaipur)

Box: A

Age-wise: Young have utilised more e-Governance Services

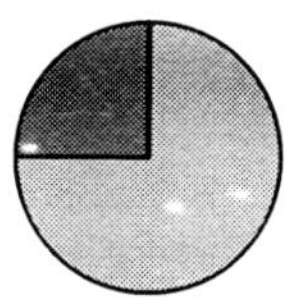

18-30 yr.	75%
31-40 yr.	25%
Above 40	0%

Box: B

Education-wise: High education group has utilised more e-Governance Services

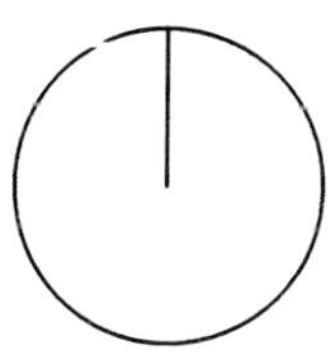

Low education group	0%
Medium education group	0%
High education group	100%

Box: C

Income-wise: High Income group has utilised more e-Governance Services

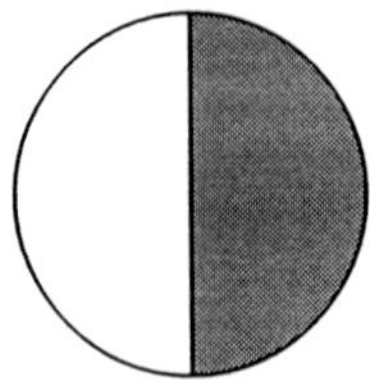

Low income group	0%
Middle income group	50%
High income group	50%

Box: D

Caste-wise: OBC and General caste have utilised e- Governance Services

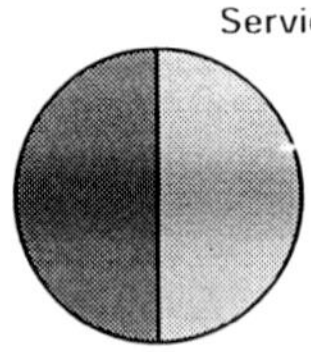

General	50%
OBC	50%
SC/ST	0%

Box: E

Sex-wise: Males have utilised more e-Governance Services

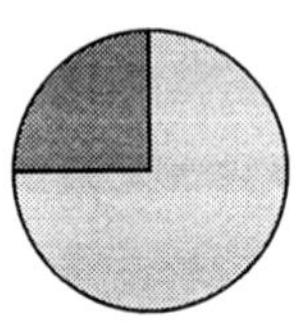

Male	75%
Female	25%

Figure: S3.1
Flow Diagram of Income Certificate given by e-Governance project (in Jaipur)

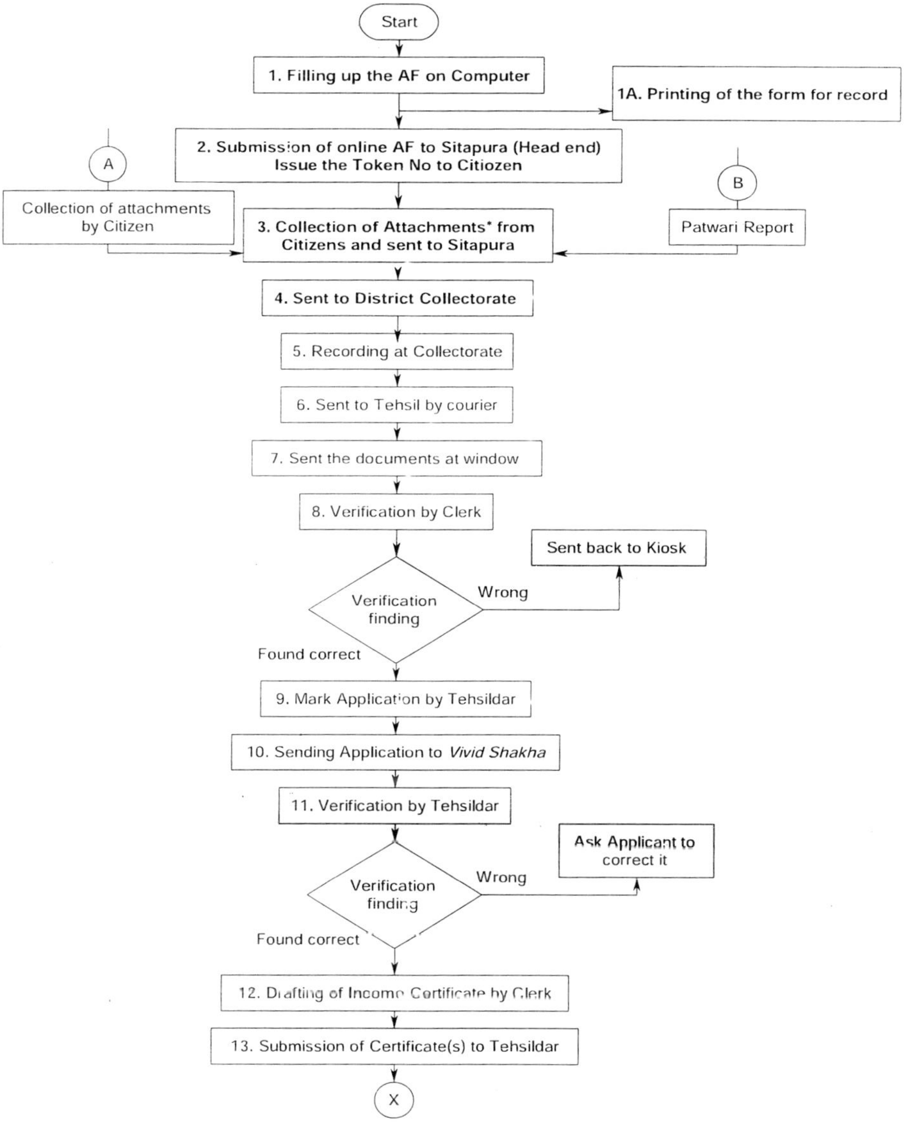

Note: Bold activities are electronic activities.

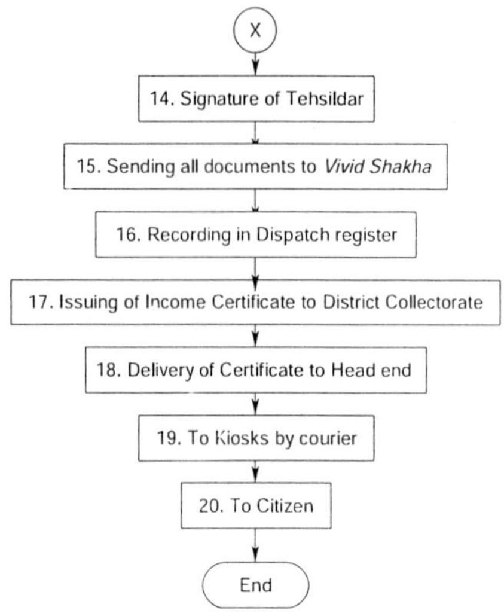
X
14. Signature of Tehsildar
15. Sending all documents to *Vivid Shakha*
16. Recording in Dispatch register
17. Issuing of Income Certificate to District Collectorate
18. Delivery of Certificate to Head end
19. To Kiosks by courier
20. To Citizen
End

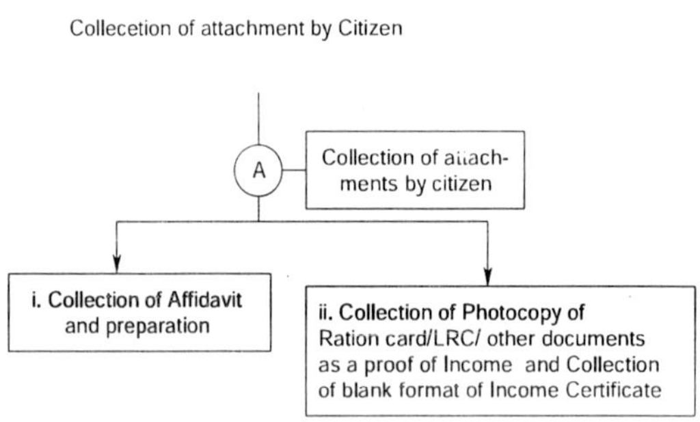
Collecetion of attachment by Citizen
A
Collection of attachments by citizen
i. Collection of Affidavit and preparation
ii. Collection of Photocopy of Ration card/LRC/ other documents as a proof of Income and Collection of blank format of Income Certificate

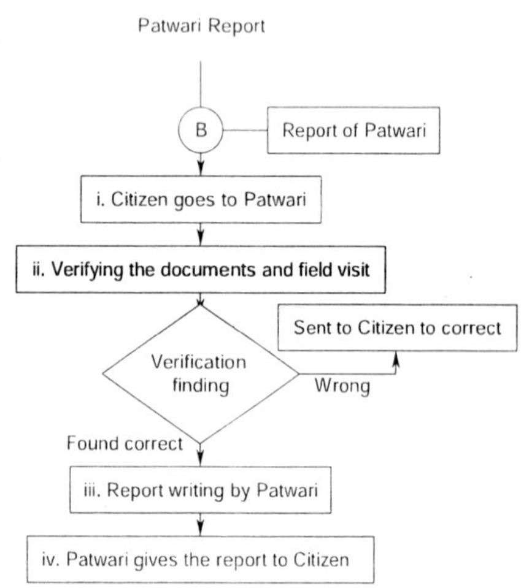
Patwari Report
B
Report of Patwari
i. Citizen goes to Patwari
ii. Verifying the documents and field visit
Verification finding
Sent to Citizen to correct
Wrong
Found correct
iii. Report writing by Patwari
iv. Patwari gives the report to Citizen

Figure: S3.2

Flow Diagram of Domicile Certificate given by e-Governance Project (in Jaipur)

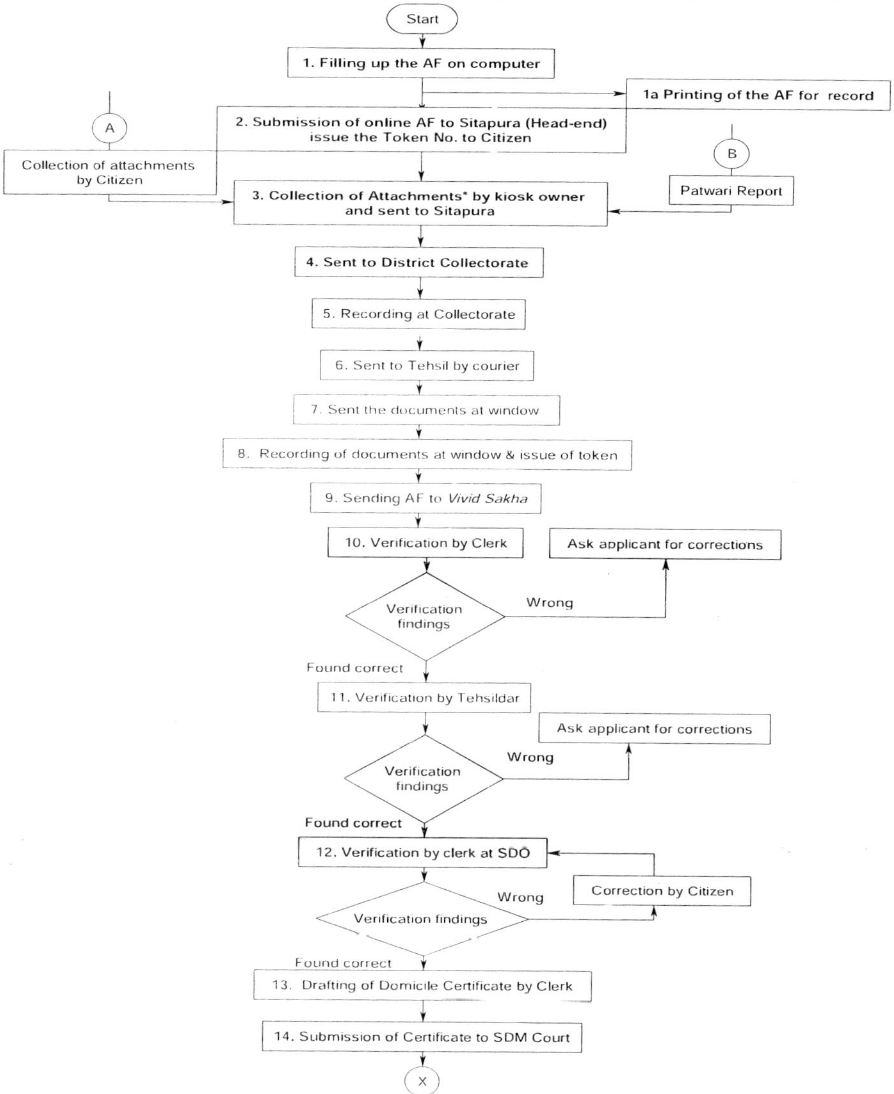

Note: Bold activities are electronic activities.

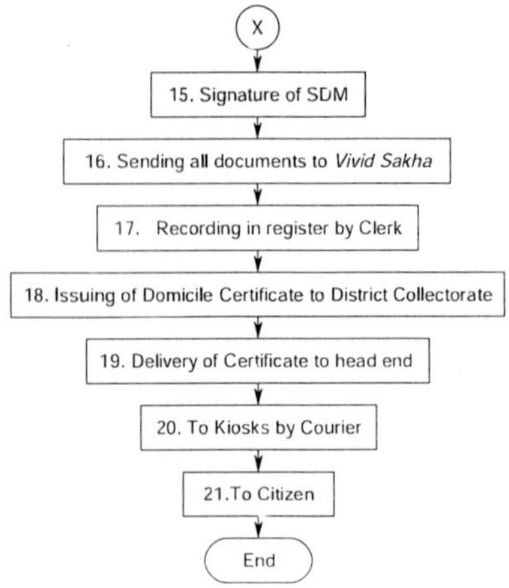

Collecetion of attachment by Citizen

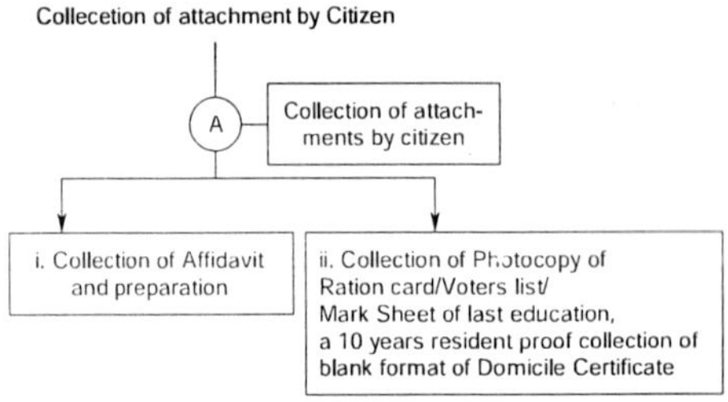

Patwari Report

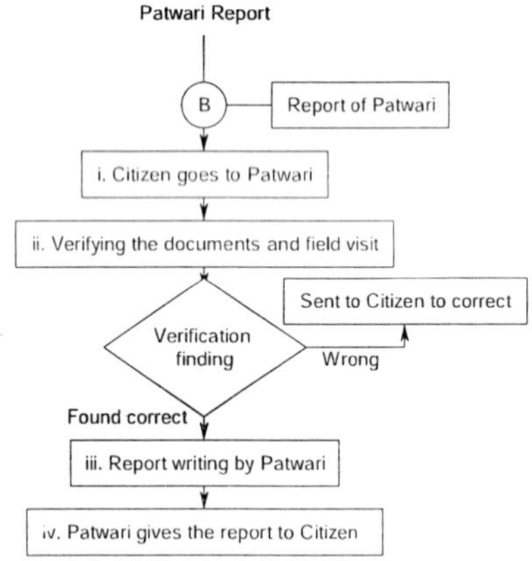

Figure: S3.3
Flow Diagram of Jamabandi Certificate given by e-Governance Project (in Jaipur)

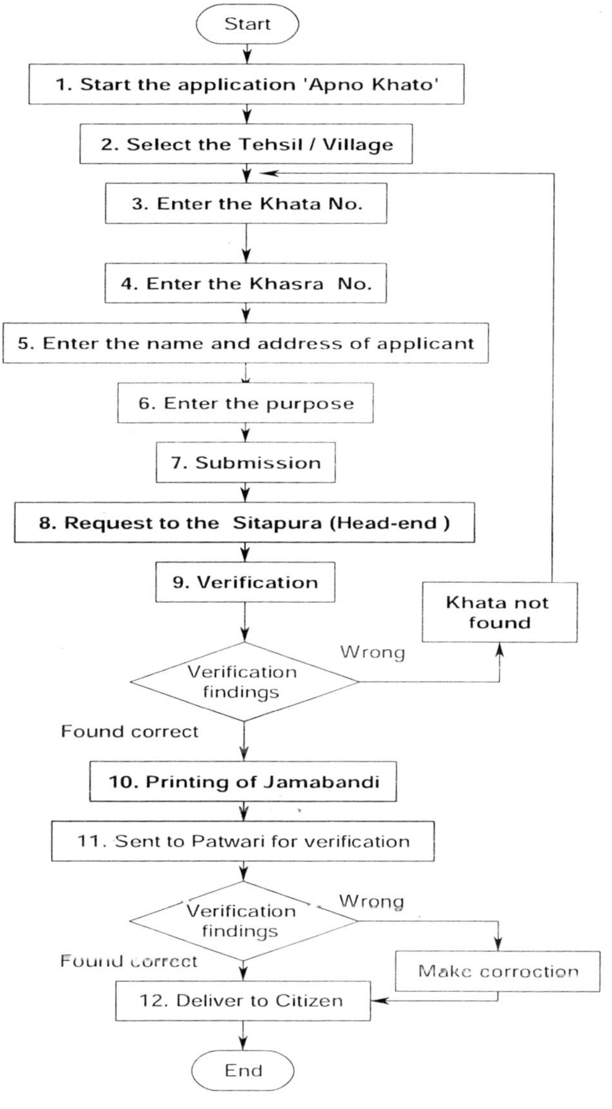

Note: Bold activities are electronic activities.

Figure: S3.4
Cause-effect Diagram (Fishbone Diagram) for Performance (Time) of delivery of Caste Certificate

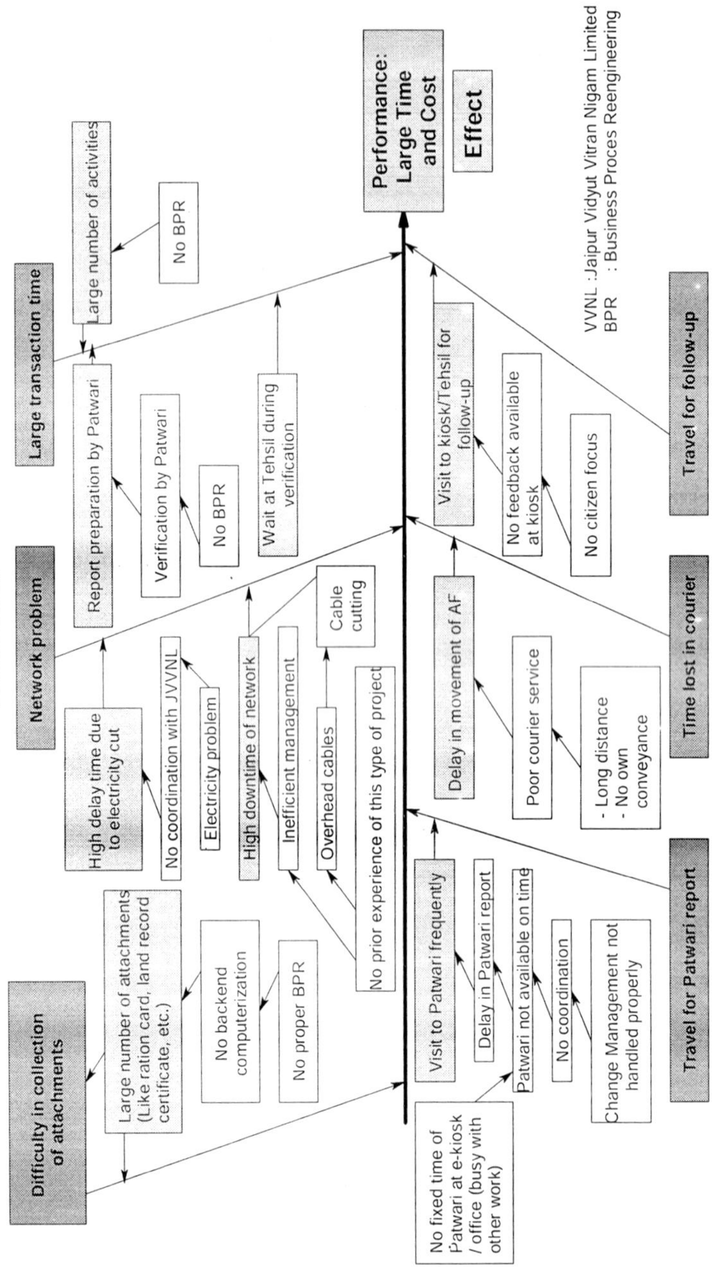

Figure: S3.5
Comparison of Performance during 02-03 and 03-04 in e-Governance Project (Chaksu Tehsil)

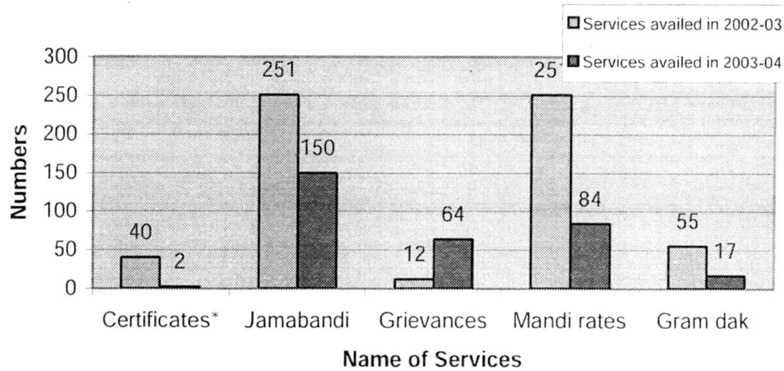

Source: e-Governance project and own analysis

Figure: S3.6
Present Status of e-Governance under e-Governance Project based on Growth Model

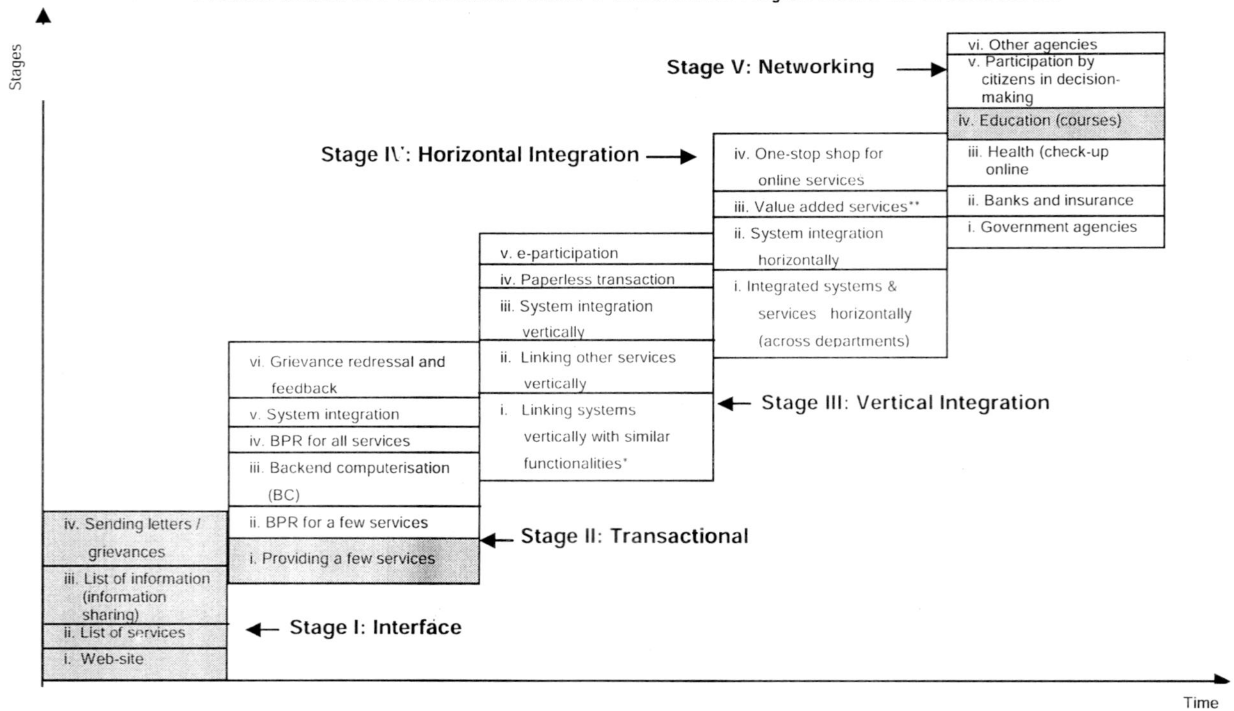

*(e.g. Patwarghar to Tehsil to Collectorate). ** Online payment, crop insurance
Note: Information sharing, service delivery, grievance redressal and feedback will be an on going and continuous process.

Figure S3.7
SWOT Analysis Diagram

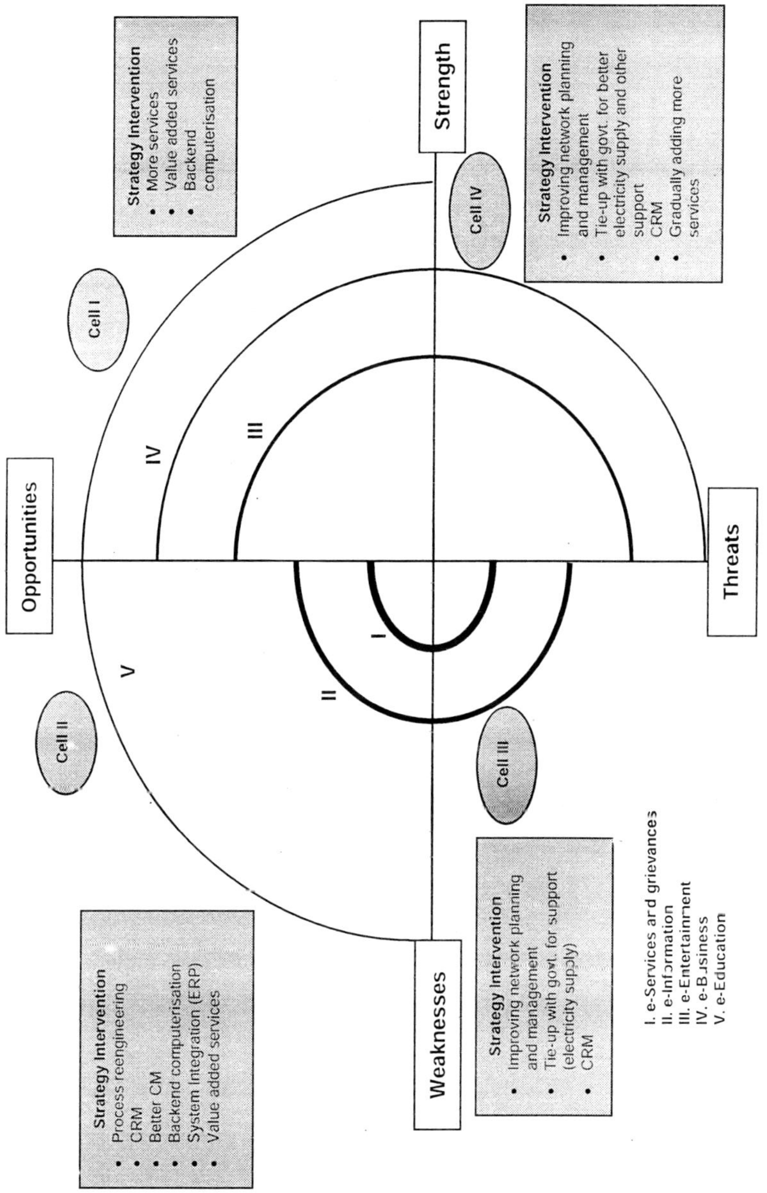

Table: S3.1A: Touch Points for Citizens and Application, and Number of Visits by Citizens for Services through Manual Processing and e-Governance Project

A1 (Caste and Domicile Certificates)

Items		Caste certificate		Domicile certificate	
		Manual	e-Governance project	Manual	e-Governance project
1. Touch points	For citizen	**Minimum** 1. Collection of AF 2. Preparation of affidavit 3. Photocopy of income certificate (for creamy-layer) 4. Goes to Patwari for Patwari report 5. For taking the report from Patwari 6. To submit at single window 7. For collecting the certificate **Maximum** 1 to 7 of minimum and 8. Ration card 9. Copy of ROR 10. Voter list 11. Two copies of parent's caste certificate, if candidate is a student 12. Mark sheet of last degree achieved 13. Identification from two Govt. employee (gazetted officers)	**Minimum** 1. Preparation of affidavit 2. Photocopy of income certificate (for creamy-layer) 3. Goes to Patwari for Patwari report 4. For taking the report from Patwari 5. To submit at e-Kiosk 6. To collecting the certificate **Maximum** 1 to 6 of minimum and 7. Ration card 8. Copy of ROR 9. Voter list 10. Two copies of parent's caste certificate, if candidate is a student 11. Mark sheet of last degree achieved 12. Identification from two Govt. employee (gazetted officers)	**Minimum** 1. Collection of AF 2. Preparation of affidavit 3. Voter list (last 10 years) 4. Mark sheet of last degree achieved 5. Goes to Patwari for Patwari report 6. For taking the report from Patwari 7. To submit at single window 8. For collecting the certificate **Maximum** 1 to 8 of minimum and 9. Ration card	**Minimum** 1. Preparation of affidavit 2. Voter list (last 10 years) 3. Mark sheet of last degree achieved 4. Goes to Patwari. For Patwari Report 5. For taking the report from Patwari 6. To submit at e-Kiosk 7. For collecting the certificate **Maximum** 1 to 7 of minimum and 8. Ration card

Contd...

<table>
<tr><th colspan="2" rowspan="2">Items</th><th colspan="2">Caste certificate</th><th colspan="2">Domicile certificate</th></tr>
<tr><th>Manual</th><th>e-Governance project</th><th>Manual</th><th>e-Governance project</th></tr>
<tr><td></td><td>For appli-cation</td><td>1. Citizen
2. Patwari
3. Single window
4. Vivid Shakha
5. Tehsildar
6. Vivid Shakha
7. Single window</td><td>1. Citizen
2. Patwari
3. e-Kiosk
4. Head-end
5. Single window (Collectorate)
6. Single window (Tehsil)
7. Vivid Shakha
8. Tehsildar
9. Vivid Shakha
10. Single window (Tehsil)
11. Single windows (Collectorate)
12. Head-end
13. e-Kiosk</td><td>1. Citizen
2. Patwari
3. Single window
4. Vivid Shakha
5. Tehsildar
6. SDM
7. Vivid Shakha
8. Single window</td><td>1. Citizen
2. Patwari
3. e-Kiosk
4. Head-end
5. Single window (Collectorate)
6. Single window(Tehsil)
7. Vivid Shakha
8. Tehsildar
9. SDM
10. Vivid Shakha
11. Single window (Tehsil)
12. Single windows (Collectorate)
13. Head-end
14. e-Kiosk</td></tr>
<tr><td colspan="2">2 No of visits</td><td>Minimum
1. Collection of AF
2. Goes to Patwari (for giving the document)
3. For photocopy of income certificate
4. For preparation of affidavit</td><td>Minimum
1. Goes to Patwari (For Giving the document)
2. For preparation of affidavit
3. For photocopy of income certificate</td><td>Minimum
1. Collection of AF
2. For preparation of affidavit
3. For collection of voter list
4. For photocopy of mark sheet of last degree achieved</td><td>Minimum
1. For preparation of affidavit
2. For collection of voter list
3. For photocopy of mark sheet of last degree achieved</td></tr>
</table>

Contd...

Items	Caste certificate		Domicile certificate	
	Manual	e-Governance project	Manual	e-Governance project
	5. Goes to Patwari for taking the report 6. For submission of AF at single window 7. For collecting the certificate from Tehsil **Maximum** 1 to 7 and 8. For photocopy of ration card 9. For collection of copy of ROR 10. For collection of voter list 11. For photocopy of parent's caste certificate, if candidate is a student 12. For photocopy of mark sheet of last degree achieved 13. For identification from two Govt. employee (Gazetted officers) 14th & 15th visits for follow-up	4. Goes to Patwari for taking the report 5. For submission of AF at e-Kiosk 6. For collecting the certificate from e-Kiosk **Maximum** 1 to 6 and 7. For photocopy of ration card 8. For collection of copy of ROR 9. For collection of voter list 10. For photocopy of parent's caste certificate, if candidate is a student 11. For photocopy of mark sheet of last degree achieved 12. For identification from two Govt. employee (Gazetted officers) 13th & 14th visits for follow-up	5. To Patwari (for giving the document) 6. To Patwari for taking the report 7. For submission of AF at e-Kiosk 8. For collecting the certificate from e-Kiosk **Maximum** 1 to 8 and 9. For photocopy of ration card 10th & 11th visits for follow- up	4. To Patwari (For giving the document) 5. To Patwari for taking the report 6. For submission of AF at e-Kiosk 7. For collecting the certificate from e-Kiosk **Maximum** 1 to 7 and 8. For photocopy of ration card 9th & 10th visits for follow-up

A2: (Income Certificate and Jamabandi)

Items		Income certificate		Jamabandi	
		Manual	e-Governance project	Manual	e-Governance project
Touch points	For citizen	**Minimum** 1. Collection of AF 2. Preparation of affidavit 3. Goes to Patwari. For Patwari Report 4. For taking the report from Patwari 5. To submit at single window 6. For collecting the certificate **Maximum** 1 to 6 of minimum and 7. Ration Card 8. Certificate employer (incase the candidate is employee) 9. Copy of ROR 10. Voter list 11. Mark sheet of last degree achieved 12. Copy of original income certificate (for Govt. employees)	**Minimum** 1. Preparation of affidavit 2. Goes to Patwari for Patwari report 3. For taking the report from Patwari 4. To submit at e-Kiosk 5. For collecting the certificate **Maximum** **1 to 5 of minimum and** 6. Ration Card 7. Certificate employer (incase the candidate is employee) 8. Copy of ROR 9. Voter list 10. Mark sheet of last degree achieved 11. Copy of original income certificate (for Govt. employees)	1. Collection of AF 2. To submit at single window 3. For collecting the certificate from single window	1. To submit at e-Kiosk 2. For collecting the certificate

Contd...

Items		Income certificate		Jamabandi	
		Manual	e-Governance project	Manual	e-Governance project
	For application	1. Citizen 2. Patwari 3. Single window 4. *Vivid Shakha* 5. Tehsildar 6. *Vivid Shakha* 7. Single window	1. Citizen 2. Patwari 3. E-kiosk 4. Head-end 5. Single window (Collectorate) 6. Single window (Tehsil) 7. *Vivid Shakha* 8. Tehsildar 9. *Vivid Shakha* 10. Single window (Tehsil) 11. Single windows (Collectorate) 12. Head-end 13. e-Kiosk	1. Citizen 2. Single window 3. Tehsildar 4. OK 5. *Nakal Lipik* 6. OK 7. Tehsildar 8. OK 9. Single window	1. Citizen 2. Kiosk owner 3. Patwari 4. Kiosk owner

Contd...

Items		Income certificate		Jamabandi	
		Manual	e-Governance project	Manual	e-Governance project
	No of visits	**Minimum** 1. Collection of AF 2. For preparation of affidavit 3. To Patwari (For giving the document) 4. To Patwari for taking the report 5. For submission of AF at e-Kiosk 6. For collecting the Certificate from e-Kiosk **Maximum** 1 to 6 and 7. Ration Card 8. Certificate employer (incase the candidate is employee) 9. Copy of ROR 10. Voter list 11. Mark sheet of last degree achieved 12. Copy of original income certificate (for Govt. employees) 13th & 14th visits for follow-up	**Minimum** 1. For preparation of affidavit 2. To Patwari (For giving the document) 3. To Patwari for taking the report 4. For submission of AF at e-Kiosk 5. For collecting the certificate from e-Kiosk **Maximum** 1 to 5 and 6. Ration card 7. Certificate employer (incase the candidate is employee) 8. Copy of ROR 9. Voter list 10. Mark sheet of last degree achieved 11. Copy of original income certificate (for Govt. employees) 12th & 13th visits for follow-up	**Minimum** 1. For collection of AF 2. For submission of AF at single window 3. For collecting the certificate from e-Kiosk **Maximum** 1 & 3 and 4th & 5th visits for follow-up	**Minimum** 1. For submission of AF at e-Kiosk 2. For collecting the certificate from e-Kiosk **Maximum** 1 & 2 and 3rd & 4th visits for follow-up

OK: Office Kanoongo, SDM: Sub-divisional Magistrate, ROR: Report of Right, AF: Application Form

Table: S3.1B: Different Attachments as required for availing Select Services

S.N.	Caste certificate		Domicile certificate	Income certificate
	ST/SC	OBC		
1.	Report of Patwari	Report of Patwari	Report of Patwari	Report of Patwari
2.	Copy of Jamabandi (ROR)	Affidavit	Voter list (last 10 years)**	Affidavit (About Income from all sources)
3.	Ration card	Income certificate*	Mark sheet of last degree achieved (history of last 10 yrs)**	Ration card
4.	Voter list	Ration card	Ration card	Certificate of employer (incase the candidate is employee)
5.	Mark sheet of last degree achieved	Mark sheet of last degree achieved	-	Copy of Jamabandi (ROR)
6.	Two copy of parents cast certificate if candidate is student	Two copies of parent's caste certificate, if candidate is a student.	-	Voter list
7.	-	Copy of ROR	-	Mark sheet of last degree achieved
8.	-	Voter list	-	Copy of original income certificate (for Govt. employees)
9.	-	Identification of two Govt. employees (gazetted officer)	-	-

*Mandatory in creamy-layer cases

** Either voter list or mark sheet

Table: S3.2: FMEA for Delivery of Caste Certificate through e-Governance Project

Activity head	Activities	Potential failure mode	Potential effect of failure	Severity	Potential cause(s)/mechanism of failure	Codes of causes	OCC	Detection techniques	Detection	RPN
A1	1.a Collection of attachments by citizen	Delay in collection	Delay in collection of attachments	7	Lack of Information about attachments; Attachments not available in time	C1	6	Complaints from citizens	7	294
	1.b Patwari report	Report delay	Delay in submission of AF	7	Patwari not available; Patwari busy in other work/ laxity in giving report	C2	5	Monitoring by higher authorities	8	280
A2	1. Filling up the AF online	Form filling unsuccessful	Token not issued; Form not filled; Harassment to the citizen	7	Equipments / technology problem; Kiosk owner not present; The web-server is not working; Computer may not work; Electricity / UPS not available	C3	7	From head-end	4	196
		Wrong information filled	Wrong information in AF	8	Deliberate mistakes	C4	2	Verification by Patwari	6	96
	1A. Printing of the AF for office record / citizen	The form not printed	Problem in record maintaining at Kiosk	2	Printer may be out of order	C5	2	Can be easily seen, if not printed	2	8
A3	2.Submission of online form to Sitapura (head-end) and issue the token number to citizen	Token not issued	No track record of the certificate can be maintained	3	Software problems; Connectivity problems	C6	4	From register at Kiosk	2	24

Contd...

Activity head	Activities	Potential failure mode	Potential effect of failure	Severity	Potential cause(s)/mechanism of failure	Codes of causes	OCC	Detection techniques	Detection	RPN
		□ Submission Unsuccessful	□ Postponing the acceptance of application	8	□ UPS / electricity problem at head-end □ Connectivity problems	C7	8	□ Software shows the message	5	320
A4	3. Collection of attachments from citizen and sent to Sitapura by Kiosk owner	□ Attachments not sent	□ AF will be rejected	7	□ Attachments not given by citizen	C8	6	□ Register of the Kiosk owner	5	210
		□ Attachments sent after a delay	□ Time lost	5	□ The Kiosk owner incognizant about which attachments are required	C9	5	□ Return of AF from Tehsil	8	200
		□ Attachments may be misplaced	□ Time lost	7	□ Courier misplaced	C10	5	□ Dispatch register of Kiosk	8	280
A5	4. Sent to district Collectorate AF electronically and attachments by courier	□ Application is not processed at the Collectorate	□ Time lost	5	□ Attachments (by courier) and the application (through intranet) get mixed up □ Delay in courier	C11	5	□ Matching (numbers, data) between the courier and the e-form	8	200
		□ Application reached by net after a delay	□ Time lost	5	□ Connectivity problem	C12	7	□ Through Pinging report of head-end	3	105
	5. Recording at Collectorate	□ Recording Missed	□ AF not processed ahead	4	□ The AF and attachments do not reach □ Human error while passing the AF forward	C13	3	□ Matching (numbers, data) between the courier and the e-form	2	24
	6. Sent to concerned Tehsil by courier	□ Documents do not reach the concerned Tehsil Properly	□ Time lost □ Harassment to the citizen	5	□ Documents mixed up between different Tehsils at Collectorate □ No proper notes maintained at he Tehsil/Collectorate of the documents □ Courier delayed	C14	3	□ Cross verifying the documents. □ Courier slip	2	30

Contd...

Activity head	Activities	Potential failure mode	Potential effect of failure	Severity	Potential cause(s)/mechanism of failure	Codes of causes	OCC	Detection techniques	Detection	RPN
		□ Documents missing	□ The process to be started again	7	□ Courier missing □ In Tehsil, documents missing	C15	4	□ Courier slip □ By register	7	196
	7. Sent the documents at single window 8. Recording of documents at single window & issue of token	□ Documents not recorded properly □ Delay in process	□ Problem in monitoring □ Harassment to the citizen	5	□ Window clerk not available □ Absenteeism, □ Deputation to other duties □ Late coming □ Large amount of work	C16	4	□ Tehsil records	3	60
	9. Sending AF to *Vivid Sakha*	□ Delay in Sending	□ Time lost	5	□ Clerk not available □ Clerk busy in other work □ Manual processes	C17	2	□ By attendance register □ By monitoring	3	30
	10. Verification by clerk	□ Verification not done	□ Time lost in the process	5	□ Attachments not proper □ AF not correct □ Manual processes	C18	6	□ Rejection numbers of the applications	2	60
	11. Drafting of caste certificate by clerk	□ Documents not processed	□ Time lost □ Harassment to the citizen	3	□ Absenteeism of concerned clerk □ Deputation to other duties □ Large amount of work. □ Late coming □ Manual processes □ Required attachment not sent	C19	3	□ Tehsil records □ By monitoring	2	18
		□ Language / spelling mistake in DF	□ Time lost □ Harassment to the citizen	7	□ Bad hand writing of clerk □ Manual processes	C20	3	□ Citizen can detect	3	63

Contd...

Activity head	Activities	Potential failure mode	Potential effect of failure	Severity	Potential cause(s)/mechanism of failure	Codes of causes	OCC	Detection techniques	Detection	RPN
	12. Submission of certificate to Tehsildar 13. Checking and signature of Tehsildar	□ Delay in Sign	□ Time lost □ Harassment to the citizen	5	□ Tehsildar not available □ To much work at Tehsildar's table □ Manual processes	C21	5	□ By monitoring □ Register pending list	2	50
	14. Sending all documents to *Vivid Sakha* 15. Recording in register by clerk	□ Delay in Recording	□ Time lost □ Harassment to the citizen	5	□ Absenteeism of concern clerk □ Deputation to other duties □ Large amount of work □ Late coming	C22	3	□ Tehsil records □ By monitoring	2	30
	16. Sending of caste certificate to district Collectorate	□ Improper processing at the Collectorate	□ Harassment to the citizen □ Time lost	3	□ Records not maintained properly.	C23	3	□ Collectorate records	3	27
A6	17. Delivery of certificate to head end 18. To Kiosks by Courier	□ Courier not sent properly or on time	□ Harassment to the citizen □ Time lost □ Accountability of the Kiosk lost	3	□ Delay in courier	C24	7	□ Not easy	5	105
A7	19. Certificate to citizen	□ Kiosk closed	□ Harassment to the citizen	5	□ Kiosk owner not present	C25	5	□ Visit by field supervision	7	175

Source: FGDs and own analysis

Occ: Occurrence, RPN: Risk Priority Number, AF: Application Form, DF: Delivery Form , UPS: Uninterrupted Power Supply

Note: see Appendix 2.2 for details about FMEA

Table: S3.3: Cumulative %age of RPN for Pareto Analysis

S. N.	Code of causes	Brief description	%age of total RPN	Cumulative %age of RPN
1.	C7	UPS/electricity problem at head end and connectivity problem (large down time)	10.39	10.39
2.	C1	Lack of Information about attachments Attachments not available in time (to citizen)	9.54	19.93
3.	C2	Patwari's absenteeism and his work style and attitude (lack of responsiveness)	9.09	29.02
4.	C10	Courier misplaced	9.09	38.10
5.	C8	Attachments not given by citizen (at Kiosk)	6.82	44.92
6.	C9	The kiosk owner incognizant about which attachments are required	6.49	51.41
7.	C11	Delay in courier	6.49	57.90
8.	C3	Equipments / technology / electricity problem Kiosk owner absent	6.36	64.26
9.	C15	Documents missing in Tehsil (due to courier)	6.36	70.63
10.	C25	Kiosk owner not present	5.68	76.31
11.	C12	Connectivity problem (large down time)	3.41	79.71
12.	C24	Delay in courier	3.41	83.12
13.	C4	Deliberate mistakes by citizen	3.12	86.24
14.	C20	Functionaries problem (grammar, writing)	2.04	88.28
15.	C16	Functionaries' problem at Tehsil - Absenteeism - Deputation to other duty - Late coming - Large amount of work	1.95	90.23
16.	C18	Attachments not proper AF not correct	1.95	92.18

Contd...

S. N.	Code of causes	Brief description	%age of total RPN	Cumulative %age of RPN
		□ Manual processes		
17.	C21	□ Tehsildar not available □ To much work at Tehsildar's table □ Manual processes	1.62	93.80
18.	C14	□ Mismatching of attachment due to lack of documentation □ Courier delayed	0.97	94.77
19.	C17	□ Functionaries' commitment at Tehsil □ Absenteeism □ Manual processes	0.97	95.75
20.	C22	□ Functionaries' problems at Tehsil - Absenteeism - Deputation - Late coming - Large amount of work	0.97	96.72
21.	C23	□ Records not maintained properly.	0.88	97.60
22.	C6	□ Connectivity / software problems	0.78	98.38
23.	C13	□ The AF and attachments do not reach □ Human error while passing the AF forward	0.78	99.16
24.	C19	□ Functionaries' problems at Tehsil - Absenteeism - Deputation - Late coming - Large amount of work □ Manual processing	0.58	99.74
25.	C5	□ Printer problem	0.26	100.00

Table: S3.4: Critical observations about the Service Delivery through e-Governance Project

Activity-head	Activities	Salient features	Critical observations	Remarks
A1	Collection of attachments by citizen	□ Number of attachments same (see Table S3.1A for all the services) □ Stamp paper/ stamps available at Kiosk	□ Number of attachments remained as before	□ No BPR
	Report of Patwari	□ Patwari was instructed to come at e-Kiosk for two days (Thursday & Saturday), so that citizens can get the report at Kiosk	□ Patwari normally did not come to Kiosk	□ Change management issues not addressed
A2	Collection of AF	□ In a few seconds AF available at the Kiosk □ Online filing of form	□ Citizen hesitated to go to Gramdoot Kiosk □ Services were not available most of the time	□ Network out of order on many occasions □ Cable cutting □ Electricity not available
	Filling of AF	□ No agent required for filling the application and as it the duty of Kiosk owner	□ Most of the times Kiosk owners were not present at Kiosk	□ No citizen focus
A3	Submission of AF	□ It was an instant activity	□ Due to electricity failure or network failure, the submission on line was delayed	□ Inefficient management
A4	At Kiosk, collection of attachments from citizen and submission to head-end	□ Attachments can be submitted at the Kiosk □ Immediate collection of attachments	□ Delay in dispatch by courier	□ Inefficient management

Contd...

Activity-head	Activities	Salient features	Critical observations	Remarks
A5	Processing in Tehsil	□ Same as earlier Tehsil system	□ First application travels to head-end, then to Collectorate & finally to Tehsil – leading to long time (this leads to unnecessary wastage of time and thus increasing the time and cost of the processing) □ Sometimes attachments got misplaced, or mismatched with AF □ Manual processing in Tehsil, as before	□ No BPR
A6	Dispatch of certificate to Kiosk	□ Citizen needs not to go to Tehsil to receive the certificate	□ Delivery of certificate from Tehsil: first it travels to Collectorate, then to head-end and finally to Kiosk (a lot of time is spent)	□ No BPR
A7	Delivery of certificate	□ Gramdoot project made a commitment to deliver certificates in 72 hours	□ The delivery of certificates gets delayed invariably □ Patwari not available at Kiosk, so citizens were not able to take his signature for Jamabandi at Kiosk	□ No change comes in the database/ records □ (records are not updated)

Source: Based on FGDs

Table: S3.5: Root Causes for Poor Usage of e-Governance Services (under e-Governance Project) Based on Fishbone Diagram

S.N.	Status of factors	Root causes	Remarks (based on discussions with citizens)
1.	Lack of awareness	□No programme of awareness building	But, not a serious problem
2.	Some difficulty in access (to e-Kiosk)	□Cost is high in setting up e-Kiosk inside the village	But, not a serious problem
3.	Some difficulty in use	□No proper training to Kiosk owners	But, not a serious problem
4.	Low opportunity cost (low performance of delivery of services)	□No backend computerization □No BPR done	Serious problem
5.	Very less number of services	□Proper feasibility study not done	Serious problem
6.	Unreliability	□Electricity failure □Network not working □Kiosk closed □Patwari not available □No BPR done	Serious problem, but manageable with proper management

Note: See Figure 3.3 also

Table: S3.6: Root Causes for Low Performance (under e-Governance Project) Based on Fishbone Diagram

S.N.	Status of factors	Root causes	Remarks (based on discussions with citizens)
1.	Difficulty in collection of attachments (large number of attachments)	□No backend computerisation □No BPR done	Serious problem (large time and cost)
2.	Large transaction / processing (large number of activities)	□No BPR done	Serious problem (large time and cost)
3.	Travel for Patwari report	□Change Management not handled properly □No fixed time of Patwari at e-Kiosk	Serious problem (large time and cost)
4.	Network problem	□No prior experience of this type of project □Electricity problem	Some problem
5..	Travel for follow-up	□No feedback available to citizens / MIS □No citizen focus	Some problem
6.	Time lost in courier	□Long distance from e-Kiosks to Tehsil	Serious problem

Note: See Figure S3.4 also

Table: S3.7: Reasons for lack of Usage of e-Governance Services (also e-Kiosk) from e-Governance Project

S.N.	Factors	Specific reasons for not using e-Governance services	Impact on usage of e-Kiosk
1.	Awareness – lack of awareness	□ No awareness building programme to reach out to citizens □ Gramdoots (Kiosk owners) were not trained adequately and they did not know how to interact with citizens to get more business	Medium
2.	Access (availability of e-Kiosk) – in some cases	□ Small number of Kiosks in the Tehsil few (14-15 for 296 Village) □ Mostly Kiosks out of villages (at some distance)	Minor
3.	Ease of use – for some categories of users	□ Women and illiterates found it difficult to use	Minor
4.	Opportunity cost (or performance of delivery of services) – service delivery of poor quality	□ Processes of service delivery remained almost same as before □ Almost same time and cost in availing services as incase of manual system □ Charges for taking Jamabandi from e-Governance project Kiosk high at Rs. 30, whereas the Tehsil charges is Rs 20 □ Patwari unable to come to Kiosk to sign Jamabandi	Major
5.	Security of data – not enough provisions from the System's perspective (though citizens were not so much concerned)	□ Not much of a problem	Minor (but important from the point of view of system security)*
6.	Number of services – very less number of services	□ A few number of services provided at the Kiosk, so citizens were not keen to go to Kiosks	Major

Contd...

S.N.	Factors	Specific reasons for not using e-Governance services	Impact on usage of e-Kiosk
7.	Reliability – poor reliability	□ High down time due to unreliable electricity supply or cable cutting □ Kiosks used to be closed on many occasions □ Unreliable quality of other services e.g. in case of colour photograph (colours were not good), old information for *mandi bhav*, etc. □ Availability of getting services within stipulated time was not reliable	Medium

Source: FGDs* i. Only password protection (that can be hacked and interchanged), no digital signature or bio-matrix Provision, ii. No data recovery system at the server end (like SAN)

Table: S3.8: Month-wise Certificates (under e-Governance) Issued by e-Governance Project in Jaipur District

S. N.	Months	Total Numbers
1.	April,2003	8
2.	May,2003	57
3.	June,2003	34
4.	July,2003	148
5.	August,2003	129
6.	September,2003	21
7.	October,2003	10
8.	November,2003	4
9.	December,2003	3
10.	January,2004	3
11.	February,2004	19
12.	March,2004	0

Source: e-Governance Project and own Analysis.

Table: S3.9: Month-wise Grievances (under e-Governance) Issued by e-Governance Project in Jaipur District

S. N.	Months	Total Numbers
1.	April, 2003	42
2.	May,2003	52
3.	June,2003	90
4.	July,2003	59
5.	August,2003	92
6.	September,2003	42
7.	October,2003	16
8.	November,2003	17
9.	December,2003	19
10.	January,2004	20
11.	February,2004	25
12.	March,2004	17

Source: e-Governance Project and own analysis

Table: S3.10: E-governance Project Performance vis-à-vis Manual System (of Tehsil Services) in Jaipur District

(02-03)

S. N.	Services		E-governance Project (in Jaipur District)	In Jaipur District (by manual system)		Percentage of services by e-Governance project w.r.t. manual system
1.	Jamabandi		2526	15893		15.89%
2.	Certificates	Caste	436	62822	87995	0.95%
		Income		5948		
		Domicile		19225		
3.	Other Tehsil Services	Mutation	0	23370	51131	0%
		No Dues		16895		
		Seema Gyan		1527		
		Wealth		355		
		Allotment of Govt. land for public purpose		184		
		Division of land		277		
		Deed (for sale of land)		8523		
		Deed (Release)				
		Deed (Lease)				
		Deed (Power of Attorney)				
		Deed (Mortgage)				
	Total		**2962**		**1,55,019**	**1.91%**

Source: e-Governance project, Jaipur Collectorate, and own analysis

Table: S3.11: Comparison Performance during 02-03 and 03-04 of e-Governance Project (Chaksu Block)

S.N.	Name of services	Services availed by citizens		%age of change	Remarks
		2002-03	2003-04		
1.	Certificates*	40	2	□95 (Decrease)	-
2.	Jamabandi	251	150	□40.23 (Decrease)	-
3.	Grievances	12	64	□433.33 (Increase)	Grievance redressal picked momentum after January, 2003 and by March, 2004, the number has reduced to less than 20 (see Figure 3.9)
4.	*Mandi* rates	251	84	□66.53 (Decrease)	-
5.	*Gram dak*	55	17	□69.10 (Decrease)	-

Source: e-Governance project and own analysis.

*Caste, income, domicile certificates

Table: S3.12: Gap Analysis for IT System Design

S.N.	Factors		Existing scenario	Expected scenario	Gap
1.	IT infrastructure	At head-end	Satisfactory	-	-
		At Kiosk	Satisfactory	-	-
		At Tehsil	Not provided	Required (computer, printer, connectivity, etc.)	Hardware infrastructure at Tehsil
2.	Process simplification		Not carried out for any service	BPR is must for improving efficiency	Business process reengineering (BPR)
3.	Knowledge of processes, Acts, reports, etc.		Not available as and when required	Need for making relevant information available in a user-friendly form	Knowledge management (KM)
4.	At Kiosk, services in the form of a package		No integrated database for different services prepared	Integrated database required	System Integration (SI)
5.	Quality services to citizen		Lack of citizen focus	Citizen relationship management required	CRM
6.	Linking different levels of the same department		Not attempted	Required for adding efficiency and better monitoring	Vertical integration (VI)
7.	Linking different service departments		Not attempted	Required for giving more services to citizens	Horizontal integration (HI)

Source: Own analysis, based on FGDs
Vertical integration: From *Patwarghar* to Tehsil to Collectorate
Horizontal integration: Connecting different departments like primary education, health at the same level

Table: S3.13: Gap Analysis for Delivery of Different Services by e-Governance Project

S.N.	Service type	Services	Parameters	Performance			Reasons for lack of performance
				Existing scenario	Expected scenario	Status (due to gap)	
1.	E-governance services	i. Certificate	Time	20-25 days	3 days	More time	□ Patwari was not able to visit e-Kiosk for report □ No citizen database □ Connectivity problem □ Interrupted electricity supply □ No BPR
			Cost	Rs. 200-250	Rs. 10-15	More cost	
			Number of visits	2-4	2	More visit	
			Citizens' perception	E-kiosks are not able to provide services	To the citizens' satisfact-ion	Low satisfaction level	
		ii. Jamabandi	Time	2-10 days	Online,	More time	□ Patwari was not able to visit e-Kiosk for signature Jamabandi □ No updation of data
			Cost	Rs. 20-25	Rs. 10-20	More cost	
			Number of visits	2-3	1	More visit	
			Citizens' perception	E-kiosks are not able to provide services	To the citizens satisfact-ion	Large dis-satisfaction	
		iii. Grievances	Time	1-2 months in a few cases, otherwise grievances are not resolved	1-7 days	More time	□ Manual processing □ Weak delivery system, e.g. infrastructure, logistics, etc. insuff-icient in primary education, health, etc.
			Cost	Rs. 50-100	Rs.10 (for travelling)	More cost	

Contd...

S.N.	Service type	Services	Parameters	Performance			Reasons for lack of performance
				Existing scenario	Expected scenario	Status (due to gap)	
			Number of visits	3-4	1	More visits	□ No backend computerisation □ Routine way of handling
			Citizen perception	E-kiosks are not able to provide services	To the citizens satisfaction	Large dis-satisfaction	
2.	Others services	i. Photos	Quality	Poor	Good quality	Gap in quality	□ No business forecasting □ Poor quality of equipments for taking photos
			Time (days)	10	3-4	More time	
		ii. Mandi rate	Timely information	Up to date data not provided	Online	Timely information not available	□ No tie-up with other agencies
3.	Rural convergence	i. Cable TV	Citizen perception	Poor	To the citizens' satisfaction	Low satisfaction level	□ Small business □ Inadequate equipments □ Scattered network □ High maintenance □ Few channel □ Marketing strategy not strong
			Cost	Rs. 150	Rs. 100-120	More cost	
			Picture quality	High noise	Digital quality	More quality	

Contd...

S.N.	Service type	Services	Parameters	Performance			Reasons for lack of performance
				Existing scenario	Expected scenario	Status (due to gap)	
	ii.	Computer education	Citizen perception	-Certificates not given to students -Quality of education is not good		Low satisfaction level	□Kiosks owners did not have teaching skills □Small business □Poor citizen relationship
	iii.	Internet	Availability	Not available		Low satisfaction level	□Connectivity problem □Interrupted electricity supply □Slow speed
			Speed	28 kbps (1:16)	56 kbps non sharable		
			Cost	Rs.30 per hours	Rs. 30 per hours		

Source: FGDs

BPR: Business process reengineering

* Taken from citizen charter, or otherwise taken from service provider, or if not available from these sources, taken from citi zens, as per their requirements

Table: S3.14: Why-Why Analysis for Fact ors Affecting Usage of e-Governance System

S.N.	Factors	Status	Why	Why	Why	Why
1.	Awareness	Poor	Citizens not informed	No programme of awareness building	Lack of understanding of citizens' needs	No proper marketing strategy
2.	Access (availability of e-Kiosk)	Available, but at distance	Mostly e-Kiosks are outside the village	Cost is high for setting up e-Kiosk inside the village, as fiber cable cost is more	-	-
			Most of the time e-Kiosks remain disconnected from head-end	Cable cutting Lack of proper management	Overhead cabling	Lack of prior experience to manage network
3.	Ease of use	No serious problem	-	-	-	-
4.	Opportunity cost (performance of delivery of services)	Poor	Time lost in sending application by courier	Manual handling	Processes not reengineered	No BPR
			Delivery time is high	Internal processing of Tehsil is manual	Processes not reengineered	No BPR
5.	Security of data	Just satisfactory	Not much data protection required	This system is not totally electronic but only a small portion of it	-	-
6.	Number of services	Very less	Only a few services are provided	Detailed study of processes of other services and re-design of processes were not done	Proper system study lacking	Lack of knowledge about successful models

Contd...

S.N.	Factors	Status	Why	Why	Why	Why
			□ Other services like information of *mandi* rates were not successful due to lack of daily updation	□ No up-to-data available	□ No proper tie-up other with agencies	-
7.	Reliability	Poor	□ Not sure to get the delivery of service in time	□ Sometimes attachments got missed while transferring from one place to another	□ Dependability on the manual process	□ Internal processing of Tehsil is not re-engineered and automated (No BPR and backend computerisa-tion)
			□ Electricity failure	□ UPS, battery problem	□ Quality of equipments was not good	-
				□ Electricity cut	□ No proper tie-up with JVVNL	-
			□ Network failure	□ Cutting of overhead fiber cable	□ Lack of experience of such type of network	-

Note: see Table 3.9 also
BPR: Business process reengineering
JVVNL: Jaipur Vidyut Vitran Nigam Limited

Table: S3.15: Why-Why Analysis for Factors Affecting Quality of Services (Performance of Delivery of Services)

S.N.	Factors	Status	Why	Why	Why
1.	IT Infrastructure	□ Satisfactory at head-end, but not at e-Kiosk	□ Problem was in network management	□ Overhead fiber cabling	□ No prior experience □ No proper network planning
		□ No IT infrastructure at Tehsil	□ Lack of funding support	□ Lack of proper assessment at the system design stage	□ Lack of prior experience and knowledge of other successful models
2.	Business Process Reengineering (BPR)	□ Not carried out	□ BPR was not the priority	□ Quality of service was not a core issue	□ Lack of citizen focus in operational terms □ Lack of resources
3.	Delivery system (DS)	□ Inadequate capacity	□ Inadequate infrastructure, manpower and logistics support	□ Lack of proper assessment of system	□ Inadequate system understanding □ Pilot testing not carried out to check feasibility
		□ Lack of commitment	□ Patwari was not available to give report at e-Kiosk	□ Lack of coordination between service provider and officials of Tehsil	□ Lack of proper change management
4.	Electricity	□ Unreliable	□ No fix time for electricity	□ Short supply of electricity	□ Lack of coordination

Contd...

S.N.	Factors	Status	Why	Why	Why
					with electricity department (JVVNL)
5.	Citizen relationship management (CRM)	□ Poor	□ Kiosk owner does not explain and behave properly □ Grievances are not handled at e-Kiosk satisfactorily	□ No proper training to Kiosk owner	□ Lack of focus on customer (citizen)

Note: see Table 3.10 also

BPR: Business process reengineering

CRM: Customer relationship management

JVVNL: Jaipur Vidyut Vitran Nigam Limited

Table S3.16: Overall Preference by Males and Females: A Select List

S.N.	Sectors	Male			Female		
		I	S	G	I	S	G
1.	Education	2.14	3.61	1.83	1.66	3.22	1.06
2.	Drinking water	2.31	3.32	3.11	2.33	3.13	2.15
3.	Health	2.61	3.92	3.21	2.65	4.46	3.61
4.	Women and child welfare	2.65	3.89	1.01	2.03	3.84	0.95
5.	Social welfare	2.91	3.52	2.23	3.32	3.71	2.15
6.	Poverty alleviation	2.74	3.45	3.02	2.37	3.09	2.75
7.	PDS	2.88	3.96	3.02	2.60	4.11	2.44
8.	Agriculture	2.88	3.16	3.68	2.51	2.12	3.17
9.	Irrigation	2.66	2.39	1.38	1.92	1.58	1.80
10.	Animal husbandry	2.40	3.35	3.47	2.85	3.00	3.47
11.	Tehsil	2.88	2.71	2.47	2.79	2.40	2.44
12.	Electricity	2.18	3.83	3.65	1.62	2.58	3.21
13.	Road	1.68	4.23	1.70	2.29	3.33	1.78
14.	Others	2.38	1.65	3.35	1.88	1.27	3.00
	Total	**35.30**	**46.99**	**37.13**	**32.82**	**41.84**	**33.98**

I: Information, S: Service, G: Grievance

Table S3.17: Information, Services and Grievances liked by all Castes– A Select List

S.N.	Sectors	I/S/G	Items	Mean		
				C1	C2	C3
1.	Education	S	Scholarship	3.00	3.64	3.00
2.	Drinking water	S	Making water available	3.79	4.32	3.58
3.	Health	I	Type of diseases	3.59	3.56	4.42
		I	Family planning	2.90	2.83	3.33
		S	Making medicines available	3.90	3.97	4.42
		S	Expert advice on health	4.07	4.14	4.67
4.	Women and child welfare	S	Organising immunisation programme	3.86	4.00	3.25
5.	Social welfare	I	Social welfare programme for different categories (SCs, STs, OBC etc.)	3.69	4.40	4.28
		I	Schemes for BPL families	3.18	4.13	3.60
		S	Insurance and family welfare schemes	3.31	4.00	3.53
6.	Agriculture	I	Loan schemes	3.82	3.93	3.35
		G	Non-availability of quality seeds, fertilizer, pesticides	3.51	4.33	3.68

I: Information, S: Service, G: Grievance
C1: General caste, C2: OBC, C3: SC & ST

Table S3.18: Information, Services and Grievances Liked by Males, Middle-aged Group, OBC, High Education, and Middle Income Group

S. N.	Categories	I/S/G	Groups		
			Male		**Female**
1.	Gender	I	35.30		32.82
		S	46.99		41.84
		G	37.13		33.98
2.	Age		Young	Middle-aged group	Aged (above 40 year)
		I	35.43	37.72	31.49
		S	47.38	48.38	43.68
		G	35.57	39.32	34.30
3.	Caste		General	OBC	SC&ST
		I	33.82	37.91	32.84
		S	45.73	48.82	43.08
		G	34.52	39.74	33.93
4.	Education		Low education group	Medium education group	High education group
		I	29.99	35.77	39.55
		S	41.95	46.90	50.82
		G	33.21	37.26	37.57
5.	Income		High income group	Meddle income group	Low income group
		I	32.47	35.28	36.10
		S	43.70	47.81	44.35
		G	33.89	37.73	36.38

I: Information, S: Service, G: Grievance

Table S3.19A: Information, Services and Grievances Preferred by Males, Youn g, General, Higher Education Group, High Income Group Citizens (better off / prosperous) – A Select List

S. N.	Sectors	I/S/G	M/A1/C1/E3/I3
1.	Education	I	Results for 10th and 12th classes
		S	Computer education
		S	Providing education to children
		G	Late coming of teachers
2.	Drinking water	I	Quality of water
		S	Making water available
		G	Poor quality of drinking water
3.	Animal husbandry	G	Requirement of veterinary Doctor in rural areas
4.	Electricity	S	Electricity connection
		G	Electricity failure – for agriculture pump sets
5.	PDS	S	Timely availability of essential commodities
6.	Irrigation	I	Sources of irrigation
		S	Timely availability of water for irrigation
7.	Tehsil	S	Domicile certificate
		S	Mutation
		S	Sale deed
		S	Conversion of agriculture land into non-agriculture land
8.	Agriculture	S	Purchase of seeds, fertiliser, pesticide, implements
		S	Mandi rates
		S	Expert advice on agriculture
9.	Other	I	Employment notification
		S	Driving license
		S	e-mail
		S	Internet browsing
		S	Local News

M: Male, A1: Young, C1: General, E1: Low education group, I3: High income group

Table: S3.19B: Preferred by Females, Aged (above 40 year), Low Education group, Low Income Group and SC&ST Citizens (Vulnerable group) – A Select List

S. N.	Sectors	I/S/G	F/A3/C3/E1/I1
1.	Education	I	Schemes for BPL families
		G	Irregularities in mid-day meal
2.	Health	I	Health Information
		S	Immunisation
		S	Making medicines available
3.	Animal husbandry	I	Information of diseases
		I	Schemes for BPL families
		S	Supply of feed
		S	Expert advice on cattle management
4.	Women and child welfare	I	Schemes for BPL families
		S	Organising immunisation programme
5.	Social welfare	I	Social welfare programme for different categories
		S	Old age and widow pension
6.	Poverty alleviation	I	Schemes for BPL families
		G	Name not included in BPL list
7.	PDS	I	Schemes for BPL families
		I	Items available at fair price shops
		S	Ration card
		G	Complaints of BPL / antyodaya cards holder
8.	Tehsil	I	Schemes for BPL families
		S	Caste certificate
		S	Income certificate
		S	Land certificate
		G	Non-availability of Patwari
9.	Road	G	Bad road

F: Female, A3: Aged (above 40 years), C3: SC & ST, E1: Low education group, I1: Low income group.

Table: S3.20: Overall Mean of Information, Services and Grievances of Different Sectors

S. N.	Sectors	Information	Services	Grievances	Total	Ranks
1.	Health	2.62	4.08	3.32	10.02	1
2.	PDS	2.83	3.99	2.91	9.73	2
3.	Electricity	2.11	3.68	3.60	9.39	3
4.	Agriculture	2.82	2.97	3.59	9.38	4
5.	Animal husbandry	2.45	3.31	3.47	9.23	5
6.	Poverty alleviation	2.67	3.39	2.97	9.03	6
7.	Social welfare	2.99	3.55	2.22	8.76	7
8.	Drinking water	2.32	3.27	2.83	8.42	8
9.	Tehsil	2.87	2.67	2.46	8.00	9
10.	Road	1.75	4.12	1.71	7.58	10
11.	Women and child welfare	2.47	3.88	0.99	7.34	11
12.	Others	2.32	1.60	3.31	7.23	12
13.	Education	1.99	3.50	1.61	7.10	13
14.	Irrigation	2.57	2.29	1.43	6.29	14
	Total	**34.78**	**46.30**	**36.42**	–	–

Perception of functionaries about the Delivery of services (Tables from S3.21 to S3.26)

Table: S3.21

	Quality of service is a top priority with our organisation	Responsible for the services delivered to the public	Work is a mere routine work	Exact status of the applications to the citizens
	%	%	%	%
Strongly disagree	4.6	1.0	3.1	-
Disagree	4.6	8.8	23.1	13.8
Neither agree/Nor disagree	3.1	1.0	-	3.1
Agree	63.1	70.8	64.6	67.7
Strongly agree	24.6	16.9	6.39.	15.4

Table: S3.22

	Individual initiative is encouraged	Equipped with old instruments which hinder their performance	Behave in a friendly manner with my colleagues	Seniors always behave in a friendly manner with me
	%	%	%	%
Strongly disagree	-	1.5	1.5	-
Disagree	13.8	10.8	9.2	9.4
Neither agree / Nor disagree	4.6	4.6	-	3.1
Agree	69.2	67.7	60.0	70.3
Strongly agree	12.3	13.8	29.2	17.2

Table: S3.23

	Training of new techniques should be imparted to all of us to update our knowledge	Multimedia knowledge is essential	Innovative techniques to improve performance
	%	%	%
Strongly disagree	-	-	7.8
Disagree	10.8	4.7	
Neither agree / Nor disagree	1.5	-	-
Agree	64.6	71.9	81.3
Strongly agree	23.1	23.4	10.9

Table: S3.24

	Not always necessary to be courteous with public while delivering services to them	Extra courtesy while dealing with senior citizens and women
	%	%
Strongly disagree	6.3	-
Disagree	33.3	-
Neither agree / Nor disagree	1.6	1.6
Agree	52.4	65.6
Strongly agree	6.3	32.8

Table: S3.25

	Follow a rule to have a time limit to provide service to people	I always make all efforts to complete deadlines.	Deadlines for providing services at our organisation are realistic. We usually meet them.
	%	%	%
Strongly disagree	1.5	1.5	-
Disagree	7.7	4.6	6.3
Neither agree / Nor disagree	1.5	1.5	4.7
Agree	66.2	73.8	76.6
Strongly agree	23.1	18.5	12.5

Table: S3.26

	Observes transparency in all the dealings	Punctual worker
	%	%
Strongly disagree	1.5	1.6
Disagree	-	10.9
Neither agree / Nor disagree	-	-
Agree	78.5	57.8
Strongly agree	20.0	29.7

Perception of Citizens about the Delivery System (Tables from S3.27 to S3.31)

Table: S3.27
Overall, how satisfied are you while dealing with Government Officials

Dissatisfied	Somewhat dissatisfied	Neither satisfied / Nor dissatisfied	Somewhat satisfied	Satisfied
15	21	-	3	2
35.7%	52.4%	-	7.1%	4.8%

Table: S3.28
Do you feel that the Government Officials give you all Information?

Always gives	Sometimes gives	Maybe	Never gives	Cant say / DK
9	12	5	13	3
21.4%	28.6%	11.9%	31.0%	7.1%

Table: S3.29
What is the general Behaviour of the Officials while dealing with you?

Very cordial	Cordial	Neither cordial / Nor hostile	Hostile	Very hostile
4	3	4	16	15
9.5%	7.1%	9.5%	38.1%	35.7%

Table: S3.30
Does the services provided by the Government Official are dependable?

	Yes	**No**
No	7	35
%	16.6%	83.4%

Table: S3.31
Do the Officials take Responsibility of the Services provided to you?

	Yes	**No**
No	17	25
%	40.5%	59.5%

Perception of Panchayat Members about the Delivery System

Table: S3.32
Do you take up matters with concerned Officials about the Problems?

	Yes	**Sometimes**	**Difficult to reach**	**No**
No	21	-	1	3
%	84%	-	4%	12%

Table S3.33: Status of Delivery System in Basic Services at Village Level

S.N	Delivery system	Present status of delivery of services	Manpower	Infrastructure	Logistics, inputs, equipments, material etc.	Work culture	Monitoring & supervision	Autonomy (provided for expenditure)	Rules & procedure
1	Primary education	□ Quality of education is poor □ Dropout rate high □ Participation of parents in education is less □ Preference for private schools among richer	□ Shortage of teachers □ Training is not properly given □ Shortage of type IV staff	□ 2-3 rooms in a school □ No toilet, drinking water facility □ No play ground	□ Teaching-aids are provided but not sufficient and not properly maintained □ MDM provided by Govt. Furniture not available □ Other than grains, no utensils and fuel provided by Govt.	□ Quality of education not given priority Responsive-ness towards children is missing	□ Lack of monitoring and supervision by higher officials □ No feedback from parents □ Local panchayat representa-tives do not monitor properly	□ Teachers do not have autonomy for meeting contingency for teaching-aids, sports	□ District officials have to take actions for any repair and maintenance and supply of new equipments, so process is long and provisioning is delayed
2.	Health	□ Quality of health check-up not good □ Unavaila-bility of medicines □ Large distance between health centers and villages □ General	□ Shortage of health-worker □ No in-service training is given	□ On an average one room for sub-center for each GP is not sufficient □ CHC and PHC lack Infrastruc-ture	□ No equipments for health check-up provided □ No adequate medicines provided □ No vehicle to ANMs for village to village visit or ambulance	□ Lack of concern for citizens for providing services like medicines, health check-up □ Lack of Responsive-ness □ Lack of commitment to patients	□ Regular monitoring and supervision by senior doctors not adequate	□ Doctors or staff do not have autonomy to utilise the funds according to local needs such as medicines	□ Centralised purchasing systems for medicines, equipments, etc. It delays supply

Contd...

S.N	Delivery system	Present status of delivery of services	Manpower	Infrastructure	Logistics, inputs, equipments, material etc.	Work culture	Monitoring & supervision	Autonomy (provided for expenditure)	Rules & procedure
		awareness on immunisation and nutrition not present			□ Modern equipments are missing				
3.	Drinking water	□ Total quantum of potable water supplied is not sufficient □ Tanks are not connected to households □ Water quality is poor (the amount of fluoride content is more than permissible limit)	□ Shortage of field engineers □ Training is not provided	□ The capacity of tanker is not sufficient to fulfill demand □ No treatment plant for removing fluoride	□ No proper Infrastructure for supply to individual houses □ Though tanker is provided in GP but it is only at head-quarters not at village level. □ Inadequate equipments and vehicle to mechanic for repairing hand pumps	□ Quality of water is not satisfactory and not given priority by the department (lack of sensitivity to quality)	□ There is no monitoring of water quality and availability at village □ Local panchayat is not active in taking action for quality improvement of water □ No action for making those wells functional, which are defunct at village level	□ Local panchayat has no authority to work and monitor the availability and quality.	□ Long procedures delay the installation
4	Agriculture	□ No information centre about technology transfer □ No information about crop diseases □ No information	□ Lack of VAW for Demonstration and training to people in villages	□ Due to Unavailability of permanent buildings for seeds, godowns, training, etc. work is affected	□ Supply of inputs such as seeds is delayed due to logistics problems □ Inadequate equipments for demonstration	□ Lack of Responsiveness	□ Regular monitoring and supervision is not done by higher officials	□ AAO does not have autonomy for meeting contingency (for crop disease, etc.)	□ Long procedure for supplying seeds, fertilisers, and pesticides, hamper the timely action

Contd...

S.N.	Delivery system	Present status of delivery of services	Manpower	Infrastructure	Logistics, inputs, equipments, material etc.	Work culture	Monitoring & supervision	Autonomy (provided for expenditure)	Rules & procedure
		about sale price of agriculture product			□ No vehicles for field visits				
5	PDS	□ Storage problem for food items □ Information is not provided in time □ Quality of materials is very poor □ All food items not available regularly	□ Manpower for supervision is not sufficient □ Lack of manpower for distribution	□ Lack of storage godowns	□ Transportation of commodeties is affected to remote villages □ No accurate measurement equipments □ No particular place for distribution	□ Lack of good behaviour □ Irregular distribution of food, at will of dealer	□ Lack of supervision by higher officials	-	□ Rules for transparency (display of commodeties prices) are not followed
6.	Animal husbandry	□ Treatment of cattle's disease is not available at village level □ Artificial insemination not done in time	□ One staff available at one field centre	□ No veterinary centre at GP level	□ No equipments for saving semen □ No equipments for artificial insemination □ Inadequate equipments to doctors □ Lack of medicines	□ Lack of responsiveness	□ Lack of supervision by higher officials	□ Doctors don't have autonomy for purchasing the equipments & medicines □ Doctors don't have autonomy for visiting at home for seeing the cattle	□ Centralised purchasing system for medicines, equipments, etc. It delays supply

Contd...

S.N	Delivery system	Present status of delivery of services	Manpower	Infrastructure	Logistics, inputs, equipments, material etc.	Work culture	Monitoring & supervision	Autonomy (provided for expenditure)	Rules & procedure
7.	Tehsil office	□ Delay in making certificates to citizens	□ Patwari has to cover a large number of villages and cases / records	□ Lack of office infrastructure □ Insufficient record room	□ Equipments such as computers, generator, photocopy machine, etc not available □ No furniture available □ No vehicles for field staff □ Lack of almirah and racks for documents	□ Lack of responsiveness	□ Lack of supervision by higher officials due to heavy work load	□ No provision to make expenditure for meeting day to day contingency	□ Collectorate level purchasing system
8	Family care & women and child health care (ICDS)	□ Food available for children and mother is inadequate. □ No effort made to disseminate information about nutrition and immunization	□ Training is inadequate and irregular	□ Inadequate facility at AWC □ No drinking water facility □ *Murmure* and biscuits provided by deptt. □ Inadequate storage space	□ No pots / utensils for distributing the food □ No storage faculty for food □ No almirah for cash	□ Lack of responsiveness □ Parents not willing to send their children □ Feedback from parents is not taken	□ Lack of supervision by higher officials (supervisor and CDPO) □ Local panchayat representatives (sarpanch / upsarpanch) do not monitor properly	□ Centralised purchasing system of medicines, equipments, etc delays supply	□ State level purchasing system
9	Bank - poverty	□ Loan is not given in	□ One bank for fifty	□ Lack of infrastruc-	□ Good infrastruc-	□ Lack of concern	□ Poor monitoring	-	□ Rules for timely

Contd...

S.N	Delivery system	Present status of delivery of services	Manpower	Infrastructure	Logistics, inputs, equipments, material etc.	Work culture	Monitoring & supervision	Autonomy (provided for expenditure)	Rules & procedure
	alleviation	time	villages	ture	ture from department □ No vehicles provided to field officers	over timely sanction of loans □ Lack of commitment to citizens □ Lack of responsiveness	and supervision		provisioning of loan are not followed
10	Panchayat	□ Panchayat is not able to provide the basic services to people (even sanitation) □ Panchayat functioning is dominated by a few (sarpanch, influential people) □ Women do not get voice in the panchayat	□ One panchayat secretary for 1-3 GPs □ Panchayat members do not have sufficient knowledge of rules, schemes, appropriate technologies for day-to-day working □ Dummy panchayat members (women members elected where their husbands or male members cannot contest)	□ Lack of infrastructure	□ Lack of furniture like tables, chairs, etc.	□ Lack of awareness & training □ Lack of responsiveness □ Lack of commitment	□ Poor monitoring and supervision	□ Lack of autonomy to panchayats □ Lack of proper rules for conducting gram sabha □ Lack of procedural details and guidelines for local level planning	-

Source: FGDs and field visits
MDM: Mid day meal

Table: S3.34: Problem for Functionaries engaged with Delivery System

S.N	Department name Functionaries	Training	Motivation	Difficulty in achieving high targets	Workload other than departments job (Approx. * %age in a Year)	Internal environment	External environment
1.	Primary education	□ No training at the time of joining □ Only in-service training by DPEP after some time of joining	□ Lack of motivation in teacher □ Promotion avenues less □ Promotion not based on performance □ No benefits / incentive for good performance	□ Less support from parents □ Engaged in non-teaching work □ Lack of proper training and equipment □ Lack of proper teaching environment	□ About 40 to 45% of total working time consumed in: □ Pulse polio □ Census □ Training □ BPL survey □ MDM during school time □ Election □ Protocol	□ Inside environment is not healthy; rooms are mostly in dilapidated condition, dirty and are not cleaned regularly	□ Some of them are in the busy locality, it also affect the school teaching environment
2.	Health	□ Training provided only at the time of joining □ No in-service training	□ Lack of motivation in doctors, nurses and ANM to take care of patients □ Promotion not based on performance □ No benefits / incentive on good performance	□ Inadequate logistics support □ Engaging in non health related work □ Lack of proper environment	□ About 40 to 45% of total working time consumed in: □ Census □ Survey □ Election □ Protocol	□ No cleanliness inside the health center. Due to lack of resources, infrastructure and manpower, it is not maintained	□ Outside of the health center is not clean either and is filthy in some cases due to medical waste
3.	Drinking water	□ Training provided only at the time of joining □ No in-service training	□ Lack of motivation to workers for solving the problems of public in time □ Promotion not based on performance	□ Limited sources of natural water □ High fluoride content in water □ Lack of infrastructure □ Lack of resources	□ More than 30 to 40% of total working time consumed in: □ Travel □ Election □ Protocol	□ The regular cleaning of water tank is not done in time □ Dirty water around tube well / tap water station	-
4.	Family care & women	□ Training provided	□ Lack of	□ Lack of training	-	□ Local panchayat	-

Contd...

S.N	Department name Functionaries	Training	Motivation	Difficulty in achieving high targets	Workload other than departments job (Approx. * %age in a Year)	Internal environment	External environment
	and child welfare (ICDS)	only at the time of joining □ No in-service training	motivation among AWWs to take care of children and mothers	to AWW □ Lack of logistics support		representatives (sarpanch / upsarpunch) do not monitor properly □ Centralised purchasing systems of medicines, equipments, etc delays supply	
5.	Animal husbandry	□ Training provided only at the time of joining □ No in-service training □ No special training	□ No motivation programme for doctors and field staff □ Promotion not based on performance	□ No advanced technology □ Lack of logistics Support	-	- -	
6.	PDS	□ Training provided only at the time of joining □ No in-service training	□ Lack of motivation in retailer	-	-	- -	
7.	Tehsil Office	□ Training provided only at the time of Joining □ No in-service training	□ Lack of motivation in Patwari □ Promotion not based on performance □ No benefits / incentive on more collection of tax	□ No e-Governance system □ High workload on Patwari	□ More than 40 to 45% of total working time consumed in: □ Pulse polio □ Census □ Report preparation □ Election □ Travel □ Protocol	-	-
8.	Agriculture	□ No special training to agriculture	□ Lack of motivation	□ Short supply of agricultural inputs	□ About 30 to 40% of total working time consumed	- -	

Contd...

S.N	Department name Functiona-ries	Training	Motivation	Difficulty in achieving high targets	Workload other than departments job (Approx. * %age in a Year)	Internal environment	External environment
		officers and staff		□ Lack of awareness about new technology	in: □ Travel □ Report preparation □ Election □ Census □ Protocol		
9.	Banks (poverty alleviation)	□ Inadequate training at the time of joining	□ Lack of motivation level in bank officers	-	-	- -	
10.	Panchayat	□ Training provided only at the time of joining	□ Lack of motivation for sarpanch and panchayat secretary due to local politics	□ No support from other govt. departments □ No trained staff	-	-	□ Lack of proper sanitation and cleanliness in compound of panchayat office

Source: FGDs and field visits

* Calculations based on data collected

AWW: Anganwadi worker

Table: S3.35: System based Critical Indicators for Select e-Governance Projects

S.N.	Projects	E-governance services	Critical indicators (system based)					
			Electricity	Connectivity	BPR	Backend computerisation	MIS	Efficiency of delivery system
1.	E-governance project (Jaipur district, Rajasthan) (2003-04)	(i) Caste (ii) Income, (iii) Domicile certificate (iv) ROR (Jamabandi) (v) Grievances	Major problem	Good speed but problem due to electricity and fiber cut	Not done	Not done	Developed, but does not work at e-Kiosk	□ Inefficient for most of the e-services □ Efficient only for ROR
2.	Janmitra (Jhalawar district, Rajasthan) (2003-04)	(i) Caste (ii) Income, (iii) Domicile certificate (iv) ROR (Jamabandi) (v) Grievances	Major problem	Speed is very slow (dial-up based)	Not done	Not done	Developed, but does not work at e-Kiosk	□ Manual and insufficient for most of e-services □ Efficient only for ROR
3.	Gyandoot (Dhar district, Madhya Pradesh) (2004-05)	(i) Caste (ii) Income, (iii) Domicile certificate (iv) ROR, (v) Grievances	Major problem	Speed is very slow (dial-up based)	Not done	Not done	Not developed	□ Manual and insufficient for most of e-services □ Efficient only for ROR

Contd...

S.N.	Projects	E-governance services	Critical indicators (system based)					
			Electricity	Connectivity	BPR	Backend compute-risation	MIS	Efficiency of delivery system
4.	(i) e-Bhoomi (Bangalore urban district, Karnataka)	Related to ROR only	Major problem	NA (as Kiosks work at Tehsil only, not yet in the villages)	NA	Not done	Yes	□ Efficient for land record certificates, but only a few services of Tehsil provided
	(ii) RDS (including e-Bhoomi) (Mandia district, Karnataka) (2004-05)	(i) Caste (ii) Income (iii) Domicile certificate (iv) ROR (v) Grievances	Major problem	Good speed but problem due to interrupted electricity supply	Not done (under progress)	Not done	Developed, but does not work at e-Kiosk	□ Manual and insufficient for most of e-services □ Efficient only for ROR
5.	OLTP (Nalgonda district, Andhra Pradesh) (2004-05)	(i) Caste (ii) Income, (iii) Domicile certificate (iv) ROR (vi) Grievances	Major problem	Good speed but problem due to interrupted electricity supply	Not done	Not done	Developed, but does not work at e-Kiosk	□ Manual and insufficient for most of e-services □ Efficient only for ROR

Contd...

S.N.	Projects	E-governance services	Critical indicators (system based)					
			Electricity	Connectivity	BPR	Backend compute-risation	MIS	Efficiency of delivery system
6.	Lokmitra*	(i) Payments of a) Electricity bills b) Water bills c) Telephone bills d) house tax (ii) Online reservation (iii) Issuing death and birth certificate	No problem	Good connectivity	Done	Done	Developed	□ Efficient

Table S3.36: Process of Service Delivery through e-Kiosk in Different e-Governance Projects

S.N.	Projects	Salient services	Salient items of processes						
			Attach-ments	Submission of application form	Sending of application form, from e-Kiosk to Tehsil	Processing in Tehsil	MIS	Final certificate from Tehsil to e-Kiosk	Delivery of certificate to citizen
1.	E-governance project	(i) Certificates (ii) ROR Jamabandi) (iii) Grievances (iv) Computer education (v) Photographs Internet (vi) Horoscope (vii) Cable TV	As in case of manual system	At e-Kiosk	By courier	Manual	Not functional at e-Kiosk	By courier	By hand at e-Kiosk
2.	Janmitra	(i) Certificate, (ii) ROR Jamabandi) (iii) Grievances (iv) Salary bills (v) Insurance (vi) Stamp vending	-do-	-do-	By hand	Manual	-do-	By hand	-do-
3.	Gyandoot	(i) Certificate (ii) ROR (iii) Grievances (iv) Mandi bhav	-do-	-do-	By hand	Manual	Not develope d for e-Kiosk	By hand	-do-

Contd...

S.N.	Projects	Salient services	Salient items of processes						
			Attach-ments	Submission of application form	Sending of application form, from e-Kiosk to Tehsil	Processing in Tehsil	MIS	Final certificate from Tehsil to e-Kiosk	Delivery of certificate to citizen
4.	OLTP	(i) Certificate (ii) ROR (iii) Grievances ((iv) Gram hat (v) e-mail	-do-	-do-	By hand	Partially computerised	Not functional at e-Kiosk	By hand	-do-
5.	RDS (including e-Bhoomi)	(i) Caste, (ii) Income, (iii) Domicile certificate, (iv) ROR, (v) Grievances	-do-	-do-	By hand	Under progress		By hand	-do-
6.	e-Bhoomi	Related to ROR only	Only land related certificates are provided, and caste, income and domicile certificates are not provided by e-Bhoomi No processing is involved as in case of certificate.						
7.	Lokmitra	(i) Payment of a) electricity bills b) water bills c) telephone bills d) house tax (ii) Online reservation (iii) Issuing death and birth certificate	Payments of bills are made on the spot at e-Kiosk, so no processing is involved as in case of certificate.						

Source: Based on FGDs with citizens, Kiosk and officials (it is indicative).

Table S3.37: SERVQUAL Analysis of Delivery System

S. N.	Gaps	Nature of Gaps	Impact	Causes
1.	Gap 1	Gap between expected service by consumers (citizens) and management perception of citizen expectations	□ Inadequate assessment of citizens' requirement and expectations	□ Lack of proper assessment of the citizens' requirement for the quality of services
2.	Gap 2	Gap between management perception of consumers (citizens) expectations and translation of perceptions into service quality specifications	□ Poor system design	□ Lack of focus on building delivery system based on 'quality parameters' * or, there is a mismatch between capacity of delivery system to deliver and quality expected from it **. □ Lack of citizen-centric design □ Lack of system approach □ Focus on setting up delivery points / mechanisms offices up to block / Tehsil, but less at GP level – or less focus on delivery of services at the village level***
3.	Gap 3	Gap between service quality specifications (of service provider) and service delivery	□ Poor service levels	□ Inadequate infrastructure, field staff and equipment support at the field level, resulting in poor output of the system**** □ Inadequate capabilities of staff to deliver □ Lack of coordination among field functionaries (of departments) □ Inadequate change management by the service provider □ Inability of field staff to take citizens in confidence due to poor citizen (customer) focus
4.	Gap 4	Gap between Service delivery and external communications to consumers (citizens)	□ Incomplete / wrong communication to citizens	□ Exaggerating the likely deliverables without commensurate system capacity (raising expectations by telling citizens that they would get services at village level with ease, but it does not happen or

Contd...

S. N.	Gaps	Nature of Gaps	Impact	Causes
				children will get free primary education in the villages, but quality of education remains poor
5.	Gap 5	Gap between perceived service and expected service by consumers (citizens)	□ Delivery system not able to meet the requirements of citizens □ Citizens' dissatisfaction	□ Poor delivery system design □ Poor citizen focus like: i. Lack of interaction with citizens, ii. Lack of awareness building, iii. Lack of care of citizens grievances, iv. Citizens not able to give feedback, etc.

Note: Delivery system studied: Tehsil, primary education, health, agriculture, animal husbandry, drinking water, and PDS

*For example, 'quality parameters' like convenience, timeliness

**For example, in order to provide quality inputs to children in schools, good infrastructure and motivated teachers in desired number with teaching-aids are necessary; and similarly for good quality water, filtration/fluoride removal plants may be required. But these are not provided, which result into mismatch between capacity of delivery system to deliver and quality expected from it

***Mostly the facilities are located at Block / Tehsil level for health, Banks, veterinary centre, etc., but at the gram panchayat level, such facilities are not there and are far away from Block / Tehsil

****For example, inadequate class rooms, lack of teachers and inadequacy of teaching-aids lead to difficulty in providing education to a large number of children, and results into poor output of teaching.

Table S3.38: SWOT Analys is for Various Services

e-Services and Grievances and		e-Information	
Strength □ OFC Network □ One Kiosk set-up in most of the villages □ Government support □ No competitor	**Opportunity** □ To provide services at village level □ To generate revenue □ Partnership with government □ Building awareness through Cable TV □ Helping citizens	**Strength** □ OFC Network □ One Kiosk set-up in most of the villages □ No competitor □ Good hardware at head-end and kiosk	**Opportunity** □ To provide services at village level □ To generate revenue □ Partnership with government □ Helping citizens □ Building awareness through Cable TV
Weakness □ Poor reliability of services □ Citizens-centric system not designed □ Lack of awareness among people □ Inability of Kiosk owner to convince people □ Services & process not simplified, the existing processes automated □ Women and old are not willing.	**Threat** □ Erratic supply of electricity	**Weakness** □ Need-based information design is missing □ Lack of awareness among people □ Lack of capabilities of kiosk owner – inability to take people in confidence.	**Threat** □ Erratic supply of electricity
e-Entertainment and e-Business		**e-Education**	
Strength □ OFC Network □ One kiosk set-up in most of the villages □ No competitor □ License From Govt. cable TV broadcasting in rural areas	**Opportunity** □ To generate revenue	**Strength** □ OFC Network □ One Kiosk set-up in most of the villages □ No competitor □ 'Aptech' support	**Opportunity** □ To generate revenue □ Partnership with govt. □ Helping citizens

Contd...

Weakness	**Threat**	**Weaknesses**	**Threat**
□ Lack of capabilities of Kiosk owner – inability to take people in confidence.	□ Cable cutting in some cases □ Erratic supply of electricity	□ Need-based course design lacking □ Lack of awareness among people □ Lack of capabilities of Kiosk owner – inability to take people in confidence □ Women are less willing	□ Erratic supply of electricity

4

System Design: Process Reengineering and Organisational Development

"Potential of IT to transform business is not in question, it is how to unlock that potential that is the question and BPR seems to be providing one answer."

4.1 Business Process Reengineering (BPR) and System Redesign

The governments in developing countries like India face a difficult task of dealing with numerous functions that are required to provide needed services to citizens. They also have to find ways to interact with citizens to provide these services in a manner that is responsive and accountable to the satisfaction of the citizens. Traditionally governments are divided into numerous departments and sections, each of which develop, administer and deliver some services. The citizen needs to know which department or office is responsible for delivering, which service, and even then one often realises that his actual needs are hopelessly divided between functions of a few different offices, and that these offices are just not structured to take a unified view of meeting his specific need. Under the circumstances, even if one is able to spend all the time running around these different offices, one just may still be left unsatisfied.

The basis of e-Governance is not a simple online interaction with the citizen; it implies these complex organisational restructurings. E-Governance has to make the citizen's life easier, and not more difficult. So, when the citizen doesn't find internet as his preferred way of interaction (which is obviously so, for an overwhelming majority of citizens in countries like India), the convenience of a personal interaction needs to be at hand. This is why many state governments in India have come up with 'citizen service centres' where front-end staff, equipped with networked access to various backend offices of the government, interacts with and provides services to the citizens.

The fallout of having a superficially laid out front-end without doing even a basic organisational structural redesigning has resulted in service delivery initiatives getting stuck at a level that includes only a few services, which are as follows:

- Collection of payment for different departments

- Providing basic information pertaining to various departments
- Providing application form etc, and accepting them on behalf of various departments
- Providing record authentication services like land records, identity records and entering records like birth / death registration, vehicle registration, etc., but services that require detailed processing are not made available by e-Governance projects. It is mainly due to the fact that the process reengineering and backend computerisation have not been attempted.

4.1.1 Redesigning Carried Out: Business process reengineering (BPR) is defined as 'the fundamental re-thinking and radical redesign of business processes to achieve dramatic improvements in critical contemporary measures of performance such as cost, quality, service, and speed' (Hammer and Champy, 1993). The basic reasoning and the logic behind business process reengineering are as follows:

- ***Fundamental***
  - Why do we do what we do?
  - Why do we do it the way we do it?
- ***Radical***
  - Inventing completely new ways of accomplishing work
- ***Dramatic***
  - Achieving quantum leaps in performance (process efficiency)
- ***Processes***
  - Using inputs to create outputs of value to the customer

The structure of modern business organisations was based on the principles of scientific management and Adam Smith's idea of the division of labor. Such an approach argued that success was based on breaking complex processes into simple tasks and then optimising the performance of the individual tasks and their processes. For instance, a caste certificate from the Tehsil typically takes around 10-15 days (12 days average) (see Table 4.1) to complete from the time the villager starts to understand the procedure till the time he actually gets the certificate. Yet, only 134 minutes is the actual time (see Table 4.1) taken to complete the processing in manual process while in e-Governance project (in Jaipur), the total number of days in getting caste certificate is 20-25 days (23 days average) and actual processing time is 192 minutes, the process efficiency is reduced in the project (see Table 4.1). Therefore, it requires detailed process analysis.

Table: 4.1: Process Efficiency of Manual and e-Governance System for Caste Certificate

S.N.	Scenarios	Total number of days in getting certificate	Average time in getting certificate (in days)	Actual time of processing (in minutes)	Efficiency
1.	Manual	10-15	12	134	2.51 %
2.	e-Governance project	20-25	23	192	1.88 %

Source: Table 3.3, and Efficiency Tables 4.1A.1 and 4.1A.2 in Annexure 4.1A

The old way of thinking about IT was to use computers to automate existing processes; the new way of thinking about IT: use computers to create new ways of accomplishing work that were not feasible before.

Current competitive environment demands 'break-through' changes in: cycle-time, service-levels, costs, quality and other competitive performance measures.

> *"The old way of thinking about IT was to use computers to automate existing processes; the new way of thinking about IT: use computers to create new ways of accomplishing work that were not feasible before."*

To achieve 'break-through' levels of improvement, one must re-examine cross-functional flows of information and materials, activities and decisions, and existing hierarchies of measurement and control. One must employ modern information technologies to rethink and redefine 'core business processes'. One must re-engineer the way the business operates to achieve specific objectives for competitive success.

A study of e-Governance projects like Gramdoot, Lokmitra and Janmitra were carried out. It was found that some of the services were used very frequently by most of the citizens, while some of the services were rarely used. It was decided to concentrate on only those processes, which consumed the maximum resources and were touching the lives of maximum number of citizens [and also covered by the e-Governance project (in Jaipur)]. The short listed processes are as follows:

i. Caste certificate
ii. Income certificate
iii. Domicile certificate
iv. Jamabandi (ROR)

The study of these contemporary e-Governance projects also revealed that most of the projects were partially successful on the technology front; they failed because adequate attention was not given to the people or process aspect of the system. The systems in the Tehsil and elsewhere are in place for the last more than a few decades. The processes keep on getting changed and altered through various government orders as and when they come. The government officials, on their part issue guidelines to be followed while providing these services. Due to a large number of guidelines issued, that attempted to incrementally improve the processes, what has happened is that the processes themselves have become discontinuous and patchy. Even the officials do not have a complete list of the exact procedures to be followed. Moreover, all the records are maintained in a manual register system. Due to this, the measurement becomes difficult. As the measurements are not done properly, forecasting and the future direction cannot be assessed properly. A need was felt to map the processes and analyse them based on proper quality parameters.

The requirements varied from the official's requirement for security to the citizen's requirement of timely service at lower cost. The new requirements that were identified were:

- Database
- Software
- Network
- Citizens ID in the integrated database format

4.1.2 Four Scenarios: Based on CTQs and other system inputs, consultations with local officials and functionaries of Tehsil and keeping in view change management issues in mind, the new system should be evolved in a phased manner. Following are the incremental phases (see Table 4.2) for the implementation of the new system, which will take new system from ad hoc to sophisticated state.

Scenarios A and B are similar in nature. The necessity of these scenarios is due to the tendency of functionaries to resist the new changes. This is basically to gain the confidence of the functionaries in the new system. The only difference in these two scenarios is that, in scenario B, the attachments (also manually as a supplement) required with the application will be sent online by scanning the attachments, which will drastically reduce the time taken in sending attachments manually from Kiosk to Tehsil. In both the cases, the final delivery certificate will be delivered manually from Tehsil to Kiosk.

Scenario C will come into existence after the creation of citizen database.

Here the requirement of attachments will not be there for most of the services because of citizen database. The requirement of the attachments will be there only for those services for which dynamic data is required, e.g. services like income certificate will have such requirements. Despite having everything online, the final delivery certificate will still be delivered manually from Tehsil to Kiosk, again to gain the confidence of functionaries in the new system.

Table: 4.2: Processing in Different Scenarios

S. N.	Scenarios	Broad items	Processing
1.	Scenario A	- Application form	- Online
		- Attachments	- Manual
		- Internal processing of Tehsil	- Online
		- Delivery form	- Manual
2.	Scenario B	- Application form	- Online
		- Attachments	- Online (scanned) + Manual
		- Internal processing of Tehsil	- Online
		- Delivery form	- Manual
3.	Scenario C	- Application form	- Online
		- Attachments	- Only in case of dynamic data*
		- Internal processing of Tehsil	- Online
		- Delivery form	- Manual
4.	Scenario D	- Application form	- Online
		- Attachments	- Only in case of dynamic data*
		- Internal processing of Tehsil	- Online
		- Delivery form	- Online

Note: The common thing in all the scenarios is online internal processing of Tehsil.

* In case of change of place or caste or income.

Scenarios C & D are more or less same except, in scenario D, the final delivery certificate can now be printed at e-Kiosk, on which there should be the signature of some authorised staff from Tehsil. The re-engineered processes under the four scenarios are shown in Figures 4.1, S4.1, S4.2 and 4.2. While reengineering, the guidelines that were followed are indicated in Table S4.1

The process efficiency of these four scenarios has been calculated and compared with manual and e-Governance project (in Jaipur). It shows that in each scenario there is increase in efficiency, and in scenario D the efficiency is 73.64%, which is significantly higher than the present manual and e-Governance system (see Table 4.3 and Figure 4.3 and Tables 4.1A.1 to 4.1A.6 in Annexure 4.1A). This has been mainly due to BPR and followed by suggested backend computerisation (BC). It is suggested that 'citizen database' should be developed as a part of BC.

Figure: 4.1: Caste Certificate through e-Kiosk (Scenario A)

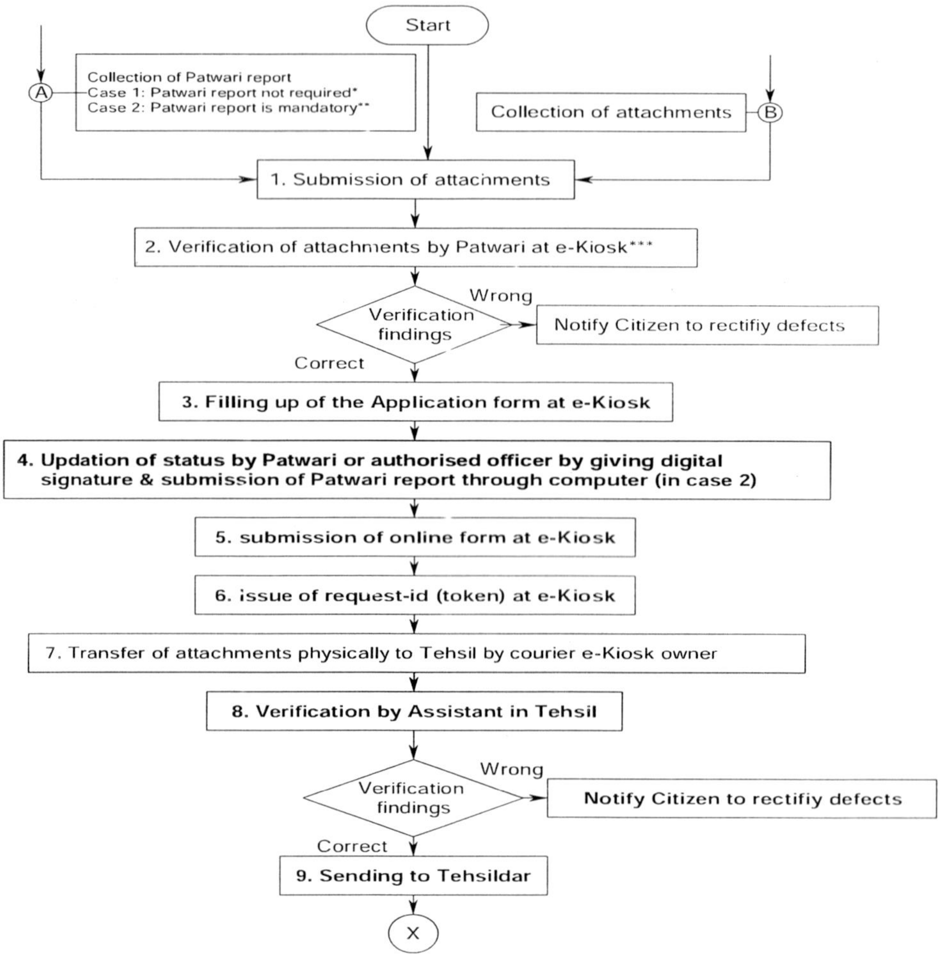

Note: Bold activities are electronic activities

*In case of the following (for caste certificate) (case 1)

- If citizen has his / her earlier caste certificate or of his father

**In case of the following (case 2)

- If citizen has come from other village in the recent past
- If citizen is not having domicile certificate / ration card
- If citizen has his/her earlier caste certificate or of his father

*** Either by Patwari or authorised staff of Tehsil

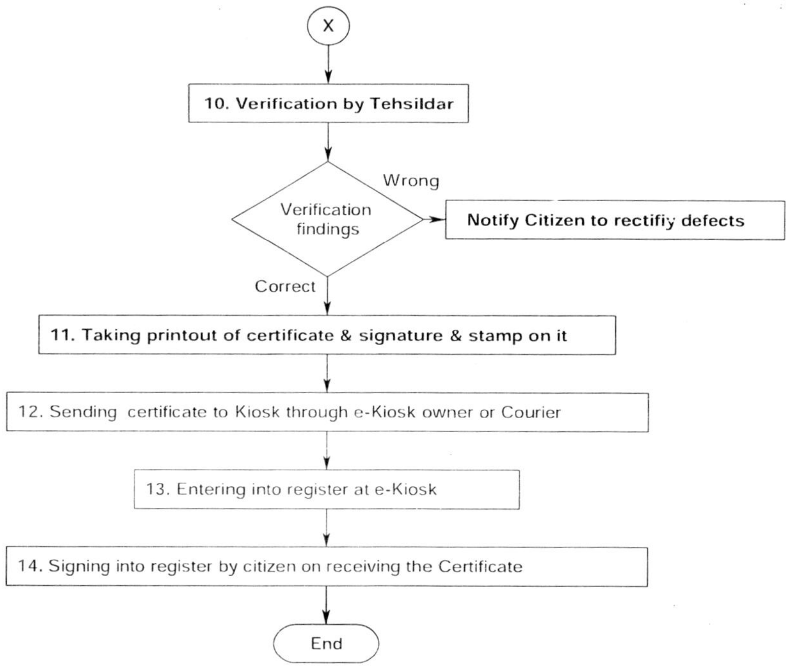

Report Patwari

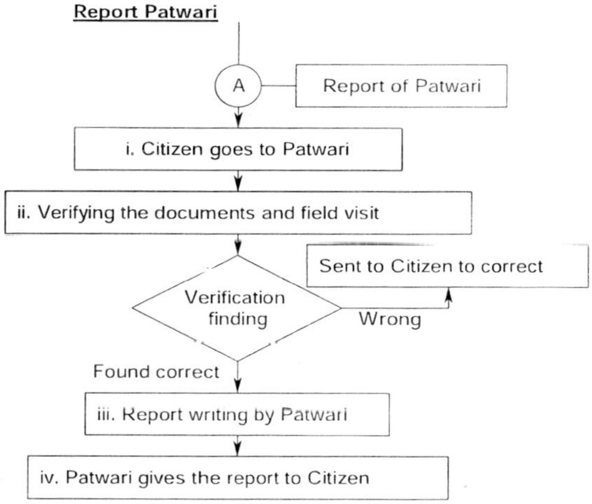

Collection of Attachments

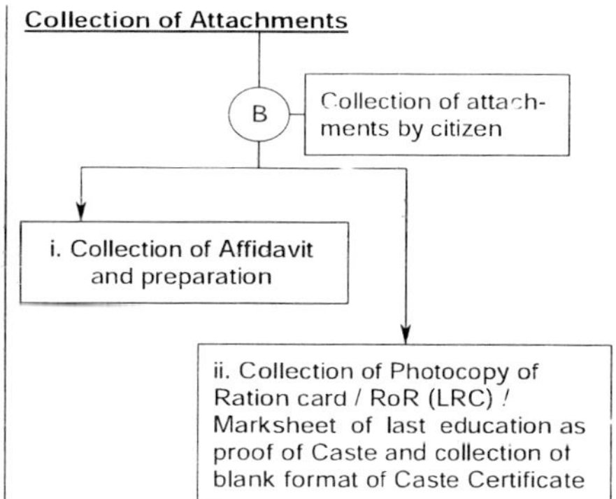

Note: Bold activities are electronic activities

Figure: 4.2 Caste Certificate through e-Kiosk (Scenario D)

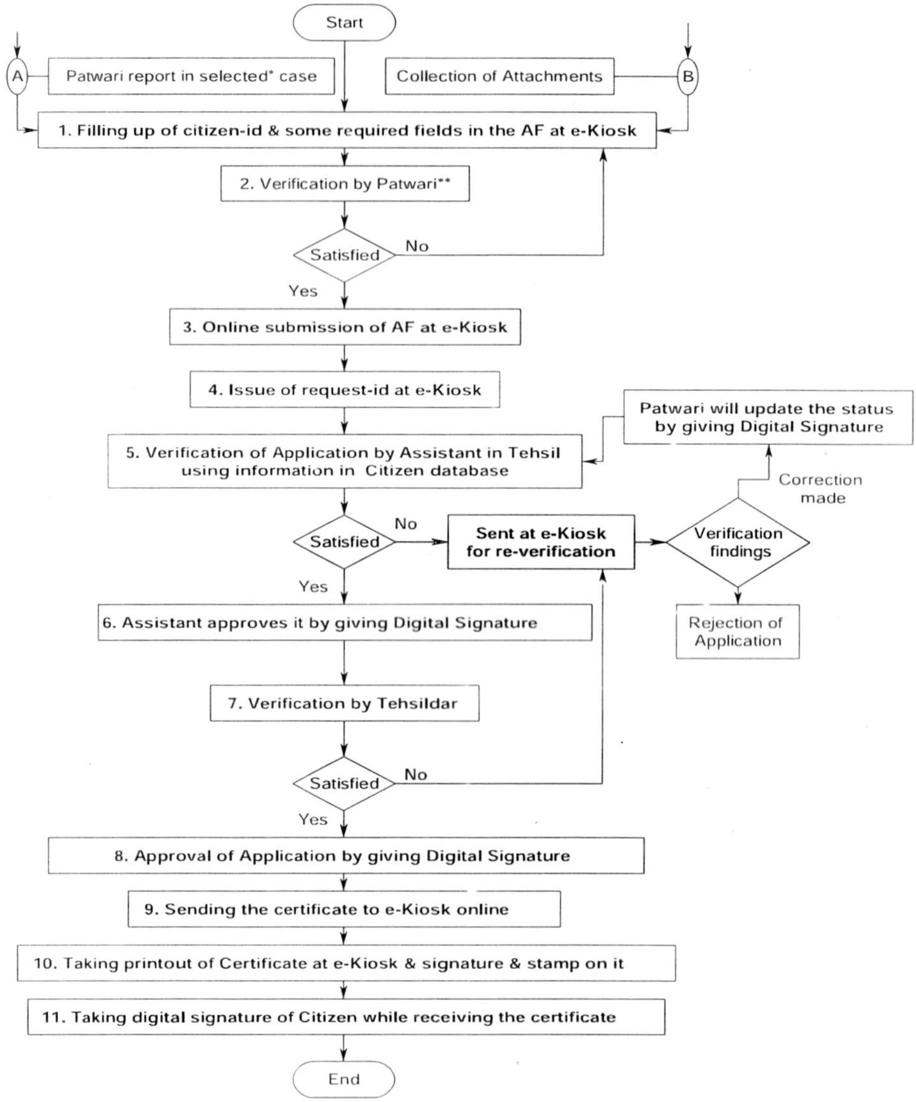

Note: Bold activities are electronic activities

*If citizen has come from other village in the recent past and his name has not been entered in citizen database

** Either by Patwari or authorised staff of Tehsil

Report Patwari (if citizen has come from other village in the recent past and his name has not been entered in citizen database)

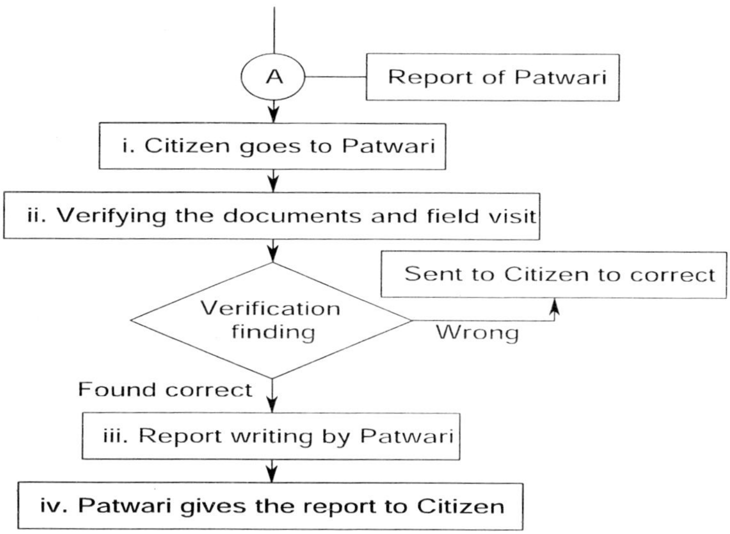

Collection of Attachment (if citizen has come from other village in the recent past and his name has not been entered in citizen database)

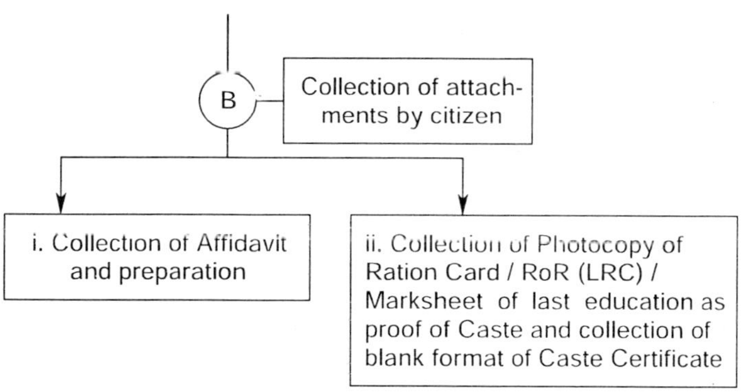

Table 4.3: Comparison of Process Efficiency among Different Modes

S.N.	Scenario	Efficiency (%)
1.	Manual Process	2.51
2.	e-Governance Process	1.88
3.	Scenario A	2.31
4.	Scenario B	2.32
5.	Scenario C	5.72
6.	Scenario D	73.64

Figure: 4.3: Comparison of Efficiency among Scenarios

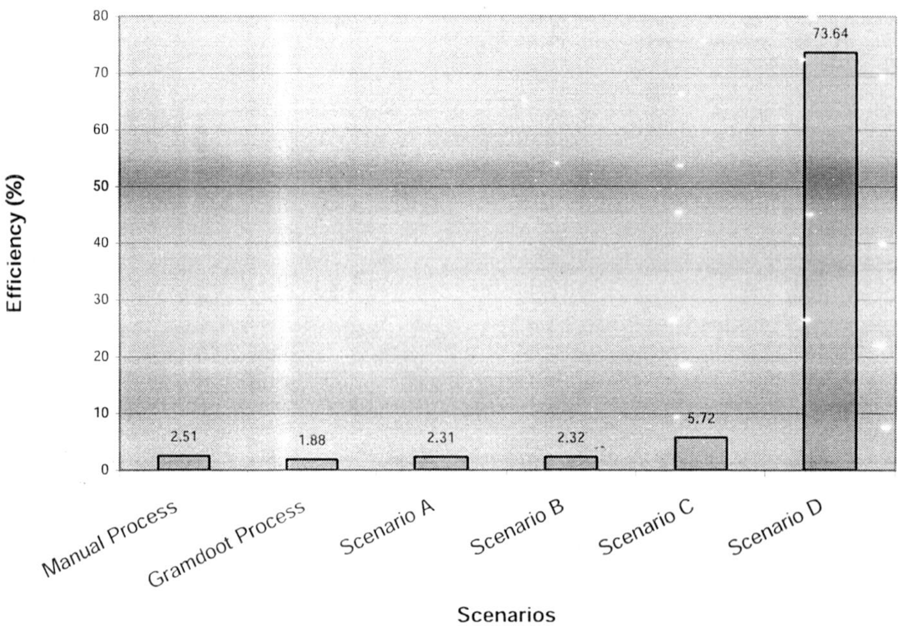

After BPR, CTQs are reflected in Table 4.4, which reflects gradual improvement from e-Governance project (in Jaipur) to scenario D. Also, it has brought out that number of mandatory (see Table 4.2A.1 in Annexure 4.2A) attachments would come down substantially. For example in case of OBC certificate number of attachments would come down from 9 to 3 (3 mandatory attachments). Similarly touch points and number of visits have come down drastically from 13 touch points and 14 visits under the project to 6 and 3 respectively under scenario D (see Table 4.2A.2 in Annexure 4.2A).

Table: 4.4: Critical Indicators for Caste Certificate by Manual processing, e-Governance Project and under different Scenarios after Computerisation in Tehsil (After BPR)

S. N	CTQs		Caste Certificate[Ψ]											
			Manual		e-Governance project		Scenario A		Scenario B		Scenario C		Scenario D	
1.	Number of activities		19		26		20		20		12		11	
2.	Activities on-line (through computer)	Number	0		4		8		8		8		10	
		%age	0		15.38		40		40		66		90.9	
3.	Touch points$	For citizen	Min	Max	Min	Max	Min	Max	Min	Max	Min	Max	Min	Max
			7	13	6	12	6	7	6	7	2	2	2	2
		For application	7		13		7		7		6		6	
4.	Number of decision-making levels		3		3		3		3		3		3	
5.	Number of visits by citizens		Min	Max	Min	Max	Min	Max	Min	Max	Min	Max	Min	Max
			7	15	6	14	5	7	5	7	2	3	2	
6.	Number of attachments	9	9		4		4		0	0		3		
7.	Total time spent by citizens to avail service *		10-15 days		20-25 days		10-12 days		10-12 days		2 days		1 day	
8.	Total expenditure by citizens in availing the service **		Rs 200-300		Rs. 200-250		Rs.50-100		Rs.50-100		Rs.20-30		Rs.20-30	
9.	Process (Throughput) efficiency (%)		2.51		1.88		2.31		2.32		5.72		73.64	

Note 1: Touch points for visits, time and cost for availing the certificates by citizens, vary depending upon the availability of attachments with citizens and follow-up to be done. *Note 2:* Touch points: It refer to the points where either 'citizen' or 'application form' has to touch during the entire process of delivery of service.

* It includes time of collection of AF, visits to Patwari, travel to e-Kiosk, Tehsil, etc. ** It includes cost of collection of AF, traveling cost, wages lost and other miscellaneous expenses. *** Required incase of dynamic data

$Number of touch points has two categories minimum (min) and maximum (max.); the first one is when the citizen has got attachments and second one is when the citizen has to collect all the attachments (number of attachments as per Table 4.2A.1 in Annexure 4.2A). (Touch points refer to the points where either citizen or application form has to touch during the entire process of delivery of certificates). ΨOBC caste certificate

4.1.3 Database Design

A. **Description of DFD:** The following are the steps involved when a citizen needs to avail the services offered by the developed system at the Kiosk (see Figure 4.4 and Table S4.2)

- Citizen shall come to the Kiosk & make a request for service delivery by filling citizen ID. If certificate is not already there in the database corresponding to that citizen ID, then only the application form will be filled and submitted.
- On submission of application form, a service request number is generated which will be given to the citizen, as a token to receive the final delivery certificate.
- Assistant in Tehsil will verify the application form by querying the citizen database and if not satisfied, will make application pending for Patwari who will then manually verify those things.
- After the verification, the Patwari will submit his remarks on the verification. If Patwari gives favourable remarks for the application, then Assistant will approve the application and makes the application pending for either Tehsildar or SDO.
- Tehsildar or SDO will look for the noting of Assistant and Patwari, and they may or may not verify the citizen database for the application. After their approval, a certificate will be generated with barcode.
- The delivery of certificate will be online, digitally signed by Tehsil / BDO and sent to the Kiosk.
- Certificate / document is printed at Kiosk and signed and stamped by local Tehsil authority (Patwari or Girdawar) and handing over to citizen.
- Informing the Tehsil office electronically by Patwari about the issue of certificate.
- Listing the information on web-site about the issue of certificate for transparency.

Note: While designing database and software, scenario D should be taken into account in order to have comprehensive design features, but interventions should be made incrementally and sequentially, starting from scenario A to scenario D.

The database design consists of data objects (or fields) as specified in the data tables (or records), which are having relationships with each other for control of various processes and for generation of MIS (see Figure 4.5).

Figure: 4.4: The DFD for the New System (Scenario D)

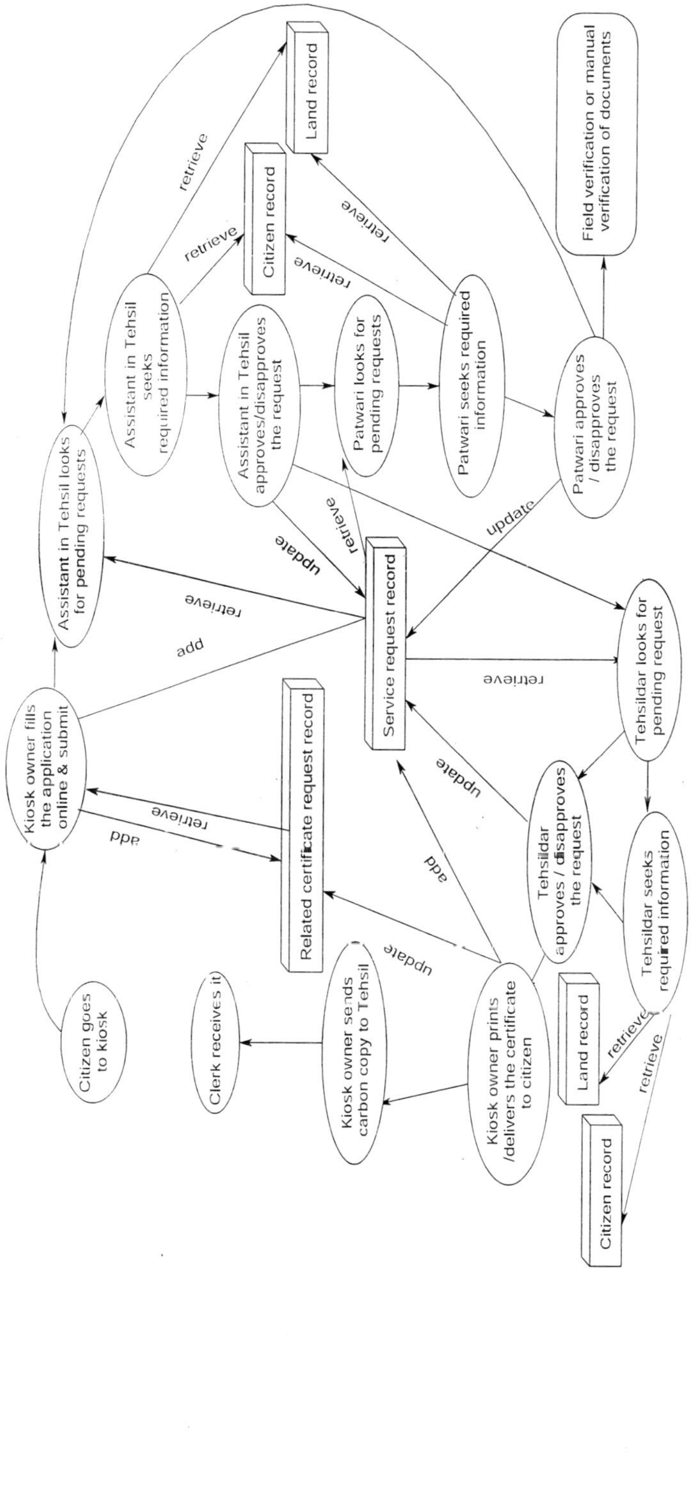

Figure: 4.5: Schema of Database

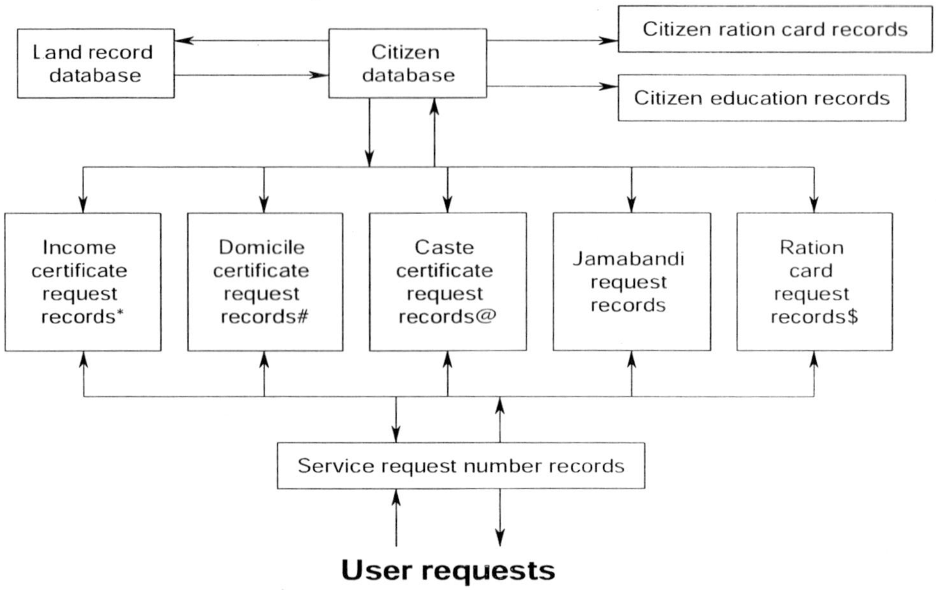

*: It indicates income certificate request record (see Table: 4.1B.7in Annexure 4.1B)
#: It indicates domicile certificate request record (see Table: 4.1B.9 in Annexure 4.1B)
@: It indicates caste certificate request record (see Table: 4.1B.8 in Annexure 4.1B)
ψ: It indicates Jamabandi request record (see Table: 4.1B.10 in Annexure 4.1B)
$: It indicates ration card request record (see Table: 4.1B.11 in Annexure 4.1B)

In this regard, citizen database design (see Annexure 4.1B) has got the following five basic records:

- Citizen master record
- Citizen asset record
- Citizen education record
- Citizen land record
- Citizen ration card record

Similarly, the service database has the following basic records:

- Service request record
- Record related to each service.
- Record related to grievances

The entity relationship (ER) diagram for citizen records and services request records are also shown in Annexure 4.1 (see Figures 4.1B.3 and 4.1B.4)

B. Cost for Development of Citizen Database: The attempt is also made to assess the cost of preparation of citizen database (see Table S4.3), and savings to Tehsil and citizens, which is reflected in Table 4.5, also see Tables 4.2B.1 and

4.2B.2 in Annexure 4.2B.

Table 4.5: Cost of Citizen Database and saving to Tehsil and Citizens

S.N.	Items	Value (lakh)	Remarks
1.	Cost of citizen database	16.71	10% maintenance cost
2.	Saving to Tehsil (yearly)	4.56	-
3.	Savings to citizens* (yearly)	4.57	-

* Savings due to lesser travel cost and wages lost.

The cost of preparation of citizen database can be recovered in six years, which appears to be a viable proposition. With backend computerisation, there would be enormous gains to citizens due to lesser time in availing services, thereby lesser cost.

C. Changes Required for New System: While evolving new system from manual system to scenario A to scenario D, certain changes are required in the following (see Table 4.6 and Tables 4.2.1 to 4.2.4 in Annexure 4.2):

- Application form
- Attachments
- Submission at e-Kiosk
- Verification
- Internal processing at Tehsil level
- Delivery form
- Delivery of certificate to citizens
- Security

The prominent changes that are to be brought by the government are listed below:

- Application form to be redesigned
- Stamp duty to be done away & replaced by single user charges
- Scanned documents should be legally accepted as an attachment
- Deputation of Patwari or authorised staff between 10 AM to 12 noon at e-Kiosk for verification of attachments at the time of submission of AF
- Report of Patwari to be typed on the computer and signed digitally using digital signatures as well as light pen
- Citizen database to be recognised as legal records throughout the district
- Digital signature should be acceptable for verification
- Internal processing of Tehsil will be fully computerised
- Delivery format needs to be redesigned (which may contain the automatically generated certificate number or some barcode number)

Scenario D

Application form : Online
Attachments : Incase of dynamic data*
Internal processing of Tehsil : Online
Delivery form : Online

Table: 4.6: Changes required for New System in Scenario D

S.N.	Description	What changes required	Type	Level & support	Benefits
1	Application form	- Application form needs to be redesigned**	AF, Rules	Govt. order required.	Simplified AF
		- Stamp duty to be done away & is replaced by single user charges.	Rules	-do-	No need to purchase stamps or stamp paper
		- Filling up the AF online at e-Kiosk, which requires only the filling of citizen id, and one or two necessary fields.	DB	-do-	Time saving
2	Attachments	- Because of centralised database, many of the attachments will not be required.	DB	-do-	Attachments not required
		- Scanned documents should be legally accepted as an attachment (in case of dynamic data such as income certificate).	Rules	-do-	Time saving due to electronic medium
3	Submission at Kiosk level	- Deputation of Patwari or authorised staff from Tehsil at e-Kiosk.	Rules	Collectorate order required	Citizen need not to go to Patwar ghar
4	Verification	- Verification of AF will be done online.	DB, Rules	Court order required	-
		- Citizen database to be recognised as legal record throughout the district.	Rules	-do-	-
		- Digital signature should be acceptable for verification.	Rules	-do-	-
5	Internal processing at Tehsil level	- Internal processing of Tehsil will be fully computerised.	Infrastructure, Rules	Govt. to provide financial support	MIS about the service delivery can be easily maintained
		- Connected to all the Kiosks.	Network	-do-	-
6	Delivery form	- Delivery format needs to be redesigned (which may contain the automatically generated certificate number or some barcode number)	DF, Rules	Govt. order required	Simplified delivery form
		- Printed form should be legally accepted.	Rules	-do-	-
		- Certificate / document is printed at Kiosk, and signed and stamped by local Tehsil authority (Patwari or Girdawar) and handing over to citizen. - While handing over certificate / document to citizen at e-Kiosk, signature of citizen with light pen or thumb impression.	Rules	-do-	Time saving in sending certificate from Tehsil to e-Kiosk
		- Informing the Tehsil office electronically by Patwari about the issue of certificate. - Listing the information on web-site about the issue of certificate			

*Attachments will be required (in case change of place or caste or income). In that case, attachments will be sent by scanning them.

** The redesigned AF for caste certificate is shown at Annexure 4.2D

Contd...

S.N.	Description	What changes required		Type	Level & support	Benefits
		Stakeholders	Security measures			
7	Security	At Kiosk (Kiosk owner & Patwari)	1. At the time of filling up of application • Login for Kiosk owner ✓ User-ID & password ✓ Biometrics (IRIS) 2. At the time of submission of AF ✓ Citizen signature using light pen	Rules	Change in relevant Act required	Preventions of unauthorised access
			3. Patwari report in case of dynamic data • Login for Patwari ✓ User- ID & password ✓ Biometrics (IRIS) ✓ Digital signature 4. At the time of delivery of certificate to citizen • Login for Kiosk owner ✓ User- ID and password ✓ Biometrics (IRIS) • Signature of citizen using light pen • Signature of issuing authority on delivery certificate			
			5. To see pending application • Login for Patwari ✓ User- ID & password ✓ Biometrics (IRIS) ✓ Digital signature 6. To see pending application • Login for Kiosk owner ✓ User- ID & password ✓ Biometrics (IRIS) ✓ Digital signature			
			7. Informing Tehsil through online about the Certificate delivered by Patwari • Login for Patwari ✓ User- ID & password ✓ Biometrics (IRIS) ✓ Digital signature 8. Barcode generated number will be printed on the delivery certificate			

Contd...

S.N.	Description	What changes required		Type	Level & support	Benefits
8		At Tehsil (Assistant, Tehsildar)	9. To see pending application • Login for (i) Tehsildar (ii) Assistant in Tehsil ✓ User- ID & password ✓ Biometrics (IRIS) ✓ Digital signature 10. For verification & updating the status of application using • Login for Patwari ✓ User- ID & password ✓ Biometrics (IRIS) ✓ Digital signature ✓ Light pen for signature			

Note: The suggestions of scenarios A, B and C are also reflected above
AF: Application form, DF: Delivery form

- Printed form should be legally accepted
- Guidelines for security (like user-ID & password, digital signature, light pen for signature, biometrics (thumb impression, IRIS)

4.2 Organisational Development (OD)

"It is not just the technology that is the key to productivity and growth, it is the ability of people to develop and use technology"

E-governance initiatives should not be seen in isolation of the role of 'people (functionaries)'. Though, IT is a big enabler, while the services are to be delivered by the delivery system, where functionaries have to use their skills to deliver, as necessary solutions can only be provided by those who are working inside. The involvement of functionaries in the service delivery, and their knowledge, skills and attitudes matter substantially. These are crucial in converting ideas into practice. If, closely examined, people are the key for 'good governance', as has been evident from field study.

Excellence in functioning will come from commitment to it. Here, human factor matters the most. It is not just the technology that is the key to productivity and growth, it is the ability of people to develop and use technology. Here, the importance of organisational development (OD) arises. It refers to the long-range effort to improve an organization's problem-solving capabilities and effectiveness to cope with changes in its external environment with the help of behavioural science, technology, research, and theory.

OD would be useful in improving organisational effectiveness of delivery system engaged in e Governance in two major ways:

First, an effective organisation (delivery system) would be able to solve its own problems (e.g. related to citizens' grievances, Kiosk management, process of preparation of certificates, network failure, etc.) and focus its attention and resources on achieving key goals. OD would help functionaries gain the skills and knowledge necessary to conduct these activities by involving them in the process.

If we take the case of BPR, it requires that old practices must be changed and new processes be designed to fully leverage new technology (IT) and management practices to meet ground realities (or field problems). And such effort would require the involvement of functionaries right from conceptual stage to process mapping to reengineering and then implementation (see BPR cycle, Figure 4.6). While re-designing the processes, the existing manpower (functionaries) needs to be utilised to the fullest extent. Here, the involvement of functionaries is critical, as the change management needs to be a 'people-centric' intervention. Outside consultants may be useful, but as the new processes are to be adapted and implemented in future by the existing functionaries of respective delivery departments, so their involvement in entire BPR cycle is essential for successful transformation. Also, it would be vital for developing system ownership at the point of delivery of services and then accountability of concerned department.

Figure 4.6: BPR Cycle
(which requires strong human input at every stage of cycle)

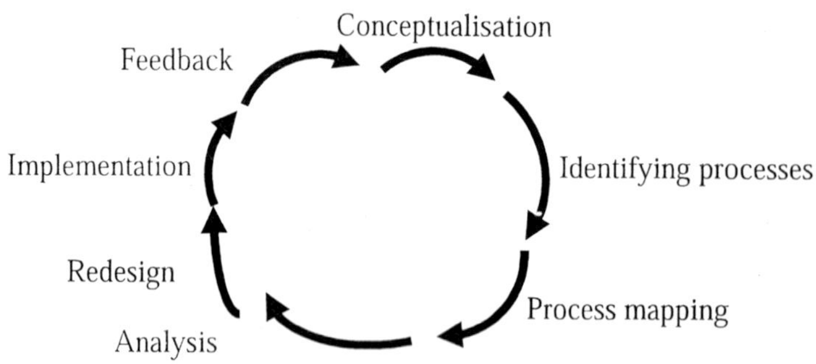

Second, an effective organisation would result into high performance and efficient delivery of services. With the changing requirements of citizens (e.g. sudden increased number of certificates or relief measures, etc.), the functionaries can respond in an effective manner and perform at high levels.

> *"OD would help functionaries gain the skills and knowledge necessary to conduct these activities by involving them in the process. ... While re-designing the processes, the existing manpower (functionaries) needs to be utilised to the fullest extent. Here, the involvement of functionaries is critical, as the change management needs to be a 'people-centric' intervention. Outside consultants may be useful, but as the new processes are to be adapted and implemented in future by the existing functionaries of respective delivery departments, so their involvement in entire BPR cycle is essential for successful transformation. Also, it would be vital for developing system ownership at the point of delivery of services and then accountability of concerned department."*

Figure 4.7A depicts how OD is vital for good governance. It highlights that good governance would require citizen focus and quality of services; and to meet them OD interventions are required to impart behavioural skills.

Figure: 4.7A: How Organisational Development (OD) is Vital for Good Governance

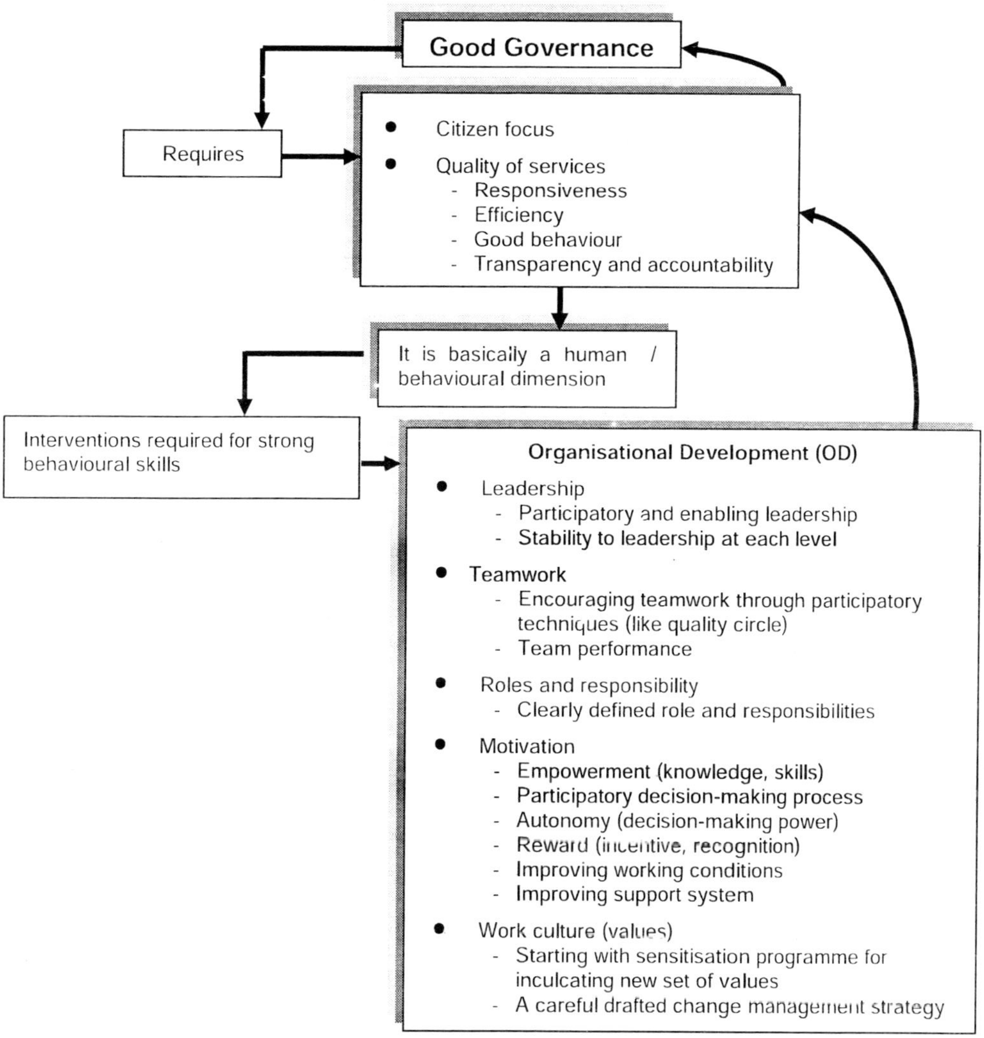

Specifically, in the context of e-Governance, OD would be vital in enhancing organisational effectiveness and managing change in terms of: *first*, preparing functionaries for the desired task through necessary behavioural skills; *second*, improving problem-solving ability to undertake the task of BPR; and *third*, adapting new technology.

Under the study of organisational behaviour, five vital issues viz., leadership, teamwork, roles and responsibility, motivation and work culture were studied through field survey and FGDs. Based on the findings (see Box 3.2 in chapter 3), it is suggested that these issues require addressal in an integrated way. And a few suggestions are given below in order to enable the delivery system to leverage technology effectively (see Table 4.7A).

- ***Leadership:*** The project leadership should be participatory type, giving encouragement to participatory way of working. This is crucial as governance involves multi-departmental and -functional activities, which would require involvement of all. The leadership should evolve into 'enabling bureaucracy' as indicated in Figure 4.8. The hallmark of participatory leadership would be to encourage 'constructive criticism'.
- ***Posting and transfer:*** Another important dimension for the organisational effectiveness is the stability of top leadership. It will call for having a right policy for transfer and posting of head of the offices.
- ***Teamwork:*** As service delivery, under e-Governance system, involves multi-departmental and - level interaction, so each member should be encouraged to work in a team for problem identification and solution.
- ***Roles and Responsibility:*** The roles and responsibilities of each team member engaged in e-Governance should be clearly identified in order to provide them clear direction and also to fix responsibility. For example, the roles of Kiosk owner, supervisor, Patwari, etc., should be clearly demarcated with regards to counseling of citizens, verification of documents, monitoring, follow-up, supervision and so on.

Figure: 4.8; Types of Bureaucratic Structure

Structure of Bureaucracy		
High	**Directional Bureaucracy** - Right rule enforcement - Extensive written rules and procedures - Hierarchy controls	**Enabling Bureaucracy** - Empowered employees - Rules and procedure as enabling tools - Hierarchy encourages constructive criticism - Hierarchy supports organisational learning
Low	**Autocratic** - Top down controls - Minimum written rules and procedures - Hierarchy controls	**Organic** - Empowered employees - Minimum rules and procedure - Little hierarchy
	Directional	**Enabling**

Social Structure

Source: Liker, 2004

Table: 4.7A: OD Interventions for Improving Effectiveness of Delivery System

S. N		Present status	Interventions	Likely impact
1.	Leadership	□ Directional	□ Participatory and enabling leadership □ Stability to leadership at each level	□ Improved work culture and motivation □ Improved organisational effectiveness □ Citizen-centric and effective organisation □ Can facilitate in achieving the objectives of e-Governance
2.	Teamwork	□ Lack of teamwork □ Individual performance	□ Encouraging teamwork through participatory techniques (like quality circle) □ Team performance	
3.	Roles and responsibility	□ Not clearly defined	□ Clearly defined roles and responsibilities	
4.	Motivation*	□ Lack of motivation	□ Empowerment (knowledge, skills) □ Participatory decision-making process □ Autonomy (decision-making power) □ Reward (incentive, recognition) □ Improving working conditions □ Improving support system	
5.	Work culture* (values)	□ Lack of citizen-focus	□ Starting with sensitisation programme for inculcating new set of values** □ A carefully drafted change management strategy	

*Note: See Tables 3.25 and 3.26.

** Values like: Punctuality, Timeliness, Responsiveness, Efficiency, ability to appreciate criticism, appreciation for Transparency and Accountability

- ***Motivation:*** For this, Herzberg's two-factor motivation-hygiene theory (see Annexure 2.2) is suggested. As brought out by the field study, among others, the working conditions for functionaries, need to be improved for raising the level of motivation. Improving working conditions would include provisioning for items like furniture; record room; sanitation; equipments such as computer, phone; canteen; toilets, etc.

Besides, 'opportunity for advancement in career' and 'recognition of good work' needs urgent consideration for motivating them and raising performance level. For instance, if a functionary interacts with citizens in a friendly and responsive manner and delivers services efficiently, he should be recognised and suitably rewarded. Such initiatives will make healthy impact on the morale of the functionaries. Also, of crucial importance is the support system – infrastructural, logistics and training in order to improve the functional capacity and reach of functionaries (such support system should be identified as per the specific needs of particular delivery system, see Tables S3.33 and S3.34 in chapter 3 also).

Also, in order to enable functionaries to deliver productively, there is a need of creating enabling environment – creating performance-driven conditions (see Figure 4.7B). It is based on the premise that there is a need to create system that recognises the value of and gives support to functionaries. There is a felt need to increase their involvement and empowerment in the change management process. It will require giving them autonomy and increasing their role in decision-making. Empowerment is based on the belief that employees have the ability to take on more responsibility and authority than traditionally has been given to them, and that heightened efficiency and a better quality of work will result. Simultaneously, efforts should be to provide good working conditions (like electricity, fans, drinking water, furniture, cleanliness, etc.) at the work place. Such environment will provide motivation to personnel to put their best and deliver good results.

Besides, 'opportunity for advancement in career' and 'recognition of good work' needs urgent consideration for motivating functionaries and raising performance level. For instance, if a functionary interacts with citizens in a friendly and responsive manner and delivers services efficiently, he should be recognised and suitably rewarded. Such initiatives will make healthy impact on the morale of the functionaries.

Figure 4.7B: Performance-driven Approach

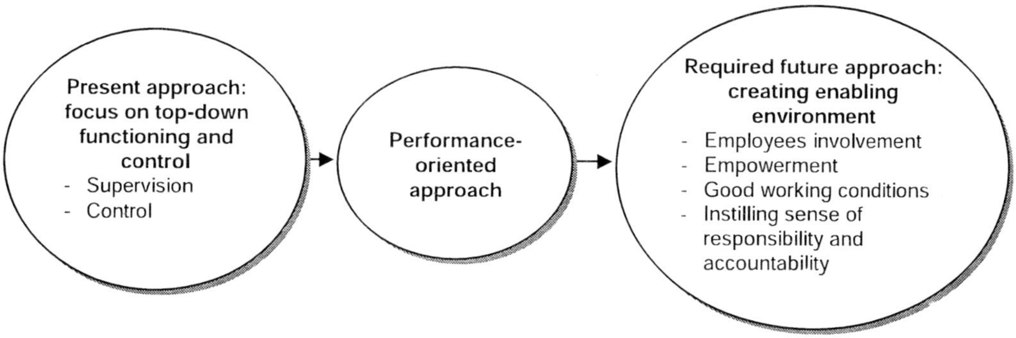

- ***Work culture:*** The culture is one ingredient in helping deliver value to customers (citizens). Like processes, it must be aligned to the strategy of the organization and managed when change is required. For good governance, the citizen-centric work culture should be evolved with a specific focus on quality indicators such as punctuality, timeliness, responsiveness and efficiency.

In the context of service sector dealing with a large number of customers (citizens in the context of governance), there is a need to develop attitude to appreciate criticism from citizens and for taking criticisms or stingy feedback in a right spirit. Also, there is a call for removing the fear of transparency and accountability among functionaries through counselling. It would require organising sensitisation programme for inculcating new set of values. In this regard, training programmes may be organised for developing emotional intelligence to better appreciate the citizen handling.

At functional level, autonomy and participation in decision-making should be encouraged by the departments. It will give functionaries the sense of involvement. And this way, they can contribute much better.

Design Features for a Participative System

In order to evolve participatory organisation in a government delivery system, it will require bringing certain design features related to organizational structure, job design, information system, career system, selection, training, reward system, personnel policies, and physical layout, as outlined in Table 4.7B. It should be such, which should give a sense of joyful setting at work place, in order to encourage functionaries to contribute their best.

Table 4.7B
Design Features for a Participative System in a Government Delivery System

• Organizational structure 1. Lean 2. Team-based 3. Participative structure • Job design 1. Individually enriched 2. Job enrichment • Information system 1. Open 2. Inclusive 3. Decentralized: team-based • Career system 1. Tracks and counseling available 2. Open job posting • Selection 1. Realistic job preview 2. Team-based 3. Potential and process-skill oriented	• Training 1. Commitment 2. Peer training 3. Interpersonal skills • Reward system 1. Open 2. Skill-based 3. Gain sharing or ownership 4. Flexible benefits 5. Egalitarian perquisites • Personnel policies 1. Stability of employment 2. Participatively established through representative group • Physical layout 1. Visibility 2. Egalitarian 3. Clean and hygienic 4. Safe and pleasant

Source: Cummings and Worley (2002) and based on own analysis

4.2.1 Breaking the Myths: During the course of discussions (while conducting field study) with various stakeholders viz., officials, field functionaries, NGOs, citizens and panchayat members, varied opinions emerged, and there was vast chasm among them. While one group of people would say that functionaries do not like the e-Governance or are not interested in work, while the functionaries would respond in an opposite way. Based on in-depth consultations and study, the following myths could be identified:

- Functionaries do not want to deliver services
- Functionaries cannot deliver services in the right way
- Functionaries are not interested in e-Governance
- Government departments cannot deliver

In this regard, the attempt was made to identify the reasons for such myths. It appears that such myths were due to poor outcome of delivery of services. It has led many to assume the above four myths. It was felt that the above is basically based on the impressions that some stakeholders have, but their impressions may not be based on in-depth study and analysis.

To overcome such a state of myths and correct the deficiencies, the five-pronged strategy is identified, which is as follows:

- *First,* understanding the field level practical difficulties faced by both citizens and functionaries, and identifying the shortcomings in the entire chain of service delivery, through a detailed diagnostic study (there is a need to have appreciation of field problems)
- *Second,* identifying critical areas where improvements would give maximum advantage
- *Third,* evolving right work culture
- *Fourth,* developing right system that can deliver
- *Fifth,* empowering functionaries

The above is summarised in Table S4.4.

Similarly, as regards citizens, it is believed by many that citizens would not like to use e-Kiosk, as they are unfamiliar with IT. If we look at the field survey, it shows that 92% of the citizens want e-Governance. But, presently, citizens do not use e-Governance services, as they do not find the e-Governance initiatives of direct relevance and there is little qualitative improvement in service delivery. It may require a diagnostic study by experts for understanding the social, political and cultural issues, and effective system design and implementation of e-Governance projects.

The purpose of mentioning above is that there is a need of breaking the myths, which are not correct and may bring biases into the decision-making process. Otherwise, it may also block the possibility of fair assessment of problems, and then taking corrective measures.

Civil Services Reforms

Why Reforms

The human resource functions have lagged for decades in public service. Due to multi-dimensional nature, anyone who has worked on e-Governance projects would understand the complexity of such tasks, especially in transformation efforts. It gets compounded due to lack of committed leadership (champions), fear of change, or administrative and political hurdles.

Earlier institutional setup dealing more with law & order and revenue related matters finds itself anachronistic for handling the citizens requirement at the grassroots level, which requires approach of working with people rather than giving command. The centralised way of decision-making and the inability to work with people do not help citizens and the cause of providing good governance. Cultural values such as lack of responsiveness, tendency not to appreciate citizens' needs, lack of appreciation for transparency and accountability among functionaries do not give confidence to citizens about public service delivery.

New Philosophy

In the light of above, if e-Governance has to a successful paradigm, a new philosophy for public service needs to be evolved. It should include an HR system that empowers the functionaries and rewards those, with outstanding citizen services. The government HR system should recognise such propositions; and personnel with a track record in citizen service should be recruited and retained into the civil service system. It requires that current HR capabilities should be assessed, critical requirements outlined, gap analysis made, and a realistic plan for transforming HR should be a priority, in parallel with business process reengineering and other internal system management. Among others, evolving the e-Governance champions, who can transform the delivery system into a citizen-centric organisation, should precede every other effort. In this scenario, the e-Governance champions should have the teams helping them achieve the transformation objectives, instead of opposing the effort, or simply passively witnessing it.

Focus of Reforms

Sustaining the effort for e-Governance will demand reforms that would address critical areas viz., citizen-centric culture, effective organisational capacity, and transparency & accountability. It calls for placing systems in right perspective. What is required is system with sound personnel management, values, institutional processes, transparency, accountability and legal framework. As the delivery departments have to meet local needs of citizens, the character of institutions should be so moulded that it should look citizen -oriented.

There is a need to make marked shift from the traditional way of approaching e-Governance by merely deploying IT and making a few changes in bits and pieces, which are familiar instances. In the context of e-Governance being usually complex and lengthy undertaking, it needs to be recognised that leveraging HR would provide for a greater chance of success for strategies' implementation under e-Governance, as human resources is a vital link. Finally, the reform process should focus on four crucial aspects. These are: *first,* creating participatory organisations; *second,* citizen-centric work culture; *third,* capabilities for efficient service delivery; and *fourth*, culture of innovation and improvement. It would be something for the government to look into, and mainstream these vitals issues of reforms into their policies, e-Governance strategies and resource allocations.

4.2.2 Change Management

"People oppose not so much the change, but the strategy or the methods of change. What is crucial is how the change is brought about."

A. Why Change Management required: The important thing about change is that it is one of the few work-related issues that are hardly discussed productively in most of the organisations (Firth,1999), while it is vital to do so. Hold any discussion with people in any organisation about change, one might be filled with the feeling of negativism or gloom. And at the personal level, what do you hear about people? Are they interested in their organisation going through change? Are they up for it, willing, capable? No. People resist change. They fear change.

In the specific context of governance, with the passage of time, people's expectations change. New things are required to be introduced. We know that the work done by us is not perfect. We know that our work does not satisfy our customer / citizen. Still we avoid change. Why we avoid is due to a variety of reasons and these are summarised in Box 4.1.

Box: 4.1
Reasons for avoiding Change

Change is a big thing for organisations because

- They (functionaries) will resist it
- Major disruption is going to happen, which will cost money
- Change is complex in large organisations and just thinking about doing it will take up lots of our already over-stretched time
- We're not very good at it, on a personal or group level
- It's not clear whether the unknown future might turn out to be worse than the present known
- We're just not sure
- Even if we do OK with this change, we just know there'll be another one coming soon
- Change initiatives in organisations like ours have produced job losses, anger, resentment, higher stress, loss of trust, confusion. Why on Earth would we bother to do it again?
  and, biggest think of all,
- We'd much prefer if it weren't happening.

Source: Firth,1999

Whereas the available literature (Gupta, 2004a and Pareek, 2004) suggests, though change is difficult, still it is crucial, at personal level for increased job satisfaction, enhanced employability / marketability, openness to learning, risk management, entrepreneurial ideas (confidence building), and understanding of the basic principles of life in organisations. The benefits for a good organisation could be refocusing of vision and mission, identity and energy on achieving new goals (enhanced confidence), shedding old, redundant ways of doing things (increased agility), attracting new customers, attracting and retaining talent, learning and faster survival. And, finally, change is alien to an organisation yet needs to be accepted. Unless a change is internalised and integrated, it remains 'alien' (Firth,1999).

B. BPR and Change Management: Studies indicate (Peppard and Rowland, 2002) that projects with the right combination of human resource practices, supplier relations, and product design succeed – not necessarily those with the most advanced technology. Econometric research also suggests that while IT investments are often associated with higher productivity, complementary organisational changes are equally important (Brynjolfsson and Hitt, 1996). Frequently, business process reengineering (BPR) efforts run into serious difficulties. By some estimates, 70% of such projects fail to reach their intended goals (Bashein, Markus and Riley, 1994; Hammer and Champy, 1993), and a programme that seeks to become a 'House of Quality' more often becomes a 'House of Cards'.

BPR requires that old practices must be changed and new processes be designed to fully leverage new technology, management practices and ground realities. While re-designing the processes or organisations the existing manpower (functionaries), logistics and organisational knowledge need to be utilised to the fullest extent. Here, the involvement of people is critical, as the change management needs to be a 'people-centric' intervention. Furthermore, also organisational change almost inevitably becomes a learning process in which unanticipated obstacles and opportunities emerge (Orlikowski & Hofman, 1996) and these can be best understood and appreciated by the functionaries. Similarly, total quality management (TQM) has also tried to institutionalise continuous learning and incremental improvement.

"Even the best business companies (Collins, 2005) in the world have given top priority to having healthy work culture, developing capabilities, redesigning processes and systems to improve efficiency. Only, after that they have successfully deployed technology to further enhance efficiency. Great companies first build a culture of discipline – disciplined people who engage in disciplined thought and who take disciplined action – and create a business model... They then use technology..."

Even the best business companies (Collins, 2005) in the world have given top priority to having healthy work culture, developing capabilities, redesigning processes and systems to improve efficiency. Only after that, they have successfully deployed technology to further enhance efficiency. When we stand back to look at the rise and fall of great corporations over the long course of history, we find that technology is an accelerator of greatness already in place, never the principal cause of greatness or decline. Great companies first build a culture of discipline – disciplined people who engage in disciplined thought and who take disciplined action – and create a business model that fits squarely in the intersection of three circles: what they can be the best in the world at, a deep understanding of their economic engine and the core values they hold with deep passion. They then use technology to enhance these pre-existing variables, never as a replacement.

C. E-governance and Change Management: Holistic Perspective: The difficulties many e-Governance projects have had with the change management (Gupta, 2004c and Hammer and Champy, 1993) depend in large part on an inadequate recognition of interdependencies among technology, practices, and people. However, beneficial a new technology (in this case IT), interface, on-line processing, decision-making structure, or MIS may appear in isolation, the acid test is how it interacts – as it must – with numerous other aspects of the organisation. There is a need to recognise the critical role that interdependencies (of peoples' behaviour, work culture, citizen's requirement, processes, delivery mechanism, and technology) play in affecting outputs (Barua, Lee & Whinston, 1995). Because new technological and expectation paradigms eliminate time and space buffers as activities become more tightly linked, ignoring such interdependencies may be counterproductive.

As success often depends on coordinating the right technology, the right process and service-mix, and several right strategic and structural issues all at the same time, and a small slip-off can leave an e-Governance project worse off than if the change had never been attempted. For example, in the present case, due to inefficient personnel management, the time of delivery of services (through e-Kiosk) has been much more than in case of manual system. It was one of the major causes for not using services from e-Kiosk.

> *"Need to recognise the critical role that interdependencies (of peoples' behaviour, work culture, citizen's requirement, processes, delivery mechanism, and technology) play in affecting outputs. Because new technological and expectation paradigms eliminate time and space buffers as activities become more tightly linked, ignoring such interdependencies may be counterproductive.*
>
> *As success often depends on coordinating the right technology, the right process and service-mix, and several right strategic and structural issues all at the same time, a small slip-off can leave an e-Governance project worse off than if the change had never been attempted."*

While several studies have highlighted the importance of coordination, administrators / managers continue to have difficulty in achieving it. For instance, in the project, there was a lack of coordination between different stakeholders viz., Kiosk owner, officials of Tehsil, Kiosk owner and field functionaries of Tehsil. Due to this, many people-related problems persisted (like delay in Patwari report, signature of Patwari on computer copy of Jamabandi, etc.), and both citizens and service provider had to suffer. Often, the problem is not that the proposed system is unworkable but that the transition proves more difficult than people had anticipated (Champy, 1995). In this context, it was quite obvious that officials / managers proceeded in an adhoc manner (manual processing without having connectivity of e-Kiosk with Tehsil), implementing the most visible bits and pieces (sending application form online, scanning the attachments, which do not add much value) of a complex new system, and were unaware of hidden but critical interconnections (for example in case of certificates, role of field functionary like Patwari in giving report, or backend computerisation).

Under e-Governance project (in Jaipur), the following issues, under three heads, were expected to be addressed:

People

- How to reach out to citizens?
- How e-Kiosk owner is interacting with citizens and service delivery departments
- Patwari's visit to e-Kiosk for two days in a week

Process

- Quality issues in the delivery of services
- Manual processing
- Process redesign (making IT compatible)
- Feedback system

Technology

- Network functioning
- Hardware
- Backend computerisation

How *interdependency* of these three entities (people, process and technology) that was not addressed, has affected the output is given below (see Figure 4.9):

Figure: 4.9: People Process and Technology Interdependency – Problems Uncertainties and Constraints therein for Delivery of Certificate

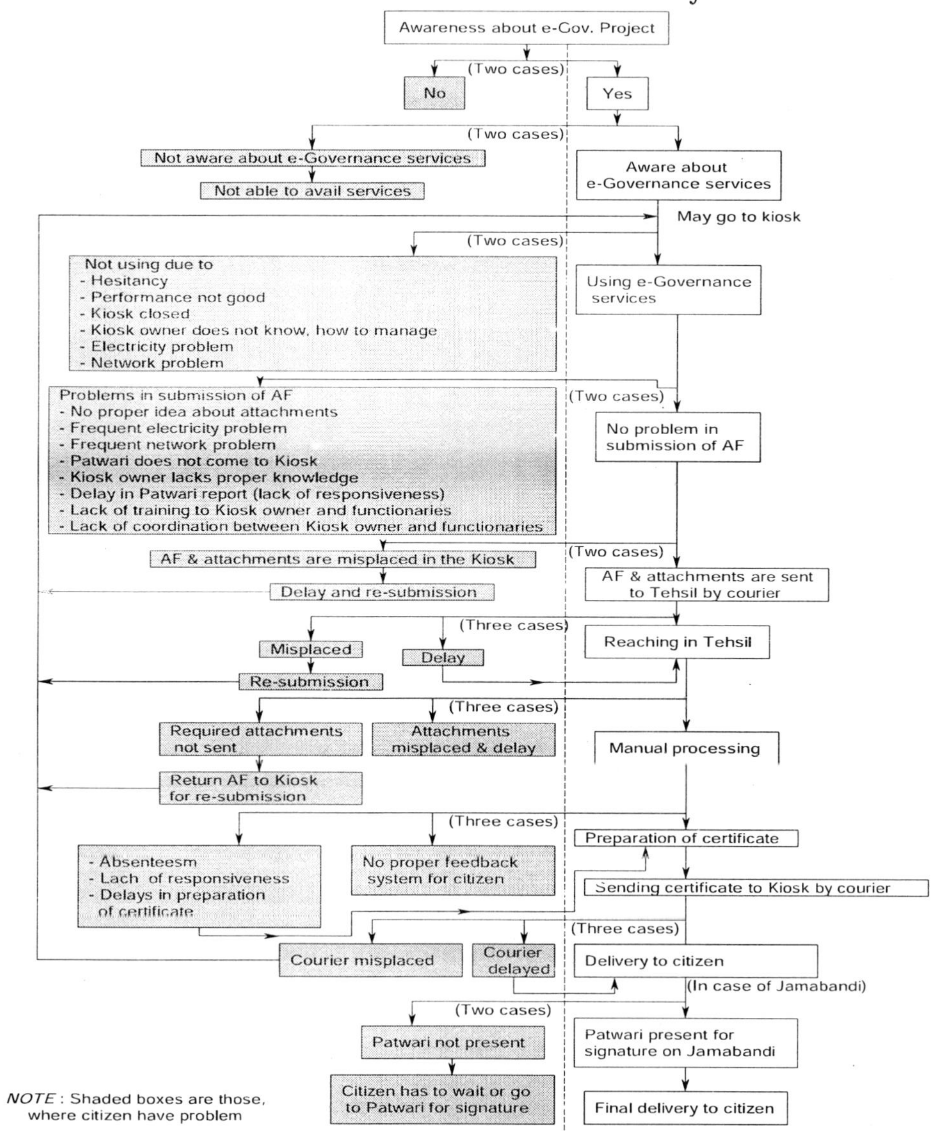

Note: The above shows about the problems, uncertainties and constraints involved in making services available to citizens through e-Kiosk.

In Chaksu Tehsil, under the present system a large number (72% respondents) of citizens were not aware about e-Governance project (in Jaipur) (see Table 3.27A1 in chapter 3), and a large percentage (44.4%) of them (those who were aware of the project) were not aware about the availability of e-Governance services from the project (see Table 3.27A2 in chapter 3).

Further, when an applicant came to a Kiosk, firstly, he was not fully aware about 'how to use' the computer or avail service from there, and the Kiosk owner had not been consistent in handling this problem in a friendly way and thus drove away some potential users. And in this process, it gave citizens opportunity of making uncharitable remarks about the e-Kiosk, and thus further discouraged some other potential users.

Whenever a citizen came to a Kiosk for availing services, on some occasions network did not work, and in some other cases, electricity was not available (and UPS did not support computer, due to long hours of electricity cut), or network used to be down. Or, sometimes, he did not bring attachments (as he was not aware and there was no system to make citizens know about this).

Problem did not end here. The attachments are required to be collected manually from different offices. It is because, no BPR has been carried out and backend computerisation was not attempted. And the old processes continued and there was no attempt to make the processes IT compatible.

Patwari was expected to visit e-Kiosk two days in a week (for signing Jamabandi and writing report), but he did not visit Kiosk on most of the occasions due to a variety of reasons. The reasons include: *first*, his own busy schedule, *second*, the e-Kiosk is about 2-5 kilometers from his office so there has been difficulty in travel, *third*, lack of commitment of Patwari, and *finally*, lack of proper rapport between Patwari on one hand and Kiosk owner and Kiosk supervisor on the hand.

Further, when application form along with attachments was submitted to e-Kiosk, it was sent to Tehsil through courier (which also caused delay), and there processing remained manual. Also, information about the submission of application form was sent to head-end and Collectorate by IT network. But, there was no system to give feedback to citizens about the status of application, as Tehsil did not have hardware and connectivity with Kiosk. After the certificate was prepared, it was sent to Kiosk through courier, which sometimes caused delay or got misplaced. In nutshell, due to host of constraints, the citizens did not get the services from e-Governance project in a satisfactory manner. And citizens had to face a number of problems before getting certificates / services.

In a way, the entire process remained manual and IT (the technology) has been used only to send information about the application from e-Kiosk to head-end and Collectorate.

In a similar way, regarding grievance redressal the Figure S4.3 reflects about the interdependency of three entities – people, process and technology, and associated problems, uncertainties and constraints.

The upshot of the above is that the issues related to people (work culture, citizen focus), process (re-design, user-friendliness, MIS, quality of services) and technology (network, hardware, software, database) were not managed to meet the changing requirements and provide services efficiently to citizens. It shows how interactions can sometimes make it impossible to successfully implement a new system in a decentralised fashion.

The import of above is that managers / administrators must plan a strategy that takes into account and coordinates the interactions among all the components of a system. The careful interactions can create a virtuous cycle of positive feedback and that should be used to amplify even small steps in the right direction.

Problem starts when managers (change agents) fail to identify feedback system and ignore it, that may push project back towards old ways of doing business or when they miss synergy that would strengthen the new and better ways they wish to establish. Ironically, the bottom-up, continuous and incremental improvement principles, empowerment and decentralised decisions associated with TQM can be less effective, but a coordinated change can. This is precisely the reason why a systematic approach for change is called for.

D. Matrix of Change: Business process reengineering efforts suffer from low success rates, due in part to a lack of tools for managing the change process. The Matrix of Change (http://ccs.mit.edu/papers) can help managers identify critical interactions among processes. In particular, this tool helps managers deal with issues such as how quickly change should proceed, the order in which changes should take place, whether to start at a new site, and whether the proposed systems are stable and coherent. The Matrix highlights interactions and complementary practices. It can help managers anticipate the complex interrelationships surrounding change. Specifically, the tool contributes to understanding issues of feasibility (stability of new changes), sequence (which practices to change first), location, pace (fast or slow), and stakeholder interests.

How the Matrix Works? For introducing BPR, Matrix of Change presents a way to capture connections and complementary practices among different practices. It graphically displays both reinforcing and interfering organisational processes. With this knowledge, a change agent can use intuitive principles to seek points of leverage and design a smoother transition. Once the broad outlines of the new system and the transition path have been charted, implementation plan can more effectively be decentralised for local implementation and optimisation.

The Matrix functions as a four step process. It provides a systematic means to judge those business practices that matter most. It highlights interactions among these practices and possible transition difficulties from one set of practices to another. It encourages various stakeholders to provide feedback on proposed changes. And, it uses process interactions to provide guidelines on the feasibility, sequence, location of change, and pace.

Steps in Preparing Matrix:

- **Step 1 - Identify Critical Processes:** The project team should first list their existing practices, and the suggested practices that create value for customers / citizens. These practices are grouped in 3 categories, viz., process, people and technology in the case of e-Governance.
- **Step 2 - Identify System Interactions:** After describing existing practices, the team should create the horizontal triangular matrix to identify complementary and competing practices / processes as illustrated in Figures 4.10 and S4.4 Complementary processes reinforce one another whereas competing practices / processes work at cross-purposes. A grid connects each process in an interference matrix, and at the junction of each grid plus signs (+) designate complementary and minus signs (-) competing practices / processes.
- **Step 3 - Identify Transition Interactions:** Next, the team should construct the Transition Matrix – a square matrix combining the horizontal and vertical matrices which helps determine the degree of difficulty in shifting from existing to target practices. The advantage of the transition matrix is that it shows the interactions involved in moving from existing practices to a new slate. The plus signs (+) designates reinforcement and minus signs (-) conflict during change.

Step 4 - Survey Stakeholders: Finally, the team should determine where various stakeholders (like citizens, functionaries) stand with respect to retaining current practices and implementing target practices. The values are as follows: '+2 'means most important, and '+1' indicates less important, '0' represents not important, '-1' means less important but change is required, and '-2' indicates most important and change is must.

Interpretations of Matrix of Change: The Matrix of change is a useful tool for addressing the following types of questions:

- **Feasibility:** Do the set of practices representing the stated goal constitute a coherent and stable system? Is our current set of practices coherent and stable? Is the transition likely to be difficult?
- **Sequence of execution:** Where should change begin? How does the sequence of change affect success?
- **Location:** Are we better off instituting the new system in a separate location or at the existing place?
- **Pace and nature of change:** Should the change be slow or fast? Incremental or radical? Which groups of practices, if any, must be changed at the same time?
- **Stakeholder evaluations:** Have we considered the insights from all stakeholders? Have we overlooked any important practices or interactions?

Drawing Matrix: Firstly, before drawing matrix, the following objectives were identified:

Immediate objectives

- Making services available in a stipulated time (1 to 3 days) at Tehsil

Future objectives

- Making services (Caste, Income, Domicile, Jamabandi certificates) available within 24 hours at village / e-Kiosk level
- Online delivery of services

Based on above, the Matrix of change has been drawn as reflected by Figure 4.10. It indicates matrix of intra-relationship among suggested practices and transition matrix (indicating transition from existing practices to suggested practices) (the matrix of intra-relationship among existing practices is indicated by Figure S4.4). The criteria for different factors viz., feasibility, sequence, location and pace and nature of change are indicated in Table 4.8).

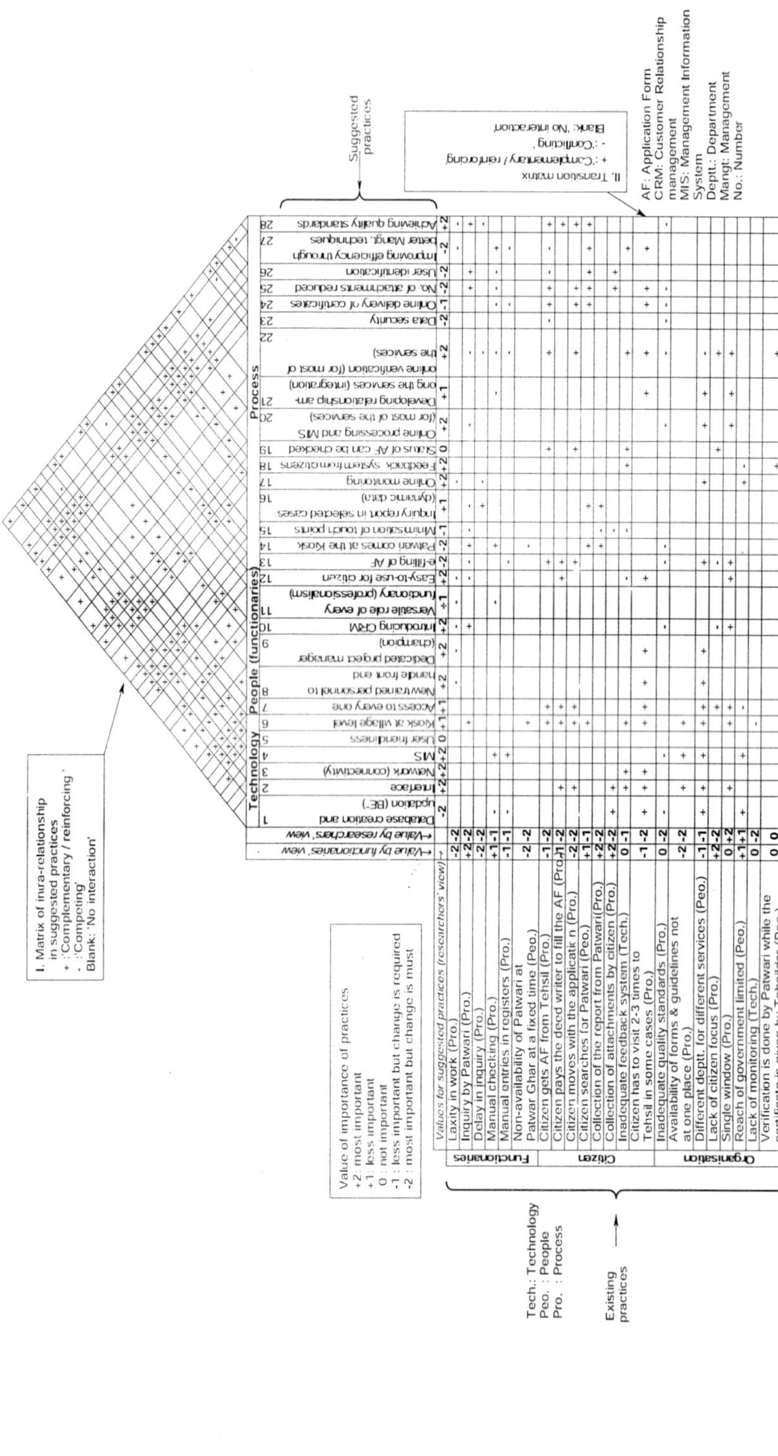

Figure: 4.10: Intra-relationship and Transition Matrix

Source: Based on FGDs

Table: 4.8: Criteria for Choosing Different Factors under Matrix of Change

S. N	Items	Criteria
1.	Feasibility	i. Based on transition matrix: Wherever there are more positive signs in this matrix, those practices will be feasible. (e.g. interface, network, Kiosk at village level). ii. Based on intra-relationship of suggested practices: Wherever there are more positive signs in an intra-relationship matrix, those suggested practices will be feasible. (e.g. MIS).
2.	Sequence of execution	i. Based on transition matrix: Wherever there are more positive signs, those practices should be implemented on priority basis (e.g. network, interface, access to everyone) ii. Based on value of suggested practices: Practices with value -2 and +2 should be given high priority. (e.g. database creation and updation, online monitoring). iii. Based on intra-relationship among suggested practices: Wherever more positive signs are reflected, those practices should be given priority. (e.g. interface, MIS, network).
3.	Location (for change)	i. Based on transition matrix: • Wherever more negative signs are in transition matrix, those suggested practice should be handled on pilot basis. (e.g. database creation and updation) • Wherever more positive signs are in transition matrix, those suggested practices should be implemented in all Kiosks. (e.g. network, interface).
4.	Pace and nature of change	i. Based on transition matrix: Wherever positive signs are more, pace and nature of change should be fast, (e.g. Kiosk at village level), and negative signs are more, pace and nature of change should be slow / cautious. (e.g. new trained personnel to handle front-end). ii. Based on value of suggested practices: Wherever there are -2, and there are positive signs in transition matrix, these practices should be changed fast (e.g. access to everyone, number of attachments reduced). iii. Based on values of exiting practices: Wherever there is difference in values of functionaries and researchers, and suggested practices are affected negatively by such difference of existing practice, the change in such suggested practices should be done cautiously (e.g. in the case of database creation and updation, it is in conflict with inquiry by Patwari).

Based on matrix of intra-relationship and transition matrix (also see Tables 4.3.1 and 4.3.2 in Annexure 4.3) the weighted value of different factors are calculated in Tables 4.9, and 4.3.3 in Annexure 4.3. The different sub-categories of factors have been given value as indicated (Table 4.10).

Table: 4.9: Total Weighted Values of Different Factors for Change of Suggested Practices

S.N	Suggested practices	Weighted values of different factors				
		Feasibility	Sequence of execution	Location (for change)	Pace and nature of change	Total value
Technology						
1.	Database creation and updation (BE* computrisation)	0.4	0.8	0.2	0.4	1.8
2.	Interface	0.6	1.2	0.4	0.4	2.6
3.	Network (connectivity)	0.6	1.2	0.4	0.4	2.6
4.	MIS	0.6	1.2	0.4	0.6	2.8
5.	User friendliness	0.6	1.2	0.2	0.6	2.6
6.	Kiosk at village level	0.6	1.2	0.2	0.6	2.6
People (functionaries)						
7.	Access to every one	0.6	1.2	0.2	0.6	2.6
8.	New trained personnel to handle front-end	0.6	1.2	0.4	0.6	2.8
9.	Dedicated project manager (champion)	0.6	1.2	0.2	0.6	2.6
10.	Introducing CRM	0.6	1.2	0.2	0.4	2.4
11.	Versatile role of every functionary (professionalism)	0.6	0.4	0.2	0.4	1.6
12.	Easy-to-use for citizen	0.6	1.2	0.4	0.6	2.8
Processes						
13.	e-filling of AF	0.6	1.2	0.4	0.6	2.8
14.	Patwari comes at the Kiosk	0.4	1.2	0.2	0.4	2.2
15.	Minimisation of touch points	0.6	0.4	0.2	0.4	1.6
16.	Inquiry report in selected case (dynamic data)	0.6	0.4	0.2	0.4	1.6

Contd...

S.N	Suggested practices	Weighted values of different factors				
		Feasibility	Sequence of execution	Location (for change)	Pace and nature of change	Total value
17.	Monitoring	0.6	0.8	0.4	0.6	2.4
18.	Feedback system	0.6	0.8	0.4	0.6	2.4
19.	Status of AF can be checked	0.6	1.2	0.4	0.6	2.8
20.	Online processing and MIS (for most of the services)	0.6	0.8	0.4	0.6	2.4
21.	Developing relationship among the services (integration)	0.6	0.8	0.2	0.2	1.8
22.	Online verification (for most of the services)	0.4	0.4	0.2	0.4	1.4
23.	Data security	0.6	1.2	0.4	0.6	2.8
24.	Online delivery of certificate	0.4	0.4	0.2	0.2	1.2
25.	Number of attachments reduced	0.4	0.8	0.2	0.4	1.8
26.	User identification	0.4	0.4	0.4	0.4	1.6
27.	Improving efficiency through better management techniques	0.4	0.4	0.4	0.4	1.6
28.	Achieving quality standards	0.4	0.8	0.4	0.4	2.0

Source: based on own analysis, AF: Application form, CRM: Customer relationship management, MIS: Management information system

S. N.	*Factors*	*Weight*
1.	*Feasibility*	*0.2*
2.	*Sequence of execution*	*0.4*
3.	*Location*	*0.2*
4.	*Pace and nature of change*	*0.2*

'No feasibility' has been assigned value 1, likewise values for other stages can be inferred from Table 4.10. The factors have been assigned weights as indicated in Table 4.11

Table: 4.10: Value for Different Sub-categories of Factors

S. N	Value (for sub-category) → / ↓ Factors	1	2	3
1.	Feasibility	No feasibility	Yes (with difficulty)	Yes
2.	Sequence of execution	Third stage	Second stage	First stage
3.	Location	Pilot	All Kiosk	-
4.	Pace and nature of change	Slow	Gradual / cautious	Fast

Box: 4.2
Rationale for Selecting Practices

Group 1: Practices (existing) those are not preferred by citizens

1. Inquiry by Patwari (process)
2. Citizen gets AF from Tehsil (process)
3. Citizen pays the deed writer to fill the AF (process)
4. Citizen moves with the application (process)
5. Collection of the report from Patwari (process)
6. Collection of attachments by citizen (process)
7. Inadequate feedback system (technology)
8. Citizen has to visit Tehsil 2-3 times in some cases (process)
9. Inadequate quality standards (process)
10. Availability of forms & guidelines not at one place (process)
11. Different departments & for different services (people)
12. Lack of citizen focus (process)
13. Lack of monitoring (technology)

Group 2: Practices, those are preferred by citizens

1. Quality standards (process)
2. Single window (process)
3. Feedback system (technology)
4. Availability of form & guidelines at one place (process)
5. Citizen focus (process)
6. Monitoring (technology)

Group 3: Practices (suggested) those are vital for new system (for e-Governance)

1. Citizen database
2. Interface at village level
3. Network
4. Feedback system
5. MIS
6. Quality standards
7. CRM
8. Trained people
9. Online processing
10. Integration of services
11. User / citizen identification
12. Patwari's availability

Source: Based on FGDs; AF: Application form; CRM: Customer relationship management
MIS: Management information system;

Table: 4.11: Weights for Different Factors

S. N	Factors	Weights
1.	Feasibility	0.2
2.	Sequence of execution	0.4
3.	Location	0.2
4.	Pace and nature of change	0.2

Box 4.2 reflects practices (existing) those are not preferred by citizens, practices those are preferred by citizens, and suggested practices those are vital for new system (of e-Governance).

Finally based on weighted values of different factors for various suggested practices, phase-wise programme is given by Figure S4.5. It is suggested that practices like 'interface', 'network', 'MIS' should get top priority while 'online' delivery of certificate should be attended in the last keeping in view the factors of change.

E. Implementation of Change Management: Introduction of change in an organisation is akin to the transplantation of an organ in a body (Pareek, 2005). An organism (a body) and an organisation have some common features. The transplanted part in a body has to be integrated with that body. It may be rejected and so a watch has to be kept to ensure that it is not and steps taken to facilitate the integration. The same applies to an organisation: it is necessary to ensure that the change gets integrated into the organisation, is stabilised, and becomes a part of the working of the organisation. This is a part of the implementation process.

Vital Points for Change

The following vital points are crucial for introducing change (Firth, 1999):

- Understand the change process – to achieve what changes in the processes are required
- Define a vision – to provide clarity to everyone associated with it, about the likely results of e-Governance at the end of, say, 10 years. Also, strategy, mission, values and goals are to be identified (see Box 4.3)
- Communicate change – inform the stakeholders clearly what changes are to be made
- Build trust and commitment to change – through communication and right actions, to win over the confidence of stakeholders
- Measure the benefits of change – the changes taking place need to be

evaluated and timely action for correction needs to be taken, and the benefits are to be communicated

- Sustain change through learning – full commitment of top leadership is crucial for sustaining the change
- Make change acceptable – where stakeholders feel free and enjoy adapting to new situation

Box 4.3: Vision and Mission

- *Vision:* A vivid picture of what it will look like when we arrive in the future
- *Strategy:* The long-term decisions and direction that will shape its path to the future
- *Mission:* A clear and tangible ways of doing business, and specific objectives to be achieved to realise vision
- *Values:* The core, unshakable beliefs about what's important
- *Goals:* Short-term milestones to be achieved on the way to the vision

Building Consensus for Change

The following five principles need to be followed for bringing consensus:

- ***Involvement:*** Ownership is all. Do everything you can to include the people in the change process. Since they'll be implementing the vision, it borders on the immoral not to give the people the opportunity to shape it. Explain the problem, then ask for ideas, ask for feedback. Encourage them to challenge your decisions if that is what they feel they need to do – not only will this help you shape your strategy more precisely, it will also tell you what the nature of resistance is towards this project. If you have information about the project, give it away to them. You'll get back credibility. If you don't have information about the project, tell them so. In return you'll gain trust. (People likely to be affected by change should be involved in finding ways to find solutions in order to minimise the adverse impact).
- ***Education to stakeholders:*** Explain why you have decided to take the route you are taking; explain what other choices you did not take and why; explain what the context is that has shaped these decisions; explain how other companies are making the same sorts of changes (thus preventing too much 'grass is always greener on the other side' mentality); explain the benefits and the anticipated costs; explain what new polices will be put in place to support the change; explain what you

believe the change will mean, positive and negative, to every single person in the group.

- ***Honesty:*** To win trust and confidence of people in the organisation.
- ***Congruency:*** Matching the actions with what you say and define. 'Congruency' is another word for alignment, which is another way of saying 'walk your talk', and could be more formally termed 'behaviour modelling'.
- ***Persistence:*** Change takes time, and people forget what was said at the time of launch. Persistence has at least three dimensions:
  - Creativity – to maintain people's interest
  - Reassurance – to tend to their changing emotional condition as they pass through transition; and
  - Reinforcement – repeating the same message consistently and testing for understanding of it in their words and action.
- ***Empowerment:*** Empowerment means allowing people the freedom and authority to do their jobs well. It does not necessarily mean letting people decide how to do everything. Empowerment must be effected by bringing right people at the appropriate level of responsibility and authority. Nothing is more annoying for customers, or indeed staffs themselves, than when the person attending to their needs has to continually refer back up the hierarchy to approve a particular request. Lack of empowerment can lead to extended lead times, dissatisfied customers, low morale amongst staff and a general inability to innovate. Harnessing the brainpower of the organisation cannot be achieved by right, hierarchical control. Saying that empowerment is good, however, and that we should all be doing it, is too superficial. We would advocate empowerment in much the same way as we would advocate technology: it should be appropriate. Empowering them to serve customers within clear guidelines on customer service and further empowering them to improve their service delivery within these guidelines is what we mean.

Action Plan for Change Management:

Cyclic Process: The change processes should follow a cycle, underlining the never-ending journey that change involves. It will have the following stages (see Figure: 4.11):

- Vision stage: creating a picture of what things could look like in an ideal world; this gives birth to a change strategy
- Analysis stage: gathering data on how things currently are

- Redesign stage: planning the tactics and refiguring the processes and systems
- Implementation stage: puts the strategy and plans into practice through introducing the new ways of working, retraining, re-education, etc.
- Review stage: an attempt both to measure success of the project and to seek new ways of pushing the organisation into a new change.

Figure: 4.11 Cyclic Process

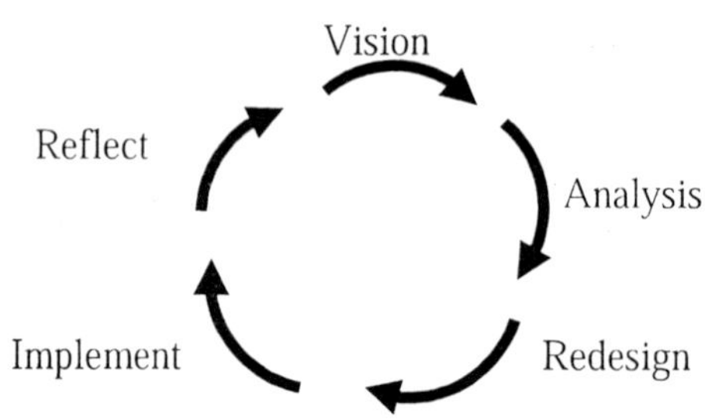

- *Implementation Plan (Steps in Change Management)*
- Initiation
- Motivation
- Diagnosis
- Information collection
- Deliberation
- Action proposal
- Stabilisation

- *Implementation Team*

The following teams are suggested at various levels:

At Top (Government) Level

- Task force
- Change agents (one in each Directorate of each department)

At Middle (District) level

- Task force
- Team leader (Champion)

Figure: 4.12 Inputs-outputs and Change Management Interaction

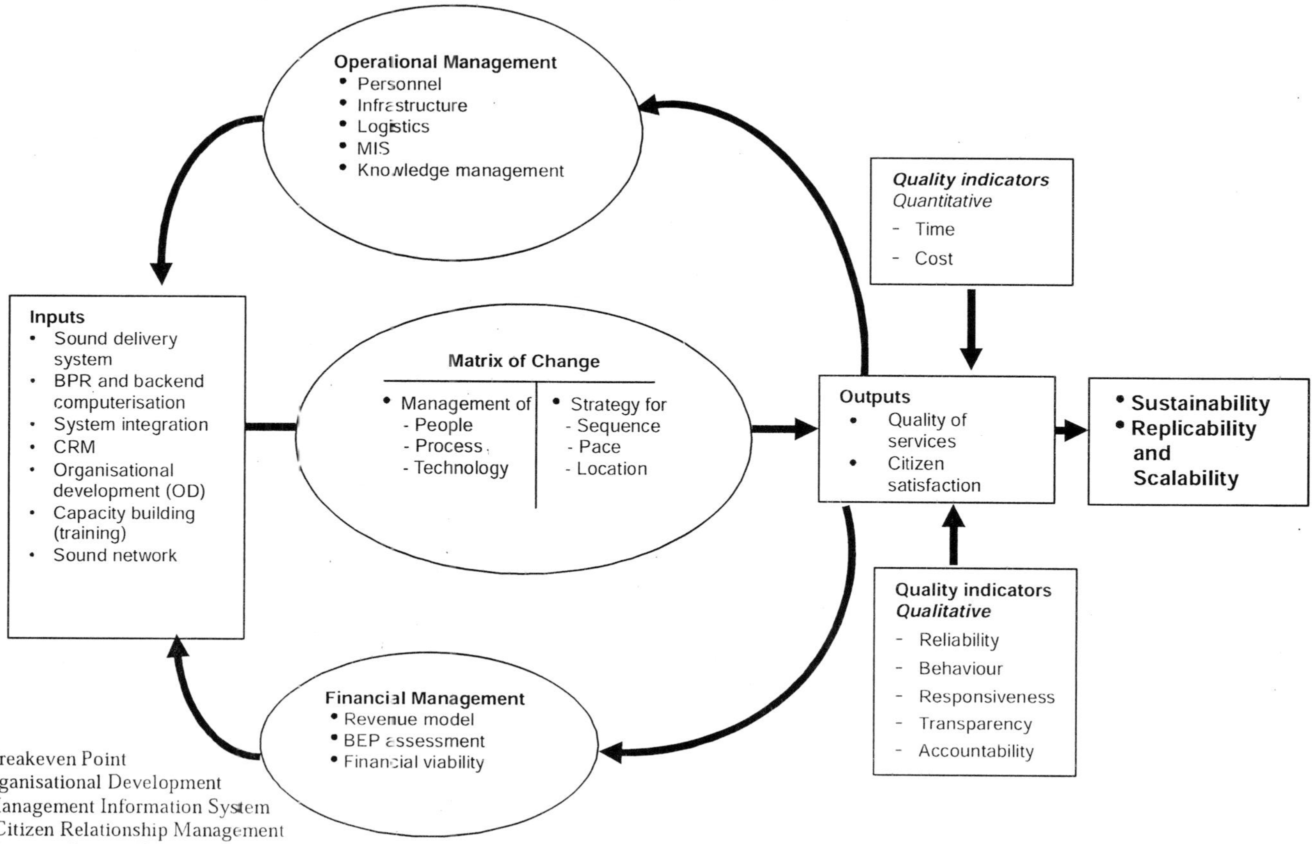

BEP: Breakeven Point
OD: Organisational Development
MIS: Management Information System
CRM: Citizen Relationship Management
BPR: Business Process Reengineering

Source: Pearce II and Robinson (1996) and based on own analysis

- Change agents (one in each department at the district level)

At Project Level

- Project team
- Team leader (Champion)
- Change agents (one in each section in a office)

The inputs-outputs and change management interaction, together with Matrix of change, is shown in Figure 4.12.

4.2.3 Capacity Building

A. **Effectiveness of Human Resources is a Key Factor**: Today, due to rising expectations of citizens and increased complexity of issues, the government organisations are faced with unprecedented change and challenge to work in innovative ways. In this context e-Governance has opened up a new opportunity to governments across the board. However, as evident from the field study, due to complexity of issues and multi-stakeholder involvement, implementing e-Governance project is a big task for any department or government. It has the potential to change the whole façade of government. It can open up a gateway of vast opportunities for citizens, seamless flow of information, on-line coordination among various agencies, and provide efficient service to the citizens. The scale of transformation is therefore huge. However what it requires in terms of resource is not just money, but also lots of expertise, special skills and commitment of the people involved (Gupta, 2004a). It will call for a well-funded and organised capacity building programme.

It assumes great significance as a good framework may be undercut, if the personnel lack training, orientation, or motivation; or if there is a lack of leadership commitment. Therefore, sincerely motivated personnel can exercise their technological skills to the highest level through continuous innovation. They need to be equipped with new skills that would enable them to work efficiently and get prepared to take risks. Special focus has to be given to behavioural skills like inter-personal skills, participatory leadership, team building and motivation.

For performing various functions, the stakeholders require enhanced capabilities. These include technical, managerial / administrative and human / behavioural capabilities. Technical capabilities relate to basic technical knowledge of different subjects concerning the delivery department.

Managerial / administrative capabilities include project management skills, quality management, etc. Human capabilities are concerned with ability to deal with other people like officials, staff members, citizens and so on. These include abilities to lead others, motivate, generate team spirit and resolve conflicts. Some of the capabilities, as may be required in the context of e-Governance, are summed-up as follows:

Technical Capabilities

Subject-based (of service delivery department)
- Laws, rules, processes, etc. governing the functioning
- Legal knowledge
- Technical knowledge based on job requirement (e.g. for health, agriculture, etc.)

Computer-based
- Computer literacy
- Database design and development
- Software design and development
- Network design

Managerial / Administrative Capabilities
- Project management
- Financial management (Revenue model and breakeven point)
- Marketing management
- CRM
- Quality management

Human / Behavioural Capabilities
- Leadership
- Teamwork
- Roles and responsibilities
- Motivation
- Inter-personal skills and emotional intelligence

Notes: The above list is indicative, not exhaustive. ii. Knowledge inputs would vary depending upon the stakeholder and the level of functioning.

Based on the field study, the capacity building programme should focus on understanding governance issues, processes (of service delivery) and BPR, and organisational issues – behavioural and cultural, besides other technical and management aspects. In this backdrop, in order to impart necessary training, the suggested modules are as follows (see Table 4.12 and Box 4.4):

Table: 4.12: Training Programme for Different Stakeholders

S. N	Participants		Duration
1	State level department coordinators		2 weeks for all modules
2	Project champion (leader) at district*		3-6 months training
3	Project teams		
	Level 1	• District department coordinators**	1 week for each module
		• District project team members***	2-3 days overview for each module
	Level 2	• Block department coordinators***	1 week for each module
		• Block project team members***	2-3 days overview for each module
	Level 3	• Field functionaries***	2-3 days overview for each module

* For project champion, a specialised course for 3-6 months should be designed and conducted by management institute or NISG

** For district department coordinators, a specialised course for one week should be designed and conducted by management institute or National Institute of Smart Government (NISG)

*** For them, the course should be designed and conducted by master trainer (by project champion and district department coordinators)

- Module I: Governance: Concepts and Philosophy
- Module II: Project management
- Module III: Management tools and techniques
- Module IV:OB & OD Issues

4.3 Strategies

It is widely acknowledged that information and communication technologies (ICTs) are effective tool in bridging rural-urban and rich-poor divide in many ways, and can play important role in accelerating economic growth. Specifically, to realise tangible advantages, e-Governance offers big opportunity for government to provide services efficiently, empowerment of people, and to usher in knowledge-based economy. It offers the scope for transformation of apparatus of Governance.

The available literature (Hammer and Champy, 1993; and Gupta, 2004) on e-Governance has brought out complex and multi-dimensional nature of e-Governance projects. Also, the projects are people-oriented and have long gestation period. The projects are influenced by both internal and external factors. They are subjected to the scrutiny of wide range of stakeholders. The need of aligning technology with other aspects such as work culture, human resource practices, capabilities, processes, systems, and external environment (social and political), is strongly felt.

It is for these reasons the decision-making require strategic management. It involves the development of long-range plans for the effective management of opportunities and threats, in light of strengths and weaknesses, while managing various and multifaceted internal activities and external environment (Pearce and Robinson, 1996). It includes defining the mission, specifying achievable objectives, developing strategies, and setting operational guidelines.

Box: 4.4: Training Modules

Module I: Governance: Concepts and Philosophy

i. Governance issues and delivery system
ii. Quality in services

Module II: Project management

i. Project management
   - Formulation
   - Planning
   - Management
ii. Revenue model and breakeven point (BPR)
iii. Marketing
   - Marketing research
   - Marketing strategy
iv. CRM

Module III: Management tools and techniques

i. BPR
ii. Quality tools
   - TQM
   - Six Sigma
   - SERVQUAL model
iii. FMEA
iv. SWOT Analysis
v. Strategic Analysis
vi. Change Management
vii. Matrix of Change

Module IV:OB & OD Issues

i. Team building
ii. Leadership
iii. Work culture
iv. Motivation
v. Change management
vi. Emotional intelligence

OB: Organisational Behaviour
OD: Organisational Development

Dimensions of Strategic Decisions for e-Governance

Typically, strategic decisions have following five identifiable dimensions that deserve strategic management attention:

- *Strategic decisions require support of top leadership:* Strategic decisions have overarching influence on every area of operation, and therefore, top-leadership involvement in decision-making is imperative. At this level, the complete understanding and anticipating broad implications and ramifications of initiatives under e-Governance are expected.
- *Strategic decisions involve both internal and external factors:* For any organisation's capacity to perform largely depends on internal work culture, ethos, capabilities of people, systems and processes. The launch of new projects or plans, in the present case e-Governance, must factor in these issues. There will be need to consider: what new capabilities are required for the people in the organisations in order to enable them to function efficiently, or, how the systems and processes are to be reengineered to meet new challenges of service delivery. Similarly, the government organisations exist in an open system, constantly interacting with various stakeholders – citizens, NGOs, political groups, business groups and so on. They impact and are impacted by external conditions. There may be changing aspirations due to demographic pattern, or technological changes, or economic conditions, or influence of culture. The strategic planners need to factor in likely changes in the society.
- *Strategic decisions involve the allocation of large resources:* Strategic decisions characteristically involve substantial resource development to realise short and long term objectives on a sustained basis. The manpower, physical assets (infrastructure, IT hardware, etc.), or budget needed should be adequately pooled.
- *Strategic decisions involve Multifunctional Issues:* A strategic decision is coordinative. Decisions about factors such as customer (citizen)-mix, service-mix, or organizational structure necessarily involve a number of departments, functions, divisions, or program units. Each of these areas will be affected by the allocation or reallocation of responsibilities and resources related to the decision.
- *Strategic decisions are future-oriented and have significant Long-term Impact:* Strategic decisions in case of e-Governance are going to affect the way services are delivered in the next ten years (may in the next 2-3 decades)

and thus, will altogether change the style, stance and substance of governance. So the decisions commit the government departments for a long period of time, and such decisions are going to impact both government and citizens substantially.

Strategy Formulation Process for e-Governance

To deal effectively with all the factors that affect the ability of a project to perform, grow in a sustained way, need is to design strategic management processes, which will facilitate the optimal positioning of the project in its new environment. Such positioning will allow more accurate anticipation of environmental changes and improved preparedness for reacting to unexpected internal or external (citizens') demands. Typically, strategic management will involve attention to critical areas such as (see Figure 4.13).

- determining the mission, including broad statements about its purpose, philosophy, and goals;
- assessment of internal conditions and capabilities, and the external environmental factors;
- analysis of possible options, identifying the desired options, and selecting right choice to achieve the desired objectives;
- designing implementing strategy (decisions for systems & processes design; matching of people, structure, process and technologies; and rewards systems); and
- review and evaluation of the success of the strategic process to serve as a basis for control and as an input for future decision-making.

Levels of Strategy formulation

Though there are going to be some overlapping areas, typically there can be three levels of strategy formulation: government, project, and functional (see Figure 4.14).

- **Government level strategy** should overall define its direction in terms of its general approach towards application of IT for improving efficiency and effectiveness of government services and empowering people; and should address issues like key areas of e-Government and e-services, network design, data centre, organisational structure, capacity building and system architecture.

Figure 4.13: Strategic Management Process for e-Governance

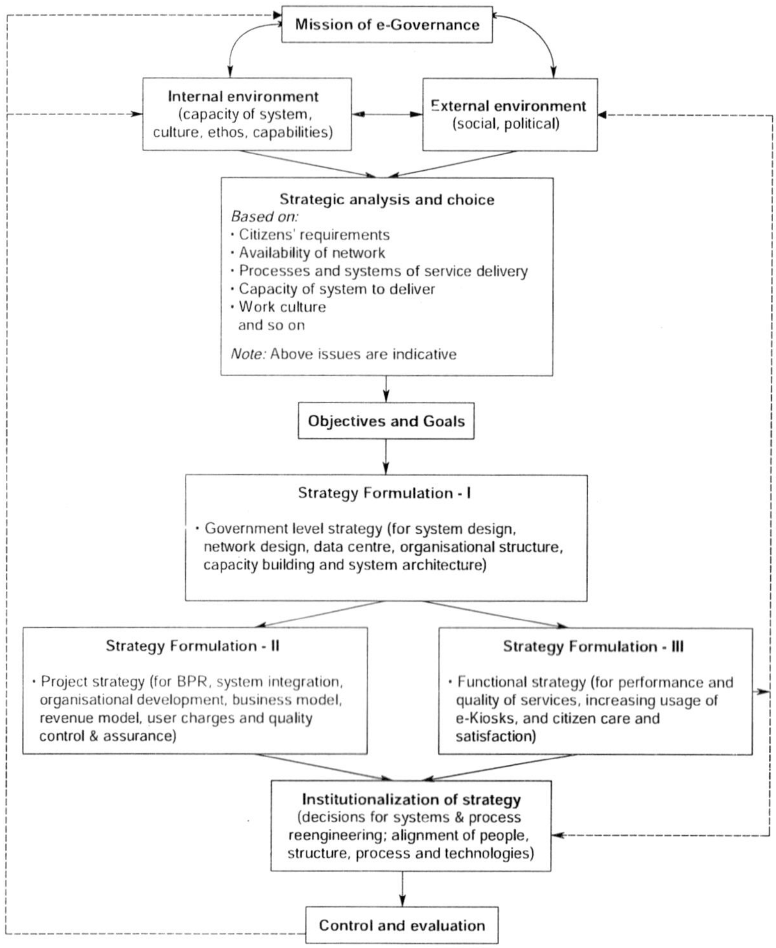

- **Project strategy** is needed at the service delivery level, and it should lay its emphasis on improvement in the service levels. It should specifically deal with citizen requirements study, BPR, system integration, organisational development, business model, revenue model, user charges and quality control & assurance

- **Functional strategy** is the approach taken by a functional area, such as marketing of services, performance and quality of services, increasing usage of e-Kiosks, and citizen care and satisfaction. It should be concerned with developing and nurturing a distinctive citizen-centric culture to meet varied expectations of citizens.

Figure 4.14: Level of Strategy

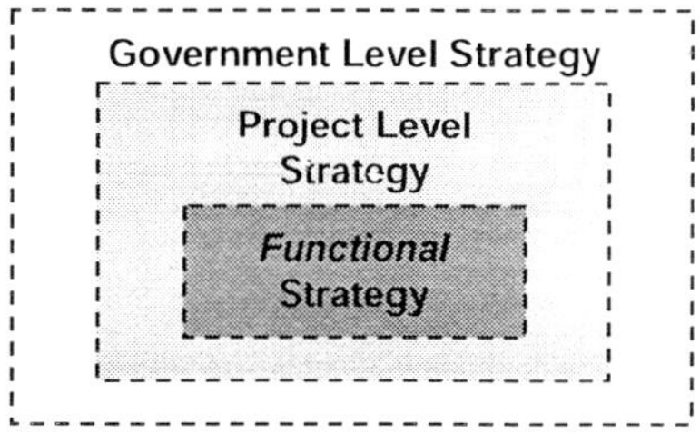

The strategic analysis is attempted for the following four vital aspects of e-Governance project:

- For system design
- For addressing citizens' requirements
- For increasing usage of e-Kiosks
- For enhancing performance of service delivery

4.3.1 For System Design: Based on SWOT analysis, there are four sets of strategies suggested which as follows (see also Figure 4.15 for strategy model) (Pearce II and Robinson, 1996):

- **Cell I (most favourable):** It calls for the 'aggressive (expansion)' type strategy. The emphasis should be laid on adding more services (certificates for land, caste, etc.) then value added services (like bank credit, insurance, etc.), and backend computerisation.
- **Cell II (somewhat favourable but constrained):** It requires 'turnaround' strategy focusing on building trust. The focus should be on process reengineering, CRM, change management, backend computerisation, system integration and value added services.
- **Cell III (most unfavourable):** This is the most difficult quadrant and it requires making efforts having 'defensive approach'.
- **Cell IV (Internal strength but unfavourable environment):** Here, it requires taking threats as challenges and building on internal strength. It requires taking initiatives for improving network planning and management, tie-up with government for support (e.g. electricity supply), CRM and gradually adding more services.

Based on above, the details of specific strategies for the system design for the following services are suggested in Table 4.13:

- e-Services and grievances
- e-Information

Figure: 4.15: Required Strategy Model for Different Quadrants

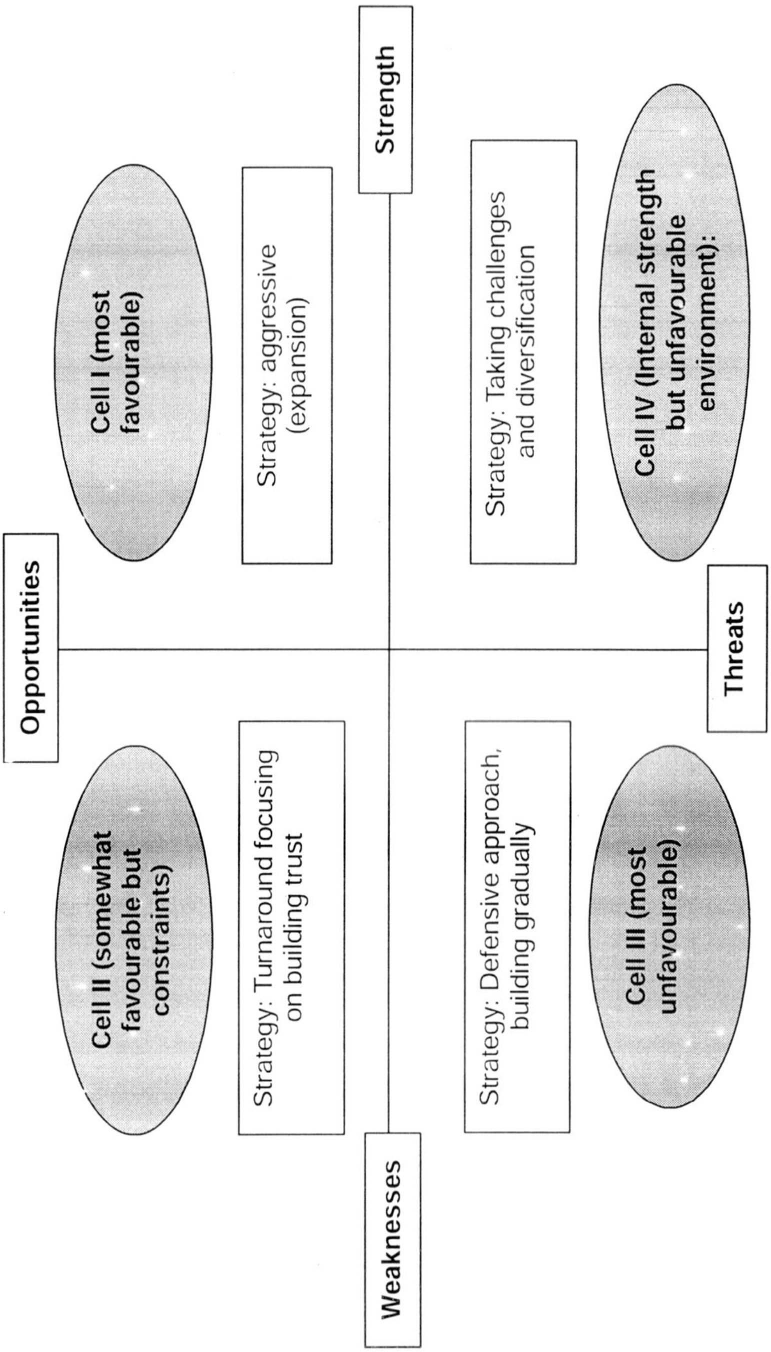

Souce: Pearce II and Robinson (1996) and based on own analysis

Table: 4.13 Specific Strategy required for different Types of Services

S. N.	Type of services	Cells	Strategy required	Specific interventions
1	e-Services and grievances	Cells II & III	Phase I - Defensive approach, building gradually Phase II - Turnaround focusing on building trust	Phase I - Improving network planning and management - Tie-up with govt. for support (e.g. electricity supply) - CRM Phase II - Process reengineering - Backend computerisation - System Integration (ERP) - CRM - Better CM - Value added services
2	e-Information	Cells II & III	Phase I - Defensive approach, building gradually Phase II - Turnaround focusing on building trust	-do-
3	e-Entertainment	Cells I & VI	Phase I - Taking challenges and diversification Phase II - Aggressive (expansion)	Phase I - Improving network planning and management - Tie-up with govt. for support (e.g. electricity supply) - CRM - Gradually adding more services Phase II - More services - Value added services
4	e-Business	Cells I & VI	Phase I - Taking challenges and diversification Phase II - Aggressive (expansion)	Phase I - Improving network planning and management - Tie-up with govt. for support (e.g. electricity supply) - CRM - Gradually adding more services Phase II - More services - Value added services - Backend computerisation
5	e-Education	Cells I & II	Phase I - Aggressive (expansion)	Phase I - More services - Value added services

Note: See Figure S3.7 (SWOT analysis) for details

- e-Entertainment
- e-Business
- e-Education

4.3.2 For Addressing Citizen Requirements: For understanding citizen requirements, the field survey was conducted. The citizens were classified in five categories and that were further broken into groups as indicated in Table 4.14. The purpose was to understand the requirement of different groups and their preferences for a variety of information, services and grievances under different sectors (see Annexure 2.1). It has added value for the formulation of strategy and positioning of the products (information, services and grievances) that may fulfill the requirements of different customers (citizens), and thus maximise the usage of e-Kiosks. And, the system design should take into account on the citizen requirement study.

Table: 4.14: Categories and Groups of Different Users (Citizens)

S. N	Categories	Groups
1.	Gender	• Male • Female
2.	Age	• Young (18-30 yrs.) • Middle-aged group (31-40 yrs) • Aged (> 40 yrs.)
3.	Income	• Low income group (BPL) • Middle income group (>BPL but < Rs. 4000pm) • High income group (income> Rs. 4000pm)
4.	Education	• Low education group (illiterate to PE) • Medium education group (>PE but < HS) • High education group (>HS)
5.	Caste	• General • OBC • SC & ST

BPL: Below poverty line; PE: Primary education; HS: High school; pm: per month

The overall strategy, for positioning of the products (information, services and grievances), should be formulated, keeping in view two vital factors: *first*, creating sustainable demand from citizens, and *second*, financial viability of e-Kiosks and service provider, the following strategies are suggested:

- Focus on information and services with maximum impact and visibility
- Awareness and confidence building programme for citizens
- Creating demand through
  - making day-to-day important information available at e-Kiosk
  - providing reliable delivery of 'a few services' in the beginning

- Services those are cost effective and are likely to give higher revenue should be given priority
- Adding services gradually based on success

For the purpose of strategy formulation, based on: *first,* the utilisation of IT, *second,* process of service delivery, and *third,* the capacity of delivery system, three types of information, services and grievances have been identified as indicated by Table 4.15.

Table: 4.15: Types of Information, Services and Grievances and their Order for Introduction for e-Governance

S. N	Types	Order	Special focus
1.	Mainly computer based	First	• Information based, where database can be prepared with available data and information, and • Information and services that can be provided at e-Kiosk through databases which would require lesser efforts for preparation and likely to give higher returns. For example: *mandi bahv,* Jamabandi, weather forecast, guidelines for schemes, etc.
2.	Computer and delivery system (department) based	Second	• Services, which would require BPR and backend computerisation. For example: caste, income, domicile, mutation certificate, etc.
3.	Mainly delivery system (department) based	Third	• Services and grievances that would require interface at e-Kiosk but delivery system would play major role. It would require improving capacity of concerned delivery system to provide services efficiently. For example: providing agriculture inputs, health services, drinking water, etc. would require major improvements in delivery system

A. **Citizen Requirement Study and Strategy Formulation:** For the field survey, the information, services and grievances were identified in the structured formats (see Annexure 2.1) for all the sectors that are of concern to the citizens. It was important to take into account all possible information, services and grievances as may be required by citizens at the time of identification of customer (or citizen) requirement. Based on such assessment, requirements can be classified in the order of preference by citizens and priority of the project management (it is also important to have priority of the management as there may be a large number of preferences of citizens, but it may not be possible for management to provide all of them at one point of time. But such preferences can definitely provide a road map for future add-ons). Based on field survey, the strategies are suggested for the following:

From the point of view of 'product' (information, services, grievances) positioning:

- Separate strategy for (see Tables 4.16A & 4.16B):
  - Information sharing
  - Service provisioning
  - Grievances redressal, to citizens

From the point of view of 'users' priority

- Strategy for degree of preferences by citizens (see Tables 4.5.1A & 4.5.1B in Annexure 4.5)
- Separate strategy for different categories viz. gender, income, education, caste and age (see Table S4.5 and Figure S4.6)
- Separate strategy for better off / prosperous and vulnerable groups (see Tables 4.6.1A and 4.6.1B in Annexure 4.6)

From the point of view 'service provider'

Based on:

- Degree of technical convenience and ease of service provider to meet citizens' needs (see Tables 4.17A to 4.17D)
- Urgency and importance of information, services and grievances (see Tables 4.4.1A to 4.4.1E in Annexure 4.4)

Phase-wise Programme (based on Technical Convenience and Ease of Service Provider) for System Design (see Tables 4.17A, to 4.17D).

4.3.3 Increasing the Usage of e-Kiosks: The Strategic Analysis Model as shown in Figure 4.16 is applied to decide about the strategic interventions to be made in each of the factor for improving usage / performance, based on the combined effect of 'present status' and 'weightage'.

The logic used here is that efforts are to be maximum, where the weightage has been high (or the contribution in improving the performance is maximum) and also the present status is low. It implies that the factors that have low present status, but have high contribution factor (weightage) in the performance should be given high priority in terms of making efforts to improve its status.

From Figure 4.16, it is clear that for increasing usage of e-Governance services, 'significantly large efforts' are to be made for the factor 'opportunity cost (or improving performance of delivery of services)'. It means that there is a strong case to improve the performance of delivery of services only then would the citizens use e-Governance services.

Table: 4.16A Overall Strategy for promoting Information, Services and Grievances under e-Governance

S. N.	I / S / G	Immediate strategy	Short term strategy	Long term strategy
1.	Information	*Focus on providing* - Urgent information needs like employment notification, mandi rates, health information, etc.	*Focus on providing* - Information related to socio-economic development	- Main focus on citizen satisfaction and revenue generation - Information that require making network with other agencies
2.	Services	*Focus on providing* - Certificate required on day-to-day basis like caste, income, RORs, domicile, ration card, etc.	*Focus on providing* - Services to be added after BPR and backend computerisation	- Main focus on citizen satisfaction and revenue generation - Services those require system integration and networking like crop loan, insurance, etc.
3.	Grievances	- Grievances of urgent needs like electricity failure for household, non-availability of health worker, late coming of teachers, etc.	- Grievances that require strengthening delivery system (e.g. primary education, health, drinking water, etc.) like infrastructure, funds, facilities, manpower and logistics	- Main focus on citizen satisfaction and revenue generation - Grievances that require online interaction and processing (backend computerisation) of grievances like delay in pension, non-availability of scholarship, etc.

Table: 4.16B Overall Strategy for Designing System for Information, Services and Grievances under e-Governance

S.N.	I / S / G	Immediate strategy	Short term strategy	Long term strategy
1	Information	*Focus on* - Database for select information - Listing of important information - Providing interface at village level - Providing accurate information	*Focus on* - Improving MIS - Improve work culture - Training	*Focus on* - Integrated information database (automatic updation) - Backend computerisation - Making network with other agencies (horizontal and vertical integration)
2	Services	*Focus on* - Listing of important services - Providing the interface at village level	*Focus on* - BPR - Backend computerisation - Improving MIS - Improve work culture - Training - Improving the capacity of delivery system	*Focus on* - Horizontal & vertical integration - System integration - Integrated provisioning of services like ROR, mutation, deeds, loan and insurance
3	Grievances	*Focus on* - Listing of important grievances - Providing the interface at village level	*Focus on* - Improving work culture - Improving MIS - Training	*Focus on* - Backend computerisation - Improving the capacity of delivery system

Table: 4.17A: Phase I (in the first year): Requires Less Effort an Easy to Provide (Information, Services and Grievances) by Service Provider

S.N	Type*	I/S/G	Items
1	Mainly computer based (T1)	I	Health information
		I	Land records
		I	Timings of busses and bus routes
		I	Employment notification
		I	Cattle health care and controls
		I	Last date of depositing bill payment
		I	Guidelines for accessing the certificates
		I	Telephone numbers of all departments
		I	Information about electricity cut
		I	Availability of forms
		I	Last date of depositing bill payment
		I	Artificial insemination
		S	Computer education
		S	Internet browsing
		S	E-mail
		S	Horoscope
2	Computer and delivery system (department) based (T2)	S	Land certificate
3	Mainly delivery system (department) based (interface with computer) (T3)	S	Immunisation
		S	Making medicines available
		G	Irregularities in mid-day meal

Table: 4.17B: Phase II (from the second year): Requires More Preparation by Service Provider and BPR (for Information, Services and Grievances)

S.N	Type*	I/S/G	Items
1	Mainly computer based (T1)	I	Daily mandi rates
		I	Schemes for BPL families (all group)
		I	Type of diseases
		I	Items available at fair price shops
		I	Loan schemes
		I	Rates of commodities
		I	Subsidy for different schemes
		I	Fertiliser use
		I	Water table
		I	Cropping pattern
		I	Results for 10th and 12th classes
		I	Type of scholarship
		I	Schemes for handicaps
		I	Insurance of cattle
		I	Number of hospitals
		I	Number of schools
		I	Number of teachers

S.N	Type*	I/S/G	Items
		I	Number of night schools and locations
		I	Number of children and mothers covered
		I	Village-wise status of development works
		I	Sources of irrigation
		I	Area under different sources of irrigation
		I	Production of crops
		I	Number of hand pumps
2	Computer and delivery system (department) based (T2)	S	Ration card
		S	Caste certificate
		S	Income certificate
		S	Domicile certificate

Table: 4.17C: Phase III (from the third and fourth year): Requires both Intensive BPR and Integration with other Agencies (for Information, Services and Grievances)

S.N	Type*	I/S/G	Items
1	Computer and delivery system (department) based (T2)	S	Loan for self-employment
		S	Payment of government dues (electricity, phone, etc.)
		S	Crop loan
		S	Gun license
		S	Driving license
		S	Sale deed
		S	Mutation
		S	Conversion of agriculture land into non-agriculture land
2	Mainly delivery system (department) based (interface with computer) (T3)	S	Expert advice on health
		S	Expert advice on agriculture
		S	Expert advice on cattle management
		S	Marketing of handicrafts
		S	Marketing of agriculture produce
		S	Training for self-employment
		S	Supply of feed
		G	Street cattle

Table: 4.17D: Phase IV (from the third to fifth year): Requires Improving Capacity of Delivery System (for Information, Services and Grievances)

S.N	Type*	I/S/G	Items
1.	Mainly delivery system (department) based (interface with computer) (T3)	S	Repair of tube wells
		S	Nutritional programme for pre-school children and mothers
		S	Purchase of seeds, fertiliser, pesticide, implements
		S	Supply of quality animals under Loan scheme
		S	Timely availability of essential commodities
		S	Providing education to children
		G	Delay in pension
		G	Electricity failure – for household
		G	Electricity failure – for agriculture pump sets
		G	Requirement of new hostels

S.N	Type*	I/S/G	Items
		G	Poor quality of implementation of work
		G	Late coming of teachers
		G	Non-availability of school building / drinking water / toilets / playground, etc.
		G	Closing of schools
		G	Higher prices of essential commodities
		G	Complaint against retailer
		G	Irregularities in mid-day meal
		G	Vacancies of teachers

Note 1: Phases are indicative / suggestive, actual timeframe to be devised based on state-specific requirements.

Note 2: The above items are indicative, some more may be added based on local requirements.

*For the purpose of strategy formulation. Based on: *first,* the utilisation of IT, *second,* process of services delivery, and *third,* the capacity of delivery system, three types of information, services and grievances have been identified

As regards 'number of services', 'large efforts' are required to increase the number of services at e-Kiosks so that citizens find it convenient to access more services through the Kiosk. It is important that the Kiosk should provide a package of services that are commonly required by citizens (see Table 4.18).

Table: 4.18: Strategy required for increasing Usage of e-Governance Services

S.N	Factors	Present status	Weightage of factors	Strategic efforts required
1.	Awareness	Medium	Low to medium	Some efforts
2.	Access (availability of e-Kiosk)	Medium	Low	Limited effort
3.	Ease of use	Medium	Low	Limited efforts
4.	Opportunity cost (or Performance of delivery of services)	Low	High	Significantly large efforts
5.	Security of data	Medium	Low	Some efforts
6.	Number of services	Low	Medium	Large efforts
7.	Reliability	Low	Low to medium	Some efforts

Note: See Table 3.9 for details.

Simultaneously, 'some efforts' are required to improve the 'security of data' and 'reliability' of functioning of e-Kiosk. It implies that the security of operations by Kiosk owner and functionaries should be raised, as also data security should be upgraded. And, down time should be reduced by having improved supply of electricity (together with UPS) and better network management, so that when citizens go to e-Kiosk, they find it ready for usage.

4.3.4 Enhancing the Performance of Service Delivery: Based on Figure 4.16 and Table 4.19, for improving quality of services (or performance of delivery of services), 'significantly large efforts' are required for business process reengineering (BPR) and backend computerisation. It is in a way is the most important factor. Also 'large efforts' are required for improving delivery system (DS), so as to reach out to citizens effectively and deliver services efficiently.

Table: 4.19: Strategy Required for Enhancing Quality of Services (Performance of Delivery of Services)

S.N	Factors	Status (Present value)	Factor contributing in Performance (Weight)	Strategic efforts required
1.	IT infrastructure	High	Low	No effort
2.	Business Process Reengineering (BPR) and backend computerization	Low	High	Significantly large efforts
3.	Delivery System (DS)	Low to Medium	Medium	Large efforts
4.	Electricity	Low	Low	Limited efforts
5.	Citizen Relationship Management (CRM)	Low	Low to Medium	Some efforts

Note: See Table 3.10 for details.

Figure: 4.16: Strategic Analysis Model

Weightage of a factor				
High	Limited efforts	Large efforts	Significantly large efforts	High
Medium	Limited efforts	Some efforts	Large efforts	Medium
Low	No effort	Limited efforts	Limited efforts	Low
	High	Medium	Low	
	Present status of factors			

No effort – Limited efforts – Some efforts - Large efforts – Significantly large efforts

To conclude, if the performance of delivery of services is to be improved, the maximum attention is to be paid to two vital factors viz., *first*, business process reengineering (BPR) and backend computerisation, and *second*, improving capacity of delivery system (DS).

The afore-mentioned strategies are summarised in Table 4.20.

4.3.5 Strategy for e-Governance System in a District: It needs to follow growth model, starting from stage I to stage V (Stage I: Interface; Stage II: Transactional; Stage III: Vertical Integration; Stage IV: Horizontal Integration; and Stage V: Networking). Initially in the vertical integration there should be focus on one department by linking village level unit to Block / Tehsil to District to State head-quarters. And in the next stage (Horizontal Integration), other departments are to be added at each level as shown in Figure 4.17.

Figure 4.17: Strategy for e-Governance System in a District

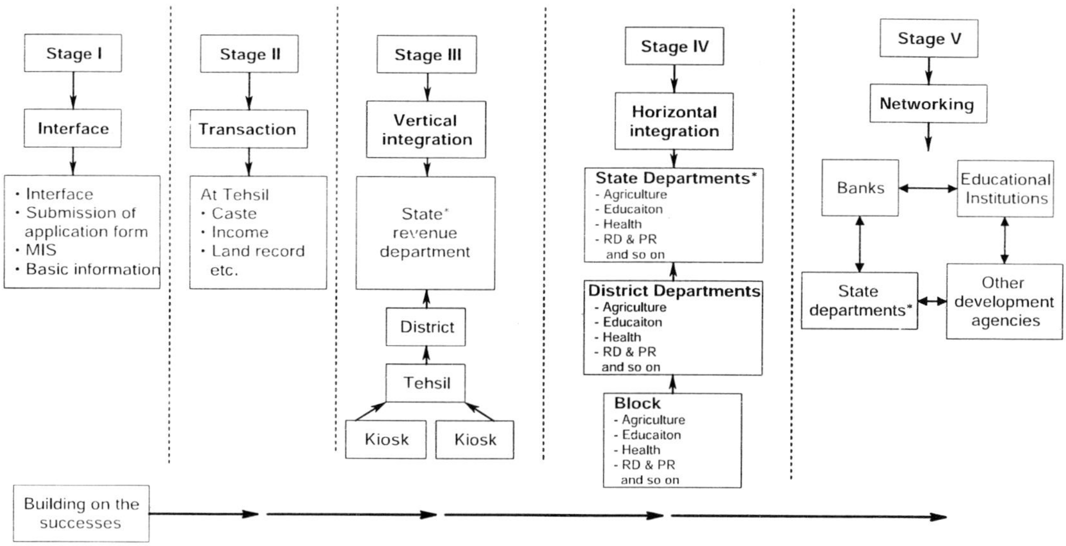

* Developing data centre [System Integration (SI), Citizen Relationship Management (CRM), and Knowledge Management (KM)]

4.3.6 Citizen-centric Approach for e-Governance: Citizen-centric approaches to government transformation are at the leading edge of public service reform in an increasing number of countries around the world. The countries (like Austria, UK, Italy) which are making most rapid progress in the direction of citizen-centric government are doing so because they see very hard, quantifiable benefits which go to the heart of public sector efficiency and the creation of public value (http:/www.intel.com). Need of the hour is to understand the underlying know-how about the cultural, political and contextual factors which have contributed to success.

Globalisation is driving up the customer expectations. In most cases citizens are being exposed to commercial and other services delivered via the internet. The known examples of this include Amazon, eBay, and MSN, and search engines such as Yahoo. These global services are setting the standard and driving up the customer expectations.

Table: 4.20: Strategy Framework

S.N	Items	Strategy required
1.	For system design i. e-Services and grievances ii. e-Information iii. e-Entertainment iv. e-Business v. e-Education	As per SWOT analysis (see Figure 4.15)
2.	For addressing citizens' requirements	The following to be considered: • Separate strategy for (see Tables 4.16A & 4.16B): - Information sharing - Service provisioning - Grievances redressal, to citizens • Strategy for degree of preference by citizens (see Tables 4.5.1A & 4.5.1B in Annexure 4.5) • Separate strategy for different categories viz. gender, income, education, caste and age (see Table S4.5) • Separate strategy for better off / prosperous and vulnerable groups (see Tables 4.6.1A & 4.6.1B in Annexure 4.6) • Based on (see Tables 4.17A to 4.17D & 4.4.1A to 4.4.1E in Annexure 4.4): • Degree of technical convenience and ease of service provider to meet citizens' needs (see Table 4.17A to 4.17D) • Urgency and importance to citizens (see Tables 4.4.1A to 4.4.1E in Annexure 4.4)
3.	For increasing usage of e-Kiosks	Based on Strategic Analysis Model (see Figure 4.16) *Maximum efforts are required for:* • Enhancing opportunity cost (or improving performance of delivery of services) • Number of services at e-Kiosk
4.	For enhancing Performance of Service Delivery	Based on Strategic Analysis Model (see Figure 4.20) *Maximum efforts are required for:* • Business process reengineering (BPR) and backend computerisation, and • Improving capacity delivery system (DS)

In India, the launch of NeGP has further provided a fillip. Notwithstanding high potential offered by e-Governance, except for some successes in providing land related certificates and collection of utility bills, the success is still alluding. The prominent reason attributed to sub-optimal performance is lack of citizen-centric approach in identifying citizens' requirements, portal design, process design, and IT system design. To reap the maximum benefits of e-Governance, a citizen-centric approach to service delivery is essential if governments are to improve service delivery to citizens; reduce cost of government service delivery and improve delivery of public policy objectives. A citizen-centric approach will enable governments to achieve essential efficiency gains and improve service delivery levels, improve citizen satisfaction with government services and improve quality of life (Mehra, 2004).

Citizen-centric Philosophy

Amidst the tremendous pressures coming from the rising aspiration of citizens, the need is to understand and accept the significance of citizen-centered philosophies. A number of successful case studies (Gupta 2004) incorporating citizen-centric approach in the e-Governance setting have been reported. In this approach, the focus is on the citizen. Ultimately, the objective is to build a system that delivers services, which fulfill citizens' requirements. The citizens' requirements and aspirations thus, form the very premise of citizen-centric approach.

While identify citiznes' requirements, it is also important to identify the various groups of citizens due to their particular and different preferences. The importance / degree assigned to such requirements of varied groups are the essence of this approach. The paper attempts to highlight the different requirement of varied groups, and presents how those can be utilised for system design.

Citizen-centricity is all about turning the focus of government around - looking at the service delivery though the eyes of the citizens (so that the needs of the citizens come first) rather than operational or other imperatives of the government system. It is hoped that a citizen-centric approach will enable government to:

- achieve essential efficiency gains and improve service delivery levels
- increase usage of online services, thereby improve sustainability and encourage investment in e-Governance
- improve citizen satisfaction with government services

- improve quality of life

Key Principles of Citizen-centricity

Presently, citizen-centric government is a much-talked about subject in the discourses on governance. It is an evolving art rather than a known science (http:/www.intel.com). So there is no fixed template for success. However, based on experience some principles for evolving successful citizen-centric delivery models are listed in Box 4.5.

Box 4.5 Principles for Citizen-centric e-Governance Design

- A holistic approach to customer focus
- Web-centric delivery
- Building a credible brand
- Value addition by large efficiency gains
- Continuous improvement, building trust and confidence

The citizen-centric approach should be such, which encourages citizens (see Figure 4.18) to avail e-services from citizen portal. It should provide *first,* easy and affordable access; *second,* motivation to citizens in terms of providing host of services at citizen portal; and *third,* it should provide confidence to citizens that the e-Kiosks provide credible services. Simultaneously, Citizen must feel that there is a value addition for him. It should add value (see Figure 4.19) to citizens by way of providing value added services, creating trust and confidence and value creation for quality of life.

Figure 4.18: Encouraging Citizens through Citizen-centric Approach

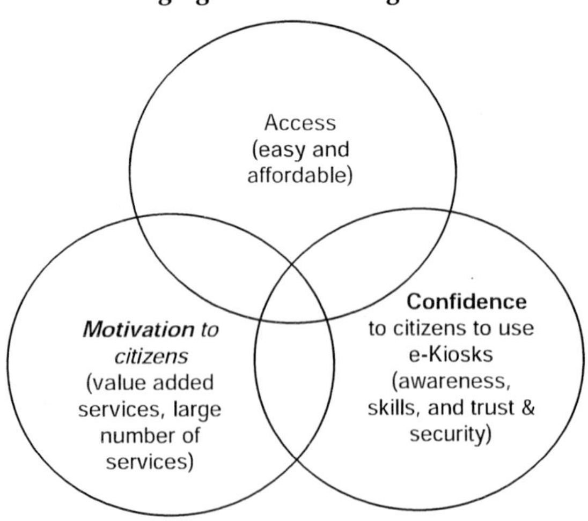

Figure 4.19: Creating Value for Citizens

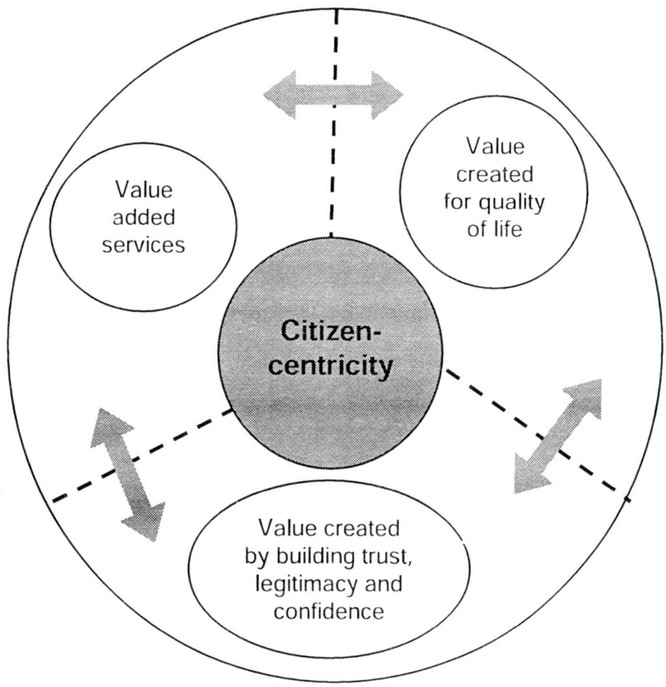

Framework for citizen-centric e-Governance system

The framework for citizen-centric e-Governance system is reflected in Figure 4.20. It specifically looks into the specifics about the following process and system management:

- citizen-centric service management
- citizen-centric communication management
- citizen care and management

The Table 4.21 outlines the issues that are to be handled in order to build citizen-centric e-Governance system. Among others, the following are vital for building such system:

Figure 4.20: Citizen-centric Framework for e-Governance

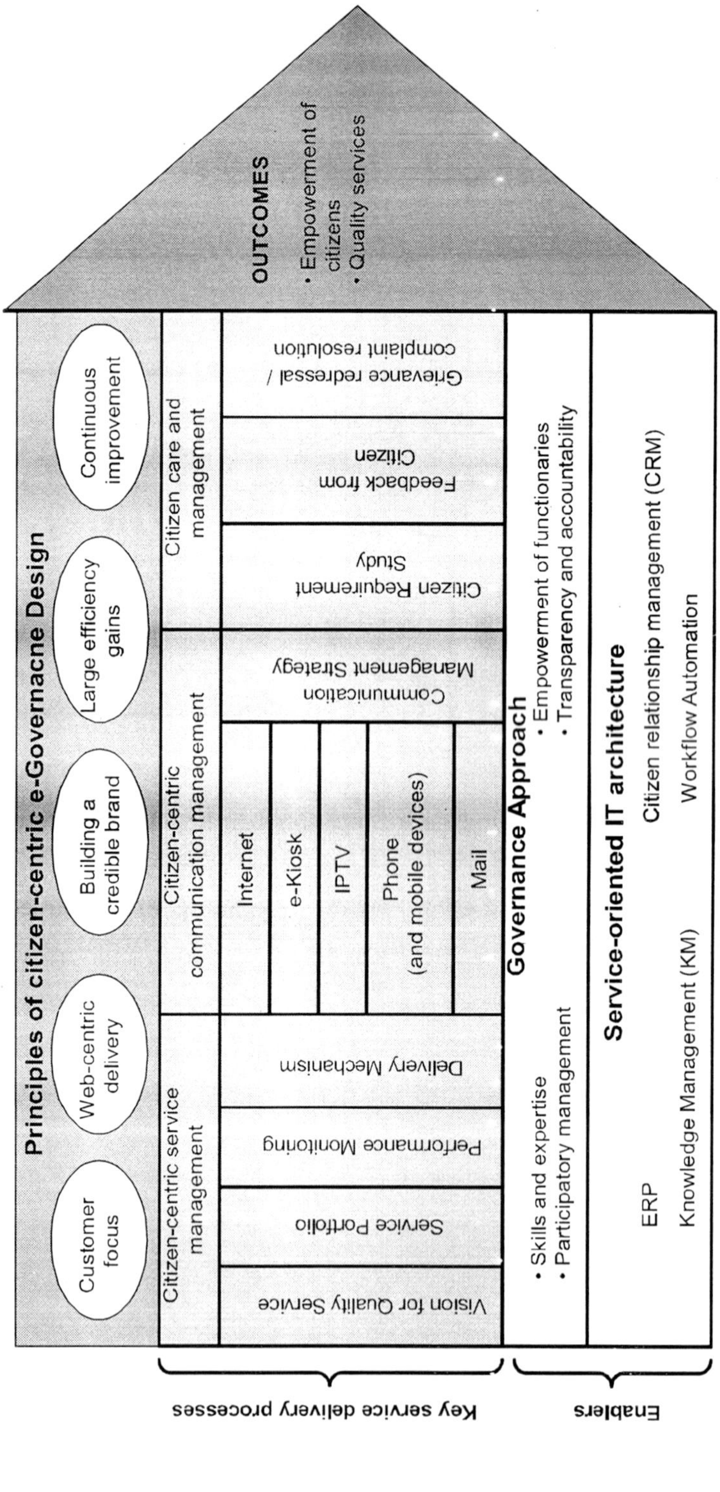

Source: www.intel.com and own analysis

- focus of vision and mission on citizens
- availability of a good number of services through citizen portal
- emphasis on developing brand for e-Kiosks through awareness building and credible delivery of services
- right communication channels for easy access
- citizen requirement study (or market research)
- systems of participatory management and quality culture
- robustness of IT infrastructure

Table 4.21 Issues for Citizen-centric e-Governance System

S.N.	Component	Elements	Issues to be addressed
1	Principles of citizen-centric e-Governance Design	Citizen focus	Focus of vision and mission on Citizens
		Web-centric delivery	Availability of a good number of services through web
		Building a credible brand	Emphasis on developing brand for e-Kiosks through awareness building and credible delivery of services
		Large efficiency gains	Availability of services within minimum possible time and large reduction in comparison to manual delivery
		Continuous improvement	Whether the quality culture is evolved, and management systems put in place for continuous improvement
2	Citizen-centric service management	Vision of Quality Service	Whether citizens' requirements and expectations reflected in service delivery policy
		Service portfolio (type and number of services)	Whether there is a right service-mix and a good package of services at e-Kiosks for citizens
		Performance monitoring	Monitoring of service delivery by officials manager and timely action by them
		Delivery mechanism	Whether delivery system (of concerned department / agency) has adequate capacity to deliver
3	Citizen-centric communication management	Internet (at office / home)	Whether right communication channels placed for easy access
		e-Kiosks	
		PITV	
		Phone (and mobile devices)	
		Mail	
4	Citizen-centric citizen management	Citizen requirement study (CRS)	Whether citizen requirement study done (or market research carried out)
		Feedback from citizens	Whether citizens can provide feedback
		Grievance redressal / complaint resolution	How efficient is complaint resolution mechanism
5	Enablers		

S.N.	Component	Elements	Issues to be addressed
	5.1 Governance Approach	- Skills and expertise - Empowerment of functionaries - Participatory management - Transparency and accountability	Whether systems of participatory management and quality culture established in the service department / agency
	5.2 Service-oriented IT architecture	- Hardware and software	- Robust IT infrastructure - Backend computerisation (including system integration, CRM) - Data security
6	Outcomes	Empowerment of citizens	Overall quality policy of service department / agency for citizen care
		Quality services	

Source: Figure 4.20 and own analysis

4.4 System Design

4.4.1 Preamble: Though IT is a great enabler in improving efficiency, but for good governance, the focus should be on 'citizen' and 'quality' of services. And, the organisations (delivery systems) should be built in such a way, that the processes, people (functionaries) and systems are aligned with IT. To achieve it, the need is:

- to involve[1] concerned stakeholders in the governance process effectively
- to continuously improve the capabilities of stakeholders (functionaries, IT professionals, etc.), reengineer processes, and to enhance capacity of delivery system in order to leverage IT effectively for providing quality services to citizens

4.4.2 Areas that Need Urgent Attention

- Environment building – with two fold aim, *first*, creating information society, and, *second*, involvement of functionaries of departments at every level from State to District to Block to Village level
- Evolving a work culture of 'quality' in official functioning
- Efficient and reliable network for connectivity
- Business process reengineering (BPR) and backend computerisation

[1] It is vital that system ownership should be developed at the point of delivery of services. It would require that the functionaries be involved right from conceptual stage to process mapping to reengineering and then implementation, as the change management needs to be a 'people centric' intervention. Outside consultants / companies may be useful in providing technical inputs, but as new processes are to be adapted and implemented in future by the existing functionaries of respective delivery departments, so their involvement in entire BPR cycle is essential for successful transformation. This way the concerned delivery departments would have a sense of system ownership.

- Strengthening capacity of delivery system[2]

4.4.3 Core Measures

Preparation of State organisational chart

The chart is suggested in Figure 4.21. Here, the emphasis is on five issues:

- A separate SRS group for each department (in SRS, the functionaries of concerned departments must be integral part of it. They must be a part of both SRS as well as implementation team, and be involved right from conceptual stage to study to analysis to reengineering and then implementation)
- Experts at State and district levels to be provided
- Formation of dedicated district project team, project implementation team
- Organic linkages among different teams and groups for better communication and monitoring
- Fair representation to all stakeholders (citizens, panchayat and civil society members, IT consultants, management experts, officials) (it is important as governance is a multiple stakeholder issue)

Teams Formation

- Formation of core group at State level (see Figure 4.21 for organisational chart e-Governance project)
- Formation of SRS team for each department (or whichever department to be taken)
- Formation of district project team, project implementation team

Strategy and programme design (see Box 4.6)

- Strategy for sensitisation for functionaries for good governance and evolving a work culture of 'quality' in office functioning
- Strategy for sensitisation of members of core group, SRS team, district project team, project implementation team about 'quality' issues
- Strategy for evolving work culture for participatory management
- Strategy for creating information society
- Strategy for awareness building for citizens

---

[2] **Delivery system**: The term delivery system refers to agencies or organisations through which development programmes are implemented to ensure availability of inputs and / or services such as delivery of certificates through Tehsil, agriculture inputs, marketing of agricultural produce, health services, primary education, drinking water and so on. In the report various departments like Tehsil, Education, Health, PHED, etc. (see Chapter 2, section 2.2) are referred as Delivery Systems, for their respective service provisioning.

Figure: 4.21: Organisational Chart for e-Governance Project

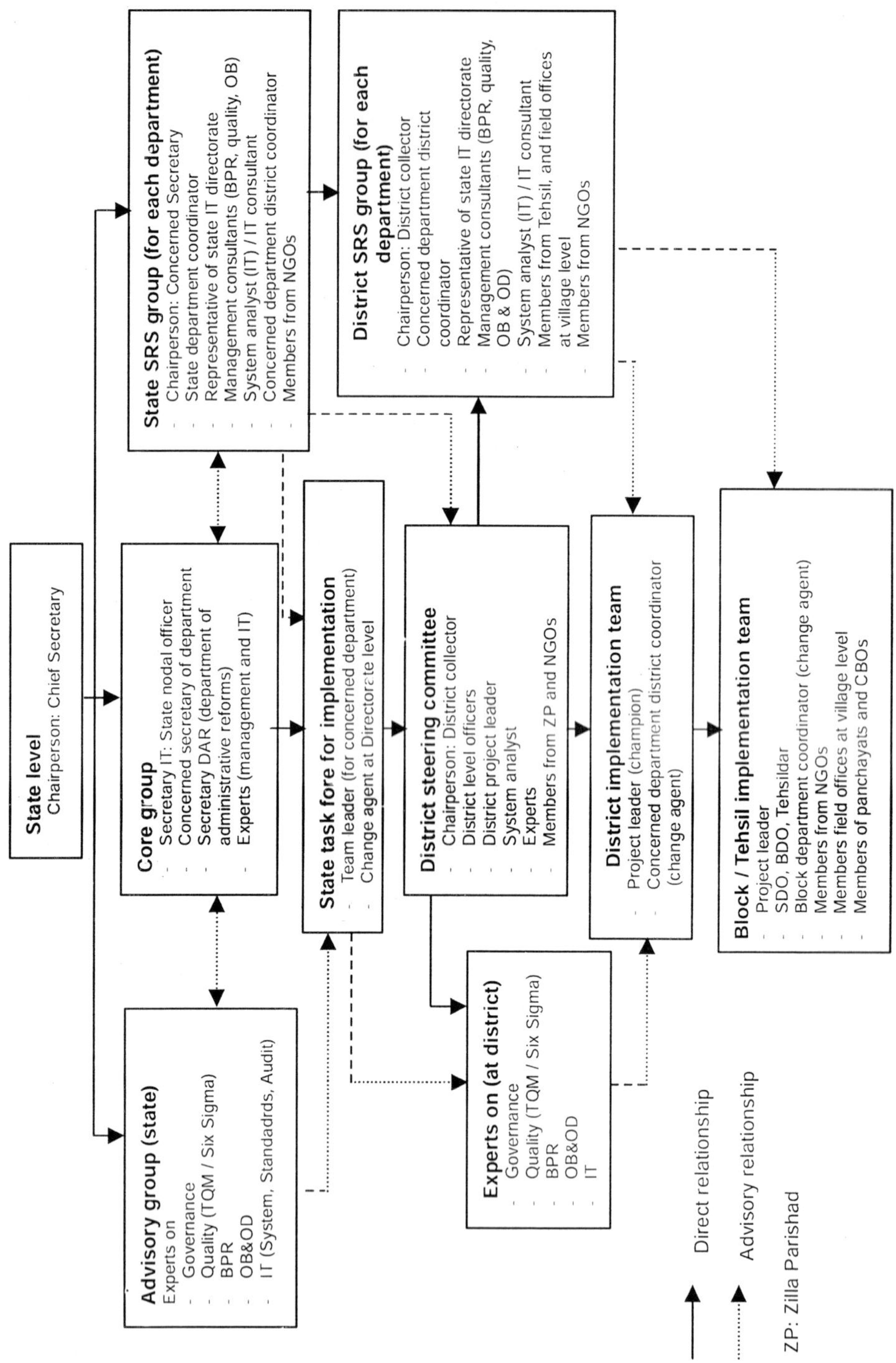

Strategy for implementation

- Quality circles formation for participatory management
- Process approach – learning by doing
- Ownership of system

Box: 4.6
Vital Actions Needed for e-Governance

For creating right apparatus for governance
- Creating information society
- For evolving work culture for 'quality', 'participatory management' and 'citizen-centric management'
- Capacity building of delivery system
- Efficient and reliable network for connectivity
- BPR and backend computerisation

For implementation
- Formation of dedicated district steering committee and project implementation team
- Quality circles formation
- Enhancing capabilities – evolving learning organisation
- Process approach – learning by doing
- Defining ownership of system

4.4.4 Initiating System Requirement Study (SRS): There is a need that each State government should launch an in-depth system requirement study (SRS)[3], before a e-Governance project (in Jaipur) is started. The study should be carried out by a multi-disciplinary team comprising of government officials (in administration and IT), private sector professionals and academics, besides members from NGOs and panchayats. The SRS should be given top priority for successful designing of the project. Among others, for successful study, it should have following important features:

First, keeping in view the nature of service delivery, the study should have study groups at three levels:

- Level I: At district level
- Level II: At block / Tehsil

[3] Though such study has been undertaken earlier by State IT departments, but from the study of report, it appears that it is not comprehensive and covers only a few issues, and vital issues concerning governance and quality of services (see Box 3.3) are not covered. And that too, study is based on observations, rather than a detailed study of issues and analysis using management tools and techniques.

- Level III: Gram panchayat / Patwarghar level (village / Kiosk level)

Second, the study should have following groups at all the three levels

- Group 1: Management (regarding quality and process reengineering) and administration
- Group 2: IT

Third, team formation, as indicated in Table S4.6.

Fourth, the members of the group, before they undertake study, should be imparted training about the following:

- What is 'good governance'
- Quality issues
- Quality tools (BPR, TQM) (only basic knowledge will be adequate)
- Steps in BPR
- Customer (citizen) management
- Participatory techniques (e.g. how quality circles work)
- Government rules and procedures (especially how to access them)
  (Other issues could be added and the methodology for training should be identified as per local requirements)

Fifth, listing of processes of delivery and their mapping, followed by analysis and BPR

- It may require framing specific questions for data collection (see guidelines for BPR, Table S4.1)
- Issues to be covered in the study, as reflected by Table 2.1 and the framework of the study as given in Figure 2.1 (see Chapter 2) (as per local requirements, the specific issues need to be identified).

Sixth, all members should be provided access to the following vital items:

- All information from departments under study

Seventh, participatory approach for FGDs, information gathering, taking suggestions and decision-making (Special care needs to be taken that the views of two important stakeholders viz., citizens and field functionaries at lower level are taken)

4.4.5 System Design Steps: Designing e-Governance project is as much a problem of understanding the concepts of governance as placing required systems in right perspective. Based on the analysis of e-Governance projects and the problems analysed therein, there is a need to provide underpinnings of first efficient delivery system and then effective management systems in order to leverage IT. And, so, for developing a sound system (see Box 4.7 for vital ingredients for designing system for e-Governance), the steps are listed below (see Figure 4.22):

Box: 4.7: Five Vital Ingredients for Designing System for e-Governance

- ***First:*** Quality of services, through e-Kiosk, should be a touchstone of judging good governance. This premise should be at the core of design of e-Governance project.
- ***Second:*** Citizen-centric processes and work culture to be evolved
- ***Third:*** Effective capacity of delivery system to provide services
- ***Fourth:*** Alignment of people (functionaries), processes and system, and technology (IT)
- ***Fifth:*** Change management strategy

Step 1: Understanding concept of good governance
Step 2: Citizen requirement study
Step 3: System requirement study (SRS)
Step 4: Identify BPR requirements
Step 5: Benchmarking services or setting quality standards
Step 6: Identify IT requirements
- Network
- Hardware
- Software
- Backend computerisation

Step 7: Identify requirements for efficient delivery system
- People (functionaries)
- Process
- Infrastructure and logistics
- Work environment and culture

Step 8: Team Building (including quality circles)
Step 9: Pilot testing
Step 10: Planning for implementation
Step 11: Placing IT System Suitably
- Network
- Hardware
- Software
- System Integration (SI)
- Knowledge Management (KM)

Figure: 4.22: Steps in e-Governance System Design and Implementation

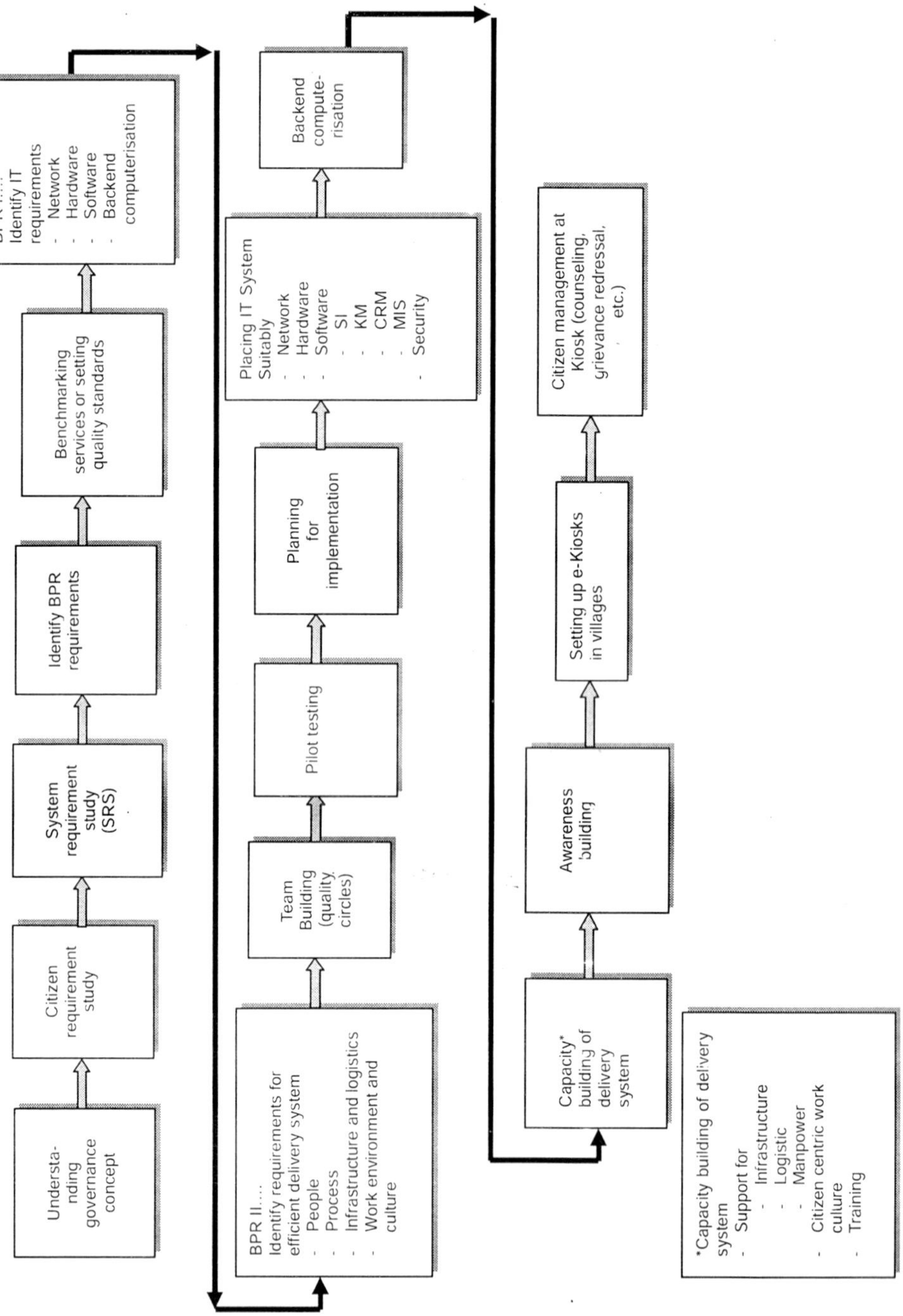

- Citizen Relationship Management (CRM)
- Management Information System (MIS)
- Security

> *"Designing e-Governance project is as much a problem of understanding the concepts of governance as placing required systems in right perspective. Based on the analysis of e-Governance projects and the problems analysed therein, there is a need to provide underpinnings of first efficient delivery system and then effective management systems in order to leverage IT"*

Step 12: Backend computerisation
Step 13: Capacity building of delivery system (infrastructure, logistics and manpower support)
Step 14: Awareness building
Step 15: Setting up e-Kiosks in villages
Step 16: Citizen management at Kiosk (counseling, grievance redressal, etc.)

Checklist that is to be taken into consideration for e-Governance system design is listed in Box 4.8.

Box: 4.8: Checklist for e-Governance System Design

- ***First***, whether citizens requirements have been identified?
- ***Second***, whether the parameters for good governance have been identified?
- ***Third***, whether the quality parameters have been defined and benchmarked for different services?
- ***Fourth***, whether the processes are simplified and synchronised with IT?
- ***Fifth***, whether the backend computerisation has been carried out?
- ***Sixth***, whether the delivery departments have been aligned with the 'service' requirements and have capacity to provide efficient services to citizens?
- ***Seventh***, whether the citizens have been made aware about the services to be provided by the e-Governance system?
- ***Eighth***, whether work culture is tuned to the requirement of 'citizen care management'?
- ***Ninth***, whether there is reliable IT connectivity and electricity?
- ***Tenth***, whether the service provider and e-Kiosks are financially viable?

Suggested Growth Model

The suggested growth model is given by Figure S2.4 it will have following five stages:

Stage I: Interface
Stage II: Transactional
Stage III: Vertical Integration
Stage IV: Horizontal Integration
Stage V: Networking

Based on the recommendation as discussed above, the five stage e-Governance service model is reflected in Table 4.22.

Table: 4.22 Five Stage e-Governance Service Model

	Stage I Interface and cataloguing	**Stage II** Service transaction	**Stage III** Vertical Integration	**Stage IV** Horizontal Integration	**Stage V** Networking
Time period	0-1 year	1-3 years	2-5 years	3-7 years	5-7 years
Focus	**Interface** - Information sharing	**G2C** - Service delivery* - Grievances redressal	**G2E** - Feedback	**G2G** - Integrated service delivery* - Grievances redressal	**G2B** - Participation in decision-making
Key Inputs* for Delivery System (People and process)**	- Training for sensitisation about 'good' governance	- Initiating BPR - Change management - Improving capacity of delivery system**	- BPR - Capacity building - CRM - Change management (work culture improvement)	- Change management for inter-departmental coordination - Integrating services - Capacity building	- Seamless integration - Mechanism for participation by citizens
Performance criteria	- Accuracy (of information)	- Efficiency (time and cost) - Convenience - Reliability	- Reliability - Transparency - Accountability	- Efficiency - Reliability	- Efficiency
IT system	- Web-development - Connectivity - PC at Kiosk level	- Good Network (64kbps to 128kbps) - Backend computerisation	- System integration (ERP) - Knowledge management (KM) - CRM Software	- Good bandwidth (128kbps to 256kbps) - System integration (ERP) - Knowledge management (KM) - CRM Software	- Integrated database - High bandwidth (256kbps)
Benefits	- Building relationship	- Services at village level	- Efficient services	- Efficient decision- making - Integration of services	- Enhanced convenience

* Services are to be identified as per citizen requirement study, ** Capacity building will be an incremental process,
*** Based on system requirement study (SRS)

Note: Information sharing, service delivery, grievance redressal and feedback will be an ongoing and continuous process.

4.4.6 Citizen-centric e-Governance System Design – Process Approach: A citizen-centric government is something much more fundamental than simply a collection of departments providing services to citizens. It involves rethinking the entire service delivery system - across all agencies, and all levels of government - from a citizen perspective. Moreover, user needs typically cut across the organisational structures and hierarchies of government. So a true citizen focus requires a holistic approach, appreciated by all the levels of government.

Citizen-centricity demands a single view of the citizen, within single service architecture, based around web technology. To begin and then sustain, it demands building a credible service delivery points, value addition by large efficiency gains, and continuous improvement, building trust and confidence. Delivering citizen-centric services needs to be seen as an ongoing and incremental process rather than a one-time exercise. There is no better way of understanding what is involved in moving to citizen-centric online delivery, and understanding customer needs, than to process approach. System design should be keeping in view, ***first,*** creating sustainable demand from citizens, and ***second,*** viable revenue model for financial viability of e-Kiosks and service provider

While designing system, in the light of CRS, the following aspects need to be taken into consideration:

- Focus on information and services with maximum impact and visibility
- Awareness and confidence building programme
- Creating demand through
  - making day-to-day required information (by citizens) available at e-Kiosk
  - providing reliable delivery of 'a few services' in the beginning (to win citizens' confidence)
- Services those are cost effective and are likely to give higher revenue should be given priority
- Adding services gradually based on success

Typically, under process approach, service delivery will include the following steps as outlined in Figure 4.23:

- Understanding citizen
  - Citizen requirement study (CRS)
- Identifying key processes
- Defining standards
- Aligning processes to meet desired standards
- Quality management system (QMS) design
- Effective service delivery

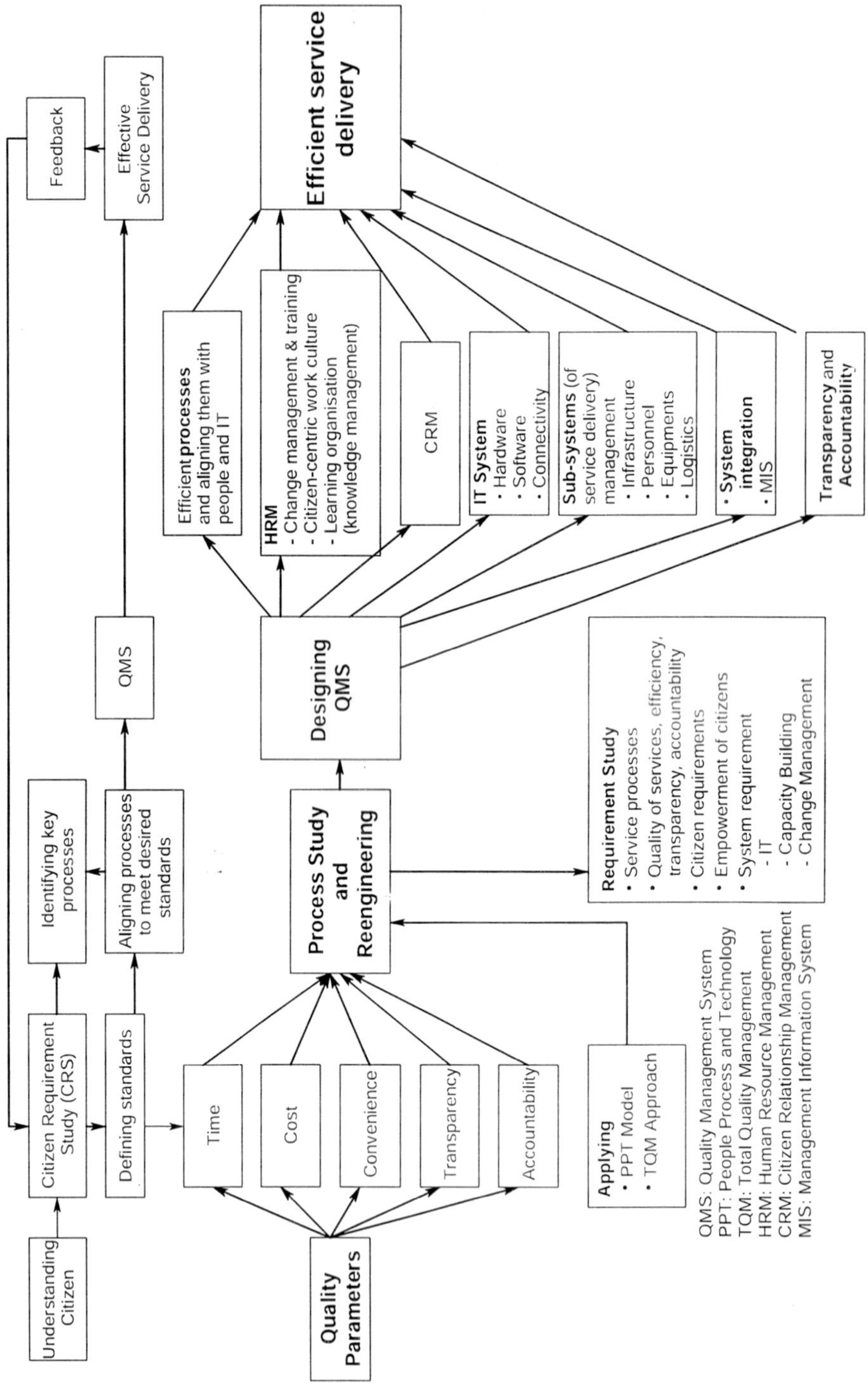

Figure 4.23: Citizen-centric e-Governance System Design (of e-Governance for one Service Department in a District)

Figure: S4.1 Caste Certificate through e-Kiosk (Scenario B)

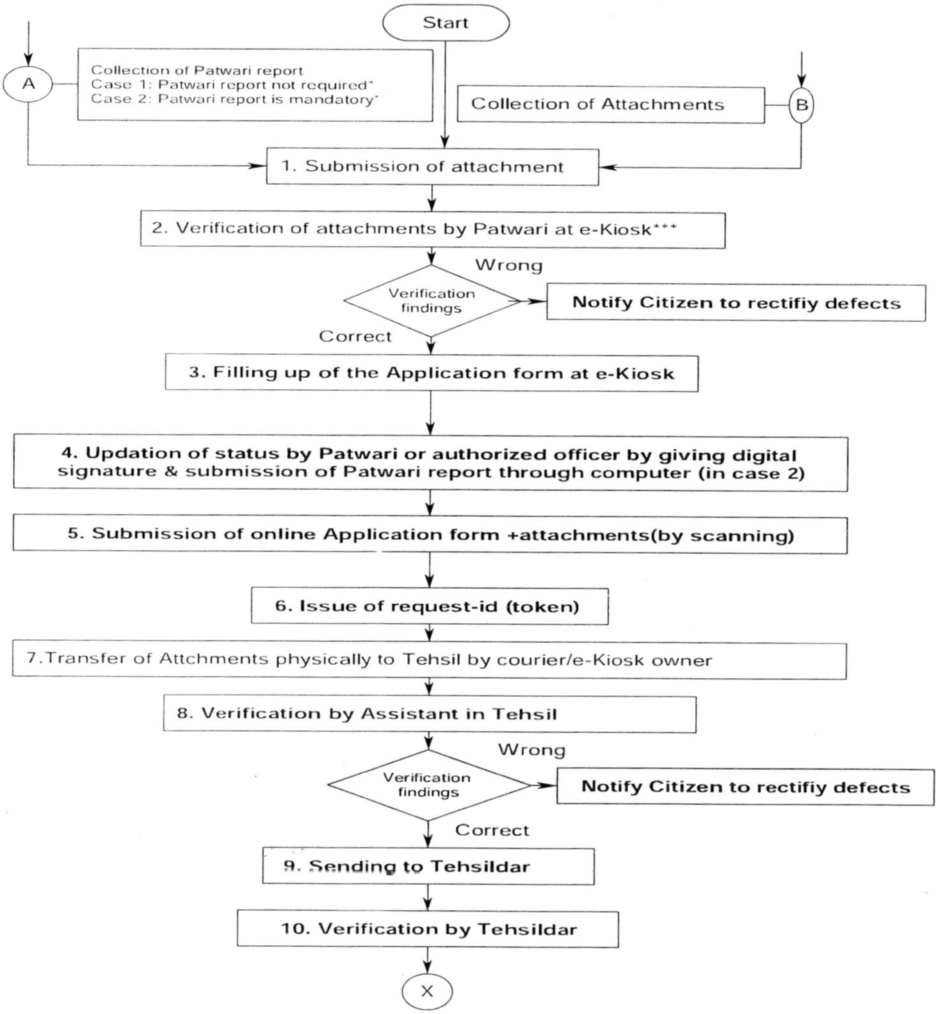

*In case of the following (for caste certificate) (case 1)

- If citizen has his/her earlier caste certificate or of his father

**In case the following (case 2)

- If citizen has come from other village in the recent past
- If citizen is not having domicile certificate / ration card
- If citizen has his/her earlier caste certificate or of his father

*** Either by Patwari or authorised staff of Tehsil

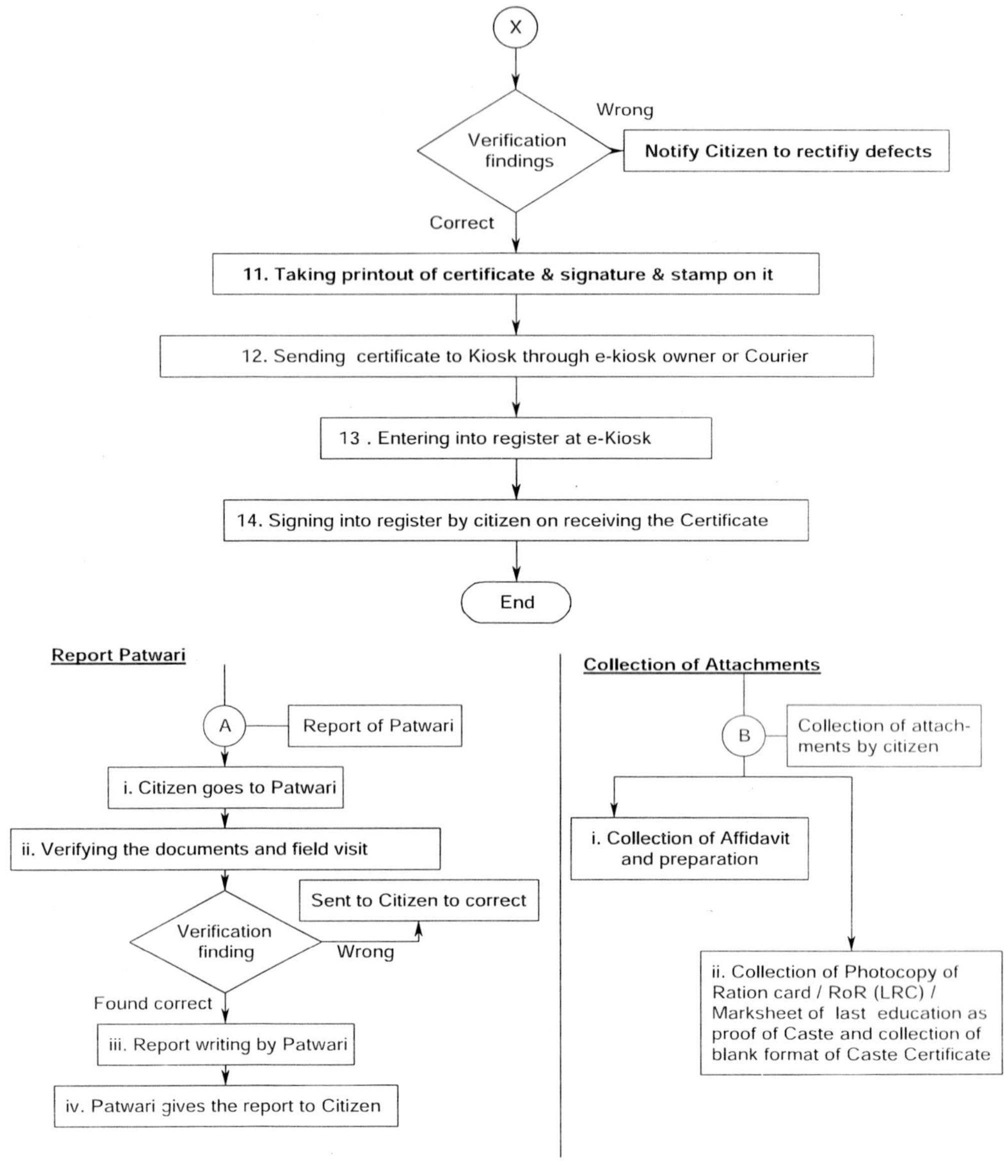

Note: Bold activities are electronic activities

Figure: S4.2 Caste Certificate through e-Kiosk (Scenario C)

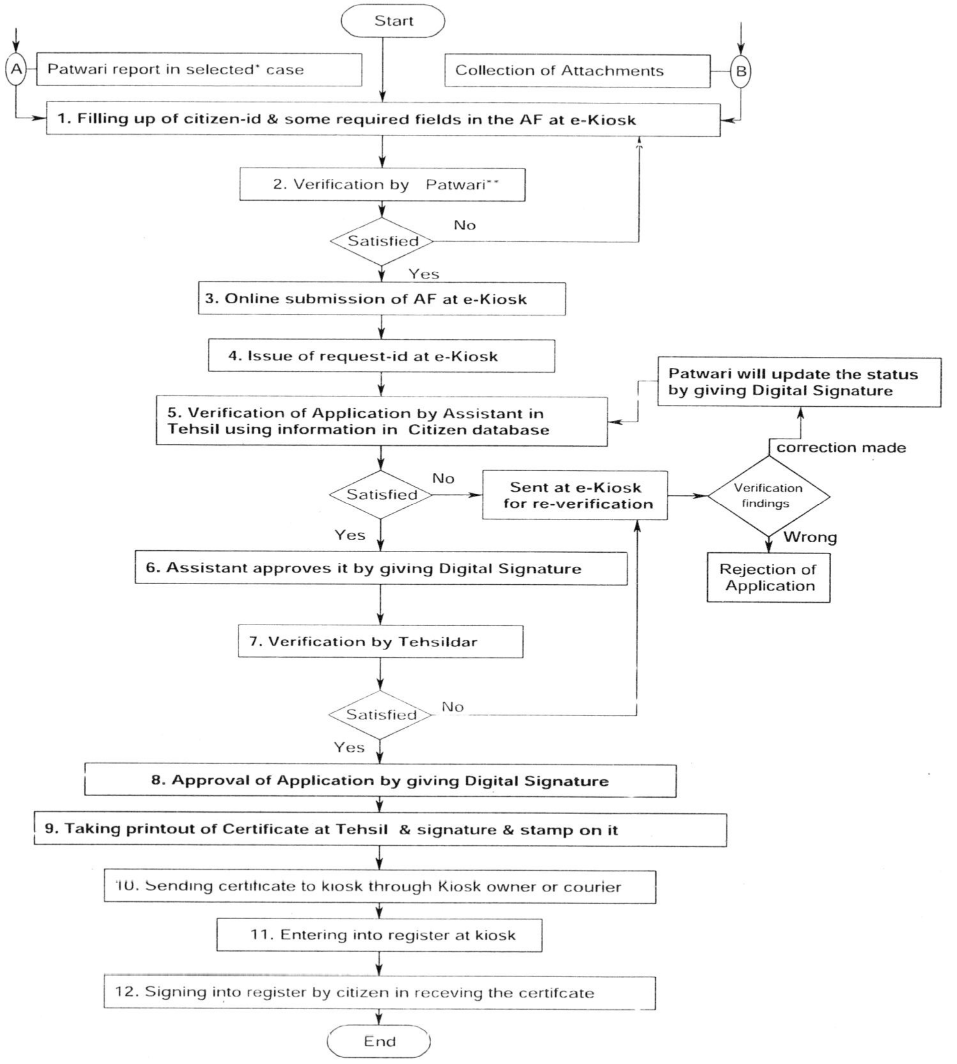

Note: Bold activities are electronic activities

* If citizen has come from other village in the recent past and his name has not been entered in citizen database

** Either by Patwari or authorised staff of Tehsil

Report Patwari (if citizen has come from other village in the recent past and his name has not been entered in citizen database)

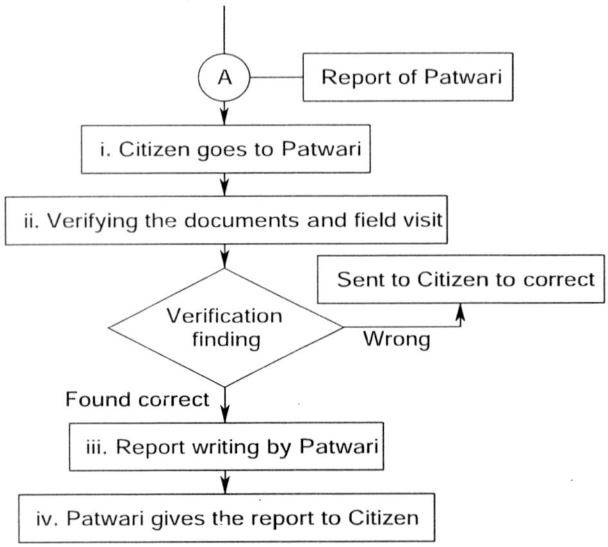

Collection of Attachments (if citizen has come from other village in the recent past and his name has not been entered in citizen database)

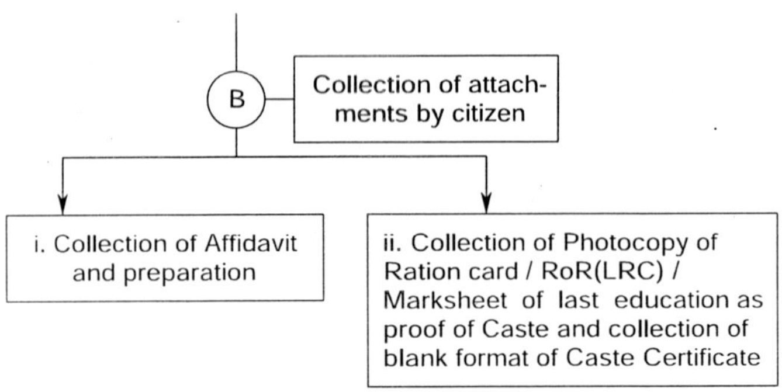

Figure: S4.3 People, Process and Technology Interdependency – Problems, Uncertainties and Constraints therein for Grievance Redressal

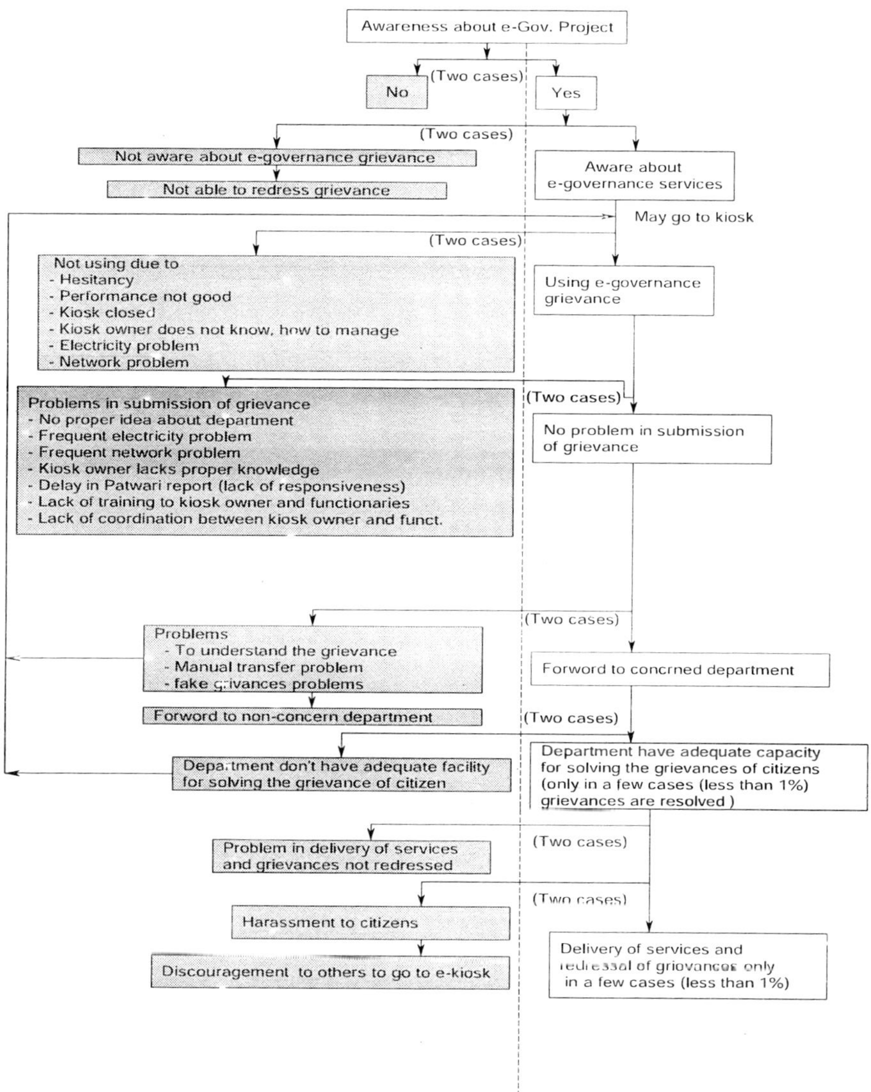

Note: The above shows about the problems, uncertainties and constraints involved in grievance redressal to citizens through e-Kiosk.

Figure: S4.4 Matrix for Intra-relationship among Existing Practices

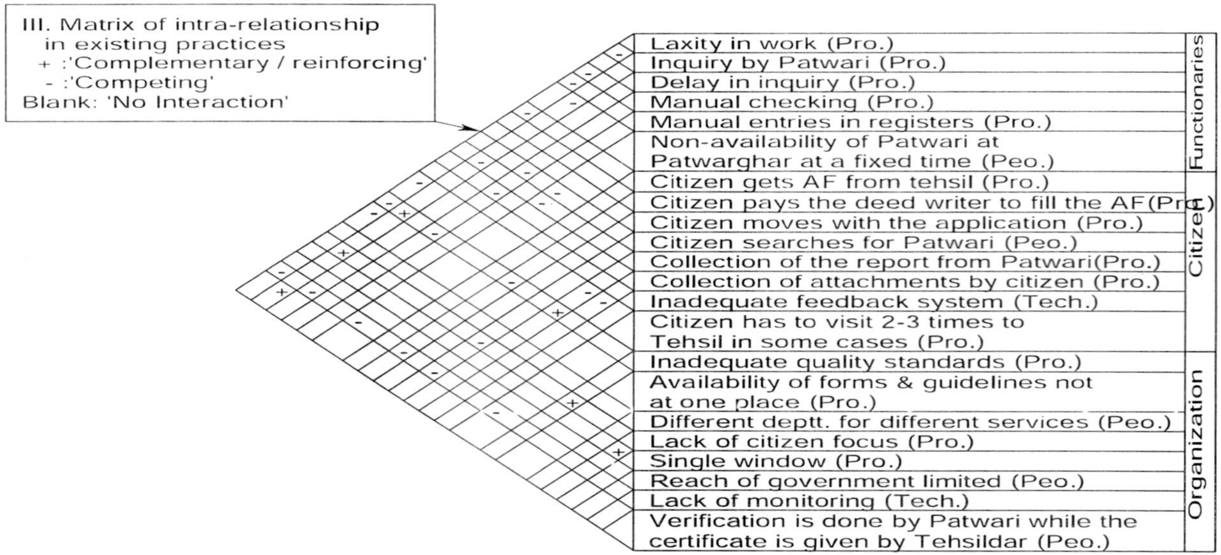

Source : Based on FGDs
Pro. : Process
Peo. : People
Tech. : Technology
AF : Application form
Deptt. : Department

Figure: S4.5 Phases for introducing Suggested Practices

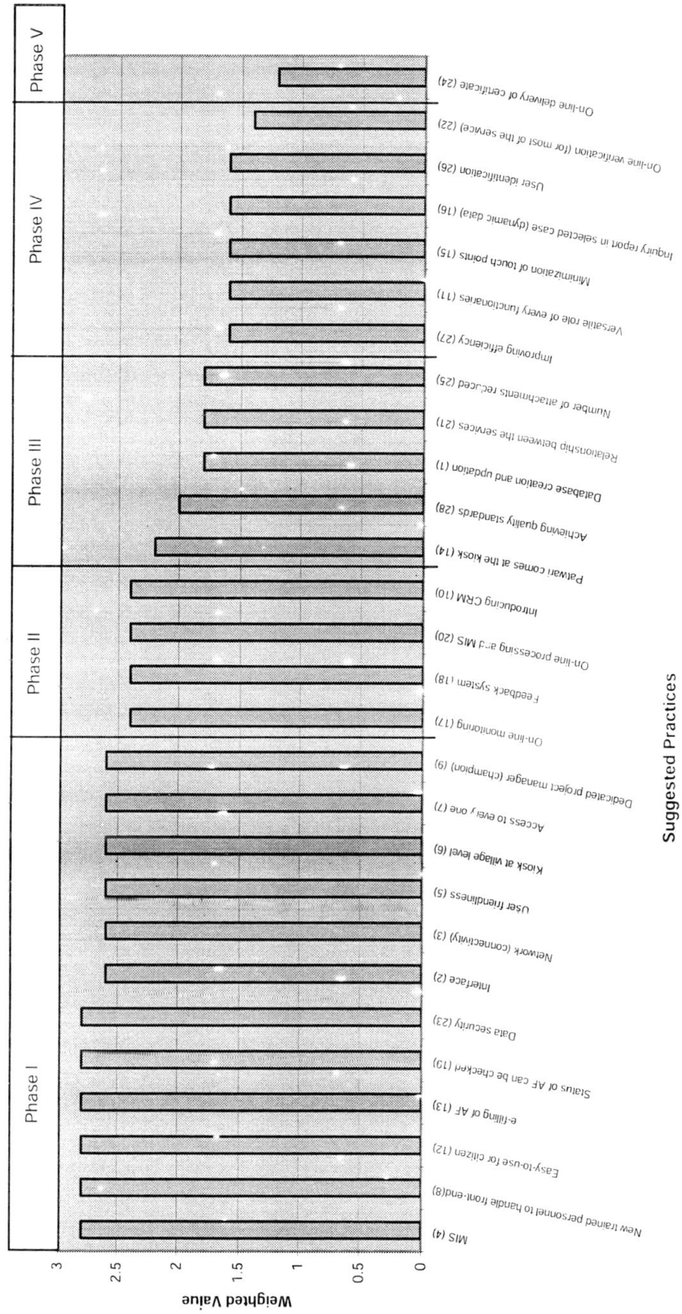

Source: Based on Table 4.9
Note: Figure in parenthesises indicates serial number (S.N.) of suggested practices.

Figure: S4.6 Preferences for Information, Services and Grievances by different Groups

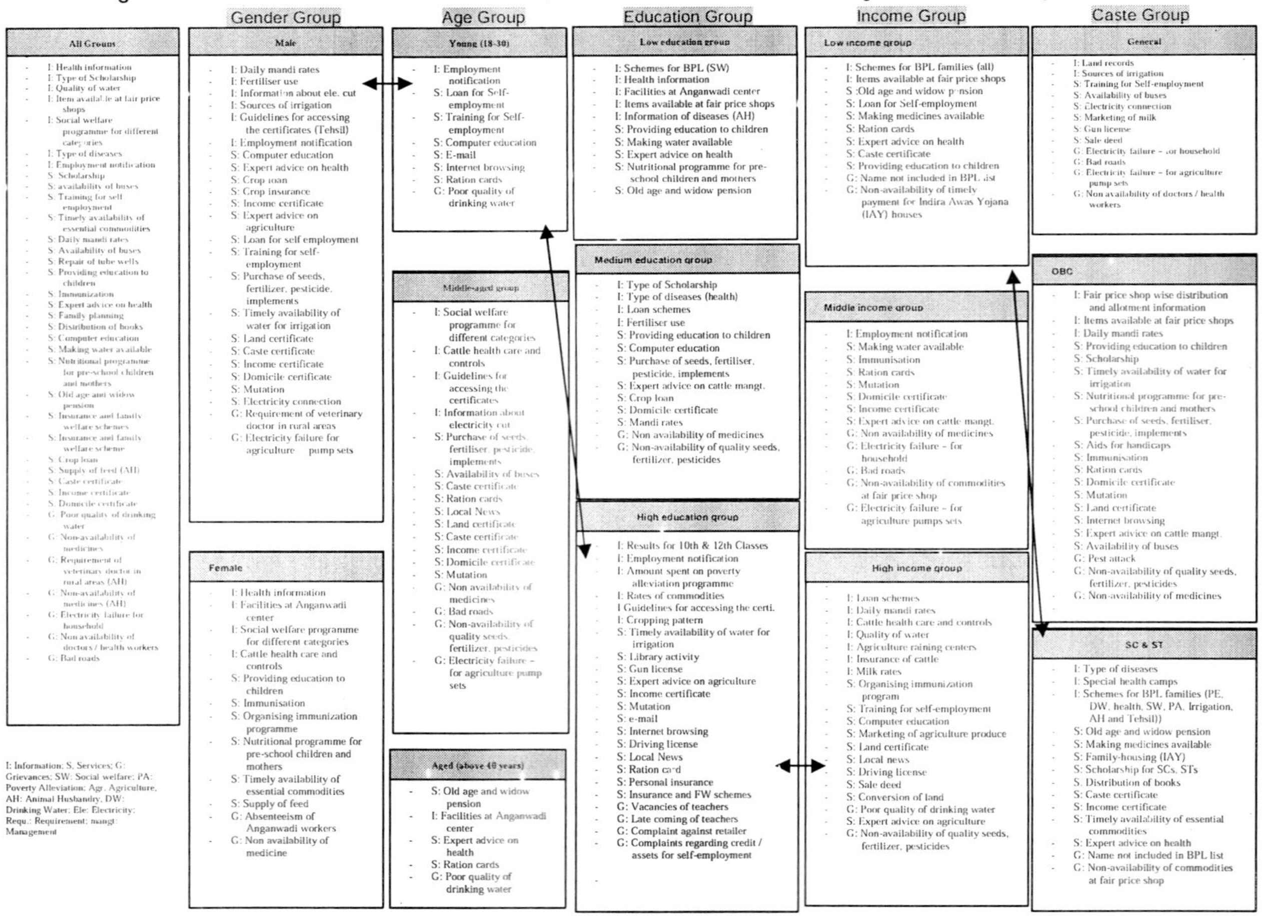

Table S4.1: Process Mapping and BPR Guidelines

S.N.	Major steps	Type	Details	Remarks
1.	Study of process	Basic information of processes	□ Identifying the services □ Identifying the processes involved in providing the services □ Identification of owner of processes □ Stakeholders involved in processes □ Final output of services □ Collection of guidelines for providing services □ Collection of application forms & delivery forms (blank & filled)	□ Interviewing 2-3 functionaries and citizens for quick assessment of services, various process parameters □ Data collection through □ Consultation with functionaries, citizens and other stakeholder □ Field survey □ Focused group discussions (FGDs)
		Identifying the process steps	□ Identifying all the activities from beginning till end of process □ Identifying the measurable process parameters (like time, cost, etc.) □ Identifying the minimum, maximum, average value of these parameters	
		Process mapping	□ Draw each activity of process in a sequence: FD I □ Draw movement of application form among stakeholders in the process: FD II □ Verifying with the functionaries (office staff) and citizens and then finalise FD I and FD II	
		Other information from office	□ Data for 2-3 years for the number of applications for each service □ Prescribed time to availing service as per citizen charter □ Registers maintained for procedure to availing the service □ Prescribed cost for availing services as per citizen charter	

Contd...

S.N.	Major steps	Type	Details	Remarks
		Citizen perspective	□ Work culture 'quick' assessment (interviewing 2-3 citizens) □ Identifying the actual cost incurred by citizens to get the service □ Identifying the actual time incurred by citizens to get the service □ Frequency of availing services □ Existing source of information available to a citizen □ Number of visits made by citizens □ Field survey for detailed assessment about process parameter (functionaries) □ Field survey for detail assessment about process parameter (interviewing 30-50 citizens)	
2.	Analysis		□ FMEA □ Pareto analysis □ Identifying CTQs i. Identifying decision-making points ii. Identifying the number of activities involved in the process iii. Identifying the touch points for citizens and application form iv. Identifying the number of visits made by citizens in availing the service v. Identifying activities taking minimum time vi. Identifying 'non-value' adding activities vii. Time for availing services viii. Cost for availing services ix. Behaviour of functionaries	-

Contd...

S.N.	Major steps	Type	Details	Remarks
			x. Responsiveness of functionaries xi. Transparency xii. Accessibility □ Fishbone diagram □ CE analysis □ Process (Throughput) efficiency □ Problems faced by functionaries (office staff) □ Constraints in the delivery system	
3.	Process redesigning	Principles for process reengineering	□ How to reduce total cycle time □ How to reduce cost to citizens □ How to reduce touch points □ How to improve responsiveness □ How to bring transparency (MIS) □ How to bring accountability (MIS) □ How to improve citizen satisfaction	-
		AF & DF design	□ AF redesign □ DF redesign	□ Based on the extent of computerization of process for delivery of service
		Database design	□ Concept of integrated database and citizen-id.	□ Identifying the data flow in the new process □ Identifying entities involved in new process
		Database creation	□ Creating the database and database table □ Drawing relationship-entity diagram.	□ Identifying data tables required in database □ Identifying data fields □ Identifying the relation among different entities involved in new process.
		Security	□ Digital signature □ Biometrics	□ Identifying security concerns

AF: Application form, DF: Delivery form, MIS: Management Information System FEMA: Failure modes and effect analysis, CTQs: Critical to quality characteristics, CE: Cause and effect, FD: Flow diagram, FGDs: Focused group discussions.

Table: S4.2: User Profile of Stakeholders in the Proposed System

S. N	User	Functions	Database tables to be accessed	Type of access
1.	Kiosk owner	- Fills up the application online	Citizen_record	Query
		- Submits the application	Service_request	Insert
			Related_certificate_request_record	Insert
		- Checks the status of any application	Service_request	Query
		- Prints the application when approved	-	-
		- Collects money from citizen	-	-
		- Sends the carbon copy of the certificate to Tehsil	-	-
2.	Patwari	- Checks for pending applications	Service_request	Query
		- Queries various databases to get relevant information	Citizen_record	Query
			Education_record	Query
			Asset_record	Query
			Ration_card	Query
			Land_record	Query
		- Approves / disapproves the application based on the information collected	-	-
		- Adds remarks if required	Service_request	Update
			Related_certificate_request_record	Update
3.	Assistant in Tehsil	- Checks for pending applications	Service_request	Query
		- Queries various databases to get relevant information	Citizen_record	Query
			Education_record	Query
			Asset_record	Query
			Ration_card	Query
			Land_record	Query
		- Approves / disapproves the application based on the information collected	Service_request	Update
		- Adds remarks if required	Service_request Update	
			Related_certificate_request_record	Update
4.	Tehsildar	- Checks for pending applications	Service_request	Query
		- Looks for the approval of Patwari and Assistant in Tehsil	Service_request	Query
		- Final approval / disapproval of application	Service_request	Update, delete
5.	SDO	- Checks for pending applications	Service_request	Query
		- Looks for the approval of Patwari and Assistant in Tehsil	Service_request	Query
		- Final approval / disapproval of application	Service_request	Update, delete

Access: Query, Update, Insert, Delete

Table: S4.3: Cost for Development of Citizen Database

S.N.	Item	Rate	Population	Time consumption (man-days)	Per days salary (Aprox.) (in Rs)	Wages expenditure (total salary) (in Rs)	Total TA/DA @Rs.175 (in Rs)	Others expenditure (Stationeries etc.) (in Rs.)	Total expenditure (in Rs)	(Total expenditure – salary)
1	Survey	112 record / day / team$ (4 families/ hour/team$)	175000	{(175000/112) *2} = 3125	318#	3125*318 = 993750	3125*175 = 546875	175000*1=175000	1715625	721875
2	Verifying data	200 records /day / team$	175000	(175000/200)* 2 = 1750	318#	1750*318 = 556500	1750*175 =306250	175000*0.05 =8750	871500	315000
3	Taking the grievances from citizen	-	15% of 175000	(57*2)* 2 = 228	318#	228*318 = 72504	228*175 =39900	175000*0.05 =8750	121154	48650
4	Data feeding	10 p / entry	175000	-	-	-		525000	525000	525000
5	Quality check	500 records / day	175000	175000/500 = 350	318#	350*318 = 111300	350*175 =61250	-	172550	61250
6	Total	-	-	-	-	-	-	-	3405829	1671775

Source: based on FGDs and own analysis

$Two members in a team

Average salary of Govt employee (clerk) is Rs. 7000 and 22 days average working days in a month)

Preparation (data feeding cost)

One citizen cost = 30 (fields/ record) x 0.1(10 Paisa / entry) = Rs 3

One Tehsil cost =175000(population of Chaksu) x 3 (Rs) = Rs 525000

Table: S4.4: Myths about the Functionaries and Citizens

S. N	Myth	Status based on study*	Reasons for poor state of functioning (which gives rise to myths)	Remarks (Strategy required for improvement)
1.	Functionaries do not want to deliver services	☐ Functionaries are interested to deliver work/ service	☐ Functionaries do not get enough support system and resources to carry out their job ☐ Lack of enough knowledge and skills with functionaries ☐ Working conditions of functionaries are poor	☐ A diagnostic study by experts for understanding the field problems ☐ Improving support system and working conditions of functionaries
2.	Functionaries can not deliver services in the right way	☐ Functionaries are interested to learn new skills to perform better	☐ It is mainly due to lack of enough knowledge and skills with functionaries ☐ Functionaries do not get enough support system and resources to carry out their job ☐ Long process and obsolete rules, which delay the work	☐ A well-organised capacity building programme for the functionaries ☐ Developing professional culture in the functionaries
3.	Functionaries are not interested in e-Governance	☐ Functionaries keen about e-Governance	☐ Functionaries do not get enough opportunity to express themselves ☐ Wide gap between opinion-makers and thinking of functionaries ☐ High failure of e-Governance projects	☐ A diagnostic study by experts for understanding the field problems and the views of functionaries

Contd...

S. N	Myth	Status based on study*	Reasons for poor state of functioning (which gives rise to myths)	Remarks (Strategy required for improvement)
4.	Government departments can not deliver	☐ Lack of efforts and resources by government to develop sound delivery system ☐ Unhealthy work culture	☐ Poor state of delivery system** makes it difficult / impossible to deliver (see Tables S3.33 & S3.34 for details)	☐ Improving capacity of delivery system ☐ Developing professional culture in the functionaries
5.	Citizens will not like to use e-Kiosk, as they are unfamiliar with IT	☐ Citizens are very keen to use e-Governance services	☐ Presently citizens do not find the e-Governance initiatives of direct relevance and there is little qualitative improvement in service delivery	☐ A diagnostic study for understanding the social, political and cultural issues, and effective system design and implementation of e-Governance projects

* Field survey and FGDs

** Poor infrastructure, manpower and logistics support (as brought out by field study)

Table: S4.5: Strategy to Attract Citizens of Different Categories for Usage of e-Governance Services

S. N	Categories	Groups	Immediate strategy	Short term strategy	Long term strategy
1.		All Groups	□ Awareness building □ Highlight the services of immediate usage like health information, information about electricity cut, availability of forms, weather forecast, employment notification, etc.	□ Highlight the services which are likely to give higher revenue and preferred by male, high-income and higher-educated people (who can afford)*, where chances of success are high □ Awareness building with a special focus on women and marginalised group □ Highlight the services liked by all groups (see Figure: S4.6) □ Focus on: Jamabandi (LRC), guidelines for accessing certificates, mandi bhav, phone numbers of all departments, quality of water, timely availability of essential commodities, non-availability of medicines, etc. □ Involvement of local representatives □ Discounts on special occasions □ Involvement of NGOs	□ Involvement of local representatives □ Involvement of NGOs □ Good quality of services □ Good citizen management □ Reliable services □ Reliable network □ Create information society
2.	Gender	Male	□ Focus on certificates and licenses	□ Highlight the services liked by male (see Figure: S4.6) □ Focus on: crop loan, crop insurance, mandi rate, milk rates, certificates (caste, income, domicile and land), etc.	-

Contd...

S. N	Categories	Groups	Immediate strategy	Short term strategy	Long term strategy
		Female	□ Discount in select services □ Implement ladies first rule	□ Awareness building □ Discount in select services □ Implement ladies first rule □ Making them aware about their rights under various Acts. □ Making them aware about various benefits entitled to them (under government schemes) □ Highlight the services liked by female (see Figure: S4.6) □ Focus on: facilities at Anganwadi centers, immunization, health information, guidelines for schemes for all departments, non-availability of medicines, etc.	□ Empowerment: improving education and awareness
3.	Age	Young	□ Providing services like internet, e-mail, computer education	□ Highlight the services liked by young (see Figure: S4.6) □ Focus on: computer education, e-mail, internet, etc.	-
		Middle-aged group	-	□ Highlight the services liked by middle-aged (see Figure: S4.6) □ Focus on: certificates of Tehsil (caste, income, domicile and land) purchase of seeds, local news, etc.	-
		Aged (above 40 years)	-	□ Highlight the services liked by aged (see Figure: S4.6) □ Focus on: old age and widow pension, etc.	-
4.	Education	Low education group	-	□ Highlight the services liked by low education group (see Figure: S4.6) □ Focus on: health, social welfare, PDS, poverty alleviation, etc. □ Making them aware about various benefits entitled to them (under government schemes)	□ Empowerment: improving education and awareness

*The purpose of this strategy is to start those services, which are going to be most successful and likely to be used. After initial success, other services are to be added and citizens of other groups (women and marginalised) should be encouraged

Contd...

S. N	Categories	Groups	Immediate strategy	Short term strategy	Long term strategy
		Medium education group	-	□ Highlight the services liked by middle-educated (see Figure: S4.6) □ Focus on: purchase of seeds, crop loan, fertilizers use	□ Empowerment: improving education and awareness
		High education group	□ Providing services like internet, e-mail, computer education	□ Involve them in socio? economic development of nation □ Highlight the services liked by high educated (see Figure: S4.6) □ Focus on: e-mail, local / national news, internet browsing, etc.	-
5.	Income	Low income group	-	□ Making the aware about their rights under various Acts. □ Making them aware about various benefits entitled to them (under government schemes) □ Highlight the services liked by low income group (see Figure: S4.6) □ Focus on: health, social welfare, PDS, poverty alleviation, etc.	□ Empowerment: improving education and awareness
		Middle income group	-	□ Highlight the services liked by middle income group (see Figure: S4.6) □ Focus on: mutation, ration cards, domicile, income certificate, etc.	-
		High income group	□ Providing services like internet, e-mail, computer education	□ Highlight the services liked by high income group (see Figure: S4.6) □ Focus on: mandi rates, training for self-employments, etc.	-
6.	Caste	General	-	□ Highlight the services liked by general caste (see Figure: S4.6) □ Focus on: land records, sources of irrigation, etc.	-

Contd...

S. N	Categories	Groups	Immediate strategy	Short term strategy	Long term strategy
		OBC	-	• Highlight the services liked by OBC (see Figure: S4.6) • Focus on: health, social welfare, PDS, poverty alleviation, etc.	-
		SC&ST	• Information about poverty alleviation programmes	• Information about poverty alleviation • Making them aware about their rights under various Acts. • Making them aware about various benefits entitled to them (under government schemes) • Highlight the services liked by SC & ST (see Figure: S4.6) • Focus on: health, social welfare, PDS, poverty alleviation, etc.	• Empowerment: improving education and awareness

Note: Though any provisioning for providing information or services can be utilised by any group, but in order to encourage a particular group (e.g. female or SC & ST) a special focus has to be given on a certain information / services / grievances.

Table: S4.6: Framework for System Requirement Study (SRS) at District Level

S. N	Levels	Team members	Training for		Job and responsibility
		SRS team leader	General items	Specialised	
1.	*Level I*: At district level	□ District collector □ Project champion (ieader) □ SDO □ IT specialists □ Academics □ Concerned district department coordinator	□ What is 'Good Governance' □ Quality issues □ Quality tools (BPR, TQM) (Only basic knowledge will be adequate) □ Customer (citizen) satisfaction □ Participatory techniques (e.g. how quality circle works) □ Government rules and procedures	□ Management □ Techniques for analysis (FMEA, Fishbone diagram, SWOT) □ Detailed inputs on quality, BPR, and TQM	□ Design of the study □ Supervision and consultations □ Analysis □ (All above in consultations with □ members of other teams at □ levels II and III) □ Assisting the members of other teams at levels II and III in data collection on a regular basis (besides collecting some sample data on their own)
2.	*Level II*: At block / Tehsil	□ SDO □ Tehsildar □ IT programmer □ Network specialist	-do-	-	□ Member of SRS team for study and analysis

Contd...

	Levels	Team members	Training for		Job and responsibility
		SRS team leader	General items	Specialised	
3.	*Level III*: Gram panchayat / Patwarghar	☐ Tehsildar ☐ Patwari and 1-2 other field functionaries ☐ IT programmer ☐ Members from NGOs ☐ Members of panchayats and CBOs ☐ 2-3 citizens (who can express well about their problems)	-do-	-	☐ Member of SRS team for study and analysis

5

Lessons Learnt and Way Ahead

"For the e-Governance initiatives to be successful, it requires coherent integration of IT and delivery institutions (people and processes) – the scale of success is immense."

5.1 Salient Concerns

The analysis presented in the preceding sections categorically brings out the problems besetting the e-Governance projects. The problems have been at every level – conceptual, designing the system and management of implementation. The specific areas where projects have not been effective are:

- In appreciating the concept of 'governance' and 'quality' parameters in service delivery
- In developing IT compatible processes – for efficient delivery of services
- In backend computerisation
- In awareness building
- In improving information sharing and ensuring citizens' participation in the decision-making process
- In improving the capacity of delivery system – the capacity of delivery mechanism in terms of manpower, infrastructure, logistics and work culture has not improved to improve its capacity to deliver effectively
- In making service provider, e-Kiosks and departments accountable to people – mechanism for 'quality audit' is not placed. [System ownership is lacking. (Many stakeholders are involved in e-Governance projects, but there is no accountability at the point of delivery of services. It leads to shifting of responsibility from one to another.)]

5.1.1 Behavioural Dimension: In the case of e-Governance, which requires a shift from a traditional way of working to a new mode of working with technology (IT) and new processes, the behavioural issues like leadership, work culture, attitudes, motivation, commitment and teamwork play vital role in building capabilities and effective delivery system in order to manage technological change better and in giving desired shape to the delivery of services. And unless right measures are initiated for bringing new set of ethos for evolving right kind of leadership (which should be participatory), teamwork, citizen-centric work culture and having motivated and empowered functionaries, the technology (IT) would make little impact, and achieving the goals of good governance would be a distant possibility.

Based on system study, the critical findings about the e-Governance are grouped in Box 5.1 and key areas of concern are reflected in Box 5.2.

Box 5.1: Critical Findings: Performance-based

- Poor quality of service delivery
- Citizen dissatisfaction
- Number of e-Governance services availed by citizens came down drastically in one year (from 02-03 to 03-04) in the project.
- Less than 2% of Tehsil services were accessed in a year (02-03)
- Less than 1% of families have accessed e-Governance services (02-03)
- The revenue earned by most of the e-Kiosks is much less than breakeven point (BEP), thus Kiosks are financially unviable
- Projects are at Interface and Transactional stages (as per growth model) and have to go a long way before start meeting citizens' needs substantially
- E-governance Kiosks turning into business centres

Note: Based on study of e-Governance project (in Jaipur) in particular and Gyandoot, Janmitra, OLTP and RDS projects in general

Box 5.2: Key Areas of Concern

Delivery system–based

Delivery System

- Lack of infrastructure, manpower and logistics support
- Poor capabilities of functionaries
- Lack of coordination
- Capacity of delivery system not improved to deliver services efficiently

Process

- Processes not simplified
- No business process reengineering (BPR)
- No backend computerisation

People

- Work culture not citizen-centric
- Lack of team work
- Lack of motivation

Management

- Lack of initiatives for citizen relationship management (CRM), knowledge management, system integration (ERP) and change management

IT system–based

- High down time of network (more than 60%)
- Low bandwidth

Performance–based

- 'Quality standards' not followed for delivery of services

5.2 Way Ahead

For the last one decade, several e-Governance projects are being implemented in all the States in the country. The available studies indicate that they have not met with the desired success due to host of constraints. In spite of problems, the potential of such projects cannot be under estimated, if necessary corrective measures are taken and requisite support is provided.

In order to augment efforts under e-Governance, both States and Central governments are making concerted efforts. The Government of India has planned a national level initiative – National e-Governance Plan (NeGP) (http://www.mit.gov.in) for increased transparency, efficiency and effectiveness for delivery of services.

5.2.1 Future Strategy: Though IT is providing important inputs in the area of governance, much more needs to be done in the areas of improving government processes, enhancing capacity of delivery system and IT network. There is a need for synchronising the processes and organisational capacity with the efficacy of information technology (IT) to generate synergy in the system and to realise full potential of IT.

The government processes need to be redesigned and be IT compatible alongside technology implementation, otherwise the result will be working with inefficient processes. They need simplification, standardisation and to be user-friendly, before they can be adopted and adapted by people. Institutional capacity needs to be improved. The work culture needs to be changed from a traditional department-centric thinking to a citizen-centric and user-friendly approach. The portals should be designed around citizen needs. Development of database of information having locally relevant content and application is required. Among others, it should have programme-based information; resource-profile of district, blocks and gram panchayats; and user-friendly interactive interface.

As discussed in Chapter 2, the study has focused on PPT model for aligning process, people and technology for harmonious relationship. In designing e-Governance system, information technology (IT) and delivery system [processes and other systems, and people (functionaries)] must be aligned to the needs of the customers (citizens). The entire exercise of system design is iterative. While considering people or technology, or the processes, one needs to revisit each other, with the changing requirements of process or people or technological opportunities or constraints, necessary corrections are to be made. The processes of the organisation (system) need to be identified and designed. The desired level of skill, knowledge, attitude and motivation of the people needs to be identified to operate processes. Technology, in the context of e-Governance, which would include network, hardware and software, needs to be correctly chosen. This alignment is crucial in order to leverage IT effectively and to have high performance for achieving the objective of good governance. The Box 5.3 presents the linkage between right system and good governance.

Box: 5.3 Links Between Systems and Good Governance

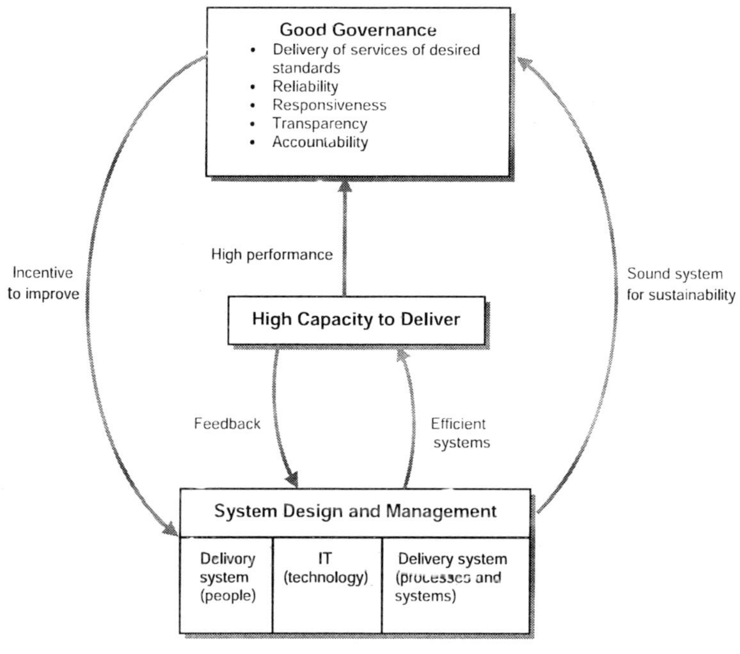

Note: Delivery system comprises of people (functionaries), processes and other sub-systems like infrastructure, logistics, manpower, legal aspect and so on.

5.2.2 Opportunities for Future: The ICTs have ushered in enormous possibilities that can have a fundamental impact on human society. There has not been any other technology in the history of mankind that has touched so many lives in such a short period of time. India has made great strides in the area of Information Technology (IT) in the last decade. Benefits of IT have been felt in all spheres of socio-economic life in the country. Notwithstanding existing problems besetting the e-Governance, it has a big role to play in providing good governance. For future, the e-Governance offers the following opportunities for people and local institutions:

- **Information sharing:** E-kiosk can become an information and knowledge storehouse for database on resources and development programmes, technology, weather conditions, inputs for production, marketing, finance, education and so on. If people-friendly environment is created, people at the village level can benefit immensely from such information and knowledge.

- **Bridging rural-urban divide:** There is consensus emerging that information and communication technologies (ICTs) are central to the creation of the emerging global knowledge-based economy and can play an important role in accelerating growth, in promoting sustainable development, facilitating eradication of poverty in developing countries as well as in their effective integration into the global economy. Likewise, within the country economy, IT can facilitate mainstreaming the backward regions and bridging rural-urban divide.
- **Services at village level:** With the emergence of ICTs, it is possible to locate service centres closer to the citizens (clients). Such centres may consist of a Kiosk in the government office, or a service Kiosk located close to the citizens, or the use of a personal computer in the home or office. With the setting up of Kiosks at the village level, citizens can utilise them as 'One Stop Shop' for availing basic services at the village level.
- **Efficient delivery of services:** With the improvement in processes, the delivery of services can be expedited.
- **Grievance redressal and feedback:** Nearness of e-Kiosk with people provides an opportunity to send grievances to concerned departments and making them more responsive. Prompt feedback mechanism will facilitate, better appreciation of the problems of people and the timely attendance of their basic needs. For example, to name a few, the attendance of children in the school can be increased, the absenteeism of teachers can be checked, health services like immunisation can be provided in time and the availability of essential commodities can be managed better.
- **Community mobilisation and people's participation:** E-kiosk can be a forum for people to express their problems and needs. It can be a forum for educating people about various development programmes, and eliciting valuable views on the problems arising out of the implementation of programmes. The feedback can be suitably used for mid-course correction wherever necessary. Thus, in achieving the millennium development goals (MDGs), e-Kiosks can play a vital role.
- **Generating synergy through convergence of programmes:** If organised meticulously through databases and GIS, e-Kiosks can help panchayats in better coordination with departments and other panchayats regarding the

funds and implementation of various programmes in order to bring synergy at the village level and improving the reach of delivery mechanism.

- **Transparency and accountability of local institutions:** With proper interface with departments, e-Kiosk can become a platform for exchange of views (among citizens, panchayats and departments) on development matters as also a ready and effective forum of accountability. This would add strength to the grassroots governance.

5.2.3 Prerequisites: For leveraging IT effectively and achieving the objectives of good governance, based on field study, the following pre-requisites are suggested in order to align delivery system (people, processes, and other systems), IT (technology) and quality standards (see Figure 5.1):

***First,* putting governance first:** Positioning right standards of good governance is the most important matter. Among others, fundamentally it would entail three vital ingredients: *first,* putting citizens first (through empowerment) – information sharing and participation in decision-making process by citizens; *second,* making 'quality' services available to citizens; and, *third,* responsive citizen management.

***Second,* IT compatible processes:** It would require BPR for re-designing processes and making them IT compatible, so that the processes are user-friendly, simple, standard and efficient. Thus, enabling the citizens to get services efficiently.

***Third,* good IT infrastructure:** It should include:

- Reliable and high bandwidth network: For quick and reliable transmission of application form and information, and for verifying status.
- Backend computerisation: Preparing integrated database is essential so as to take decisions fast and on-line.
- Security system: To ensure that the data is fully secured and recovered in the event of any breakdown, which will provide confidence to users (citizens) as well as service provider

***Fourth,* quality standards (efficient delivery system):** It is vital for making e-Governance an attractive proposition to citizens, as unless the services are made available to citizens with expected quality standards, citizens would not use e-services.

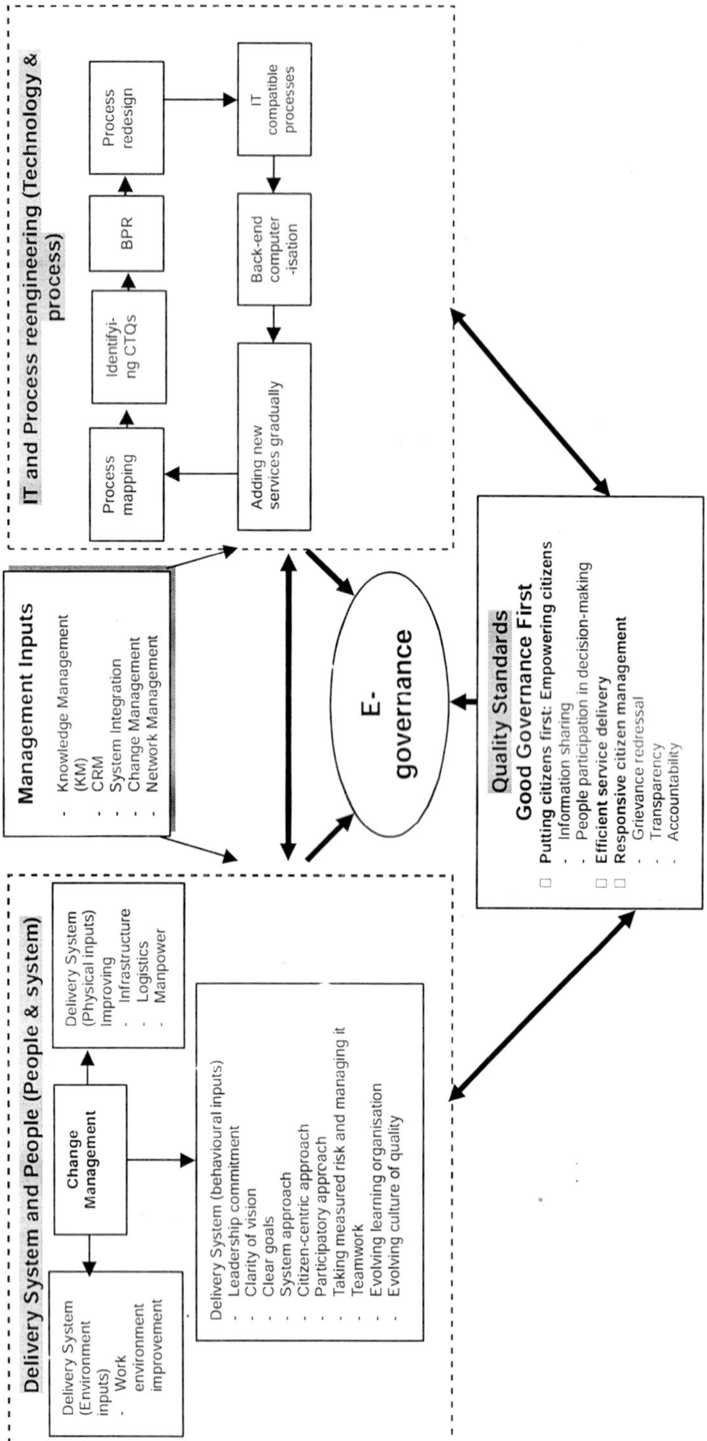

Figure: 5.1: Interventions for e-Governance (System Approach)

Fifth, **sufficient number of services:** It is important that the citizens be provided with all the basic services through e-Kiosk in the form of a package, in order to retain their interest in the system; and also to provide enough revenue to e-Kiosk to recover the expenses.

Sixth, **Management systems:** Required for knowledge management, citizen relationship management (CRM), system integration (ERP), change management, and network management

Seventh, **transparency and accountability:** It is essential for maintaining public confidence in governance, justifying and ensuring the overall legitimacy of the e-Governance system.

5.2.4 Challenges: The e-Governance projects, as evident from field study, are beset with numerous problems. Though the States in the country are taking several initiatives, yet much more needs to be done before good governance can be achieved through these projects. Although the challenges are many, yet the following, as analysed from the study, stand out as having considerable early priority:

- **Bringing a Culture of Quality and Citizen-centric Functioning:** Good governance call for evolving sound value system that promotes values like 'quality', 'citizen-centric' approach (valuing 'responsiveness', 'good behaviour' 'participatory and transparent decision-making', 'accountability to people'). It will require bringing changes at all levels in attitudes and beliefs that are deep-rooted in past cultural values. It will also require making shift in overall design and strategy as shown in Figure 5.2.
- **BPR and Backend Computerisation:** It would require in-depth understanding and study of government processes and then reengineering them to make them IT compatible to enhance process efficiency. It will require teams of dedicated and competent people to carry out this task.
- **Improving Capacity of Delivery System:** The sound delivery system is crucial for reaching out to citizens effectively and efficiently. Presently, everything gets stuck up after the application leaves from e-Kiosk (to any delivery department), as the delivery mechanism is not effective to provide services qualitatively. The system needs improvement for all the major services like primary education, health, drinking water, agriculture inputs, veterinary and credit. It would call for strengthening infrastructure, logistics and manpower, along with improving capabilities across the levels viz. district, block and gram panchayats, which is going to be a huge exercise.

Figure: 5.2: Reversing the Approach for System Design and Strategy

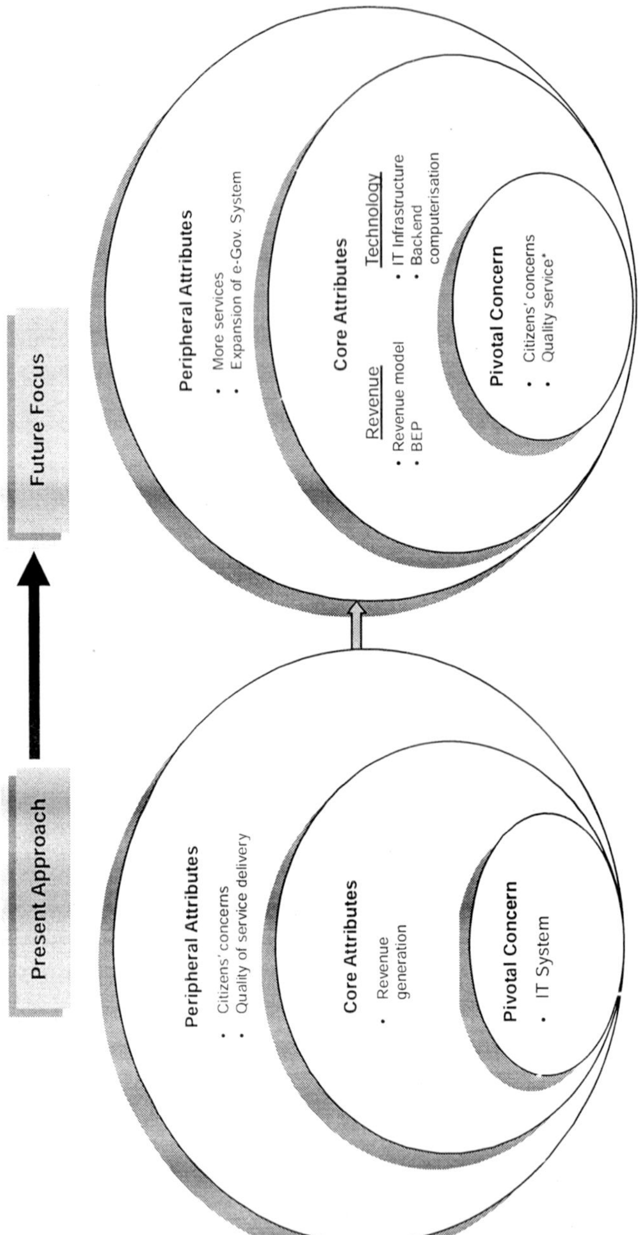

*Quality parameters: Time, Cost, Reliability, Behaviour, Responsiveness, Transparency and Accountability

- **Transparency and Accountability Mechanism:** In order to instill confidence of citizens in local institutions, mechanism for transparency and accountability is important. It would require serious efforts to beat the present culture used to of taking decisions without the knowledge of citizens and also without being accountable to them.
- **Political Will for Resources and Reforms:** Good governance will entail making a large number of interventions in the areas of institutions and IT, which would be possible through good investments in programmes for capacity building of delivery system, IT infrastructure, backend computerisation and so on.

5.2.5 Future Agenda: While designing the e-Governance project, the concept of good governance should be adequately understood and it should be judged by the 'quality' of delivery of services, of information sharing with the citizens, of participation in the process of governance – local resource planning, implementation of projects, policy formulation. It would require evolving quality parameters and ensuring them through improved systems. In this backdrop and in the light of elaborate description in Chapter 4, the recommendations are summarised in Box 5.4 for e-Governance project design.

A. Harnessing Full Potential of IT: In the backdrop of above discussion, for designing e-Governance projects, it is important to look at the following vital questions:

From Institutional perspective

- How do the personnel in the departments respond to citizens' problems?
- Whether the processes are user-friendly?
- Whether the processes need changes due to change of time?
- Whether the processes are IT compatible?
- Whether delivery system has capacity to provide quality services to citizens?

From citizens' perspective

- Whether the citizens are able to get quality services or the grievances are redressed in time?
- And, whether there is consistency in providing services?

B. Action plan

In the Context of

- Lack of focus on 'quality' of services
- Poor capacity of delivery system to deliver services effectively
- Long and cumbersome processes

- Potential benefits of e-Governance

Box 5.4: Recommendations for e-Governance Project Design

Vision
- Improving socio-economic opportunities and the quality of life; and bridging rural-urban divide, through leveraging IT

Mission
- To strive for providing 'quality' services to citizens, using resources effectively

Goals
- Evolving citizen-centric work culture
- Evolving culture of 'quality' in office functioning
- Creating information society
- Effective delivery system to deliver 'quality' services

Step-wise action plan
- Understanding the governance issues and putting governance first
- Detailed citizen requirement study
- In-depth system requirement study (SRS)
- Vision and mission should be clearly defined
- Roadmap / growth model should be properly identified
- Participatory leadership needs to be evolved
- Local project champion should be developed (at District / Tehsil)
- Dedicated project team with clear roles and responsibilities should be formed at State, District and Tehsil levels
- Process re-engineering should be top priority
- Installing reliable communication network
- Adequate resources from State and Central governments
- Backend computerisation (citizen database) should be carried out based on BPR
- Citizen-centric work culture to be evolved
- Awareness building programme

Specific key programmes
- Capacity building of delivery system to deliver effectively and efficiently
- Good IT network
- BPR
- Organisational development (OD)
- System integration (integrating databases of different services) for integrated service delivery
- Citizen relationship management (CRM)
- Knowledge management (KM)

Programme Focus

Action research to evolve operational and financial model's for:

- Improving capacity of delivery system
- IT infrastructure
- BPR

- Backend computerisation (including citizen database)
- System integration
- Citizen relationship management (CRM)
- Knowledge management (KM)

Reform areas

- Institutional reforms – evolving citizen-centric effective delivery system. Reforms are required in the areas of work culture, leadership, team building and working conditions

Essentialities

- Political will for reforms and resources (for improving capacity of delivery system, IT infrastructure, backend computerisation)

Expected results

- Efficient availability of basic services to citizens
- Socio-economic opportunities to people
- Transparent and accountable functioning
- Good governance

5.2.6 Implications: In the backdrop of above, the improved process efficiency and organisational effectiveness, and information networking, would provide a new dimension to the concept of e-Governance. With the improvements that would follow, it would generate a great deal of interest in citizens to access more and more services from government as well as private agencies. Making interventions as suggested have potential to create significant multiplier and network effects. This can trigger a virtuous cycle of socio-economic development – leading to good governance. It would bring in scalability and replicability to the efforts under e-Governance (see Figure S5.1).

5.2.7 Concluding Remarks: The study has evidently brought out that IT, though vital, by itself is very unlikely to create improvements if it is not accompanied by appropriate institutional innovations. It is precisely the reason (due to weak systems of delivery of services) the concept of e-Governance has not gained widespread adoption by the citizens, and it is raising problems of replicability and scalability of their applications. The present efforts under e-Governance though positive and encouraging are yet mainly in the area of providing scope to people in villages to access some information about the government programmes and to represent to departments either for service or grievances, but not so much on grievance redressal and availing quality service delivery.

There have been many e-Governance initiatives taken up in the country. But what is observed is that the focus in most of these cases is on computerisation and automation using IT, without much attention paid to other vital issues of delivery system (like processes, functionaries). As a result, such projects have not sustained after the roll-out. The problems such as lack of BPR and backend computerisation and poor capacity of delivery system, are common (in varying degrees) across the States (and such problems have affected all the e-Governance projects, where study was made). Though there have been definitely design problems, but service provider cannot be faulted so much, as BPR, backend computerisation and sound delivery system are to be provided by the State governments. And without them, e-Governance projects in rural areas for the service delivery would find it hard to succeed.

Good governance means that the processes and institutions produce results that are consistent, reliable and meet the desired standards. Also, it requires that institutions and processes are sensitive to the problems of people and try to serve all stakeholders within a reasonable timeframe. In the context of delivery of services, the quality can be measured in terms of reliability, consistency, responsiveness, timeliness, and desired standard.

The sustainability of system is closely tied to the reform processes in the current system of government. Reforms must be an all-embracing phenomenon, touching every aspect of the government – work culture, citizen management, organisational functioning and so on. Then the e-Governance model chosen will impact the way reform processes are handled.

In sum, the success of e-Governance initiatives hinges on institutional changes than only on introduction of IT. For the e-Governance initiatives to be successful, it requires coherent integration of IT and delivery systems (people and processes) – the scale of success is immense.

Figure: S5.1 Through Interventions – Virtuous Cycle of Functioning of e-Governance to Leverage full Potential of IT

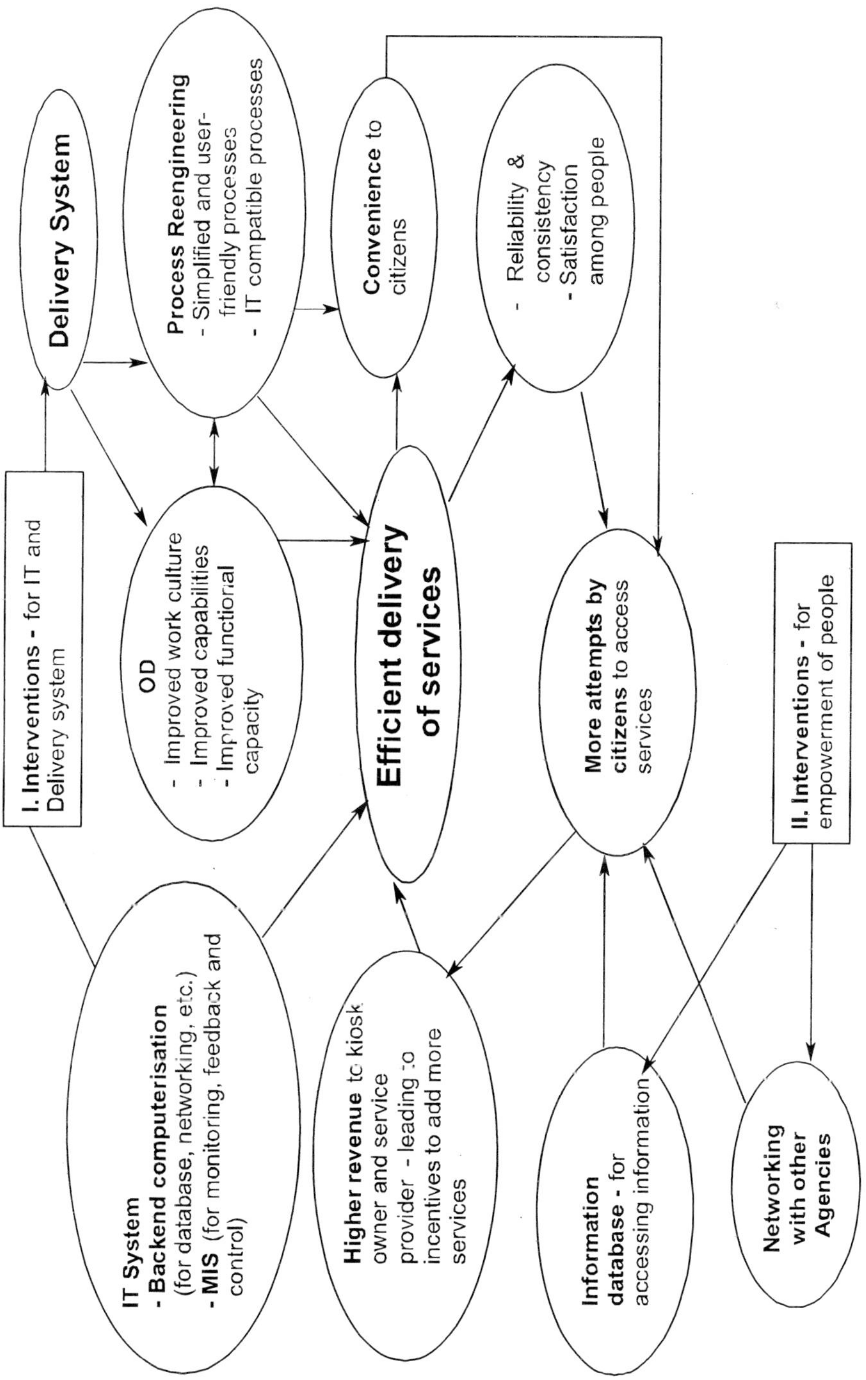

Annexures

Annexure 2.1

Sample Survey Schedule for Requirement of Information, Services and Grievances of Citizens, for e-Governance Project

1. Name of GP: ....
2. Name of the village:...........
3. Name of the respondent:..........
4. Ward member / up-sarpanch / sarpanch / Citizen:...........
5. Age:

18-30	31-40	41-50	51-60	More than 60
1	2	3	4	5

6. Education

Illiterate	Just literate	PE	PE to HS	HS to HS	Graduate or more
1	2	3	4	5	6

7. Income

Destitute	BPL	APL	Rich	Very rich
1	2	3	4	5

8. Caste:

General	OBC	SC	ST	Others
1	2	3	4	5

9. M / F:

Male	Female
1	2

1 2 3 4 5
(Least important) (Most important)

S.N.	Sector	No.	Services*	Scale (1-5)**	Not required	Frequency of usage***				
						Weekly	Monthly	In 3 months	6 months-1 year	Yes, but Rarely
1.	Education									
	Information	1.	Type of scholarship							
		2.	Number of schools							
		3.	Number of children attending schools by age, caste and gender							

* *Note:* List of sectors covered: i. Education, ii. Drinking water, iii. Health, iv. Women and child welfare, v. Social welfare, vi. Po verty alleviation, vii. PDS, viii. Agriculture, ix. Irrigation, x. Animal husbandry, xi. Tehsil, xii. Electricity, xiii. Road, xiv. Others, **Scale of the importance: It shows about the importance given by citizens from 1 to 5 ('1' means least important and '5' means most impor tant)., *** Frequency of usage of service: under this category, the follo wings have been taken: 'weekly', 'monthly', 'in three months', 'in six months to one year' and 'rarely'.

Annexure 2.2 Herzberg's Motivation-hygiene Theory

Frederick Herzberg's two-factor, motivation-hygiene theory is another type of need theory and is one of the most popular theories of motivation in business today. Herzberg developed his theory after surveying hundreds of accountants, engineers, and other managerial personnel. It provides additional assistance in understanding the role of motivation in organizations (Luthans, 1998).

Herzberg's research caused him to categorize various needs of individuals into two groups: (1) hygiene factors, or what he called "dissatisfiers," and (2) motivation factors, what he labels "satisfiers." Hygiene and motivation factors include the items listed in Figure 1 below.

The hygiene factors are dissatisfiers because if all of them are present in a work situation, people will not be dissatisfied; their presence, however, does not really motivate people. However, take away any of the hygiene factors from a job and extreme dissatisfaction can occur. For example, lower pay, bad supervision, or a hazardous or uncomfortable workplace can create substantial dissatisfaction among employees. A hot stuffy classroom in September with a professor who is ill prepared and allows no taking or any break for a full 110-minute class period can cause considerable dissatisfaction among students and severely weaken the motivation to learn the course material.

Motivation requires the opportunity to meet the needs for employee autonomy, competence, and achievement. And this is where the motivational factors come into play. These factors are aspects of the task or work itself. They include challenge, chance for personal growth, and performance feedback. In other words, as viewed by the employee, work with these characteristics means motivational factors are present.

Figure 1: Hygiene-motivation Factors

Group I – Hygiene factors	Group II – Motivation factors
1. Money and compensation	1. Work itself – challenging
2. Personal life	2. Added responsibility
3. Working conditions	3. Opportunity for advancement
4. Working relationships	4. Management recognition for good work
5. Status	5. Opportunity for personal growth
6. Job security	
7. Company policy and administration	
8. Quality of supervision	

These factors contribute heavily to the satisfaction of the employee and have a positive effect on his or her performance

Annexure 2.3 Guidelines for Process Mapping

S.N.	Major steps	Type	Details	Remarks
1.	Study of process	Basic information of processes	☐ Identifying the services ☐ Identifying the processes involved in providing the services ☐ Identification of owner of processes ☐ Stakeholders involved in processes ☐ Final output of services ☐ Collection of guidelines for providing services ☐ Collection of application forms & delivery forms (blank & filled)	☐ Interviewing 2-3 functionaries and citizens for quick assessment of services, various process parameters. ☐ Data collection through ☐ Consultation with functionaries, citizens and other stakeholder. ☐ Field survey ☐ Focused group discussions (FGDs)
		Identifying the process steps	☐ Identifying all the activities from beginning till end of process ☐ Identifying the measurable process parameters (like time, cost, etc.) ☐ Identifying the minimum, maximum, average value of these parameters	
		Process mapping	☐ Draw each activity of process in a sequence: FD I ☐ Draw movement of application form among stakeholders in the process: FD II. ☐ Verifying with the functionaries (office staff) and citizens and then finalise FD I and FD II	
		Other information from office	☐ Data for 2-3 years for the number of applications for each service ☐ Prescribed time to availing service as per citizen charter ☐ Registers maintained for procedure to availing the service ☐ Prescribed cost for availing services as per citizen charter	

Contd...

S.N.	Major steps	Type	Details	Remarks
		Citizen perspective	□ Work culture 'quick' assessment (interviewing 2-3 citizens) □ Identifying the actual cost incurred by citizens to get the service □ Identifying the actual time incurred by citizens to get the service □ Frequency of availing services □ Existing source of information available to a citizen □ Number of visits made by citizens □ Field survey for detailed assessment about process parameter (functionaries) □ Field survey for detail assessment about process parameter (interviewing 30-50 citizens)	-
2.	Analysis		□ FMEA □ Pareto analysis □ Identifying CTQs i. Identifying decision-making points ii. Identifying the number of activities involved in the process iii. Identifying the touch points for citizens and application form iv. Identifying the number of visits made by citizens in availing the service v. Identifying activities taking minimum time vi. Identifying 'non-value' adding activities vii. Time for availing services viii. Cost for availing services ix. Behaviour of functionaries x. Responsiveness of functionaries xi. Transparency xii. Accessibility □ Fishbone diagram □ CE analysis □ Process (Throughput) efficiency □ Problems faced by functionaries (office staff) □ Constraints in the delivery system	-

Annexure 3.1

Table 3.1.1: Critical Behavioural Indicators

S.N.	Project name	Behaviorual Issues				
		Leadership	Role and responsibility	Team work	Motivation	Work culture
1.	e-Governance	a) Not clear about vision and mission b) Enthusiastic but less participatory	c) Roles of different stakeholders (service provider, Tehsil staff, field staff) not clearly defined	d) Lack of coordination among different stake-holders	e) Kiosk owner de-motivated	f) Lack of citizen focus g) Lack of responsiveness h) Lack of concern for timeliness
2.	Janmitra	-do-	-do-	-do-	-do-	-do-
3.	Gyandoot	-do-	-do-	-do-	-do-	-do-
4.	e-Bhoomi*	i) Enthusiastic but less participatory	j) Roles of different officials and field staff clearly defined	k) Good team work	l) Good motivation to officials and field functionaries	m) Responsiveness
	RDS (including e-Bhoomi)	□ Not clear about vision and mission □ Enthusiastic but less participatory	□ Roles of different stakeholders (service provider, Tehsil staff, field staff) not clearly defined	□ Lack of coordination among different stake-holders	□ Kiosk owner de-motivated	□ Lack of citizen focus □ Lack of responsiveness □ Lack of concern for timeliness
5.	OLTP	-do-	-do-	-do-	-do-	-do-
6.	Manual process	□ Directional less participatory	□ Roles of different stake holders Tehsil staff, field staff) defined, but due to heavy workload they are not followed	□ Lack of coordination	□ Lack of motivation in field and official staff	□ Lack of citizen focus □ Lack of responsiveness □ Lack of concern for timeliness

Source: Based on FGDs with citizens, Kiosk and officials (it is indicative).

**Provides only a few services related to ROR and only at Tehsil level (not in the villages), so there are not many complications as in case of other projects

Table: 3.1.2: Strength, Weakness and Challenges of e-Governance Projects

S.N.	Project name	Strength	Weaknesses	Challenges
1.	e-Governance	☐ Support of district administration ☐ Sufficient number of e-Kiosks ☐ Strong network backbone	☐ Interrupted electricity supply ☐ Connectivity problem ☐ Manual processing (no BPR) ☐ Very limited (3-5) e-Governance services ☐ Quality of services (time, cost, etc.) of service delivery is poor ☐ Lack of system ownership	☐ How to provide electricity on a sustained basis ☐ How to ensure good connectivity ☐ How to do BPR & backend computerisation ☐ How to bring citizen-centric work culture ☐ How to add more services
2.	Janmitra	☐ Support of district administration ☐ Sufficient number of e-Kiosks ☐ Weak network	-do-	-do-
3.	Gyandoot	☐ Support of district administration ☐ Sufficient number of e-Kiosks ☐ Weak network	-do-	-do-
4.	RDS (including e-Bhoomi)	☐ Support of district administration ☐ Limited number of e-Kiosks ☐ Weak network	-do-	-do-
5.	OLTP	-do-	-do-	-do-
6.	e-Bhoomi	☐ Support of district administration and State IT department	☐ Very limited services only related to ROR ☐ E-kiosks only at Tehsil level (not in the villages)	☐ How to provide more services of Tehsil ☐ How to provide good connectivity to e-Kiosk in villages ☐ How to do BPR & backend computerisation ☐ How to bring citizen-centric work culture

Source: Based on FGDs with citizens, Kiosk and officials (it is indicative).

Table 3.1.3: Indicative Performance of (Time Spent and Cost Incurred) in Availing Caste Certificate by Citizen

S.N.	Projects	Time spent (days)*			Cost incurred by citizens (in Rs.) **			Visits by citizens	Citizen satisfaction	Remarks
		Min	Max	Avg	Min	Max	Avg			
1.	e-Governance (in Jaipur)	20	25	23	200	250	225	6-12	No	□ Not much difference in comparison to manual processing, so it is not an attractive proposition, citizens prefer to go to Tehsil (through manual system)
2.	Janmitra	6	18	12	50	250	150	4-6	No	-do-
3.	Gyandoot	6	20	13	40	225	125	3-4	No	-do-
4.	e-Bhoomi***	NA						-	□ One to a limited Extent (for those who can come to Tehsil)	□ Only certificates related to land records given □ e-Kiosk only at Tehsil (not in the villages)
	RDS*** (including e-Bhoomi)	6	12	8	40	175	125	3-4	No	□ Not much difference in comparison to manual processing
5.	OLTP	4	15	9	40	150	100	3-4	No	-do-
6.	Manual process	10	15	12	200	300	250	6-13	No	-

Source: Based on FGDs with citizens, Kiosk owners and officials (it is indicative).
Min: minimum, Max: maximum, Avg: Average
* It includes time for collection of attachments, visits to e-Kiosk, Tehsil, etc.
**It Includes cost of application form, fees, traveling cost, wages lost, etc.
*** Caste, income and domicile certificates not provided by e-Bhoomi (but for collection of RORs, citizen have to come to Tehsil, and incur expenditure for traveling)

Table 3.1.4: Indicative Number of Applications under e-Governance Projects (Overall Performance) (Average per Kiosk per month)

S.N.	Projects	Number of e-Governance services						Other all services		
		Grievances			Certificates					
		Min	Max	Avg	Min	Max	Avg	Min	Max	Avg
1.	e-Governance	2	5	4	5	25*	6	10	20	15
2.	Janmitra	5	20	8	10	220*	30	10	20	15
3	Gyandoot	2	15	5	5	150*	25	25	90	45
4.	i. e-Bhoomi	NA								
	ii. RDS (including e-Bhoomi)	-	-	15	-	-	20	-	-	30
5.	OLTP	3	18	6	10	28*	15	7	30	12

Source: Based on FGDs with citizens, Kiosk owners and officials.

*For Kiosk in town or near Tehsil

Table 3.1.5: Indicative Income under e-Governance Projects (Overall Performance) (Average per Kiosk per month)

S.N.	Projects	Income from (in Rs.)											
		E-governance*			Other** services						Total		
					Mandi rates			Others					
		Min	Max	Avg	Min	Max	Avg	Min	Max	Avg	Min	Max	Avg
1.	e-Governance	120	550	160	42	108	52	550	820***	820	712	1478***	1032
2.	Janmitra	250	4600	680	-	-	-	500	2000***	1000	750	6600***	1680
3.	Gyandoot	120	3150	550	-	-	-	100	3000***	800	220	6150***	1350
4.	e-Bhoomi	NA											
	RDS (including e-Bhoomi)	-	-	550	-	-	-	-	-	500	-	-	1050
5.	OLTP	30	180	60	-	-	-	150	200	175	180	280***	235

Source: Based on FGDs with citizens, Kiosk owners and officials.

*Caste, Income, Domicile certificates; ROR, and grievances.

**Mandibhav, horoscope, computer education, Cable TV, photo copy, etc.

*** These e-Kiosks (hardly 10 % of total number of Kiosks) are working well as they are in towns or near Tehsil. Also the income in these Kiosks is mainly from non-e-Governance services and as far as e-Governance services are concerned there is manual processing of certificates not electronic processing (while in far-off / remote (15-20 kms away from Tehsil) villages, Kiosks are almost non-functional)

Annexure 3.2

3.2.1 Case Studies on e-Governance Project

Case Study 1: *Lack of management by service provider (Kadera Gram Panchayat, Chaksu Tehsil, Jaipur District)*

Arif was the e-Governance Kiosk owner at Kadera. The Kiosk was operational for ten months. Since the e-Governance service was not successful at Kadera, Arif shifted the e-Governance Kiosk to Chaksu. Here too, after a number of problems with the Sitapura office, he was forced to close the Kiosk after 3-4 months. For services like income and caste certificates, it requires filling online application forms and enclosures to be e-mailed or couriered to Sitapura head-end. Arif said that the follow-up was not done satisfactorily at the head-end and finally the application forms were returned without providing the final certificate or document. Similarly, certificates from Aptech were promised for computer education, but were not given to candidates. Arif suffered loss of face and reputation due to this. He also stated that timely redressal of complaints regarding connectivity, cable cutting, etc. was not done. It led to closure of the e-Kiosk.

It indicates that the demand for services through e-Governance project was there, even if it took longer time to obtain certificates through the project, but due to poor management, services were not provided satisfactorily to citizens.

Case Study 2: *Lack of care by e-Kiosk owner – A lack of citizen focus (Muhana Gram Panchayat, Sanganer Tehsil, District Jaipur)*

When Krishan Yadav went to the e-Kiosk for obtaining a caste certificate, he was told to furnish the required documents along with the fees. After completing the above formalities he was told that he would receive his certificate within three days. After three days, when he went to the e-Kiosk, he was told that he would get the certificate after a few days. The reason told to him was that the application had not reached Sanganer till then because of some fault in the cable lines. When the applicant went to the Kiosk after a few days he found out that the Kiosk had been shifted to another place. After several days the applicant met the e-Governance Kiosk owner. On enquiry he told Krishan that he himself had not received his salary, and he would not be able to help the applicant in any way.

Krishan decided to talk to higher authorities. The authorities assured him that the Kiosk would be reopened in a few days. After reopening, when the applicant went to the Kiosk, he was asked to furnish the application fees and the required documents once again. Later, when after collecting the necessary documents he reached the Kiosk, he was told that the Kiosk had been shifted to another place and that the owner had run away.

The applicant became so frustrated that he never recommended anyone to go to the Kiosks and labeled e-Kiosk as unreliable.

It shows that until and unless there is a feedback system which is transparent and the applicant knows what exactly is happening, uncertainty will remain in his / her mind.

Case Study 3: *Lack of sincerity of Kiosk owner (Shivdaspura Gram Panchayat, Chaksu Tehsil, Jaipur District)*

Kailash Choudhary was the Kiosk owner and used to come from Chaksu (20 km from Shivdaspura). The timings of Kiosk were 9.30AM to 5.30PM but he always came late and went early.

On further discussion, villagers told that the facility of e-Governance services were good but due to lack of knowledge and the interest on the part of the Kiosk owner, they were unable to get services. When discussed with Kailash Choudhary, he told that he had not got the salary for the last thirteen months, thus leaving him de-motivated. The payment was not made because revenue generated by the e-Kiosk was low. The above shows that lack of sincerity of the Kiosk owner resulted in an ill-functioning e-Kiosk. No efforts were also made to set it right by the service provider.

Case Study 4: *Lack of proper land database by e-Kiosk service provider (Chaksu Tehsil, Jaipur District)*

There was incident that took place at Chaksu Tehsil Kiosk. One citizen came from nearby village and wanted a copy of Jamabandi. Arif (the Kiosk owner) entered his Khata number and Khasra number in computer, and then he found that the Jamabandi was not displayed properly, so he made a call to head-end. After inquiry it was found that the data in Jamabandi was outdated, finally the citizen had to take the Jamabandi from Tehsil computer centre.

It indicated that the data at e-Governance Kiosk was not updated.

Case Study 5: *Patwari's availability for report writing for and signature on Jamabandi (Kotkhawda Gram Panchayat, Chaksu Tehsil, Jaipur District)*

During the field visit of village Kotkhawda, Surendra told us about the unavailability of the Patwari in office when needed. On detailed discussion with Surendra he explained that a few months back he wanted a caste certificate for which he needed the report of Patwari. He made 5-6 rounds to Patwarghar, but he was not successful. At last one of his friends Rajeev Mishra suggested that

Patwari would be available at Tehsil and he should search him there. So the next day he went to Tehsil and found that Patwari was on leave that day. Next day, he was able to find Patwari at the Tehsil, and he requested the Patwari for the report. The Patwari told him to come after two days.

Although two days later he received his report, Surendra told that his certificate was delayed only because of non-availability of Patwari in his office.

It indicates the importance of the Patwari's presence in his office.

Case Study 6: *Non-availability of Patwari for signing Jamabandi at e-Kiosk (Shivdaspura Gram Panchayat, Chaksu Tehsil, Jaipur District)*

Kailash Choudhary (Kiosk owner at Shivdaspura) told that citizens do not come to the e-Kiosk, as they are not able to get the signature of Patwari at e-Kiosk. The Patwari is supposed to come to e-Kiosk twice a week for necessary paper work. Kailash Choudhary told that one citizen Harinarayan came to Kiosk and got computerised Jamabandi copy from the e-Kiosk, but he could not get the signature from Patwari, and so he had to go to Tehsil for the signature.

3.2.2. Case Studies on Grievances Redressal through e-Governance Project

Case Study 7: *Complaints against the poor quality of education through e-Kiosk (Shivdaspura Gram Panchayat, Chaksu Tehsil, Jaipur District)*

During a discussion in the village of Shivdaspura (GP) some villagers informed that they had earlier sent a complaint regarding poor quality of education in their village. The complaint was sent through e-Governance e-Kiosk to Collectorate.

On inquiry it was found that the complaint was marked to the district education officer (DEO) who in turn sent it to the block elementary education officer (BEEO). He informed that he was not able to do much as there is a shortage of teachers, and those who are posted are not provided proper training. So they are not able to impart education properly to children. Villagers also expressed that there is a poor infrastructure in the school (like three rooms, no toilets and drinking water facility) and adequate teaching-aids are also not available. Even after four months, the grievance has not been redressed.

The above shows that there is a need to improve the teacher's strength, school infrastructure, etc. in order to provide quality education to children.

Case Study 8: *Complaints against the drinking water through e-Kiosk (Bara Padampura Gram Panchayat, Chaksu Tehsil, Jaipur District)*

During consultation with villagers of Bara Padampura it was revealed that villagers had complained about poor quality of drinking water due to fluoride, through e-Kiosk to Collectorate.

After one month the villagers received a letter regarding their complaint, which was sent to the PHED. The department found that their complaint was genuine but it had no funds to install the new plant for removing the fluoride in the water. The villagers also expressed that they are suffering from many diseases due to fluoride in water like pain in knees, deformation of bones, yellow teeth, etc.

The above matter shows that without funds administration is helpless.

Case Study 9: *Complaints against electricity (Barkhera Gram Panchayat, Chaksu Tehsil, Jaipur District)*

During the focused group discussion in the village of Barkhera in Shivdaspura GP, the citizens expressed that they faced a major problem of electricity shortage especially during crop sowing month, May and June. They also told that they had complained to Collector through e-Kiosk in Shivdaspura and also received a token indicating that the complaint would be resolved within 21 days.

With this hope, the villagers kept waiting for one month before getting an answer from Jaipur Vidyut Vitran Nigam Limited (JVVNL). JVVNL expressed their helplessness in solving the problem due to non-supply from the other end. Nevertheless they promised to change the transformer as soon as they would get it from their head office.

The case indicates that JVVNL at block level has little control over the operational management and is unable to rectify the problems.

Case Study 10: *Complaint about the poor quality of MDM and its irregularity (Dadanpura Gram Panchayat, Chaksu Tehsil, Jaipur District)*

During the field visit of village Dadanpura, it was noticed that they had complained about the poor quality of food in MDM and its irregularity. The complaint was made through the e-Kiosk from Shivdaspura.

On detailed discussion with some people of the village, it was revealed that one month after the complaint, villagers got the answer through the school. It said, 'we have fully attempted at solving your problem and we have also given strict instructions to the headmaster of the Dadanpura school that this type of carelessness shouldn't be repeated in future.' The headmaster told that food is prepared from the material received from the Block. Sometimes the quality of grains is not good and on some occasion the material is not supplied in time. He added that they do not have proper utensils and water to cook food, which affects the quality of cooked food.

The villagers also told that the children don't wish to eat Ghooghri (MDM) because it is tasteless and half-cooked, but children are forced to eat it, due to which children sometimes complain of stomach ache and loose motion.

The above four case studies indicate that e-Kiosk was able to send the complaints to Collectorate, but these complaints were not resolved in time due to a variety of factors such as inadequacy of manpower and infrastructure, low capabilities, lack of commitment, lack of resources and equipments and so on. Due to this, citizens stopped sending grievances through e-Kiosk.

Thus for good governance, IT is important for connectivity, but for efficient delivery of services, delivery system should be first strengthened.

3.2.3 Case Studies on Service Delivery by different Service Departments

Case Study 11: *Presence of high percentage of fluoride in water and its effect on human life (Kumhariyawas Gram Panchayat, Chaksu Tehsil, Jaipur District)*

The presence of high percentage of fluoride in the water has resulted into diseases in the village. For the last ten years, Mahadev is sick. Initially his body started swelling and then developed joint pain. As years passed by he realised that along with these physical problems his intake of food deteriorated and he also developed stomach ache and chest pain. He said that he could feel and see the downfall in the quality of water because of which not only Mahadev but also many villagers in this panchayat has developed many health problems. Many villagers under this panchayat have been handicapped.

It shows that the most essential thing of life (i.e. water) is not provided purely to citizens, and due to this citizens do face many diseases, and also their lives become shorter day-by-day.

Case Study: 12: *Difficulties with SHGs (Chandlai Gram Panchayat, Chaksu Tehsil, Jaipur District)*

Asha Devi is working as Anganwadi worker for the last eight years. She has acquired expertise in her work and doing good work with the village people. As a worker she has been entrusted with certain tasks in the centre that are related to the service delivery of the ICDS package. Similarly, Asha Devi is supposed to form SHGs of women but in this task she faces problems. Women do not deposit their money at the right time because of which the group was functioning very irregularly. Once Asha Devi was requested by Meena, member of a SHG group to give her a loan of Rs 200 from the group with the assurance that she would return the loan with interest very soon. But Meena did not return the amount and left the group for which Asha Devi had to refund the group amount from her own pocket. From then onwards Asha Devi feels very de-motivated to help any of the group members and try her level best to motivate the members to maintain all the rules and regulation of the groups as decided by the group when it was formed. It indicates that in the field there are so many problems like finance, behavior, and management of people.

Case Study 13: *Not getting ration in time (Chandlai Gram Panchayat, Chaksu Tehsil, Jaipur District)*

Ramjilal, son of Kasturi Chand Khatik stated that he had not received wheat for the last two months. He failed to come and collect ration on the day, which the retailer declared that he would distribute ration. But after that within the span of two months, Ramji came minimum eight times to take ration but did not receive as the retailer denied to give. On asking the reason, some people told that the person for distribution is not in the village. Ramji gets ration under Antodaya card. He gets 35 kg wheat per month at the cost of Rs 2/-. But during these two months he purchased wheat from the market at the cost of Rs 7/- per kg. Usually he purchased wheat for two months (70 kg) at the cost of Rs 140, but because of irregular working culture of retailer, he had to purchase 70 kg wheat spending Rs 490. Ramji moreover added that the quality of the wheat was not upto the level of satisfaction and the behaviour of the retailer was not good. He concluded that today he received the ration, as researchers were present while he came to collect the ration.

It shows the irregularity in PDS supply and quality of material. Both need to be improved by proper monitoring and strict action.

Case Study 14: *Delay in delivering of seeds (Teetriya Gram Panchayat, Chaksu Tehsil, Jaipur District)*

Sitaram, who is a farmer, has his livelihood solely dependent on agriculture. He got the seeds from the department after the season for sowing got over. He said that the procedure for getting seeds from the department is too lengthy because of which cultivators suffer. He stated that the procedure is long and it takes a long time before seeds are delivered.

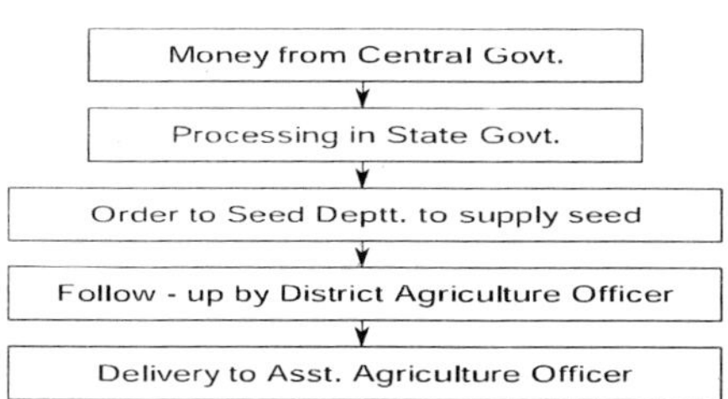

The procedure is shown in the left. It is a long process and by the time they receive the seeds the season for sowing gets over. So villagers suggested that if seeds are directly delivered to village panchayat then that would take less time and farmers can do their agriculture operation on scheduled time.

The above shows about the long processes of delivery system and due to which, citizens have to suffer.

Case Study 15: *Non-availability of services of animal husbandry (Kumhariyawas Gram Panchayat, Chaksu Tehsil, Jaipur District)*

In May'2004, Omprakash purchased a Holliston cow for Rs. 7000 from Jaipur. He took the cow for artificial breeding in the veterinary hospital paying Rs.120 to the doctor, as there was no male cow of that particular type in Kumhariyawas. But the breeding failed and doctor said that this happened because it is not possible to have successful artificial breeding in summer. Omprakash then decided to take the cow to Vatika. He took the cow to Vatika for artificial breeding where the result was positive. For this work he wasted three days and more than Rs 200 were spent. Omprakash commented that if there had been better facilities in the village or nearby villages, he would not have taken so much of trouble.

The above shows that due to non-availability of services in the villages, citizens have to face the problem like long-distance walking with their animals and high expenditure for treatment of animals.

Case Study 16: *Lack of responsiveness of teachers in government schools (Shivdaspura Gram Panchayat, Chaksu Tehsil, Jaipur District)*

Sitaram got his son Raju admitted in the government primary school at the age of six. Sitaram is a farmer and has studied up to 9th standard. He never gave attention to his son's education with a trust that teachers are taking proper care of the child and he is doing well. Moreover, Sitaram was involved in agricultural activities from early morning to sunset. After four years his son got promoted to 5th Standard. One day Sitaram suddenly found that his son wrote his own name wrong. He scolded his son and asked him to write it correctly but Raju could not correct that. Sitaram then asked him some more simple spelling but his son failed to write them too. He then decided to shift his son from the government school to private school where he had to pay Rs 40 per month as fees. Now Sitaram checks his son's copies regularly and also timely monitors the education status of Raju.

Sitaram added that being a farmer it is difficult for him to take out time to devote for his son and daughter. So he sends his children to school with full trust on teacher. But the teacher never called him to inform about the children's progress. He himself could not go because of traditional culture. All the teachers being females, from outside the village, he could only sit outside and observe.

The case reflects the lack of responsiveness of teachers in government schools and lack of parents' attention on their children.

Case Study 17: *Social reasons for high dropout rate (Dadanpura Gram Panchayat, Chaksu Tehsil, Jaipur District)*

Deokishanpura is a village of Gurjars, where certain malpractices that were followed traditionally are still prevalent. During the visit to Dadanpura village on 13th April and while conversing with the villagers, it was known that Rani Gujar got married at the age of around 9 years, because of which she had to leave her studies. Her in-laws did not want her to study further and wished that she engaged herself in household work. On the other hand, the girl insisted that she wanted to study further and did not want to be a dropout from school. However, due to constant pressure from her parents and in-laws, she eventually had to leave the school. This was one case that was highlighted as a result of our survey. However, there may be many other such cases, which never come to light.

As a consequence of this, it was realised that this is a social problem that has arisen due to the following reasons:

- Lack of awareness among the parents for education of the girl child
- Traditions demanding women be involved in household work
- Large distance to be travelled to reach school

Case Study 18: *Lack of sufficient support services and infrastructure (Chandlai Gram Panchayat, Chaksu Tehsil, Jaipur District)*

Dr. Devendre Sharma had been transferred to Chandlai PHC eight months back. Since then he is finding himself in a difficult position. No sweeper has been appointed for the PHC, so he has to look after the hygiene of the hospital himself. Every month he has to shell out Rs.2000 from his own pocket for electricity bill and sweeper. It takes long time from the department to reimburse the amount. The chair in which the doctor sits is also in a very bad condition that may crack anytime. The doctor said that he feels de-motivated for work, as there is no proper facility due to which his working capacity is hampered. At the same time the villagers blame the PHC, that it does not provide adequate services. The PHC is also responsible for 4 sub-centres, but inadequate facilities do not allow him to devote required time and attention to each. Villagers too pressurise the doctor to provide better health facilities.

Adequate facilities and good infrastructure in the health system is a must. Unfortunately, lack of them leaves the doctor handicapped and unable to deliver better results.

Case Study 19: *Lack of facilities at GP level (Kumhariyawas Gram Panchayat, Chaksu Tehsil, Jaipur district).*

Late Sangiya, wife of Kanha expired at the age of 45. She was suffering from severe stomach pain for a long time and was under treatment by the local physician. The day she expired, she had sudden severe pain. Her husband took her to the nearby dispensary of Kumhariyawas but there were no medicines and other facilities to give her immediate relief. He immediately decided to take her to Vatika but she expired on the way. Kanha laments each and every moment and feels that he could have saved his wife life if only there would have been proper health facilities in the GP.

This indicates that lack of facilities at the GP level coupled with insufficient medicines and other supporting infrastructure, is detrimental to the health of the villagers.

Annexure 4.1A: Process (Throughput) Efficiency

Table 4.1A.1: Process Efficiency of Manual Process (Caste Certificate)

S.N.	Code	Activities	Time for value added activity	Total time
1.	A1	a. Collection of attachments	30 m	3 days =1440 m
		b. Report of Patwari	30 m	2+4=6 days=2880 m (8 working hours / day)
2.	A2	Collection & filling of AF	15 m	Half day=240 m
3.	A3	Submission of AF	15 m	Half day=240 m
4.	A4	Collection of attachments by clerk	2 m	5 m
5.	A5	Processing in Tehsil	30 m	One day = 480 m
6.	A6	Delivery to single window	10 m	30 m
7.	A7	Delivery to citizen	2 m	5 m
8.		**Total**	**134 m**	**5320 m**

Efficiency (Throughput) $= \frac{\text{Actual time} \times 100}{\text{Total time}}$

$= \frac{134\text{ m} \times 100}{5320\text{ m}}$

= **2.51%**

Table 4.1A.2: Process Efficiency of Getting Caste Certificate through e-Governance Project

S.N.	Code	Activities		Actual time	Total time
1.	A1	a. Collection of attachments		15 m	3 days = 1440 m
		b. Report of Patwari		30 m	6 days=2880 m
2.	A2	Collection & filling of AF		15 m	120 m
3.	A3	Submission of AF			
4.	A4	Collection of attachments by Kiosk owner		2 m	5 m
5.	A5	Processing (After submission till certificate preparation)	Kiosk to Sitapura	15 m	2 days = 960m
			Sitapura to district Collectorate	15 m	2 days = 960 m
			Collectorate to Tehsil	15 m	2 days = 960 m
			Processing at Tehsil	30 m	1 day = 480 m
6.	A6	Dispatch of certificate to Kiosk	Tehsil to Collectorate	15 m	2 days = 960 m
			Collectorate to Sitapura	15 m	2 days = 960 m
			Sitapura to Kiosk	15 m	1 day = 480 m
7.	A7	Delivery of certificate to citizen		10m	1 day=480 m
8.		**Total**		**192 m**	**10205 m**

Efficiency (Throughput) = $\frac{\text{Actual time x 100}}{\text{Total time}}$

$= \frac{192 \text{ m x } 100}{10205\text{m}}$

= **1.88%**

Table 4.1A.3: Process Efficiency of Scenario A

S.N.	Codes	Major activities of Scenario A	Actual Time taken	Total time
1.	A1	a. Collection and submission of attachment by citizen	30m	3 days= 1440 m
		b. Collection of Patwari report Case 1: Patwari report not required* Case 2: Patwari report is mandatory**	30 m	6 days =2880 m
2.	A2	Filling up of the application form at e-Kiosk	5 m	10m
3.	A3	Submission of online form at e-Kiosk	2m	5m
		Issue of request-id (token) at e-Kiosk	1m	2m
4.	A4	Verification of attachments by Patwari at e-Kiosk***	10 m	20 m
		Transfer of attachments physically to Tehsil by courier / Kiosk owner	10 m	2 days = 960 m
5.	A5	Verification by Assistant in Tehsil	10m	15m
		Sending to Tehsildar	1m	1 m
		Verification by Tehsildar	5m	10 m
		Taking printout of certificate, signature and stamp on it	15 m	20 m
6.	A6	Sending certificate to Kiosk through Kiosk owner or courier	15 m	1.5 days = 720m
7.	A7	Entering into register at e-Kiosk	5m	15 m
		Signing into register by citizen on receiving the certificate	2m	5 m
8.		**Total**	**141m**	**6103m**

*In case of the following (for caste certificate) (case 1)

- If citizen has his / her earlier caste certificate or of his father

**In case the following (case 2)

- If citizen has come from other village in the recent past
- If citizen is not having domicile certificate / ration card
- If citizen has his / her earlier caste certificate or of his father

*** Either by Patwari or authorised staff of Tehsil

Efficiency (Throughput) = $\frac{\text{Actual time x 100}}{\text{Total time}}$

$= \frac{141 \text{ m} \times 100}{6468 \text{ m}}$

= **2.31%**

Table 4.1A.4: Efficiency of Scenario B

Codes	Major activities of Scenario B		Actual time taken	Total time
A1	a. Collection and submission of attachment by citizen		30 m	3 days = 1440 m
	b. Collection of Patwari report Case 1: Patwari report not required* Case 2: Patwari report is mandatory**		30 m	6 days = 2880 m
A2	Filling up of the application form at e-Kiosk		5 m	10 m
A3	Submission of online form at e-Kiosk		2 m	5 m
	Issue of request-id (token) at e-Kiosk		1 m	2 m
A4	Verification of attachments by Patwari at e-Kiosk***		10 m	20 m
	Transfer of attachments physically to Tehsil by courier/Kiosk owner	By scanning	10 m	20 m
		By courier	10 m	2 days = 960 m
A5	Verification by Assistant in Tehsil		10 m	15 m
	Sending to Tehsildar		1 m	1 m
	Verification by Tehsildar		5 m	10 m
	Taking printout of certificate, signature and stamp on it		15 m	20 m
A6	Sending certificate to Kiosk through Kiosk owner or courier		15 m	1.5 days = 720 m
A7	Entering into register at e-Kiosk		5 m	15 m
	Signing into register by citizen on receiving the certificate		2 m	5 m
	Total		**151 m**	**6498 m**

*In case of the following (for caste certificate) (case 1)
- If citizen has his / her earlier caste certificate or of his father

**In case the following (case 2)
- If citizen has come from other village in the recent past
- If citizen is not having domicile certificate / ration card
- If citizen has his / her earlier caste certificate or of his father

*** Either by Patwari or authorised staff of Tehsil

Efficiency (Throughput) = $\frac{\text{Actual time} \times 100}{\text{Total time}}$

$= \frac{151\text{ m} \times 100}{6498\text{m}} =$ **2.32%**

Table 4.1A.5: Process Efficiency of Scenario C

Codes	Major activities of Scenario C	Actual Time taken	Total time
A1	Patwari report in selected* case	-	-
A2 and A3	Filling up of citizen-id and some required fields in the AF at e-Kiosk	5 m	10 m
A4	Online submission of AF at e-Kiosk	2 m	5 m
	Issue of request-id at e-Kiosk	1 m	2 m
A5	Verification of application by Assistant in Tehsil using information in citizen database	10	15 m
	Assistant approves it by giving digital signature	2 m	10 m
	Verification by Tehsildar	2 m	5 m
	Approval of application by giving digital signature	2 m	2 m
	Taking printout of certificate at Tehsil, signature and stamp on it	5 m	15 m
A6	Sending certificate to Kiosk through Kiosk owner or courier	10 m	720 m
	Entering into register at Kiosk	5 m	15 m
A7	Signing into register by citizen on receiving the certificate	2 m	4 m
	Total	**46 m**	**803 m**

*If citizen has come from other village in the recent past and his name has not been entered in citizen database

Efficiency (Throughput) = $\frac{\text{Actual time} \times 100}{\text{Total time}}$

$$= \frac{46\text{m} \times 100}{803 \text{ m}}$$

= **5.72 %**

Table 4.1A.6: Process Efficiency of Scenario D

Codes	Major activities of Scenario D	Actual time taken	Total time
A1	Patwari report in selected* case	-	-
A2 and A3	Filling up of citizen-id and some required fields in the AF at e-Kiosk	2 m	2 m
A4	Online submission of AF at e-Kiosk	1 m	2 m
	Issue of request-id at e-Kiosk	1 m	2 m
A5	Verification of application by Assistant in Tehsil using information in citizen database	10 m	15 m
	Assistant approves it by giving digital signature	2 m	2 m
	Verification by Tehsildar	2 m	5 m
	Approval of Application by giving digital signature	2 m	2 m
	Sending the certificate at e-Kiosk online	1 m	1 m
	Taking printout of certificate at e-Kiosk, signature and stamp on it	5 m	5 m
A6 & 7	Taking digital signature of citizen while receiving the certificate	2 m	4 m
	Total	**28 m**	**38 m**

*If citizen has come from other village in the recent past and his name has not been entered in citizen database

Efficiency (Throughput) $= \frac{\text{Actual time} \times 100}{\text{Total time}}$

$= \frac{28 \text{ m} \times 100}{38 \text{ m}}$

$=$ **73.64%**

Annexure 4.1B

Citizen Database Design

We choose to use the relational data model, which is a type of logical database model that treats data as if they were stored in two-dimensional tables. It can relate data stored in one table to data in another as long as the two tables share a common data element. The relational data model, the most recent of the three database models, overcomes some of the limitations of the other two models: hierarchical and network database model respectively.

According to the conceptual design of our proposed database, we would have the following databases.

Citizen Database: This database contains all the information required while availing any of the government services. Citizen Database contains:

- Citizen master record
- Citizen asset record
- Citizen education record
- Citizen land record
- Citizen ration card record

Service Database: This database contains all the information needed to process an application while citizen comes for availing the service. Service database contains:

- Service request record
- Record related to each service
- Record related to grievances

The subsequent sections will explain the entities and their relationships that will be used in the design of the database.

Entities: *Entities are data objects.*

Entities Involved in Citizen Database

Citizen Master Record: A citizen record is responsible to keep / manage general information about all the citizens in the whole district / state.

Following are the attributes of this record with their data types & field size. This record will be useful while availing any of the services as it stores all the general information about the citizen, which is, required everywhere.

Some of the attributes of the above table are explained below indicating the Primary Key[1] and the Foreign Keys[2] of the table.

Table 4.1B.1: Citizen Master Record

S. N.	Field name	Data type	Field size
1.	Citizen_id	Text	Width 10
2.	citizen_sex	Text	Width 6
3.	citizen_first_name	Text	Width 25
4.	citizen_middle_name	Text	Width 25
5.	citizen_last_name	Text	Width 25
6.	citizen_fathers_or_husband's_id	Text	Width 10
7.	citizen_date_of_birth	Date*	Auto
8.	citizen_place_of_birth	Text	Width 25
9.	citizen_state	Text	Width 20
10.	citizen_district	Text	Width 20
11.	citizen_tehsil	Text	Width 20
12.	citizen_village	Text	Width 20
13.	citizen_gp	Text	Width 20
14.	citizen_house_no	Number	Integer
15.	citizen_current_address	Text	Width 50
16.	citizen_permanent_address	Text	Width 50
17.	citizen_pin_code	Number	Long Integer
18.	citizen_govt_servant	Bit**	Auto
19.	citizen_govt_organisation	Text	Width 50
20.	citizen_election_id_no	Number	Long Integer
21.	citizen_ward	Number	Integer
22.	citizen_profession	Text	Width 20
23.	citizen_ration_card_id	Text	Width 10
24.	citizen_photograph	OLE Object	Auto
25.	citizen_tel_no	Number	Long Integer

*Date is stored in its predefined format

**Bit is stored in its predefined format to store Yes or No values as 1 or 0

- Citizen_id: This is the Primary Key of this record that distinguishes one citizen from another. Every citizen n will have a unique citizen ID.

---

[1] Primary Key (PK): Every table should have one field (attribute) which is unique to each record, or at least some combination of field which together are unique to each record. There is no other way to distinguish a single record reliably. This field or combination is called the Primary Key. Primary Key value cannot be NULL.

[2] Foreign Key (FK): It is field in a database record that points to a field of another database record in another table. Usually a Foreign Key in one table refers to the Primary Key (PK) of the other table. This way references can be made to link information together.

- Citizen_fathers_or husband's_id: This is the Foreign Key to map the citizen record to the record of his / her guardian, so that if need arises; one can easily check the record of citizen's guardian.
- Citizen_ration_card_id: This is the Foreign Key to map citizen to a particular Ration Card record.
  Here are some other attributes of a table, which require explanation for their existence in the table.
- Citizen_place_of_birth: This field will be useful while availing domicile certificate.
- Citizen_govt_servant: This field will again be useful while getting domicile certificate. Government servant is eligible for domicile of a state with only 3 years of service in that state. Otherwise for common man, there is an eligibility of 10 years to get domicile of a state.

Citizen Asset Record

It contains information about all the assets citizens have. It will be useful when government officials require information about the economic condition of the citizen. This record will be also useful in case of getting income certificate.

Table 4.1B.2: Citizen Asset Record

S. N.	Field name	Data type	Field size
1.	Asset_citizen_id	Text	Width 10
2.	Asset_name	Text	Width 25
3.	Asset_amount	Number	Integer
4.	Asset_description	Text	Width 50

Some of the attributes of the above table are explained below indicating the Primary Key and the Foreign Keys of the table.

- Citizen_id & Asset_name together constitute the Primary Key, which may also be termed as the Composite Key.
- Citizen_id is the Foreign Key from 'Citizen Master Record' Table 4.1B.1 that enables to view any information related to the citizen like name, address etc.

Citizen Education Record

It contains information about the educational qualification of citizens and the education the citizen is currently pursuing.

It may not be useful right now but it may definitely be useful in future as the citizen database will grow and systems become more and more sophisticated.

Some of the attributes of the above table are explained below indicating the primary key and the foreign keys of the table.

- Education_citizen_id forms the Primary Key & the Foreign Key of this table. As a Primary Key, it enables one to identify the educational qualifications of each citizen. As a foreign key it maps to the citizen_id field in Table 4.1B.1 – citizen master record.

Table 4.1B.3: Citizen Education Record

S.N.	Field Name	Data Type	Field size
1.	Education_citizen_id	Text	Width 10
2.	Education_qualification	Text	Width 25
3.	education_institution	Text	Width 25
4.	educaton_year_of_passing	Date	Auto
5.	education_currently_pursuing	Text	Width 25
6.	education_current_institution	Text	Width 25
7.	education_type_of_course	Text	Width 9

Citizen Ration Card Record

It is nothing but the details of ration card what we can say a digital ration card.

This record will be useful while availing service for getting caste, income & domicile certificate.

Table 4.1B.4: Citizen Ration Card Record

S. N.	Field name	Data type	Field size
1.	Ration_Card_id	Text	Width 10
2.	Ration_Card _citizen_id	Text	Width 10
3.	Ration_Card _issue_date	Date	Auto
4.	Ration_Card _validity	Date	Auto
5.	Ration_Card _address	Text	Width 50
6.	Ration_Card _units_lt_12yr	Number	Integer
7.	Ration_Card _units_gt_12yr	Number	Integer

Some of the attributes of the above table are explained below indicating the Primary Key and the Foreign Keys of the table.

- Ration_Card_id is the Primary Key of the table. (Which corresponds to citizen_ration_card_id in Table 4.1B.11)
- Ration_Card _citizen_id is the Foreign Key that maps to the citizen_id field

of the 'Citizen Master Record' Table 4.1B.1

Citizen Land Record

It is an existing database, which contains information about the land record of citizens, which is kept on a server at Collectorate, updated through CD ROM on a fortnightly basis. Tehsils have been given PC's, which are used to update records. Patwari visits Tehsil every month & gets the records updated.

Table 4.1B.5: Citizen Land Record

S. N.	Field name	Data type	Field size
1.	jamabandi_new_khata_number	Text	Width 10
2.	jamabandi_citizen_id	Text	Width 10
3.	jamabandi_old_khata_number	Text	Width 10
4.	jamabandi_khasra_number	Text	Width 10
5.	jamabandi_area	Number	Auto
6.	jamabandi_khatedar_category	Text	Width 15
7.	jamabandi_land_classification	Text	Width 15
8.	jamabandi_soil_category	Text	Width 15
9.	jamabandi_source_of_irrigation	Text	Width 15
10.	jamabandi_lagaan_amount	Number	Integer
11.	jamabandi_date_of_transfer	Date	Auto
12.	jamabandi_date_of_record_update	Date	Auto
13.	jamabandi_update_officer_1_name	Text	Width 25
14.	jamabandi_update_officer_1_date	Date	Auto
15.	jamabandi_update_officer_2_name	Text	Width 25
16.	jamabandi_update_officer_2_date	Date	Auto
17	jamabandi_record_created_by	Text	Width 25
18.	jamabandi_record_created_on	Date	Auto

Some of the attributes of the above table are explained below indicating the Primary Key and the Foreign Keys of the table.

- jamabandi_new_khata_number and jamabandi_khasra_number together form the Primary Key for this table.
- jamabandi_citizen_id is the foreign key of this table, which maps to the citizen_id field in 'Citizen Master Record' Table 4.1B.1

Entities Involved in Service Database

Table 4.1B.6: Service Request Record

S. N.	Field name	Data type	Field size
1.	service_request_id	Text	Width 10
2.	service_request_citizen_id	Text	Width 10
3.	service_request_received_on	Date	Auto
4.	service_request_prescribed_date	Date	Auto
5.	service_request_status	Text	Width 20
6.	service_request_officer1_id	Text	Width 15
7.	service_request_officer1_approved_on	Date	Auto
8.	service_request _officer1_remarks	Text	Width 255
9.	service_request_officer2_id	Text	Width 15
10.	service_request_officer2_approved_on	Date	Auto
11.	service_request _officer2_remarks	Text	Width 255
12.	service_request_officer3_id	Text	Width 15
13.	service_request_officer3_approved_on	Date	Auto
14.	service_request _officer3_remarks	Text	Width 255
15.	service_request_completion_date	Date	Auto
16.	service_request_amount_paid	Number	Integer

Some of the attributes of the above table are explained below indicating the Primary Key and the Foreign Keys of the table.

- service_request_id is the Primary Key of the above Table 4.1B.6
- service_request_citizen_id is the Foreign Key that maps to the "citizen_id" field of the 'Citizen Maser Record' Table 4.1B.1

Table 4.1B.7: Income Certificate Request Record

S. N.	Field name	Data type	Field size
1.	income_certificate_id	Text	Width 10
2.	income_certificate_citizen_id	Text	Width 10
3.	income_certificate_service_request_id	Text	Width 10
4.	income_certificate_reason	Text	Width 50
5.	income_certificate_income	Number	Long Integer
6.	income_certificate_issued_by_off_name	Text	Width 25
7.	income_certificate_issued_by_off_desg	Text	Width 25
8.	income_certificate_issued_by_off_loc	Text	Width 25
9.	income_certificate_issued_on	Date	Auto

Some of the attributes of the above table are explained below indicating the Primary Key and the Foreign Keys of the table.

- income_certificate_id is the Primary Key of the above table
- income_certificate_citizen_id is the Foreign Key that maps to the "citizen_id" field of the 'Citizen Master Record' Table 4.1B.1
- service_request_id is the Foreign Key that maps to the "service_request_id" field of the 'Service Request Record' Table 4.1B.6

Apart from the above attributes, following attributes also needs some explanation:

income_certificate_issued_by_off_name, income_certificate_issued_by_off_desg & income_certificate_issued_by_off _loc store the name, designation and location of the final authority who have approved or disapproved an application.

Table 4.1B.8: Caste Certificate Request Record

S. N.	Field name	Data type	Field size
1.	caste_certificate_id	Text	Width 10
2.	caste_certificate_service_request_id	Text	Width 10
3.	caste_certificate_citizen_id	Text	Width 10
4.	caste_certificate_reason	Text	Width 50
5.	caste_certificate_creamy_layer	Bit	Auto
6.	caste_certificate_income	Number	Long Integer
7.	caste_certificate_income_id	Text	Width 10
8.	caste_certificate_caste_name	Text	Width 3
9.	caste_certificate_issued_by_off_name	Text	Width 25
10.	caste_certificate_issued_by_off_desg	Text	Width 25
11.	caste_certificate_issued_by_off_loc	Text	Width 25
12.	caste_certificate_issued_on	Date	Auto

Some of the attributes of the above Table 4.1B.8 are explained below indicating the Primary Key and the Foreign Keys of the Table 4.1B.6

- caste_certificate_id is the Primary Key of the above Table 4.1B.8
- service_request_id is the Foreign Key that maps to the "service_request_id" field of the 'Service Request Record' Table 4.1B.6
- caste_certificate_citizen_id is the Foreign Key that maps to the "citizen_id" field of the 'Citizen Master Record' Table 4.1B.1

Apart from the above attributes, following attributes also needs some explanation: caste_certificate_income & caste_certificate_income_id fields are required in case of creamy-layer OBC candidate.

Table 4.1B.9: Domicile Certificate Request Record

S. N.	Field name	Data type	Field size
1.	domicile_certificate_id	Text	Width 10
2.	domicile_certificate_service_request_id	Text	Width 10
3.	domicile_certificate_citizen_id	Text	Width 10
4.	domicile_certificate_reason	Text	Width 50
5.	domicile_certificate_living_since	Date	Auto
6.	domicile_certificate_issued_by_off_name	Text	Width 25
7.	domicile_certificate_issued_by_off_desg	Text	Width 25
8.	domicile_certificate_issued_by_off_loc	Text	Width 25
9.	domicile_certificate_issued_on	Date	Auto

Some of the attributes of the above table are explained below indicating the Primary Key and the Foreign Keys of the table.

- domicile_certificate_id is the Primary Key of the above Table 4.1B.9
- service_request_id is the Foreign Key that maps to the "service_request_id" field of the 'Service Request Record' Table 4.1B.6.
- domicile_certificate_citizen_id is the Foreign Key that maps to the "citizen_id" field of the 'Citizen Master Record " Table 4.1B.1

Table 4.1B.10: Jamabandi Request Record

S.N.	Field name	Data type	Field size
1.	jamabandi_id	Text	Width 10
2.	jamabandi_service_request_id	Text	Width 10
3.	jamabandi_citizen_id	Text	Width 10
4.	jamabandi_khata_no	Text	Width 10
5.	Jamabandi_khasra_no	Text	Width 10
6.	jamabandi_reason	Text	Width 50
7.	jamabandi_issued_on	Date	Auto

Some of the attributes of the above table are explained below indicating the Primary Key and the Foreign Keys of the table.

- jamabandi_id is the Primary Key of the above Table 4.1B.10
- service_request_id is the Foreign Key that maps to the 'service_request_id' field of the 'Service Request Record' Table 4.1B.6
- jamabandi_citizen_id is the Foreign Key that maps to the 'citizen_id' field of the 'Citizen Master Record' Table 4.1B.1

Table 4.1B.11: Ration Card Request Record

S. N.	Field Name	Data Type	Field size
1.	ration_card_id	Text	Width 10
2.	ration_card_service_request_id	Text	Width 10
3.	ration_card_citizen_id	Text	Width 10
4.	ration_card_reason	Text	Width 50
5.	ration_card_income	Number	Long Integer
6.	ration_card_income_id	Text	Width 10
7.	ration_card _issued_by_off_name	Text	Width 25
8.	ration_card _issued_by_off_desg	Text	Width 25
9.	ration_card _issued_by_off_loc	Text	Width 25
10.	ration_card_issued_on	Date	Auto

Some of the attributes of the above table are explained below indicating the Primary Key and the Foreign Keys of the Table 4.1B11

- ration_card_id is the Primary Key of the above Table 4.1B.11
- service_request_id is the Foreign Key that maps to the 'service_request_id' field of the 'Service Request Record' Table 4.1B.6
- ration_card_citizen_id is the Foreign Key that maps to the "citizen_id" field of the 'Citizen Master Record' Table 4.1B.1.

Apart from the above attributes, following attributes also needs some explanation: Ration_card_income & Ration_card_income_id fields will be useful in determining the category of ration card like Antyodaya, BPL or APL.

Entity Relational Model

This table defines the relationships: between entities, types of relationships, and their attributes.

Table 4.1B.12: Entity Relational Model

S. N.	Relationship	Entities Involved	Type
1.	Has	Citizen / Asset	1:N
2.	Has	Citizen / Land	1:N
3.	Has	Citizen / Education record	1:1
4.	Has	Citizen / Ration card	1:1
5.	For	Service request / Income certificate	1:1
6.	For	Service request / Caste certificate	1:1
7.	For	Service request / Domicile certificate	1:1
8.	For	Service request / Jamabandi	1:1
9.	For	Service request / Ration card	1:1
10.	Makes	Citizen / Service request	1:N

Relationship Descriptions

Has: This relationship type joins table citizen with land, education record, ration card, & asset to comprise the citizen database. There is a 1:N relationship between citizen & asset, & citizen & land. While a 1:1 relationship between citizen & ration card, & citizen & education record

For: This relationship type joins table service_request with income certificate, caste certificate, domicile certificate, ration card, & Jamabandi. There is a 1:1 relationship between service_request & these services.

Makes: This relationship type joins tables citizen & service_request while citizen avails any of the services. There is a 1:N relationship between citizen & service_request.

Relation Model

Figure: 4.1B.1
Schema Diagram for Service Request

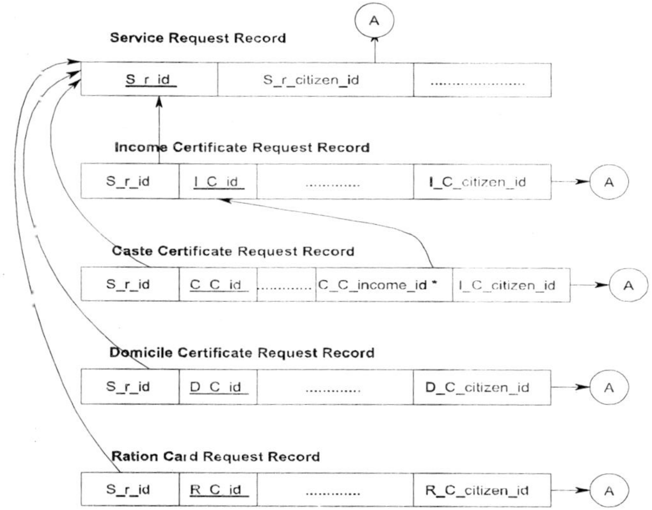

* This field will be useful when a person needs to have an OBC certificate under creamy-layer category and the person needs to show his / her income. In that case, if the person is already having an income certificate that is already there in the database, the person only needs to give the income certificate ID in this field and the certificate will be available online for the verification.

Figure: 4.1B.2
Schema Diagram for Citizen Database

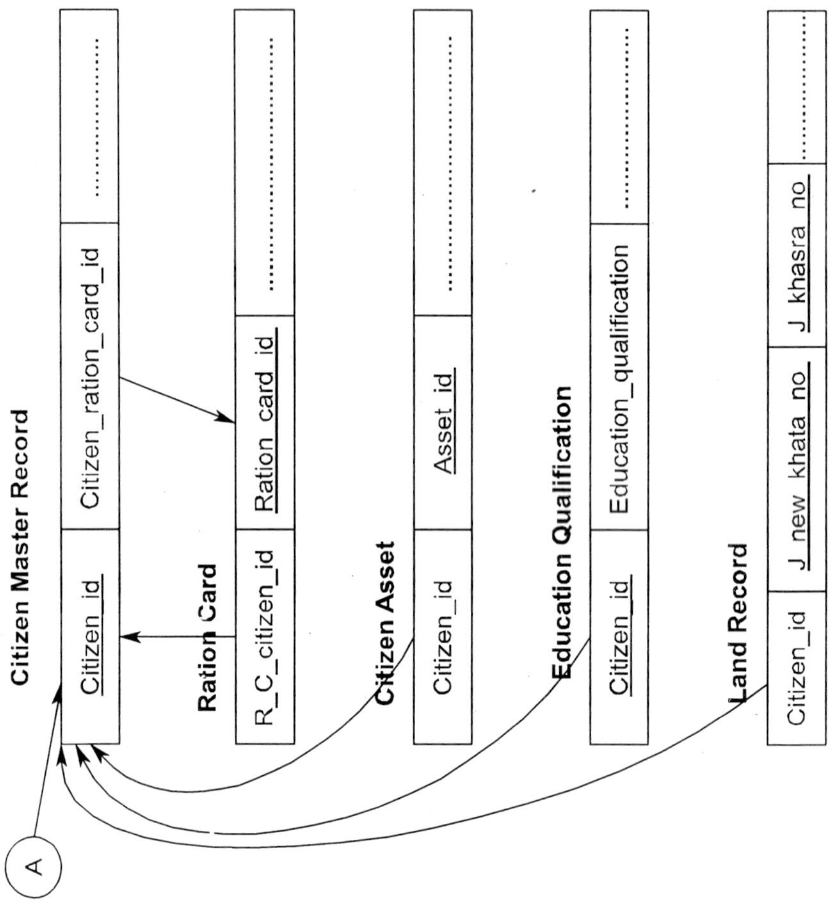

Figure: 4.1B.3
ER Diagram - Relationship Diagram for Citizen Records

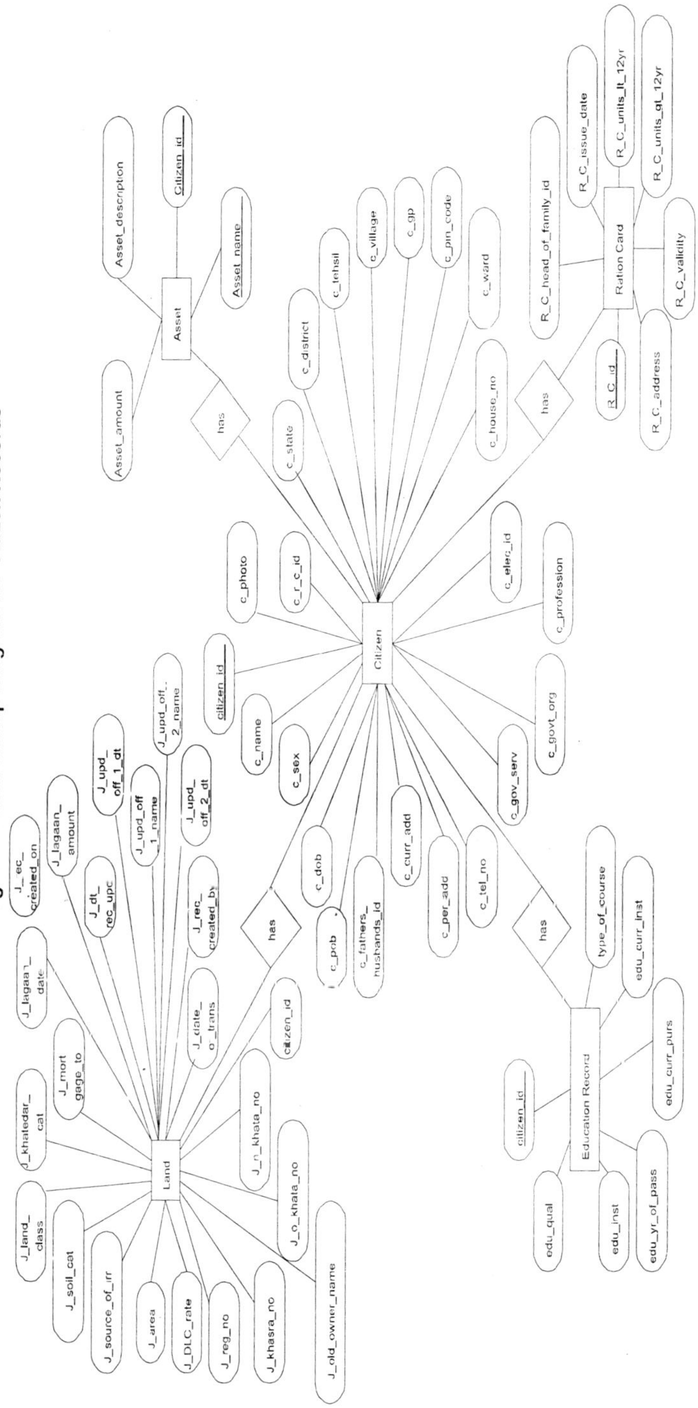

Figure: 4B.1.4
Relationship Diagram for Service Request Record

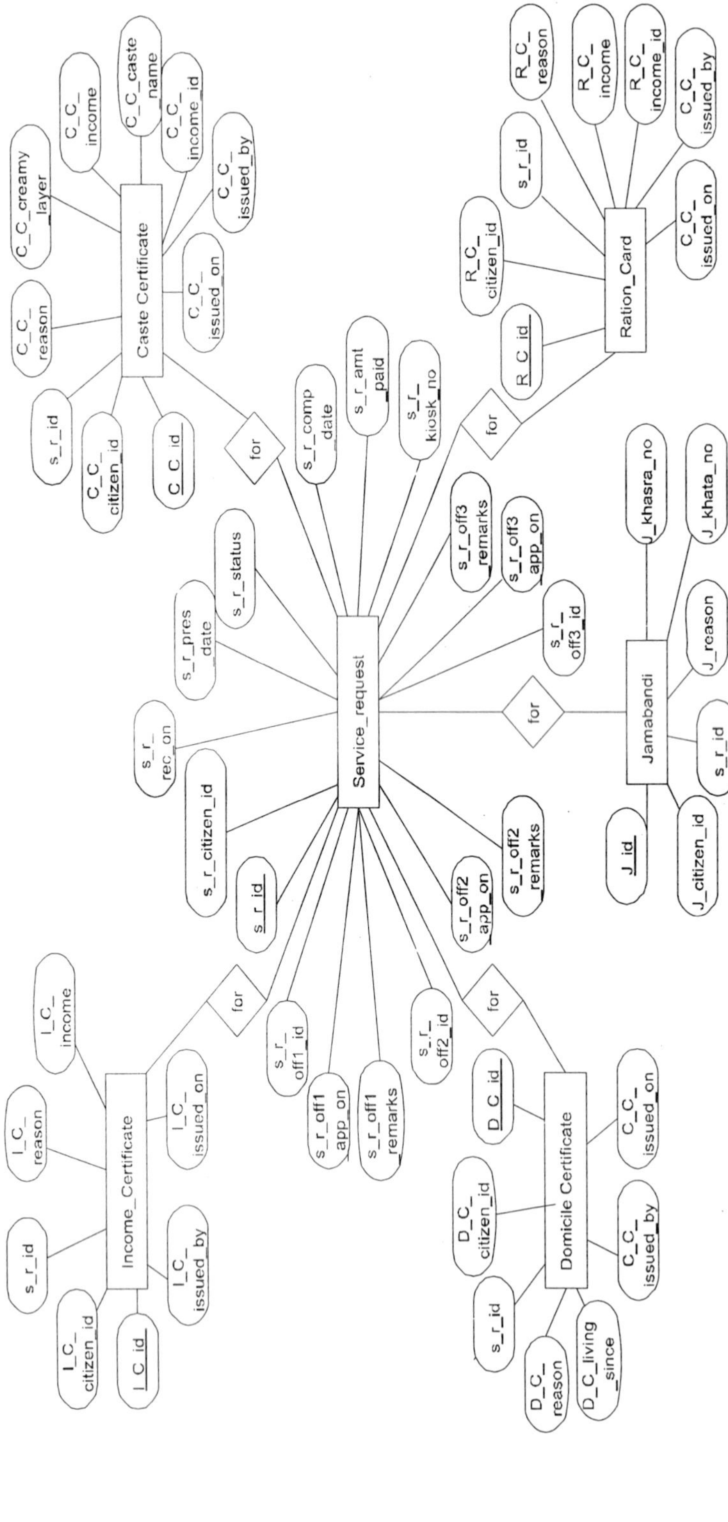

Figure: 4.1B.5
Relationship Diagram to show Relationship between Citizen Record and Service Request Record

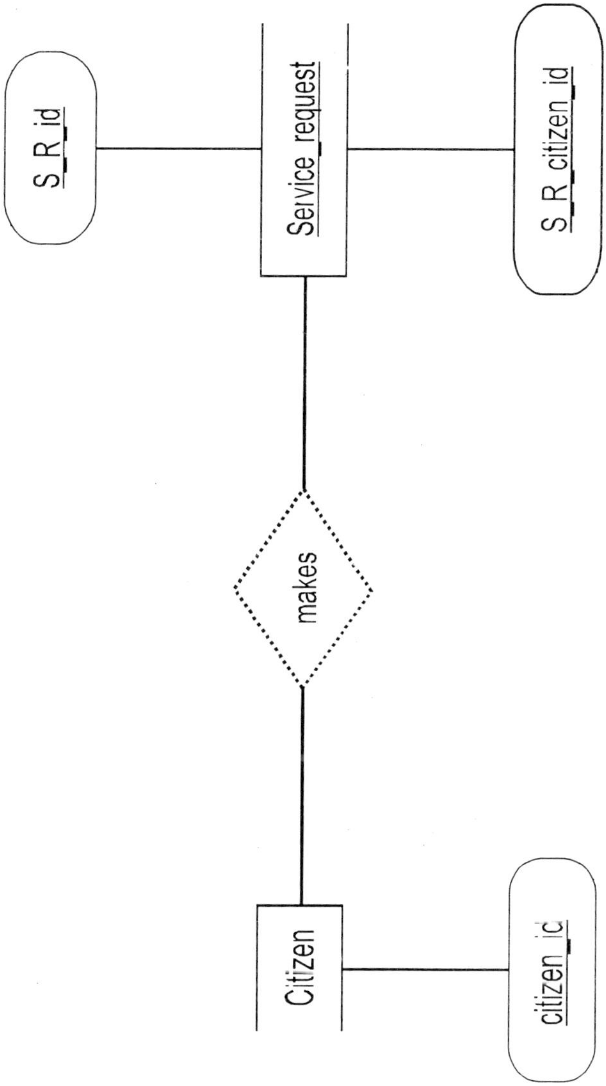

Annexure 4.2: Changes required for New System

ScenarioA

Application form	:	Online
Attachments	:	Manual
Internal processing of Tehsil	:	Online
Delivery form	:	Manual

Table 4.2.1: Changes Required for New System in Scenario A

S.N.	Description	What changes required	Type	Level & support	Benefits
1.	Application form	□ Application form to be re-designed*	AF, Rules	Govt. order required	Simplified AF
		□ Stamp duty to be done away with & replaced by single user charges.	Rules	-do-	No need to purchase stamps or stamp paper
		□ Application form to be submitted at e-Kiosk.	Rules	-do-	Citizen need not to go to Tehsil
2.	Attachments	□ Mode of sending attachments from e-Kiosk to Tehsil.	By courier or post	-do-	-
3.	Verification	□ Deputation of Patwari or authorised staff between 10 AM to 12 noon at e-Kiosk for verification of attachments at the time of submission of AF.	Rules	Collectorate order required	Citizen need not to go to *Patwarghar*
		□ Patwari report to be typed on the computer and signed digitally using digital signatures as well as light pen.	Rules	Govt. order required	-
		□ Digital signature should be accepted legally	Rules	-do-	-
4.	Internal processing at Tehsil level	□ Internal processing of Tehsil will be fully computerised.	Infrastructure & equipments	Govt. to provide financial support	MIS about the service delivery can be easily maintained

*The re-designed AF for caste certificate is shown at Annexure 2 C

Contd...

S.N.	Description	What changes required	Type	Level & support	Benefits
		• Connected to all the Kiosks	Network	-do-	-
5.	Delivery form	• A way to send delivery form from Tehsil to e-Kiosk.	By ourier or post	Collectorate order required	-
6.	Delivery of certificate to citizen	• Handing over document to citizen at e-Kiosk with signature of citizen with light pen or thumb impression. • Informing the Tehsil office electronically by Patwari about the issue of certificate. • Listing the information on web-site about the issue of certificate	Rules	Govt. order required	-
7.	Security	**Stakeholders**: At Kiosk (Kiosk owner & Patwari) **Security measures**: 1. At the time of filling up of AF • Login for Kiosk owner ✓ User-ID & password ✓ Biometrics (thumb impression) 2. At the time of submission of AF • Citizen signature using light pen 3. Patwari report • Login for Patwari ✓ User- ID & password ✓ Biometrics (thumb impression) ✓ Digital signature	Rules	Change in relevant Act required	Prevention of unauthorised access

Contd...

S.N.	Description	What changes required		Type	Level & support	Benefits
			4. To see pending application • Login for Patwari ✓ User- ID & password ✓ Biometrics (thumb impression) ✓ Digital signature 5. To see pending application • Login for Kiosk owner ✓ User- ID & password ✓ Biometrics (thumb impression) ✓ Digital signature			
		At Tehsil (Assistant & Tehsildar)	6. To see pending application • Login for (i) Tehsildar (ii) Assistant in Tehsil ✓ User-ID & password ✓ Biometrics (thumb impression) ✓ Digital signature 7. For verification & updating the status of application using • Login for Patwari ✓ User-ID & password ✓ Biometrics (thumb impression) ✓ Digital signature ✓ Light pen for signature			

AF: Application Form, DF: Delivery Form

Scenario B

Applicationform : Online
Attachments : Online+manual
Internal processing of Tehsil : Online
Deliveryform : Manual

Table 4.2.2: Changes Required for New System in Scenario B

S. N.	Description	What changes required	Type	Level & support	Benefits
1.	Application form	□ Application form to be redesigned*.	AF, Rules	Govt. order required	Simplified AF
		□ Stamp duty to be done away with & replaced by single user charges.	Rules	-do-	No need to purchase stamps or stamp paper
		□ AF to be submitted at e-Kiosk.	Rules	-do-	Citizen need not to go to Tehsil
2.	Attachments	□ Scanned documents should be legally accepted as an attachment.	Rules	-do-	Will take less time due to electronic medium
3.	Verification	□ Deputation of Patwari or authorised staff between 10 AM to 12 noon from Tehsil at e-Kiosk for verification of attachments at the time of submission of AF.	Rules	Collectorate order required	Citizen need not to go to *Patwarghar*
		□ Patwari report to be typed on the computer and signed digitally using digital signatures as well as light pen.	Rules	Govt. order required	-
		□ Digital signature should be accepted legally	Rules	- do-	-
4.	Internal processing at Tehsil level	□ Internal processing of Tehsil will be fully computerised.	Infrastructure, Rules	Govt. to provide financial support	MIS about the service delivery can be easily maintained
		□ Connected to all the Kiosks.	Network	-do-	-

*The re-designed AF for caste certificate is shown at Annexure 4.2C

Contd...

<table>
<tr><th>S. N.</th><th>Description</th><th colspan="2">What changes required</th><th>Type</th><th>Level & support</th><th>Benefits</th></tr>
<tr><td>5.</td><td>Delivery form</td><td colspan="2">☐ A way to send DF from Tehsil to e-Kiosk.</td><td>By courier or post</td><td>Collectorate order required</td><td></td></tr>
<tr><td>6.</td><td>Delivery of certificate to citizen</td><td colspan="2">☐ Handing over document to citizen at e-Kiosk with signature of citizen with light pen or thumb impression
☐ Informing the Tehsil office electronically by Patwari about the issue of certificate
☐ Listing the information on web-site about the issue of certificate</td><td>Rules</td><td>-</td><td>-</td></tr>
<tr><td rowspan="2">7.</td><td rowspan="2">Security</td><td>Stakeholders</td><td>Security measures</td><td rowspan="2">Rules</td><td rowspan="2">Change in relevant Act required</td><td rowspan="2">Prevention of unauthorised access</td></tr>
<tr><td>At Kiosk (Kiosk owner & Patwari)</td><td>1. At the time of filling up of AF
• Login for Kiosk owner
✓ User-ID & password
✓ Biometrics (thumb impression)
2. At the time of submission of AF
• Citizen signature using light pen
3. Patwari report
• Login for Patwari
✓ User- ID & password
✓ Biometrics (thumb impression)
✓ Digital signature
4. To see pending application
• Login for Patwari</td></tr>
</table>

Contd...

S. N.	Description	What changes required		Type	Level & support	Benefits
			✓ User- ID & password ✓ Biometrics (thumb impression) ✓ Digital signature 5. To see pending application • Login for Kiosk owner ✓ User- ID & password ✓ Biometrics (thumb impression) ✓ Digital signature			
		At Tehsil (Assistant & Tehsildar)	6. To see pending application • Login for (i) Tehsildar (ii) Assistant in Tehsil ✓ User- ID & password ✓ Biometrics (thumb impression) ✓ Digital signature 7. For verification & updating the status of application using • Login for Patwari ✓ User- ID & password ✓ Biometrics (thumb impression) ✓ Digital signature ✓ Light pen for signature			

Note: The suggestions of scenario A are also reflected above
AF: Application Form, DF: Delivery Form

Scenario C

Application Form : Online
Attachments : In case of dynamic data*
Internal processing of Tehsil : Online
DeliveryForm : Manual

Table 4.2.3: Changes Required for New System in Scenario C

S. N.	Description	What changes required	Type	Level & support	Benefits
1.	Application form	□ Application form needs to be redesigned**.	AF, Rules	Govt. order required.	Simplified AF
		□ Stamp duty to be done away & is replaced by single user charges.	Rules	-do-	No need to purchase stamps or stamp paper
		□ Filling up the AF online at e-Kiosk, which requires only the filling of citizen ID, and one or two necessary fields.	DB	-do-	Time saving
2.	Attachments	□ Because of centralised database, many of the attachments will not be required.	DB	-do-	Attachments not required
		□ Scanned documents should be legally accepted as an attachment (in case of dynamic data such as income certificate).	Rules	-do-	-
3.	Submission at Kiosk level	□ Deputation of Patwari or authorised staff from Tehsil at e-Kiosk.	Rules	Collectorate order required	Citizen need not to go to *Patwarghar*
4.	Verification	□ Citizen database to be recognised as legal record throughout the district.	DB, Rules	Govt. order required	-
		□ Digital signature should be acceptable for verification.	Rules	-do-	-

Attachments will be required (in case of change of place or caste or income). In that case, attachments will be sent by scanning them,
** The re-designed AF for caste certificate is shown at Annexure 4.2D

Contd...

<table>
<tr><th>S. N.</th><th>Description</th><th colspan="2">What changes required</th><th>Type</th><th>Level & support</th><th>Benefits</th></tr>
<tr><td rowspan="2">5.</td><td rowspan="2">Internal processing at Tehsil level</td><td colspan="2">□ Internal processing of Tehsil will be fully computerised.</td><td>Infrastructure, Rules</td><td>Govt. to provide financial support</td><td>MIS about the service delivery can be easily maintained</td></tr>
<tr><td colspan="2">□ Connected to all the Kiosks.</td><td>Network</td><td>-do-</td><td>-</td></tr>
<tr><td rowspan="3">6.</td><td rowspan="3">Delivery form</td><td colspan="2">□ Delivery format needs to be redesigned (which may contain the automatically generated certificate number or some barcode number)</td><td>DF, Rules</td><td>Govt. order required.</td><td>Simplified DF</td></tr>
<tr><td colspan="2">□ Print out will be taken in Tehsil only.</td><td>Rules</td><td>-do-</td><td>-</td></tr>
<tr><td colspan="2">□ A way to send DF from Tehsil to e-Kiosk</td><td>By courier or post</td><td>Collectorate order required</td><td>-</td></tr>
<tr><td>7.</td><td>Delivery of certificate to citizen</td><td colspan="2">□ Handing over document to citizen at e-Kiosk with signature of citizen with light pen or thumb impression
□ Informing the Tehsil office electronically by Patwari about the issue of certificate
□ Listing the information on web-site about the issue of certificate</td><td>Rules</td><td>-do-</td><td>-</td></tr>
<tr><td rowspan="2">8.</td><td rowspan="2">Security</td><td>Stakeholders</td><td>Security measures</td><td rowspan="2">Rules</td><td rowspan="2">Change in relevant Act. required</td><td rowspan="2">Prevention of unauthorised access</td></tr>
<tr><td>At Kiosk (Kiosk owner & Patwari)</td><td>1. At the time of filling up of AF
• Login for Kiosk owner
✓ User-ID & password
✓ Biometrics (thumb impression)
2. At the time of submission of AF
• Citizen signature using light pen</td></tr>
</table>

Contd...

S. N.	Description	What changes required		Type	Level & support	Benefits
			3. Patwari report in case of dynamic data • Login for Patwari ✓ User- ID & password ✓ Biometrics (IRIS) ✓ Digital signature 4. To see pending application • Login for Patwari ✓ User- ID & password ✓ Biometrics (thumb impression) ✓ Digital signature 5. To see pending application • Login for Kiosk owner ✓ User- ID & password ✓ Biometrics (thumb impression) ✓ Digital signature			
		At Tehsil (Assistant & Tehsildar)	6. To see pending application • Login for (i) Tehsildar (ii) Assistant in Tehsil ✓ User- ID & password ✓ Biometrics (thumb impression) ✓ Digital signature			
			7. For verification & updating the status of application using • Login for Patwari ✓ User- ID & password ✓ Biometrics (thumb impression) ✓ Digital signature ✓ Light pen for signature			

Note: The suggestions of scenarios A and B are also reflected above

AF: Application Form, DF: Delivery Form

Scenario D

Application Form : Online
Attachments : Incase of dynamic data
Internal processing of Tehsil : Online
Delivery form : Online

Table 4.2.4: Changes Required for New System in Scenario D

S.N.	Description	What changes required	Type	Level & support	Benefits
1.	Application form	□ Application form needs to be redesigned**	AF, Rules	Govt. order required.	Simplified AF
		□ Stamp duty to be done away & is replaced by single user charges.	Rules	-do-	No need to purchase stamps or stamp paper
		□ Filling up the AF online at e-Kiosk, which requires only the filling of citizen id, and one or two necessary fields.	DB	-do-	Time saving
2.	Attachments	□ Because of centralised database, many of the attachments will not be required.	DB	-do-	Attachments not required
		□ Scanned documents should be legally accepted as an attachment (in case of dynamic data such as income certificate).	Rules	-do-	Time saving due to electronic medium
3.	Submission at Kiosk level	□ Deputation of Patwari or authorised staff from Tehsil at e-Kiosk.	Rules	Collectorate order required	Citizen need not to go to *Patwarghar*
4.	Verification	□ Verification of AF will be done online.	DB, Rules	Court order required	-
		□ Citizen database to be recognised as legal record throughout the district.	Rules	-do-	-
		□ Digital signature should be acceptable for verification.	Rules	-do-	-

Attachments will be required (in case change of place or caste or income). In that case, attachments will be send by scanning them.
** The re-designed AF for caste certificate is shown at Annexure 4.2D

Contd...

S.N.	Description	What changes required	Type	Level & support	Benefits
5.	Internal processing at Tehsil level	□ Internal processing of Tehsil will be fully computerised.	Infrastructure, Rules	Govt. to provide financial support	MIS about the service delivery can be easily maintained
		□ Connected to all the Kiosks.	Network	-do-	
6.	Delivery form	□ Delivery format needs to be redesigned (which may contain the automatically generated certificate number or some barcode number)	DF, Rules	Govt. order required	Simplified delivery form
		□ Printed form should be legally accepted.	Rules	-do-	-
		□ Certificate / document is printed at Kiosk, and signed and stamped by local Tehsil authority (Patwari or Girdawar) and handing over to citizen. □ While handing over document to citizen at e-Kiosk, signature of citizen with light pen or thumb impression. □ Informing the Tehsil office electronically by Patwari about the issue of certificate. □ Listing the information on web-site about the issue of certificate	Rules	-do-	Time saving in sending certificate through Tehsil to e-Kiosk
7.	Security	**Stakeholders**: At Kiosk (Kiosk owner & Patwari) **Security measures**: 1. At the time of filling up of application • Login for Kiosk owner ✓ User-ID & password ✓ Biometrics (IRIS) 2. At the time of submission of AF • Citizen signature using light pen	Rules	Change in relevant Act required	Preventions of unauthorised access

Contd...

S.N.	Description	What changes required	Type	Level & support	Benefits
		3. Patwari report in case of dynamic data • Login for Patwari ✓ User-ID & password ✓ Biometrics (IRIS) ✓ Digital signature 4. At the time of delivery of certificate to citizen • Login for Kiosk owner ✓ User-ID and password ✓ Biometrics (IRIS) • Signature of citizen using light pen • Signature of issuing authority on delivery certificate			
		5. To see pending application • Login for Patwari ✓ User-ID & password ✓ Biometrics (IRIS) ✓ Digital signature 6. To see pending application • Login for Kiosk owner ✓ User-ID & password ✓ Biometrics (IRIS) ✓ Digital signature			

Contd...

S.N.	Description	What changes required		Type	Level & support	Benefits
			7. Informing Tehsil through online about the Certificate delivered by Patwari • Login for Patwari ✓ User-ID & password ✓ Biometrics (IRIS) ✓ Digital signature 8. Barcode generated number will be printed on the delivery certificate			
		At Tehsil (Assistant, Tehsildar)	9. To see pending application • Login for (i) Tehsildar (ii) Assistant in Tehsil ✓ User-ID & password ✓ Biometrics (IRIS) ✓ Digital signature 10. For verification & updating the status of application using • Login for Patwari ✓ User-ID& password ✓ Biometrics (IRIS) ✓ Digital signature ✓ Light pen for signature			

Note: The suggestions of scenarios A, B and C are also reflected above
AF: Application Form, DF: Delivery Form

Annexure 4.2A: Attachments, Touch Points and Number of Visits

Table 4.2A.1: Different Attachments as required for availing Select Services (After BPR for Scenarios A and B)

S.N.	Caste certificate				Domicile certificate	M/N	Income certificate	M/N
	ST/SC	M/N	OBC	M/N				
1.	Report of Patwari	M	Report of Patwari	M	Report of Patwari	M	Report of Patwari	M
2.	Copy of ROR	N	Affidavit	M	Voter list (last 10 years)	M**	Affidavit (About Income from all sources)	M
3.	Ration card	N	Income certificate	M*	Mark sheet of last degree achieved (history of last 10 years)	M**	Ration card	N
4.	Voter list	N	Ration card	N	Ration card	N	Certificate of employer (incase the candidate is employee)	N
5.	Mark sheet of last degree achieved	N	Mark sheet of last degree achieved	N			Copy of Jamabandi	N
6.	Two copy of parents caste certificate if candidate is student	N	Two copies of parent's caste certificate, if candidate is a student.	N			Voter list	N
7.			Copy of ROR	N			Mark sheet of last degree achieved	N
8.			Voter list	N			Copy of original income certificate	N
9.			Identification of two Govt. employees (gazetted officer)	N				

*Mandatory in creamy-layer cases; ** Either voter list or mark sheet; M: Mandatory; N: Non-mandatory

Table: 4.2A.2

Touch Points for Citizen and Application, and Number of Visi ts by Citizens in Manual processing, e-Governance Project, different Scenarios - A Comparative Analysis

Item		Manual	E-governance	Scenario A	Scenario B	Scenario C*	Scenario D*
Touch points	For citizens	**Minimum** 1. Collection of AF 2. Preparation of affidavit 3. Photocopy of income certificate (for creamy-layer) 4. Goes to Patwari for Patwari report 5. For taking the report from Patwari 6. To submit at single window 7. For collecting the certificate **Maximum** 1 to 7 of minimum and 8. Ration card 9. Copy of ROR 10. Voter list 11. Two copies of parent's caste certificate, if candidate is a student 12. Mark sheet of last degree achieved 13. Identification from two Govt. employee (gazetted officer)	**Minimum** 1. Preparation of affidavit 2. Photocopy of income certificate (for creamy-layer) 3. Goes to Patwari for Patwari report 4. For taking the report from Patwari 5. To submit at e-Kiosk 6. To collecting the certificate **Maximum** 1 to 6 of minimum and 7. Ration card 8. Copy of ROR 9. Voter list 10. Two copies of parent's caste certificate, if candidate is a student 11. Mark sheet of last degree achieved 12. Identification from two Govt. employee(gazetted officer)	*Minimum* 1. Preparation of affidavit 2. Photocopy of income certificate (for creamy-layer) 3. Coes to Patwari. For Patwari report 4. For taking the report from Patwari 5. To submit at e-Kiosk 6. For collecting the certificate ***Maximum*** 1 to 6 of minimum 7. Copy of one of the items from 7 to 12, as indicated under e-Governance head	*Minimum* 1. Preparation of affidavit 2. Photocopy of income certificate (for creamy-layer) 3. Goes to Patwari. For Patwari report 4. For taking the report from Patwari 5. To submit at e-Kiosk 6. For collecting the certificate ***Maximum*** 1 to 6 of minimum 7. Copy of one of the items from 7 to 12, as indicated under e-Governance head	*Minimum* 1. To submitting at e-Kiosk 2. For collecting the certificate	*Minimum* 1. To submitting at e-Kiosk 2. For collecting the certificate

*Dynamic data: In case of dynamic data (change of place or caste or income, etc.) the attachments are to be attached as in scenario A

Contd...

Item		Manual	E-governance	Scenario A	Scenario B	Scenario C*	Scenario D*
	For application	To 1. Citizen 2. Patwari 3. Single window 4. *Vivid Shakha* 5. Tehsildar 6. *Vivid Shakha* 7. Single window	To 1. Citizen 2. Patwari 3. E-kiosk 4. Head-end 5. Single window (Collectorate) 6. Single window (Tehsil) 7. *Vivid Shakha* 8. Tehsildar 9. *Vivid Shakha* 10. Single window (Tehsil) 11. Single windows (Collectorate) 12. Head-end 13. E-kiosk	To 1. Citizen 2. Patwari 3. E-kiosk 4. Tehsildar 5. Tehsildar 6. Tehsildar 7. E-kiosk	To 1. Citizen 2. Patwari 3. E-kiosk 4. Tehsildar 5. Tehsildar 6. Tehsildar 7. E-kiosk	To 1. Citizen 2. E-kiosk 3. Tehsildar 4. Tehsildar 5. Tehsildar 6. E-kiosk	To 1. Citizen 2. E-kiosk 3. Tehsildar 4. Tehsildar 5. Tehsildar 6. E-kiosk
	Number of visits	**Minimum** 1. Collection of AF 2. For preparation of affidavit 3. For Photocopy of income certificate 4. Goes to Patwari (for giving the document) 5. Goes to Patwari for taking the report 6. For submission of AF at single window 7. For collecting the certificate from Tehsil	**Minimum** 1. For preparation of affidavit 2. For Photocopy of income certificate 3. Goes to Patwari (for giving the document) 4. Goes to Patwari for taking the report 5. For submission of AF at e-Kiosk 6. For collecting the certificate from e-Kiosk	**Minimum** 1. For preparation of affidavit 2. To Patwari (for giving the document) 3. To Patwari for taking the report 4. For submission of AF at e-Kiosk 5. For collecting the certificate from e-Kiosk	**Minimum** 1. For preparation of affidavit 2. To Patwari (for giving the document) 3. To Patwari for taking the report 4. For submission of AF at e-Kiosk 5. For collecting the certificate from e-Kiosk	**Minimum** 1. For submission of AF at e-Kiosk 2. For collecting the certificate from e-Kiosk **Maximum** 1 & 2 and 3rd visit follow-up	**Minimum*** 1. For submission of AF at e-Kiosk 2. For collecting the certificate from e-Kiosk **Maximum** 1& 2 and 3rd visit follow-up

Contd...

Item		Manual	E-governance	Scenario A	Scenario B	Scenario C*	Scenario D*
		Maximum 1 to 7 and 8. For Photocopy of ration card 9. For collection of copy of ROR 10. For collection of Voter list 11. For photocopy of parent's caste certificate, if candidate is a student 12. For photocopy of mark sheet of last degree achieved 13. For identification from two Govt. employee (gazetted officer) 14. 14th & 15th visits for follow-up	**Maximum** 1 to 6 and 7. For Photocopy of ration card 8. For collection of copy of ROR 9. For collection of voter list 10. For photocopy of parent's caste certificate, if candidate is a student 11. For photocopy of mark sheet of last degree achieved 12. For identification from two Govt. employee (gazetted officer) 13. 13th & 14th visits for follow-up	**Maximum** 1 to 5 and 6. Copy of one of the items from 7 to 12, as indicated under e-Governance head 7. 7th visit for follow-up	**Maximum** 1 to 5 and 6. Copy of one of the items from 7 to 12, as indicated under e-Governance head 7. 7th visit for follow-up		

ROR: Record of Rights
AF: Application Form
Govt.: Government

Annexure: 4.2B: Cost Saving

Table: 4.2B.1: Cost Saving to Tehsil

S. N.	Name of the certificate -es (1)	Number of applicat-ions (in 2003-04) (2)	Time taken in manual process[$]		Time after BPR[$]		Saving (per certificate)		Saving (total) to Tehsil	
			Total time (3)	To office (4)	To citizen (5)	To office (6)	In total time (7)={(3)-(5)}	To office (8)={(6)-(4)}	Time (9)={(8)X(2)}	Cost (in Rs.) (9)X318[#]
1.	Caste	2700	15 days	104 m	One day	28 m	14 days	76 m	205200 m = 427.5 days	135945
2.	Jamabandi	7301	3 days	52 m	One day	9 m	2 days	43 m	313943 m = 654 days	207987
3.	Income	430	15 days	104 m	One day	28 m	14 days	76 m	32680m = 68 days	21651
4.	Domicile	1800	15 days	104 m	One day	28 m	14 days	76 m	136800m = 285 days	90630
5.	**Total**								**1434.5 days**	**4,56,213**

Source: Based on FGDs and collected data

[$]See efficiency (Table 4.1A.1 & 4.1A.6 in Annexure 4.1A) and CTQs Table 4.4.5

[#]Average salary of Govt. employee (clerk) is Rs. 7000 and 22 days average working days in a month and 8 hours in a day)

BPR: Business Process Re-engineering

Table: 4.2B.2: Cost Saving to Citizens

S. N.	Name of the certificate	Saving (total) to citizens	Saving (total) to Tehsil	
		Cost (in Rs) = (actual rounds X wages[$] +other expenditure[#]) X total issued certificate	**Time (in days)**	**Cost (in Rs)**
1.	Caste	2 days (four roundsα) wages +traveling cost = Rs 180X2700 = Rs 486000	= 427.5 days	135945
2.	Jamabandi	One days (Two rounds) wage + traveling cost = Rs 90X7301 = Rs 657090	= 654 days	207972
3.	Income	2 days wages (four roundsα) + traveling cost = Rs 180X430 = Rs 77400	= 68 days	21624
4.	Domicile	2 days wages (four roundsα) + traveling cost = Rs 180X1800 = Rs 324000	= 285 days	90630
	Total	**15,44,490**	**1434.5 days**	**456171**

Source: Based on FGαs; [$] Rs 70 / aay (minimum daily wage); *One round (time lost) =4 hours (1/2 aay); α Actual rounds = 4 (only 3 rounds out of 6 rounds to Patwari or Tehsil have been taken for the wages lost, as on some occasion citizens have other pending / routine work; [#] Rs 10 per round (traveling +other expenditure) (average) (it will vary with the distance)

S.N.	*Purpose*	*Where to*	*Round (for certificate)*	*For Jamabandi*
1.	*Report*	*Patwariβ*	*3*	*0*
2.	*For submission* *Follow up* *For issuing*	*Tehsil*	*1* *1* *1*	*1* *0* *1*
3.	*For attachments*	*Photocopier etc.*	*1*	*0*
		Total	*7*	*2*

β For searching Patwari, citizens have to go to Tehsil mostly

Annexure 4.2C: Re-designed form for Scenarios A & B Caste Certificate

Name of Applicant

Father's/Mother's Name

Reason

Caste of applicant

House No.

Village

Tehsil

District

Attachments arriving by courier(scanning)

- ☐ Report of Patwari
- ☐ Affidavit
- ☐ Income Certificate
- ○ Ration Card
- ○ Marksheet of Last Degree Achieved
- ○ Copies of Parent's Caste Certificate
- ○ Copy of ROR(LRC)
- ○ Voter List
- ○ Identification of Two Govt. Employees (1st class officer)

Submit   Cancel

Annexure 4.2D: Re-designed form for scenarios C & D
Caste Certificate

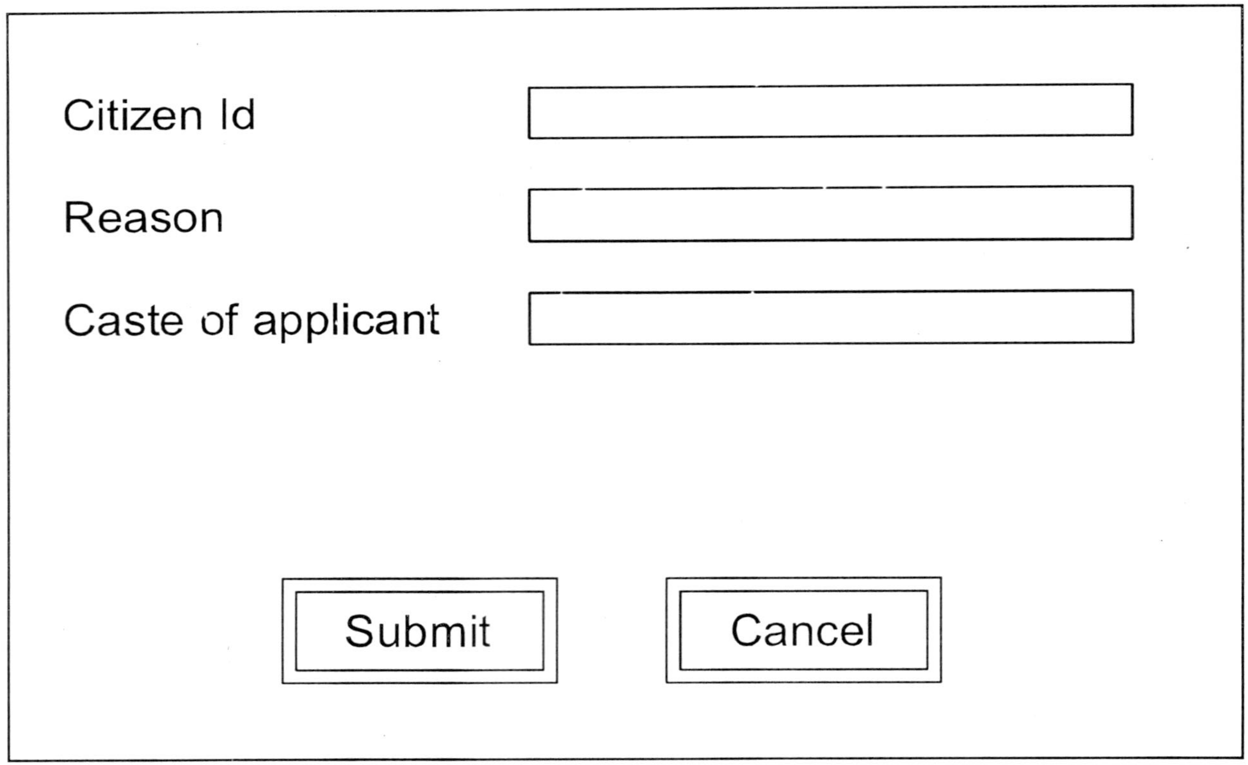

Annexure 4.3: Matrix of Change

Table 4.3.1: Number of Intra-relationship and Value for Suggested Practices

S. N.	Suggested practices	Number of Intra-relationships	Value of importance
1.	Database creation and updation (BE* computerisation)	+(19)	-2
2.	Interface	+(15)	2
3.	Network (connectivity)	+(16)	2
4.	MIS	+(19)	2
5.	User friendliness	+(13)	0
6.	Kiosk at village level	+(15), –(1)	1
7.	Access to every one	+(11)	1
8.	New trained personnel to handle front-end	+(16)	2
9.	Dedicated project manager (champion)	+(15)	2
10.	Introducing CRM	+(10)	2
11.	Versatile role of every functionary (professionalism)	+(8), –(1)	1
12.	Easy-to-use for citizen	+(5)	2
13.	e-filling of AF	+(19)	-2
14.	Patwari comes at the Kiosk	+(8)	-2
15.	Minimisation of touch points	+(7)	-1
16.	Inquiry report in selected cases (dynamic data)	+(5)	1
17.	Online monitoring	+(17)	2
18.	Feedback system	+(16)	2
19.	Status of AF can be checked	+(8)	0
20.	Online processing and MIS (for most of the services)	+(17)	2
21.	Developing relationship among the services (integration)	+(14)	1
22.	Online verification (for most of the services)	+(12)	2
23.	Data security	+(10), –(1)	-2
24.	Online delivery of certificate	+(18)	-1
25.	Number of attachments reduced	+(17)	-2
26.	User identification	+(9)	-2
27.	Improving efficiency through better management techniques	+(0), –(4)	-2
28.	Achieving quality standards	+(18), –(1)	2

* Back-end; AF: Application Form, CRM: Customer Relationship Management, MIS: Management Information System

Table 4.3.2: Recommendations for Different Factors of Matrix of Change

S. N.	Suggested practices	Feasibility	Sequence of execution	Location (for change)	Pace and nature of change
1.	Database creation and updation (BE* computerisation)	Yes (with difficulty)	Second stage	Pilot (for a single Tehsil) #	Gradual / cautious
2.	Interface	Yes	First stage	All Kiosks	Gradual / cautious (first testing and then gradually improving and implementing it everywhere)
3.	Network (connectivity)	Yes	First stage	All Kiosks	Gradual / cautious (first, testing for connectivity with 2-4 Kiosks is done and then gradually increasing the number of Kiosks)
4.	MIS	Yes	First stage	All Kiosks	Fast
5.	User friendliness	Yes	First stage	Pilot (a few Kiosks) #	Fast
6.	Kiosk at village level	Yes	First stage	Pilot (a few Kiosks) #	Fast
7.	Access to every one	Yes	First stage	Pilot (a few Kiosks) #	Fast
8.	New trained personnel to handle front-end	Yes	First stage	All Kiosks	Fast
9.	Dedicated project manager (champion)	Yes	First stage	Pilot (a few Kiosks) #	Fast (developing though training and guidance of senior management)
10.	Introducing CRM	Yes	First stage	Pilot (a few Kiosks) #	Gradual / cautious
11.	Versatile role of every functionary (professionalism)	Yes	Third stage	Pilot (a few Kiosks) #	Gradual / cautious
12.	Easy-to-use for citizen	Yes	First stage	All Kiosks	Fast
13.	e-filling of AF	Yes	First stage	All Kiosks	Fast
14.	Patwari comes at the Kiosk	Yes (with difficulty)	First stage	Pilot (a few Kiosks) #	Gradual / cautious

Contd...

S. N.	Suggested practices	Feasibility	Sequence of execution	Location (for change)	Pace and nature of change
15.	Minimisation of touch points	Yes	Third stage	Pilot (a few Kiosks) #	Gradual / cautious
16.	Inquiry report in selected cases (dynamic data)	Yes	Third stage	Pilot (a few Kiosks) #	Gradual / cautious
17.	Online monitoring	Yes	Second stage	All Kiosks	Fast
18.	Feedback system from citizen	Yes	Second stage	All Kiosks	Fast
19.	Status of AF can be checked	Yes	First stage	All Kiosks	Fast
20.	Online processing and MIS (for most of the services)	Yes	Second stage	All Kiosks	Fast
21.	Developing relationship among the services (integration)	Yes	Second stage	Pilot (a few Kiosks) #	Slow (initially can be seen at a few Kiosks)
22.	Online verification (for most of the services)	Yes (with difficulty)	Third stage	Pilot (a few Kiosks) #	Gradual / cautious
23.	Data security	Yes	First stage	All Kiosks	Fast
24.	Online delivery of certificate	Yes (with difficulty)	Third stage	Pilot (a few Kiosks) #	Slow
25.	Number of attachments reduced	Yes (with difficulty)	Second stage	Pilot (a few Kiosks) #	Gradual / cautious
26.	User identification	Yes (with difficulty)	Third stage	All Kiosks	Gradual / cautious
27.	Improving efficiency through better management techniques	Yes (with difficulty)	Third stage	All Kiosks	Gradual / cautious
28.	Achieving quality standards	Yes (with difficulty)	Second stage	All Kiosks	Gradual / cautious

Source: Based on own analysis; * BE: Back-end; # Assessment for Testing; AF: Application Form; CRM: Customer Relationship Management; MIS: Management Information System

Table: 4.3.3: Value of Different Factors of Change for Suggested Practices

S. N.	Suggested practices	Values*			
		Feasibility	Sequence of execution	Location (for change)	Pace and nature of change
Technology					
1.	Database creation and updation (BE* computerisation)	2	2	1	2
2.	Interface	3	3	2	2
3.	Network (connectivity)	3	3	2	2
4.	MIS	3	3	2	3
5.	User friendliness	3	3	1	3
6.	Kiosk at village level	3	3	1	3
People (functionaries)					
7.	Access to every one	3	3	1	3
8.	New trained personnel to handle front-end	3	3	2	3
9.	Dedicated project manager (champion)	3	3	1	3
10.	Introducing CRM	3	3	1	2
11.	Versatile role of every functionary (professionalism)	3	1	1	2
12.	Easy-to-use for citizen	3	3	2	3
Process					
13.	E-filling of AF	3	3	2	3
14.	Patwari comes at the Kiosk	2	3	1	2
15.	Minimisation of touch points	3	1	1	2
16.	Inquiry report in selected case (dynamic data)	3	1	1	2
17.	Mcnitoring	3	2	2	3
18.	Feedback system	3	2	2	3
19.	Status of AF can be checked	3	3	2	3
20.	Online processing and MIS (for most of the services)	3	2	2	3

Contd...

S. N.	Suggested practices	Values*			
		Feasibility	Sequence of execution	Location (for change)	Pace and nature of change
21.	Developing relationship among the services (integration)	3	2	1	1
22.	Online verification (for most of the services)	2	1	1	2
23.	Data security	3	3	2	3
24.	Online delivery of certificate	2	1	1	1
25.	Number of attachments reduced	2	2	1	2
26.	User identification	2	1	2	2
27.	Improving efficiency through better management techniques	2	1	2	2
28.	Achieving quality standards	2	2	2	2

Source: Based on own analysis; AF: Application Form; CRM: Customer Relationship Management; MIS: Management Information System

*

S. N.	*Value →* / *Factors ↓*	*1*	*2*	*3*
1.	*Feasibility*	*No feasibility*	*Yes (with difficulty)*	*Yes*
2.	*Sequence of execution*	*Third stage*	*Second stage*	*First stage*
3.	*Location*	*Pilot*	*All Kiosks*	-
4.	*Pace of nature of change*	*Slow*	*Gradual / cautious*	*Fast*

Annexure 4.4: System Design for Information, Services and Grievances based on Urgency and Importance

Table 4.4.1A: Group 1: Required (Information, Services and Grievances) on a Day-to-day Urgent Basis*

S. N.	Type**	Sectors	I/S/G	Items
1	Mainly computer based (T1)	Health	I	Health information
			I	Type of diseases
		Agriculture	I	Marketable surplus
			S	Mandi rates
			S	Weather forecast
		Animal husbandry	I	Milk rates
		Electricity	I	Information about electricity cut
		Road	I	Timings of busses and bus routes
		Tehsil	I	Availability of forms
		Other	I	Employment notification
			S	Local / national news
			I	Telephone numbers of all departments
2	Computer and delivery system (department) based (T2)	Tehsil	S	Land certificate
3	Mainly delivery system (department) based (interface with computer)	Education	S	Providing education to children
			G	Late coming of teachers
		Health	S	Immunisation
			S	Making medicines available
		Drinking water	S	Making water available
		Agriculture	S	Marketing of agriculture produce
		Animal husbandry	S	Marketing of milk

Note: Above are based on urgency and importance,
I: Information; S: Services; G: Grievances
* Based on field survey and FGDs

Table: 4.4.1B: Group 2: Vital, required (Information, Services and Grievances) from Time to Time*

S. N.	Type**	Sectors	I/S/G	Items
1.	Mainly computer based (T1)	Education	I	Results for 10th and 12th classes
			S	Computer education
		PDS	I	Fare price shop-wise distribution information
		Agriculture	I	Loan schemes
			I	Crop insurance
		Social Welfare	I	Scheme for BPL families (all sectors)
			I	Schemes for handicaps
		Drinking water	I	Quality of water
		Tehsil	I	Guidelines for accessing the certificates
		Animal husbandry	I	Insurance of cattle
		Others	I	Telephone numbers of all departments
			S	E-mail
			S	Internet browsing
			S	Horoscope
			S	Personal insurance
2.	Computer and delivery system (department) based (T2)	Tehsil	S	Caste certificate
			S	Income certificate
			S	Domicile certificate
			S	Mutation
			S	Sale deed
			S	Conversion of agriculture land into non-agriculture land
			S	Birth & death certificate
		PDS	S	Ration card
		Others	S	Gun license
			S	Driving license
			S	Payment of Govt. dues (electricity, phone etc.)

Contd...

S. N.	Type**	Sectors	I/S/G	Items
3.	Mainly delivery system (department) based (interface with computer) (T3)	Education	S	Library activity
			G	Closing of schools
			G	Late coming of teachers
		Women and child welfare	G	Absenteeism of Anganwadi worker
		Social welfare	G	Delay in pension
		Electricity	S	Electricity connection
		PDS	G	Complaints of BPL / Antyodaya cards holder
		Poverty alleviation	G	Non availability of timely payments for Indira Awas Yojana (IAY) houses
		Health	S	Expert advice on health
		Agriculture	S	Expert advice on agriculture
		Animal husbandry	S	Expert advice on cattle management

Note: above are based on urgency and importance
I: Information; S: Services; G: Grievances
* Based on field survey and FGDs

Table: 4. 4.1C: Group 3: Required (Information, Services and Grievances) on a Regular Basis (Monthly / Quarterly / Half-yearly*)

S. N.	Type**	Sectors	I/S/G	Items
1	Mainly computer based (T1)	Education	I	Type of scholarship
		Poverty alleviation	I	Assets created under poverty alleviation programs
		Road	I	Milestones for bus routes
		Drinking water	I	Water Table
		PDS	I	Fair price shop wise distribution and allotment information
			I	Items available at fair price shops
			I	Rates of commodities
		Electricity	I	Last date of depositing bill payment
		Irrigation	I	Sources of irrigation
			I	Area under different sources of irrigation
		Agriculture	I	Production for crops
			I	Subsidy for different schemes
			I	Fertiliser use
		Animal husbandry	I	Information about cattle fairs
2	Computer and delivery system (department) based (T2)	Education	S	Scholarship
		Animal husbandry	I	Cattle health care and controls
		Poverty alleviation	S	Loan for self-employment
3	Mainly delivery system (department) based (interface with computer) (T3)	Education	G	Delay / non-availability of scholarship
		Agriculture	S	Crop loan
			S	Purchase of seeds, fertiliser, pesticide, implements
		Health	G	Non-availability of ambulance
		Social welfare	S	Aids for handicaps
		Road	S	Availability of buses
			G	Delay in bus
		Women & child welfare	S	Nutritional programme for pre-school children and mothers

Contd...

S. N.	Type**	Sectors	I/S/G	Items
		PDS	S	Timely availability of essential commodities
		Poverty alleviation	S	Training for self-employment
		Animal husbandry	S	Supply of quality animals under loan scheme
			S	Supply of feed
			G	Street cattle
		Electricity	G	Electricity failure – for household
			G	Electricity failure – for agriculture pump sets

Note: above are based on urgency and importance
I: Information; S: Services; G: Grievances
* Based on field survey and FGDs

Table: 4. 4.1D: Group 4: Yearly Basis Usage (Information, Services and Grievances)*

S. N.	Type**	Sectors	I/S/G	Items
1.	Mainly computer based (T1)	Social welfare	I	Social welfare programme for different categories (SCs, STs, OBCs etc.)
		Health	I	Family planning
			I	Information about homeopathy dispensary
			I	Information about Ayurved dispensary
		Education	I	Type of scholarship
		PDS	I	Names of families covered
		Poverty alleviation	I	Village-wise Below Poverty Line list
			I	Village-wise status of development works
			S	Poor quality of implementation of work
			S	Construction of village assets
		Health	I	Special health camps
		Electricity	I	Rates for giving electricity connection for house hold
			I	Rates for giving electricity connection for agriculture purpose
		Drinking water	I	Village-wise drinking water resources
		Animal husbandry	I	Cattle population
		Agriculture	I	Agricultural implements used
		Women & child welfare	I	Number of children and mothers covered
2.	Mainly delivery system (department) based (interface with computer) (T3)	Education	S	Non-availability of school building / drinking water / toilets / playground, etc.
		Agriculture	S	Soil testing
		Tehsil	G	Over functioning of Patwari
			G	Non-availability of Patwari
		Irrigation	G	Over extraction of ground water
		Social welfare	G	Requirement of new hostels

Contd...

S. N.	Type**	Sectors	I/S/G	Items
		Poverty alleviation	G	Complaints regarding credit / assets for self-employment
			G	Inability of timely payment of IAY
		Animal husbandry	G	Requirement of veterinary doctor in rural areas
		Irrigation	G	Non-availability of compensation for land
			G	Name not included in BPL list

Note: Above are based on urgency and importance
I: Information; S: Services; G: Grievances
* Based on field survey and FGDs

Table 4.4.1E: Group 5: Information for Participation in Socio-economic Development Planning*

S. N.	Type*	Sectors	I/S/G	Items
1.	Mainly computer based (T1)	Health	I	Number of hospitals
		Education	I	Number of schools
			I	Number of teachers
			I	Number of night schools and locations
			I	Name of children attending school by age, caste, and general
			I	Information about professional colleges (law, medical, etc.)
			I	Information about vocational schools
		Electricity	I	Number of connections
		Agriculture	I	Agriculture implements used
		Poverty alleviation	I	Asset created under poverty alleviation programme
			I	Number of beneficiary of poverty alleviation programme
		PDS	I	Shop-wise number of family covered
			I	Total allotment of village
		Social welfare	I	Number of old age home and their beneficiaries and location
		Drinking water	I	Number of hand pumps

Note1: Above are based on urgency and importance;

Note 2: The above items are indicative, some more may be added based on local requirements;

* Based on field survey and FGDs;

** For the purpose of strategy formulation. Based on: first, the utilisation of IT, second, process of services delivery, and third, the capacity of delivery system, three types of information, services and grievances have been identified

I: Information; S: Services; G: Grievances

Annexure 4.5

Table 4.5.1A: Strategy for – Presently High Degree of Preferences (Values) for Information, Services and Grievances and in Future likely High Prospects

S. N.	Sectors	I/S/G	Items
1.	Education	S	Providing education to children
		S	Computer education
		S	Scholarship
2.	Health	I	Health information
		S	Expert advice on health
3.	Social welfare	I	Social welfare programme for different categories
		S	Old age and widow pension
		S	Insurance and family welfare schemes
4.	Agriculture	I	Fertiliser use
		I	Loan schemes
		S	Crop loan
		S	Purchase of seeds, fertiliser, pesticide, implements
5.	Tehsil	I	Guidelines for accessing the certificates
		S	Caste certificate
		S	Income certificate
		S	Domicile certificate
		S	Land certificate
6.	Animal husbandry	I	Information of diseases
		I	Cattle health care and controls
		S	Expert advice of cattle management.
7.	Road	S	Availability of buses
8.	Poverty alleviation	I	Loan for self-employment
		S	Training for self-employment
9.	Women and child welfare	S	Organising immunisation programme
10.	PDS	S	Ration card
11.	Others	I	Employment notification
		S	Personal insurance
12..	All	I	Schemes for BPL (social welfare, poverty alleviation)

Source: Based on field survey and FGDs, I: Information; S: Services; G: Grievances

Table 4.5.1B: Strategy for – Presently Low Degree of Preferences (Values) for In formation, Services and Grievances but likely Good Prospects in Future

S.N.	Sectors	I/S/G	Items
1.	Education	S	Library activity
2.	Drinking water	I	Water table
3.	Health	I	Information about Ayurved dispensary
4.	Agriculture	I	Agricultural implements used
		I	Production of crops
		I	Owner requirement
		I	Marketable surplus
		I	Subsidy for different schemes
		I	Agriculture training centres
		S	Training and demonstration
		S	Weather forecast
		S	Marketing of agriculture produce
5.	Animal husbandry	I	Artificial insemination
		I	Information about cattle fairs
		S	Insurance of cattle
		S	Supply of quality animals under loan scheme
		S	Marketing of milk
		S	Milk rates
6.	Road	I	Timings of buses and bus routes
		I	Milestones for bus routes
		G	Delay in bus
		G	Change of route
		G	Adding more buses
7.	Tehsil	I	Availability of forms
		S	Mutation
		S	Sale deed

Contd...

S.N.	Sectors	I/S/G	Items
		S	Mutation
		G	Over functioning of Patwari
8.	Electricity	I	Last date of depositing bill payment
9.	Others	I	For setting up rural industries
		I	Guidelines for schemes for all departments
		I	Telephone numbers of all departments
		I	Charter of services of all departments
		I	Charter & guideline of services in all departments
		S	Horoscope
		S	Payments of government dues (electricity, phone etc.)
		S	Matrimonial
		S	Local / national news
		S	E-mail
		S	Driving license
		S	Internet browsing
		S	Personal insurance

Source: Based on field survey and FGDs

I: Information, S: Services, G: Grievances

Note: The above items are indicative, some more may be added based on local requirements.

Annexure 4.6

Table 4.6.1A: Strategy for Better off / Prosperous Group (Male, Young, General, High Education Group, High Income Group)

S. N.	Type	Sectors	I/S/G	Items*
1.	Mainly computer based	Education	S	Computer education
		Health	I	Health information
		Animal husbandry	I	Information of diseases
		Electricity	I	Information about electricity cut
		Agriculture	I	Daily Mandi rates
		Others	S	Horoscope
			S	Matrimonial
			S	E-mail
			S	Internet browsing
		Poverty alleviation	I	Guidelines
			I	Amount spent on poverty alleviation programmes
		PDS	I	Names of families covered
2.	Computer and delivery system (department) based	Tehsil	S	Land certificate
			S	Income certificate
			S	Mutation
			S	Sale deed
			S	Domicile certificate
			S	Conversion of agriculture land into non-agriculture land
		Others	S	Driving license
			S	Gun license
			S	Local news

Contd...

S. N.	Type	Sectors	I/S/G	Items*
3.	Mainly delivery system (department) based (interface with computer)	Education	S	Providing education to children
		Health	S	Immunisation
			S	Expert advice on health
		Drinking water	S	Making water available
		Irrigation	S	Timely availability of water for irrigation
		Agriculture	S	Expert advice on agriculture
			S	Purchase of seeds, fertiliser, pesticide, implements
		Animal husbandry	S	Supply of feed
			G	Requirement of veterinary doctor in rural areas
			S	Expert advice on cattle management
		Electricity	G	Electricity failure for household
			G	Electricity failure – for agriculture pump sets
		Road	S	Availability of buses
			G	Adding more buses

* Based on field survey
I: Information, S: Services, G: Grievances

Table 4.6.1B: Strategy for Vulnerable Group [Female, Aged (above 40 years), SC&ST, Low Education Group, Low Income Group]

S. N.	Type	Sectors	I/S/G	Items*
With present high preference (of ISG) also likely high prospects**				
1.	Mainly computer based	Health	I	Health Information
		Animal husbandry	I	Information of diseases
		PDS	I	Items available at fair price shop
		All	I	Schemes for BPL families (all sectors)
2.	Computer and delivery system (department) based	Social welfare	S	Old age and widow pension
		Tehsil	S	Caste certificate
3.	Mainly delivery system (department) based (interface with computer)	Education	S	Providing education to children
		Health	S	Immunisation
			S	Expert advice on health
			S	Making medicine available
			G	Non-availability of medicines
		PDS	S	Timely availability of essential commodities
		Drinking water	S	Making water available
		Irrigation	S	Timely availability of water for irrigation
		Animal husbandry	S	Supply of feed
			G	Requirement of veterinary doctor in rural areas
		Electricity	G	Electricity failure for household

Contd...

S. N.	Type	Sectors	I/S/G	Items*
With present low preference (of ISG), but good prospects in future*				
4.	Mainly computer based	Education	I	Computer education
		Education	I	Results for 10th and 12th classes
		Health	I	Information about homeopathy dispensary
		Agriculture	S	Weather forecast
			I	Marketable surplus
		Road	I	Timing of busses & bus routes
		Others	S	E-mail
			S	Internet browsing
			S	Matrimonial
5.	Mainly delivery system (department) based (interface with computer)	Education	G	Irregularities in mid-day meal
		Road	G	Change of route
		Education	G	Late coming of teacher
		Women and child care	G	Absenteeism of Anganwadi workers
			G	Food is not given to children
		Others	I	Guidelines for schemes for all department

Note: The above items are indicative, some more may be added based on local requirements.

* For the purpose of strategy formulation. Based on: first, the utilisation of IT, second, process of services delivery, and third, the capacity of delivery system, three types of information, services and grievances have been identified

** Based on field survey

I: Information, S: Services, G: Grievances

Annexure 4.7

Table 4.7.1: Likely Users for Different Information, Services and Grievances based on Type of ISG Design

S.N.	Type*	I/S/G	Items	Main likely users
1.	Mainly computer based	I	Health information	All categories
			Information of diseases	All categories
			Employment notification	All categories
			Availability of forms	High education group
			Guidelines for accessing the certificates	High education group, middle-aged group
			Land records	General, female
			Schemes for BPL families	SC&ST
			Schemes for handicaps	OBC
			Type of diseases	SC&ST
			Loan schemes	High income group
			Fair price shop wise distribution and allotment information	OBC
			Items available at fair price shops	OBC
			Rates of commodities	High education group
			Marketable surplus	High income group
			Subsidy for different schemes	High income group
			Fertiliser use	OBC
			Cropping pattern	High education group
			Insurance of cattle	Middle-aged group
			Social welfare programme for different categories	All categories
			Family planning	All categories
			Type of scholarship	All categories
			Quality of water	All categories
			Village-wise Below Poverty Line list	High education group

Contd...

S.N.	Type*	I/S/G	Items	Main likely users
			Special health camps	SC&ST
			Rates for giving electricity connection for house hold	Middle-aged group
			Rates for giving electricity connection for agriculture purpose	High education group, middle-aged group
			Village-wise drinking water resources	High education group
			Cattle population	Middle-aged group, female group
			Agricultural implements used	High education group
			Telephone numbers of all departments	High education group
			Water table	Middle-aged group, general
			Last date of depositing bill payment	Middle-aged group
			Artificial insemination	Middle-aged group
			Information about electricity cut	Middle-aged group, high income group
			Weather forecast	High income group
			Milestones of bus routes	High income group
			Results for 10th and 12th classes	Low income group, high education group, male
			Information about electricity cut	High education group
			Daily Mandi rates	High income group
			Cattle health care and controls	High income group
		S	Computer education	High education group
			Horoscope	Middle-aged group
			E-mail	Young, high education group, male
			Internet browsing	Young
			Local / national news	Middle-aged group, high income group
2.	Computer and delivery system (department) based	S	Land certificate	Middle aged
			Loan for self-employment	Low income group, young
			Scholarship (Education)	High income group
			Payment of government dues (electricity, phone, etc.)	OBC, high education group
			Crop loan	High income group, middle education group

Contd...

S.N.	Type*	I/S/G	Items	Main likely users
			Crop insurance	High educated group, young
			Scholarship (education)	High income group
			Driving license	High education group
			Caste certificate	SC&ST, low income group, middle aged group
			Income certificate	Middle-aged group
			Domicile certificate	Middle-aged group, medium education group
			Mutation	Middle-aged group
			Sale deed	Middle-aged group
			Conversion of agriculture land into non-agriculture land	High income group
3.	Mainly delivery system (department) based (interface with computer)	S	Old age & window pension	All categories
			Expert advice on health	SC&ST, low income group, middle-aged group, low education group
			Experts advices on agriculture	High education group, high income group
			Expert advice on cattle management	OBC, middle-aged group
			Providing education to children	All categories
			Immunisation	Female, old age
			Making water available	All categories
			Timely availability of water for irrigation	OBC, high education group
			Marketing of handicrafts	Middle income group
			Marketing of milk	Young
			Nutritional programme for pre-school children and mothers	High education group, OBC
			Timely availability of essential commodities	SC&ST, middle-aged group
			Purchase of seeds, fertilizer, pesticide, implements	High education group
			Training for self-employment	High education group, young
			Supply of feed	All categories
			Marketing of agriculture produce	High income group
			Electricity connection	Middle-aged group, high education group

Contd...

S.N.	Type*	I/S/G	Items	Main likely users
			Soil testing	High educated group
		G	Requirement of veterinary doctor in rural areas	All categories
			Electricity failure for household	Middle-aged group
			Electricity failure – for agriculture pump sets	Middle-aged group, high education group, general
			Over functioning of Patwari	Middle-aged group
			Over extraction of ground water	Middle education group
			Complaints regarding credit / assets for self-employment	High education group
			Non-availability of compensation for land	High education group, middle-aged group
			Name not included in BPL list	High education group, female
			Closing of schools	High education group, high income group
			Higher prices of essential commodities	High educated group
			Complaint against retailer	OBC
			Irregularities in mid-day meal	High education group
			Vacancies of teachers	High education group

Source: Field survey and FGDs

I: Information S: Services G: Grievances

* For the purpose of strategy formulation. Based on: first, the utilisation of IT, second, process of services delivery, and third, the capacity of delivery system, three types of information, services and grievances have been identified

Annexure 4.8

Table 4.8.1: Items under e-Governance, e-Business and e-Entertainment

S.N.	Type	Item
1.	E-governance	- I: Health information - I: Facilities at Anganwadi centre - I: Social welfare programme for different categories - I: Cattle health care and controls - I: Type of scholarship - I: Quality of water - I: Guidelines for accessing the certificates - I: Agriculture training centres - I: Insurance of cattle - I: Special health camps - I: Information of diseases - I: Information about electricity cut
		- S: Nutritional programme for pre-school children and mothers - S: Old age and widow pension - S: Expert advice on health - S: Ration cards - S: Purchase of seeds, fertiliser, pesticide, implements - S: Providing education to children - S: Making water available - S: Electricity connection - S: Organising immunization programme - S: Timely availability of essential commodities

Contd...

S.N.	Type	Item
		- S: Crop loan - S: Expert advice on agriculture - S: Expert advice of cattle management - S: Loan for self employment - S: Training for self-employment - S: Timely availability of water for irrigation - S: Land certificate - S: Caste certificate - S: Domicile certificate - S: Mutation - S: Driving license - S: Repair of tube wells - S: Family planning - S: Distribution of books - S: Library activity - S: Insurance and family welfare schemes - S: Making medicines available - S: Conversion of land - S: Aids for handicaps - S: Family-housing (IAY) - S: Scholarship for SCs, STs
		- G: Poor quality of drinking water - G: Absenteeism of Anganwadi workers - G: Non availability of medicine - G: Requirement of veterinary doctor in rural areas - G: Non availability of doctors / health workers - G: Bad roads - G: Non-availability of quality seeds, fertiliser, pesticides - G: Vacancies of teachers - G: Late coming of teachers - G: Complaint against retailer

Contd...

S.N.	Type	Item
		- G: Complaints regarding credit / assets for self-employment - G: Name not included in BPL list - G: Non-availability of timely payment for Indira Awas Yojana (IAY) houses - G: Electricity failure for agriculture pump sets - G: Electricity failure – for household - G: Non-availability of commodities at fair price shop
2.	E-business	- I: Results for 10th and 12th classes - I: Employment notification* - I: Milk rates
		- S: Availability of buses - S: Mandi rates - S: Computer education - S: Insurance and family welfare schemes - S: Local news - S: Internet browsing - S: Personal insurance - S: Marketing of milk - S: E-mail - S: Supply of feed - S: Crop insurance
3.	E-entertainment	- S: Marketing of agriculture produce - S: Marketing of milk - S: Marketing of handicrafts - Cable TV - Computer games - Movies

I: Information, S: Services, G: Grievances

Appendices

Appendix 2.1: Literature for Training

A. Process Reengineering

Good governance is one, which provides quality of life to the people. One major factor, which helps attaining it, is the quality of services provided by the government as government regulates most of the activities of the citizens. The quality of service which government provides depends on the process used, the attitude of the service provider and the technology intervention. All these are intrinsically interdependent. Most of the processes currently used by the government are not customer friendly and are not focused on the needs and expectations of the people. Process reengineering is aimed at developing simple, efficient, and cost effective and customer friendly processes.

Process reengineering is all about redesigning the way we do our work. Government service providers are engaged in the process of providing services to the citizens who are their customers. A process is a set of activities taken together produces an output, which is of high value to the customer. Most of the processes were designed long back when computers and information technology were not available. Through many of these processes were not complicated when initially designed, they were modified to take care of complex situations and the plethora of rules and regulations. The result is that we have processes that look like spiders web, too complex and segmented with rigid boundaries. Many of the tasks, which form part of the process, are done to satisfy internal checks and controls. Process reengineering is essentially going back to the beginning of technology. Through computers and information technology are going to be backbone of the reengineered process, reengineering is not automating an existing process in its present form.

Reengineering was practiced in different form since the time of F.W. Taylor, the father of Scientific Management and his contemporaries like Gilbreth. However, Michael Hammer and James Campy could be credited with popularizing process reengineering in business and industry in 1990s.

What is Reengineering?

Reengineering is defined in the book "Reengineering the Corporation" co-authored by Michael Hammer and James Campy as *"fundamental rethinking and radical redesign of business processes to achieve dramatic improvements in critical contemporary measures of performance such as cost, quality service and speed."* Reengineering does not take any thing for granted. It ignores what is being done now and goes to the root and ask the question, "why do we do what we do?"

- Steps in process reengineering
- Select a process
- Collect data on the process
- Flow chart the process
- Develop a new process by critical examination

- Flow chart new process
- Develop software for the new process
- Implement

Selecting the Process

The following three points can be kept in mind while selecting a process for reengineering by an organization, which is functioning normally and is embarking on reengineering it effectiveness.

- Extent of dysfunction – having lot of problems, complaints or customer dissatisfaction
- Impact – likely to have an impact if simplified
- Feasible – feasible to implement with minimum charge in organization structure or jobs

Collecting Data and Flow-Charting

The next step is collecting data about the conversion inputs into the output and the steps involved in the process, time taken for completing each step, the person involved and the places where the work is carried out, the tools and equipments used, the value addition in each step, decisions taken, the document generated, the forms used and recording them in the form of a process chart.

Critical Examination

Critical Examination of the existing process with a view to develop a simple and more economical process is the most important step in process improvement. Critical Examination is a technique, which ensures generation of all possible alternatives in a systematic manner. During critical examination each activity is subjected to a systematic and progressive series of questions.

Identifying the Purpose of the Process

The best approach to critical examination is to start with the output. Every process has to result in an output. We should subject the output to critical examination by the following question with a view to establish the purpose of the output and need to continue it in the present form. While identifying the purpose of the process, the major questions taken into consideration are:

- What is being achieved?
- Why is it necessary to have that achievement?
- Can it be eliminated?
- What will happen if the output is not there?
- Can it be simplified, or modified?

Answer to the first question will indicate the specify output, which has also been recorded in the earlier step. Answer to the second question will give the reasons for the output. If there is no compelling justification for continuing the output, it should be eliminated. If the output is eliminated and then the process itself become redundant and can be discontinued. In that case the output cannot be eliminated, and attempt should be made to modify or simplify it.

Once the purpose of a process is established, all steps in the process are to be subjected to critical examination. Critical examination is a disciplined questioning technique, which systematically examines all governing considerations. These governing considerations are:

- Purpose
- Means
- Sequence
- Place and
- Person

The governing considerations are common to all steps through their relative importance that will vary from activity. The 'purpose' is a statement of what is being achieved and the statement of purpose should bring out this clearly. The 'means' descried the method of performance, materials and equipments used and the working condition. The 'sequence' will indicate the time of performance, preceding and succeeding activities, frequency and periodicity. The 'place' signifies the location of activity, distance, movement to and from place of activity, layout of office, etc. The 'person' signifies the individual (s) who perform the whole or part of the activity, and gives details of their skills.

Primary Questions

For carrying out critical examination, a series of questions are asked. In the first stage of questioning the 'Purpose' 'Means', 'Sequence', 'Place' and 'Person' of the activity is systematically questioned and reasons for each is sought.

The primary questions are:

- Purpose : What is being achieved? Why is it necessary?
- Means : How is it done? Why in that way?
- Sequence : When is it done? Why then?
- Place : Where is it done? Why there?
- Person : Who does it? Why that person?

The aim of the primary question is to sharply focus on fact and bring out the reason with a view to eliminate, combine, rearrange or simplify the activity.

Once the facts and reason for each activity are clearly established, each governing consideration is subjected to the secondary questions. The secondary questions are given below.

- Purpose : What else could be done?
- Means : How else could it be done?
- Sequence : When else could it be done?
- Place : Where else could it be done?
- Person : Who else could do it?

The purpose of secondary question is to generate all possible alternatives.

After generating all possible alternatives, their implications are studied one by one. Implications bring out the advantage and disadvantage of each alternative in terms of economic, technical, human, legal and political considerations. After all possible alternatives are generated and their implications studied, the most suitable alternatives should be selected to develop into a new process.

In order to carry out critical examination in systematic way, a standard format is used called critical examination sheet. The format of the critical examination sheet is given below:

Factors	Facts	Reasons	Alternatives	Implications	Selection for Development
Purpose					
Means					
Sequence					
Place					
Person					

The first vertical column is for listing facts under each governing consideration. The second vertical column is for statement of reasons for each fact listed in the first column. These two columns supply the complete background. The remaining columns are for generating alternatives, listing their advantages, disadvantages and lastly for noting the alternatives selected for development.

Use of Computers and Information Technology

Computers and information technology are drastically altering the way we think, communicate and work. Information technology can aid us at least in the following ways:

- Sharing the same database and information by several people
- Expert system to substitute programmed decisions like checking and calculations
- Creating and updating records
- Online monitoring or monitoring by exception.

Implementation

Most difficult part of process reengineering is to make people accept the fact that the way they do work is going to change. This naturally needs concerted effort on the part of the top management. Naturally, people want to be assured that their jobs are not going to be cut and their promotion chances are not going to be affected.

It will also be necessary to have a pilot run before the new process is tried to trouble shoot minor problems that are likely to crop up. The pilot run can be a parallel run with the old and new process going simultaneously.

The test for effectiveness of the process is its value addition to the customer, with cost and time reduction for the organization.

Common Pitfalls

The common pitfalls in process simplification are given below. The list is only indicative and not exhaustive.

1. Automating an existing process.
2. Fixing performance standards without changing an existing process (people will find errors in the previous step and pass on the buck)
3. Making incremental improvements. Incrementalism is the path of least resistance.
4. Do not focus on process but make improvements in the work unit.
5. Willing to settle for minor results.
6. Quite too early assuming that the process cannot be simplified.
7. Pull back when people resist change.

B. Quality in Government

The role of the government has been and is a topic of much discussion and debate both within the government and outside the government. The expectation of the general public from the government have tremendously increased with the advent of liberalization and globalization, due to better awareness of their rights, developments in information technology, and rising standards of life. the public perceive civil servants as rule based, negative, slow, inaccessible, in sensitive and corrupt. Most of the public who come in contact with the civil servants for doing some work or other are disillusioned. While part of the blame goes to the attitude of the civil servants, the major part of the blame goes to outdated processes and documentation followed by the government offices. Improvements in delivery of public services are possible if the processes are simplified and latest developments in computers and information technology are used for delivery of public services.

Business organization all over the world has only one motto 'meet and exceed the expectation of the customer'. Business organization which is now working in a globally competitive environment cannot survive unless the quality of the product and services they offer is difficult to define. The dictionary meaning of 'quality' is given below:

1. A distinguished attribute
2. Degree of excellence
3. Degree of goodness or worth
4. Reliability
5. Trustworthiness, etc.

As quality is something that bears in the mind of the customer, it will be better to look at quality from the point of view of the customer expectation. Goods or services that meet the expectation and requirements of the customer or confirm to the standards expected by the customer, can be treated as good quality. Some of the attributes of quality in terms of the customer perceptions are given below:

1. Adhering to specific standards consistently
2. At a cost, reasonable and affordable
3. Timely delivery
4. Defect free
5. Prompt servicing
6. Courteous behaviour

Government organizations do not treat the public as customers but consider them as beneficiaries. While a customer has choice, government customers do not have a choice. Choice is possible because of competition that bring in quality. But in case of most do the services rendered by the government, competition are not possible and no choice can be provided to the customer. To improve quality it is necessary to think in terms of customer satisfaction. This is possible only when the design of service delivery keep the citizen as the focal point. The present system makes the civil servants accountable to the internal hierarchy and not to the citizens. To make these service citizens friendly, it will be necessary to consider the needs and expectation of the citizens. Citizens want a good government. From the point of view of service delivery a good government is one that is helpful, open, accountable, responsive, offers information, fair, observe standards, observe right and give value for money to the citizens.

The concepts of good governance can be translated into the practical steps mentioned in succeeding paragraphs for providing citizen friendly delivery of public services.

Standards

There should be clearly laid down well-published and documented standards regarding delivery of public services. Standards can be ensured by implementing the following points:

1. Standardizing the input and output
2. Laying down time limits for rendering the output

3. Laying down timings for submitting applications and receiving the service
4. Minimum documentation
5. Single window clearance
6. Minimum delay
7. Facilities for waiting in waiting rooms with proper amenities
8. Ensure that the service provided to the citizens is free the first time and every time.
9. Specifying the procedure for receiving the service

Information

Getting information from government offices regarding the forms to be filled place the form is to be deposited, formalities to be completed, the fees to be paid, the time required for delivery of the service are generally difficult to obtain. It is therefore necessary to provide full and accurate information to the citizens about the service in local language containing information regarding the forms to be filled, where they are available, at what cost, where they are to be deposited, the timing for depositing the forms and the timings for receiving the final output and if there is a delay how to find the status of the application. This information can also be displayed either at a facilitation counter or at prominent places in front of the office.

Transparency

There is need for transparency regarding how decisions are taken and what are the inputs considered for taking decisions. Transparency can be achieved and speedy decision can be taken if the inputs for decision taking are standardized and structured at the Taluk level. Whenever a request of the citizen is rejected the reasons for the rejection have to be communicated.

Accessibility

The service provided should suit the convenience of the customers so that they can avail the services with minimum expenditure. Some of the ways for improving access is providing flexible timings, facilities for filling applications electronically and providing services close to the residence of citizens. In fact if the services can be designed after consulting the citizens and taking into account their difficulties, this problem can be easily overcome.

Redressal of Grievances

Something will go wrong in spite of well processes. As such, there is an urgent necessity for well-published complaint procedure indicating whom to complain and in what format. Once a complaint is filed, it should be acknowledged immediately and the time likely to be taken for giving a reply should be indicated in the acknowledgement itself. When things go wrong the minimum time citizens can expect be granted, there should be provision for independent scrutiny by somebody than the one who has taken the decision.

Value for Money

Most of the time the cost of delivering service is not calculated. If they are calculated, many of the public services can be handled at a lesser cost by private organizations. As such it should be necessary to examine whether the public is getting value for money on the services rendered. It is also necessary to ensure that the services should be self sustaining and self supporting.

In any process the final output is generated by value addition by a number of persons who are part of the chain. If any one, in the chain makes or delays his work, the final output will be defective or delayed. It is therefore, necessary for all the people working in the system to work together as a team and ensure that every step is performed accurately, in time and without errors.

Improving quality is possible only when processes are simplified and made efficient and effective. It will not be possible to provide quality service by using out dated technology. Extensive use of computers and information technology for data processing is necessary for delivery of quality service. This will enable the government functionaries to focus more on the customers as most of the clerical processing can be taken care of by the computers. Simultaneously government functionaries are required to change their attitude and think that they exist for providing quality services to the customers and the customers pay them.

Appendix 2.2

Failure Modes and Effects Analysis (FMEA)

Failure Modes and Effects Analysis, (Peter, Neuman, and Gavanagh, 2003) is a set of guidelines, a process, and a form to identify and prioritize potential problems (failures). By basing their activities on FMEA, a manager, improvement team, or Process Owner can focus the energy and resources in prevention, monitoring, and response plans where they are most likely to pay off. Borrowed from high-stakes industries like aerospace and defense (also now applied in service industry), FMEA is a more rigorous application of the 'potential problem analysis' concept.

Uses of FMEA

The FMEA method has many applications in a Six Sigma environment, in terms of looking for problems not only in work processes and improvements but also in data-collection activities, Voice of the Customer efforts, procedures – and even the rollout of a Six Sigma initiative. The only prerequisite is to have a complex or high-stakes situation in which you want to place a special emphasis on keeping problems at bay.

How FMEA Works

The steps and key concepts are as follows:

1. *Identify the process of product / service.*
2. *List potential problem that could arise (Failure Modes).* The basic question is: "What could go wrong?" Ideas as to potential problem may come from various sources including brainstorming, process analysis, benchmarking, etc. They can be grouped by process step or product / service component. Avoid trivial problems.
3. *Rate the problem for severity, probability of occurrence, and detectability.* Using a 1-10 point scale, give a score on each factor to each potential problem. More serious problems get a higher rating; harder-to-detect problem also get a higher score. Again, these may be judgments or be based on historical or test data.
4. *Calculate the "Risk Priority Number," or* RPN, *and prioritize actions.* Multiplying the three score together gives this overall risk rating. By adding the RPNs from all problems, one get a total risk figure for adding process or product/service. (Maximum RPN is 1,000)
5. *Develop actions to reduce the risk.* Focusing first on potential problems having the highest priority, one then can devise actions to reduce one or all factors: seriousness, occurrence, and detectability. A key benefit of the tool is to make one's management resources – which always are finite – go to best benefit.

An FMEA Example

Managers and engineers at e-Commerce company nitwit.com wanted to make sure nothing went wrong with its process for updating the on-line catalog. Here are two of the problems they identified and analyse:

1. The wrong artwork is used with a new item.
   Severity = 5
   Occurrence = 5
   Detection = 3
   RPN = 5 x 5 x 3 = 75
2. Buyers can't place an order for an item.
   Severity = 8
   Occurrence = 5
   Detection = 6
   RPN = 8 x 5 x 6 = 240

Based on this assessment, they focused on the concern about not being able to place orders (as RPN is more) and developed preventive measures to ensure that all new product numbers are posted to the ordering system.

Appendix 2.3

Pareto Chart

Pareto diagram is named after Vilfredo Pareto, who studied the distribution of wealth in 19th century Italy, that is, the number of people in various income classes (Mohanty and Lakhe, 2002). Pareto diagram is a special type of histogram that helps to determine which problems to solve and in what order. The bar in Pareto is rearranged in descending order of their heights, showing the individual contribution of each factor as well as the cumulative contributions.

Appendix 2.4

The Cause and Effect Diagram (Fishbone diagram)

The Cause and Effect or Fishbone diagram has for years been one of the favorites for quality teams and still is used by Six Sigma improvement teams (Pande, Neuman, and Gavanagh, 2003). Cause and Effect analysis lets a group start with an 'effect' – a problem, or in some cases a desired effect or result – and create a structured list of possible causes for it. Benefits of the Cause and Effect diagram include the following:

- It's a great tool for gathering group ideas and input, being basically "structured brainstorming" method.
- By establishing categories of potential causes, it helps ensure that a group thinks of many possibilities, rather than just focusing on a few typical areas (e.g., people, bad materials).
- It helps get the analyse phase started. Using a Cause and Effect diagram to identify some "prime suspect" causes, as the AutoRec team has done, provides the focus to help begin process and data analysis.

Upstream from the customer (in the inputs or process), is call factors of variation – "the Xs'. The downstream or Output variation that is the result of the changes in the Xs is call "the Ys'. We can apply the same principle of X and Y to the Cause and Effect model: the "effect" or problem is the Y, and the possible root causes that appear on the "bones" are the Xs.

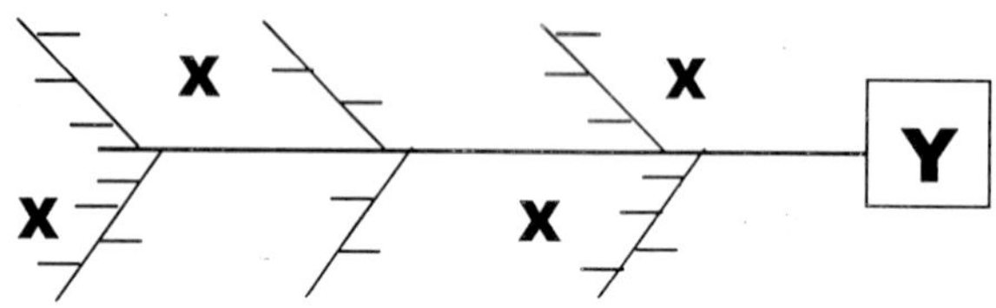

Appendix 2.5
Matrix of Change

What is Matrix of Change?

Business process reengineering efforts suffer from low success rates, due in part to a lack of tools for managing the change process. The Matrix of Change (http://ccs.mit.edu/papers) can help managers identify critical interactions among processes. In particular, this tool helps managers deal with issues such as how quickly change should proceed, the order in which changes should take place, whether to start at a new site, and whether the proposed systems are stable and coherent. The Matrix highlights interactions and complementary practices. It can help managers anticipate the complex interrelationships surrounding change. Specifically, the tool contributes to understanding issues of feasibility (stability of new changes), sequence (which practices to change first), location, pace (fast or slow), and stakeholder interests.

How the Matrix Works?

For introducing BPR, Matrix of Change presents a way to capture connections and complementary practices among different practices. It graphically displays both reinforcing and interfering organizational processes. With this knowledge, a change agent can use intuitive principles to seek points of leverage and design a smoother transition. Once the broad outlines of the new system and the transition path have been charted, implementation plan can more effectively be decentralized for local implementation and optimisation.

The Matrix functions as a four step process. It provides a systematic means to judge those business practices that matter most. It highlights interactions among these practices and possible transition difficulties from one set of practices to another. It encourages various stakeholders to provide feedback on proposed changes. And, it uses process interactions to provide guidelines on the feasibility, sequence, location of change, and pace.

Steps in Preparing Matrix

Step 1 - Identify Critical Processes: The team should first list their existing practices, and the suggested practices that create value for customers / citizens. These practices are grouped in 3 categories, viz., process, people and technology.

Step 2 - Identify System Interactions: After describing existing practices, the team should create the horizontal triangular matrix to identify complementary and competing practices / processes as illustrated in Figure. Complementary processes reinforce one another whereas competing practices / processes work at cross-purposes. A grid connects each process in an interference matrix, and at the junction of each grid plus signs (+)

designate complementary and minus signs (-) competing practices / processes.

Step 3 - Identify Transition Interactions: Next, the team should construct the Transition Matrix – a square matrix combining the horizontal and vertical matrices which helps determine the degree of difficulty in shifting from existing to target practices. The advantage of the transition matrix is that it shows the interactions involved in moving from existing practices to a new slate. The plus signs (+) designate reinforcement and minus signs (-) conflict during change.

Step 4 - Survey Stakeholders: Finally, the team should determine where various stakeholders (like citizens, functionaries) stand with respect to retaining current practices and implementing target practices. The values are as follows: '+2 'means most important, and '+1' indicates less important, '0' represents not important, '-1' means less important but change is required, and '-2' indicates most important but change is must.

Interpretations of Matrix of Change

The Matrix of Change is a useful tool for addressing the following types questions:

- *Feasibility*: Do the set of practices representing the stated goal constitute a coherent and stable system? Is our current set of practices coherent and stable? Is the transition likely to be difficult?
- *Sequence of execution*: Where should change begin? How does the sequence of change affect success? Are there reasonable stopping points?
- *Location*: Are we better off instituting the new system in a separate location or at the existing place?
- *Pace and nature of change*: Should the change be slow or fast? Incremental or radical? Which groups of practices, if any, must be changed at the same time?
- *Stakeholder evaluations*: Have we considered the insights from all stakeholders? Have we overlooked any important practices or interactions?

Appendix 2.6

SWOT Analysis

SWOT is an acronym for the internal strengths and weaknesses of a business and environmental opportunities and threats facing that business (Pearce and Robinson, 1996). SWOT analysis is a systematic identification of these factors and the strategy that reflects the best match between them. It is based on the logic that an effective strategy maximizes a business's strengths and opportunities but at the same time minimizes its weaknesses and threats. This simple assumption, if accurately applied, has powerful implications for successfully choosing and designing an effective strategy.

Opportunities

An opportunity is a major favorable situation in the firm's environment. Key trends represent one source of opportunity. Identification of a previously overlooked market segment, changes in competitive or regulatory circumstances, technological changes, and improved buyer or supplier relationships could represent opportunities for the firm.

Threats

A threat is a major unfavorable situation in the firm's environment. It is a key impediment to the firm's current and / or desired future position. The entrance of a new competitor, slow market growth, increased bargaining power of key buyer of supplier, major technological change, and changing regulations could represent major threats to a firm's future success.

Strengths

A strength is a resource, skill, or other advantage relative to competitors and the needs of markets a firm serves or anticipates serving. A strength is a distinctive competence that gives the firm a comparative advantage in the marketplace. Financial resource, image, market leadership, and buyer / supplier relations are examples.

Weaknesses

A weakness is a limitation or deficiency in resources, skills, and capabilities that seriously impedes effective performance. Facilities, financial resources, management capabilities, marketing skills, and brand image could be sources of weaknesses.

Appendix 2.7

Strategic Analysis

The search for alternative strategies is both incremental and creative in that strategists begin by considering alternatives they are familiar with and think will work (Pearce and Robinson, 1996). These are usually incremental alternations of past strategies. Systematic comparison of external and internal factors is often used to search for alternative strategies. Creativity can be important in this internal / external comparison. The search for multiple alternatives depends on systematic comparison of the strengths, weaknesses, risks and trade-offs of each alternative. Several alternatives are generated and systematically evaluated in a comparative framework. The quality of the ultimate choice is thereby logically enhanced. Evaluation of alternative strategies is much the same whether new alternatives or the old strategy is considered. The focus is the future. Both old and new strategies must be subjected to the same systematic evaluation if a logical choice is to be made.

The Process of Strategic Analysis

(Time ↓)

Corporate-level strategy	Business-level strategy
• Analysis of the overall company portfolio of businesses in terms of relative business unit strength matched with relative business unit strength matched with relative industry attractiveness and stage of development. • Identification of probable corporate performance if the current business unit portfolio is maintained with respective strategies. • Comparison of this projected corporate performance with tentative corporate objectives to identify major performance gaps. • Identification of alternative portfolios (including different strategy combinations at the business unit level) to close performance gaps. • Evaluation of the alternatives and strategic choice.	• Analysis of the match between the business's current strategic position (company profile) and the major strategic opportunities and threats (environmental analysis) that exist or will exist in the planning time period. • Examining the probable results of pursuing the current strategy in light of the new business-environment match. • Comparison of these results with tentative business objectives to identify major performance gaps and strategic concerns. • Identification of alternative strategies to close performance gaps and confront (or avoid) strategic concerns. • Evaluation of the alternatives and strategic choice.

The process of strategic analysis and choice involves five incremental phases. Figure 10-1 identifies these phases at the business and corporate levels. Because strategic choice is a judgmental / analytical process meant to ascertain the future impact of one or more strategies on corporate (and / or business unit) performance, the answers to three basic questions are sought:

1. How effective has the existing strategy been?
2. How effective will that strategy be in the future
3. What will be the effectiveness of selected alternative strategies (or changes in the existing strategy) in the future?

Appendix 2.8

Analytic Hierarchy Process (AHP)

Abstract

The objective of this paper is to develop a theoretically sound approach for determining the most appropriate product from a given set of options in a particular segment. A methodology using an analytic hierarchy process (AHP) is suggested as a means of formalizing the process of determining the suitability of a car (for example) in the given segment to a potential buyer. The AHP has been applied to a variety of business decisions and processes requiring high degree of subjective judgement. Although the AHP process is a subjective requiring high degree of discretion upon the judgement of the decision-maker, it does so in a manner that is more systematic and consistent than traditional subjective decision-making.

Methodology

The Analytic Hierarchy Process (AHP) is a powerful and flexible decision making process to help people set priorities and make the best decision when both qualitative and quantitative aspects of a decision need to be considered. By reducing complex decisions to a series of one-on-one comparisons, then synthesizing the results, AHP not only helps decision makers arrive at the best decision, but also provides a clear rationale that it is the best. Designed to reflect the way people actually think, AHP was developed in the 1970's by Dr. Thomas Saaty, while he was a professor at the Wharton Schools of Business and continues to be the most highly regarded and widely used decision-making theory. The AHP process is useful for systematically evaluating qualitative criteria. AHP attempts to resolve conflicts and analyze judgments through a process of determining the relative importance of a set of activities or criteria. The AHP can be summarized in terms of three basic components:

First, the principal problem is decomposed into a hierarchy. The top level of the hierarchy represents the overall objective of the process. In the approach discussed in this paper, this top level is the most suitable car in a given segment for a given set of potential customer.

Once the top level of the hierarchy has been defined, then the overall objective of the process is broken down into components. These factors compose the second level of the hierarchy.

Subsequently, each element in the second level spans a group of sub elements in the third level. This process is repeated until the final level is reached.

The final level represents the array of possible outcomes. In the case, the array of possible outcomes is the weightings of various assets held in a portfolio.

Within each level of hierarchy, the relative importance of all elements derived from a single element in the next higher level must be determined. For example, suppose element 1 in level 2 is decomposed in level 3 into three sub elements, a, b, and g. the AHP determines the relative importance of these three sub elements by constructing a complete set of pair wise comparisons among them. A nine-point scale is used for these comparisons. A score of 9 signifies highest level of importance for an element relative to other elements, and a score of 1 / 9th signifies an element is much less important. If comparison a and b is assigned 1, a and b are considered of equal importance the comparison of b to a would be assigned the reciprocal value. Interpretations for the pair wise comparisons are summarized in Table 1. A complete set of such scores constitutes a pair wise comparison matrix. At the final level of the hierarchy each possible outcome must be considered relative to a single sub element of the previous level.

In the third and final phase of the AHP the pair wise comparison matrices are evaluated by solving for their eigenvalues. The eigenvalues represent the weighting functions for each set of pair wise comparison matrices. Each set of lower level eigenvalues are then scaled by the eigenvalues corresponding to the next level in the hierarchy. Continuing the process of eigenvalue extraction and weighting through the levels of the hierarchy leads to a global weighting scale. The global priorities for the final level reflect the decision-maker's relative weights for the alternatives.

Table 1: Interpretations for the Pair-wise Comparisons

Ratings of Absolute Importance	Explanation
α to β = 1	Two activities contribute equally to the objective and are of the highest importance.
α to β = 3	Experience and judgement moderately favor α over β.
α to β = 5	Experience and judgement strongly favour α over β.
α to β = 7	α is strongly favored over β and its dominance is demonstrated in practice.
α to β = 9	The evidence favoring α over β is the highest possible.
α to β = 2,4,6,8	When compromise if needed. Reciprocals If activity α has one of the above numbers assigned to it when compared with activity β, then β has the reciprocal value when compared to α.

Setting up a problem as a hierarchy is an efficient and intuitive way of dealing with complexity and identifying the relevant components of the problem. AHP is flexible in allowing decision-makers to structure a hierarchy to fit individual needs and preferences. In addition, in a group setting, using AHP to structure a problem may help to isolate areas of disagreement so that more attention can be focused on them in order to achieve consensus.

Appendix 2.9

Process (Throughput) efficiency

Process (Throughput) efficiency is a key indicator of an organization's value adding efficiency (Peppard Joe and Rowland Philip, 2002) and is defined as:

$$\text{Throughput efficiency} = \frac{\text{Work content time}}{\text{Total time in system}} \times 100\%$$

While it does not tell us whether or not the value adding stages are being performed efficiently it does tell us how much of the time is definitely not contributing to the goals of the process. As an example of measuring throughput efficiency and what it indicates consider the progress of a simple purchase order from the manager in a department to the supplier:

Action	Time of action	Transit/wait time
Complete purchase order form send to senior manager for signature	10 minutes	1 day
Senior manager sign from sends form to finance control	1 minute	1 day
Finance book spend and sign order sends from to purchasing	3 minutes	1 day
Buyer review order form buyer issues order to supplier	5 minutes	1 day
Total times	19 minutes	4 days

$$\text{Throughput efficiency} = \frac{\text{19 minutes}}{4 \times 8 \times 60 + 12 \text{ (an 8 hour day)}} \times 100\%$$

$$= \frac{19}{1932} \times 100\%$$

$$= 1\% \text{ approximately}$$

Appendix 3.1

Citizens Requirement Study

Categories and Groups of Citizens

S.N.	Categories	Groups
1.	Gender	• Male • Female
2.	Age	• Young (18-30 yrs.) • Middle-aged group (31-40 yrs.) • Aged (> 40 years)
3.	Income	• Low income group (BPL) • Middle income group (>BPL but < Rs.4000pm) • High income group (income > Rs.4000pm)
4.	Education	• Low education group (illiterate to PE) • Medium education group (>PE but <HS) • High education group (>HS)
5.	Caste	• General • OBC • SC& ST

BPL: Below poverty line; PE: Primary education; HS: High school; pm: Per month

For identification of requirements, questionnaires were developed for a variety of information, services and grievances (under different sectors) availed by citizens in rural areas (see Annexure 2.1)

The response was taken for 'scale of importance' and 'frequency of usage'

- Scale of the importance: It shows about the importance given by citizens from 1 to 5 ('1' means least important and '5' means most important).
- Frequency of usage: under this category, the followings have been taken. These are: 'weekly', 'monthly', 'in three months', 'in six months to one year' and 'rarely'.

Note: The mean of the scale of importance and frequency of usage has been calculated using SPSS package, which is used in the following tables.

Table 3.1.1: Top three Information, Services and Grievances based on Mean of Scale of importance for all the Groups

S.N.	Sectors	I/S/G	S.N.	Items	Importance (mean value)
1.	Education	I	1	Type of Scholarship	3.00
			2	Distribution of books	2.43
			3	Number of schools	2.26
			4	Schemes for BPL families	2.25
		S	1	Providing education to children	4.51
			2	Computer education	3.54
			3	Scholarship	3.38
		G	1	Vacancies of teachers	2.40
			2	Non-availability of school building / drinking water / toilets / playground, etc.	2.22
			3	Late coming of teachers	1.92
			4	Absenteeism	1.83
2.	Drinking water	I	1	Quality of water	3.60
			2	Village-wise drinking water resources	2.45
			3	Water table	2.23
		S	1	Making water available	4.08
			2	Repair of hand pumps	3.14
			3	Repair of tube wells	2.58
		G	1	Poor quality of drinking water	3.65
			2	Non-installation of tube-well	2.49
			3	Non-functioning of tube-well or pipe water supply system	2.36
3.	Health	I	1	Health information	3.79
			2	Type of diseases	3.67
			3	Special health camps	3.33
			4	Family planning	2.91
		S	1	Expert advice on health	4.18
			2	Immunisation	4.05
			3	Making medicines available	4.00
		G	1	Non availability of medicines	3.83
			2	Non availability of doctors / health workers	3.44
			3	Non availability of ambulance	2.70
4.	Women and child welfare	I	1	Facilities at anganwadi centre	3.20
			2	Number of children and mothers covered	2.17
			3	Schemes for BPL families	2.05
		S	1	Nutritional programme for pre-school children and mothers	3.88

S.N.	Sectors	I/S/G	S.N.	Items	Importance (mean value)
			2	Organizing immunization programme	3.87
		G	1	Anganwadi centre not working	1.17
			2	Food is not given to children	1.09
			3	Absenteeism of anganwadi workers	0.72
5.	Social welfare	I	1	Social welfare programme for different categories (SCs, STs, OBCs etc.)	4.03
			2	Schemes for BPL families	3.49
			3	Schemes for handicaps	3.17
		S	1	Old age and widow pension	4.29
			2	Insurance and family welfare schemes	3.50
			3	Scholarship for SCs, STs	3.22
		G	1	Delay in pension	3.13
			2	Delay / non-availability of scholarships	2.40
			3	Irregularities in running of hostels / old age homes / orphanages	2.09
6.	Poverty alleviation	I	1	Schemes for BPL families	3.50
			2	Village-wise status of development works	3.46
			3	Village-wise below poverty line list	3.00
		S	1	Loan for self-employment	3.96
			2	Training for self-employment	3.80
			3	Family-housing (IAY)	3.00
		G	1	Name not included in BPL list	3.55
			2	Poor quality of implementation of work	3.11
			3	Complaints regarding credit / assets for self-employment	2.81
7.	PDS	I	1	Schemes for BPL families	3.51
			2	Items available at fair price shops	3.48
			3	Fair price shop wise distribution and allotment information	3.23
		S	1	Ration cards	4.10
			2	Timely availability of essential commodities	3.87
		G	1	Non-availability of commodities at fair price shop	3.64
			2	Non-functioning of fair price shops	3.32
			3	Complaints of BPL / antyodaya cards holder	2.83
8.	Agriculture	I	1	Loan schemes	3.65
			2	Fertiliser use	3.53

S.N.	Sectors	I/S/G	S.N.	Items	Importance (mean value)
			3	Soil nutrients	3.45
			4	Cropping pattern	3.32
		S	1	Purchase of seeds, fertilizer, pesticide, implements	4.07
			2	Crop loan	3.38
			3	Crop insurance	3.28
			4	Expert advice on agriculture	3.28
		G	1	Non-availability of quality seeds, fertilizer, pesticides	3.70
			2	Pest attack	3.48
9.	Irrigation	I	1	Sources of irrigation	3.13
			2	Schemes for BPL families	2.51
			3	Area under different sources of irrigation	2.06
		S	1	Timely availability of water for irrigation	4.03
			2	Digging canals	1.96
			3	Repair of canals	0.89
		G	1	Over extraction of ground water	2.40
			2	Non-availability of compensation for land	2.14
			3	Illegal irrigation from canals / ponds / river	0.98
10.	Animal husbandry	I	1	Information of diseases	4.04
			2	Cattle health care and controls	3.80
			3	Insurance of cattle	2.84
			4	Milk rates	2.60
		S	1	Supply of feed	4.15
			2	Expert advice of cattle management	3.83
			3	Marketing of milk	2.76
		G	1	Requirement of veterinary doctor in rural areas	4.45
			2	Non-availability of medicines	3.93
			3	Street cattle	2.02
11.	Tehsil	I	1	Guidelines for accessing the certificates	3.40
			2	Land records	3.16
			3	Availability of forms	2.85
		S	1	Domicile certificate	3.78
			2	Land certificate	3.52
			3	Caste certificate	3.42
		G	1	Non-availability of *Patwari*	3.08
			2	Complaint against *Patwari*	2.68

S.N.	Sectors	I/S/G	S.N.	Items	Importance (mean value)
			3	Over functioning of *Patwari*	1.63
12.	Electricity	I	1	Information about electricity cut	3.11
			2	Rates for giving electricity connection for house hold	2.32
			3	Last date of depositing bill payment	2.17
		S	1	Electricity connection	3.68
		G	1	Electricity failure for household	3.81
			2	Electricity failure for agriculture pump sets	3.38
13.	Road	I	1	Timings of buses and bus routes	2.47
			2	Milestones for bus routes	1.03
		S	1	Availability of buses	4.12
		G	1	Adding more buses	2.84
			2	Delay in bus	1.37
			3	Change of route	0.92
14.	Others	I	1	Employment notification	4.26
			2	For setting up rural industries	3.17
			3	Guidelines for schemes for all departments	2.21
		S	1	Local news	2.45
			2	Personal insurance	2.43
			3	Driving license	2.41
			4	National news	2.00
		G	1	Bad roads	3.94
			2	Non-functioning of bus	2.67

I: Information, S: Services, G: Grievances

Table 3.1.2: High Value of Scale of Importance and High Frequency for Information, Services and Grievance for all Categories

Sectors	I/S/G	S.N.	Items	Mean of scale	Mean of frequency				
					0-1	1 to 2	2 to 3	3 to 4	4 to 5
Education	S	1	Providing education to children	4.51				3.75	
Health	S	3	Expert advice on health	4.18				3.99	
DW	S	2	Making water available	4.08				3.93	
Health	S	1	Immunisation	4.05				3.43	
Health	S	2	Making medicines available	4.00				3.99	
WCW	S	1	Nutritional programme for pre-school children and mothers	3.88				3.50	
WCW	S	2	Organising immunization programme	3.87				3.05	
Health	G	2	Non availability of medicines	3.83				3.42	
DW	G	1	Poor quality of drinking water	3.65				3.05	
DW	I	4	Quality of water	3.60				3.14	
Education	S	4	Computer education	3.54					4.07
Social W	S	1	Old age and widow pension	4.29				3.41	
PDS	S	2	Timely availability of essential commodities	3.87				3.28	
Animal H	G	1	Requirement of veterinary doctor in rural areas	4.45				3.70	
Others	I	1	Employment notification	4.26				3.45	
Animal H	S	2	Supply of feed	4.15				3.79	
Road	S	1	Availability of buses	4.12				3.93	
Animal H	I	6	Information of diseases	4.04				3.35	
Irrigation	S	3	Timely availability of water for irrigation	4.03				3.36	
Others	G	1	Bad roads	3.94				3.31	
Animal H	G	2	Non-availability of medicines	3.93				3.49	
Animal H	S	4	Expert advice of cattle management	3.83				3.14	
Electricity	G	1	Electricity failure for household	3.81				3.94	

DW: Drinking Water, WCW: Women and Child Welfare, Social W: Social Welfare, Poverty A: Poverty Alleviation, PDS: Public Distribution System, Animal H: Animal Husbandry,
I: Information, S: Services, G: Grievances

Table 3.1.3: High Value of Scale of Importance and Medium Frequency for Information, Services and Grievance for all Categories

Sectors	I/S/G	S.N.	Items	Mean of scale	Mean of frequency				
					0-1	1 to 2	2 to 3	3 to 4	4 to 5
PDS	S	1	Ration cards	4.10			2.25		
Agriculture	S	1	Purchase of seeds, fertilizer, pesticide, implements	4.07			2.91		
Social W	I	1	Social welfare programme for different categories (SCs, STs, OBCs etc.)	4.03			2.82		
Poverty A	S	3	Loan for self-employment	3.96			2.34		
Poverty A	S	4	Training for self-employment	3.80			2.67		
Agriculture	G	2	Non-availability of quality seeds, fertilizer, pesticides	3.70			2.74		
Agriculture	I	10	Loan schemes	3.65			2.27		
PDS	G	1	Non-availability of commodities at fair price shop	3.64			2.90		
Poverty A	G	3	Name not included in BPL list	3.55			2.38		
Agriculture	I	3	Fertiliser use	3.53			2.38		
PDS	I	6	Schemes for BPL families	3.51			2.51		
Social W	S	2	Insurance and family welfare schemes	3.50			2.59		
Poverty A	I	7	Schemes for BPL families	3.50			2.75		
Animal H	I	2	Cattle health care and controls	3.80			2.98		
Electricity	S	1	Electricity connection	3.68			2.11		

DW: Drinking Water, WCW: Women and Child Welfare, Social W: Social Welfare, Poverty A: Poverty Alleviation, PDS: Public Distribution System, Animal H: Animal Husbandry, I: Information, S: Services, G: Grievances

Table 3.1.4: High Value Scale of Importance and Low Frequency for Information, Services and Grievance for all Categories

Sectors	I/S/G	S.N.	Items	Mean of scale	Mean of frequency				
					0-1	1 to 2	2 to 3	3 to 4	4 to 5
Health	I	3	Type of diseases	3.67		1.57			
Tehsil	S	4	Domicile certificate	3.78		1.94			
Tehsil	S	1	Land certificate	3.52		1.87			

I: Information, S: Services, G: Grievances

Table 3.1.5: Low Value Scale of Importance and High Frequency for Information, Services and Grievance for all Categories

Sectors	I/S/G	S.N.	Items	Mean of scale	Mean of frequency				
					0-1	1 to 2	2 to 3	3 to 4	4 to 5
Health	I	2	Number of hospitals	2.03				3.53	
Health	I	6	Schemes for BPL families	2.01				3.04	
Others	S	10	Local news	2.45				3.16	

I: Information, S: Services, G: Grievances

Table 3.1.6: Low Value Scale of Importance and medium frequency for Information, Services and Grievance for all Categories

Sectors	I/S/G	S.N.	Items	Mean of scale	Mean of frequency				
					0-1	1 to 2	2 to 3	3 to 4	4 to 5
DW	G	3	Non-installation of tube-well	2.49			2.03		
DW	I	1	Village-wise drinking water resources	2.45			2.08		
Education	I	7	Distribution of books	2.43			2.16		
DW	G	2	Non-functioning of tube-well or pipe water supply system	2.36			2.12		
Education	G	3	Late coming of teachers	1.92			2.10		
Education	G	2	Absenteeism	1.83			2.04		
PDS	I	2	Shop wise, number of families covered	2.44			2.07		
PDS	G	5	Complaint against retailer	2.39			2.07		
Agriculture	S	7	Marketing of agriculture produce	2.36			2.44		
Agriculture	S	5	Weather forecast	1.82			2.12		
Road	I	1	Timings of buses and bus routes	2.47			2.32		
Electricity	I	3	Last date of depositing bill payment	2.17			2.23		
Animal H	G	3	Street cattle	2.02			2.06		
Others	S	11	National news	2.00			2.85		

DW: Drinking Water, WCW: Women and Child Welfare, Social W: Social Welfare, Poverty A: Poverty Alleviation, PDS: Public Distribution System, Animal H: Animal Husbandry, I: Information, S: Services, G: Grievances

Table 3.1.7: Low Value Scale of Importance and Low Frequency for Information, Services and Grievance for all Categories

Sectors	I/S/G	S.N.	Items	Mean of scale	Mean of frequency				
					0-1	1 to 2	2 to 3	3 to 4	4 to 5
Education	G	1	Vacancies of teachers	2.40		1.74			
Education	I	2	Number of schools	2.26		1.35			
Education	I	10	Schemes for BPL families	2.25		1.67			
DW	I	2	Water table	2.23		1.95			
Education	G	5	Non-availability of school building / drinking water / toilets / playground, etc.	2.22		1.72			
WCW	I	1	Number of children and mothers covered	2.17		1.86			
Education	I	6	Results for 10th and 12th classes	2.13		1.18			
Education	I	4	Number of teachers	2.07		1.46			
WCW	I	3	Schemes for BPL families	2.05		1.72			
Education	I	8	Information about vocational schools	1.97		1.13			
DW	I	5	Schemes for BPL families	1.96		1.54			
DW	I	3	Capacity of tanks	1.91		1.74			
DW	I	6	Number of hand pumps	1.76		1.52			
Health	I	8	Information about ayurvedh dispensary	1.66		1.26			
Education	I	3	Number of children attending schools by age, caste and gender	1.64		1.06			
Education	G	8	Irregularities in mid-day meal	1.62		1.71			
Education	I	9	Information about professional collages (law,medical,etc.)	1.59		1.01			
Health	I	7	Information about homeopathy dispensary	1.56		1.55			
Education	G	7	Delay / non-availability of scholarships	1.37		1.15			
WCW	G	1	Anganwadi centre not working	1.17		1.01			
WCW	G	3	Food is not given to children	1.09		1.05			
Education	G	4	Closing of schools	1.01		1.24			

Sectors	I/S/G	S.N.	Items	Mean of scale	Mean of frequency				
					0-1	1 to 2	2 to 3	3 to 4	4 to 5
WCW	G	2	Absenteeism of anganwadi workers	0.72	0.79				
Education	I	5	Number of night schools and locations	0.62	0.49				
Education	G	6	Delay in payment of salary to staff	0.52	0.55				
Agriculture	I	11	Subsidy for different schemes	2.42		1.91			
Social W	G	2	Delay / non-availability of scholarships	2.40		1.88			
Poverty A	G	2	Non-availability of timely payment for indira awas yojana (IAY) houses	2.40		1.66			
PDS	G	3	Higher prices of essential commodities	2.39		1.93			
PDS	I	5	Total allotment of the village	2.15		1.68			
PDS	I	4	Names of families covered	2.11		1.83			
Social W	G	1	Irregularities in running of hostels / old age homes / orphanages	2.09		1.65			
Poverty A	I	4	Amount spent on poverty alleviation programmes	2.07		1.55			
Poverty A	I	6	Assets created under poverty alleviation programs	2.05		1.66			
Poverty A	I	5	Guidelines	2.01		1.75			
Agriculture	I	7	Marketable surplus	1.64		1.47			
Social W	I	3	Number of orphanages and their beneficiaries and locations	1.54		1.21			
Social W	G	4	Requirement of new hostels	1.25	0.99				
Agriculture	I	6	Owner requirement	1.22		1.32			
Animal H	S	1	Supply of quality animals under loan scheme	2.49		1.83			
Others	S	9	Personal insurance	2.43		1.45			
Others	S	5	Driving license	2.41		1.63			
Irrigation	G	1	Over extraction of ground water	2.40		1.80			

Sectors	I/S/G	S.N.	Items	Mean of scale	Mean of frequency				
					0-1	1 to 2	2 to 3	3 to 4	4 to 5
Animal H	I	7	Information about cattle fairs	2.36		1.92			
Electricity	I	4	Rates for giving electricity connection for house hold	2.32		1.91			
Others	I	3	Guidelines for schemes for all departments	2.21		1.80			
Tehsil	S	5	Mutation	2.19		1.22			
Irrigation	G	4	Non-availability of compensation for land	2.14		1.46			
Tehsil	I	4	Schemes for BPL families	2.07		1.50			
Irrigation	I	2	Area under different sources of irrigation	2.06		1.93			
Electricity	I	5	Rates for giving electricity connection for agriculture purpose	2.03		1.66			
Others	S	2	Payment of government dues (electricity, phone, etc.)	1.97		1.89			
Irrigation	S	1	Digging canals	1.96		1.04			
Others	I	4	Telephone numbers of all departments	1.95		1.79			
Animal H	I	3	Artificial insemination	1.82		1.67			
Animal H	I	1	Cattle population	1.66		1.40			
Tehsil	G	2	Over functioning of Patwari	1.63		1.59			
Others	S	7	Horoscope	1.58		1.29			
Tehsil	S	6	Sale deed	1.40		1.00			
Road	G	1	Delay in bus	1.37		1.87			
Tehsil	S	7	Conversion of agriculture land into non-agriculture land	1.24	0.81				
Road	I	2	Milestones for bus routes	1.03		1.23			
Others	S	8	Matrimonial	1.00	0.94				
Irrigation	G	2	Illegal irrigation from canals / ponds / river	0.98	0.73				
Others	S	6	Gun license	0.98	0.72				
Others	S	1	Marketing of handicrafts	0.94		1.09			
Others	S	3	e-mail	0.94		1.16			
Road	G	2	Change of route	0.92		1.32			
Electricity	I	1	Number of connections	0.91	0.94				

Sectors	I/S/G	S.N.	Items	Mean of scale	Mean of frequency				
					0-1	1 to 2	2 to 3	3 to 4	4 to 5
Others	S	4	Internet browsing	0.90	0.98				
Irrigation	S	2	Repair of canals	0.89	0.66				
Irrigation	G	5	Non-availability of water at the tail-end of canal	0.89	0.64				
Irrigation	G	3	Repair and maintenance of canals	0.76	0.68				
Animal H	I	4	No. of poultry units	0.40	0.66				
Others	I	5	Charter of services of all departments	0.00	0.00				

DW: Drinking Water, WCW: Women and Child Welfare, Social W: Social Welfare, Poverty A: Poverty Alleviation, PDS: Public Distribution System, Animal H: Animal Husbandry, I: Information, S: Services, G: Grievances

Table 3.1.8: Medium Value Scale of Importance and Medium Frequency for Information, Services and Grievance for all Categories

Sectors	I/S/G	S.N.	Items	Mean of scale	Mean of frequency				
					0-1	1 to 2	2 to 3	3 to 4	4 to 5
Education	S	2	Scholarship	3.38			2.49		
Health	I	5	Special health camps	3.33			2.53		
WCW	I	2	Facilities at anganwadi center	3.20			2.75		
DW	S	3	Repair of hand pumps	3.14			2.45		
Health	G	3	Non availability of ambulance	2.70			2.07		
DW	S	1	Repair of tube wells	2.58			2.01		
Social W	I	4	Schemes for BPL families	3.49			2.54		
Agriculture	G	1	Pest attack	3.48			2.57		
Poverty A	I	1	Village-wise status of development works	3.46			2.65		
Agriculture	I	2	Soil nutrients	3.45			2.38		
Agriculture	S	4	Crop loan	3.38			2.17		
PDS	G	2	Non-functioning of fair price shops	3.32			2.76		
Agriculture	I	1	Cropping pattern	3.32			2.16		
Agriculture	S	8	Crop insurance	3.28			2.02		
Agriculture	S	9	Expert advice on agriculture	3.28			2.55		
PDS	I	1	Fair price shop wise distribution and allotment information	3.23			2.82		
Social W	S	3	Scholarship for SCs, STs	3.22			2.38		
Social W	S	4	Aids for handicaps	3.20			2.12		
Social W	I	5	Schemes for handicaps	3.17			2.29		
Social W	G	3	Delay in pension	3.13			2.39		
Poverty A	G	1	Poor quality of implementation of work	3.11			2.41		
Agriculture	I	9	Schemes for BPL families	3.06			2.16		
Poverty A	I	2	Village-wise below poverty line list	3.00			2.24		
PDS	I	7	Rates of commodities	2.88			2.66		
PDS	G	4	Complaints of BPL / antyodaya cards holder	2.83			2.19		

Sectors	I/S/G	S.N.	Items	Mean of scale	Mean of frequency				
					0-1	1 to 2	2 to 3	3 to 4	4 to 5
Poverty A	G	4	Complaints regarding credit / assets for self-employment	2.81			2.15		
Agriculture	I	4	Agricultural implements used	2.81			2.07		
Agriculture	I	12	Agriculture raining centers	2.76			2.08		
Agriculture	S	2	Training and demonstration	2.73			2.27		
Tehsil	I	2	Guidelines for accessing the certificates	3.40			2.27		
Others	I	2	For setting up rural industries	3.17			2.68		
Irrigation	I	1	Sources of irrigation	3.13			2.45		
Tehsil	G	1	Non-availability of Patwari	3.08			2.54		
Tehsil	I	1	Availability of forms	2.85			2.01		
Road	G	3	Adding more buses	2.84			2.32		
Tehsil	G	3	Complaint against Patwari	2.68			2.22		
Others	G	2	Non-functioning of bus	2.67			2.56		
Animal H	I	5	Schemes for BPL families	2.57			2.07		

DW: Drinking Water, WCW: Women and Child Welfare, Social W: Social Welfare, Poverty A: Poverty Alleviation, PDS: Public Distribution System, Animal H: Animal Husbandry, I: Information, S: Services, G. Grievances

Table 3.1.9: Medium Value Scale of Importance and High Frequency for Information, Services and Grievance for all Categories

Sectors	I/S/G	S.N.	Items	Mean of scale	Mean of frequency				
					0-1	1 to 2	2 to 3	3 to 4	4 to 5
Health	G	1	Non availability of doctors / health workers	3.44				3.17	
Health	I	4	Family planning	2.91				3.40	
Education	S	3	Library activity	2.56				3.25	
PDS	I	3	Items available at fair price shops	3.48				3.34	
Agriculture	I	8	Daily mandi rates	3.28				3.16	
Agriculture	S	6	Mandi rates	3.10				3.07	
Electricity	G	2	Electricity failure for agriculture pump sets	3.38				3.45	
Electricity	I	2	Information about electricity cut	3.11				3.57	
Animal H	S	3	Marketing of milk	2.76				3.53	
Animal H	I	9	Milk rates	2.60				3.05	

PDS: Public Distribution System, Animal H: Animal Husbandry,
I: Information, S: Services, G: Grievances

Table 3.1.10: Medium Value Scale of Importance and Low Frequency for Information, Services and Grievance for all Categories

Sectors	I/S/G	S.N.	Items	Mean of scale	Mean of frequency				
					0-1	1 to 2	2 to 3	3 to 4	4 to 5
Education	I	1	Type of Scholarship	3.00		1.90			
Poverty A	S	2	Family-housing (IAY)	3.00		1.60			
Poverty A	S	1	Construction of village assets	2.78		1.84			
Agriculture	S	3	Soil testing	2.74		1.93			
Social W	I	2	Number of old age homes and their beneficiaries and locations	2.70		1.87			
Agriculture	I	5	Production	2.64		1.88			
Poverty A	I	3	Number of beneficiaries of poverty alleviation programmes	2.62		1.88			
Tehsil	S	2	Caste certificate	3.42		1.97			
Tehsil	S	3	Income certificate	3.17		1.86			
Tehsil	I	3	Land records	3.16		1.86			
Animal H	I	8	Insurance of cattle	2.84		1.90			
Irrigation	I	3	Schemes for BPL families	2.51		1.93			

Social W: Social Welfare, Poverty A: Poverty Alleviation, Animal H: Animal Husbandry, I: Information, S: Services, G: Grievances

Appendix 5.1

Evaluation of e-Governance Projects

For measuring the efficacy of e-Government system to deliver services efficiently

I. Internal Factors

Categories

1. IT
2. Delivery System
3. Internal Functioning
4. Rules and Procedures
5. No. of services, Scalability and Revenue

II. External Factors

Categories

1. Citizens
2. External Environment
3. Government Policies
4. Infrastructure

Factors

Internal

S.N.	Category	No.	Factors
1.	IT	1	Connectivity
		2	Hardware
		3	Software
		4	Data Security
		5	Manpower
2.	Delivery System	1	Manpower
		2	Capabilities
		3	Infrastructure
		4	Supporting equipments
3.	Internal Functioning	1	Processes
		2	Work culture & Concern for Quality
		3	Provision for Participation in decision-making by citizens
4.	Rules and Procedures	1	Transparency
		2	Accountability
		3	Rules and legal matters
5.	No. of services, Scalability and Revenue	1	Revenue generation and BEP
		2	Scope of services to people
		3	Scalability

External

S.N.	Category	No.	Factors
1.	Citizens	1	Citizens needs assessment
		2	Education level of citizens
		3	Acceptability by citizens
2.	External Environment	1	Social and economic environment
		2	Political environment
3.	Government Policies	1	Government polices
		2	Government support
4.	Infrastructure	1	Electricity
		2	Location of e-Kiosk

Details

I. Internal Factors

Factors affecting a System (e-Governance)

1. IT

S.N.	Internal Factors							
	Factors	Sub-factors						
		No.		Scale				
				5	4	3	2	1
	1. IT							
1.	Connectivity	1	Connectivity to Kiosks (Reach ability)					
		2	Speed					
		3	Outside to G					
		4	G TO G					
2.	Hardware	1	At head end					
		2	At Kiosk					
		3	At govt. level					
3.	Software	1	Software development after BPR					
		2	Back-end support					
4.	Data Security	1	Type of system (How effective)					
5.	Manpower	1	No. of manpower (adequacy)					
		2	Capabilities					

2. Delivery System

S.N.	Internal Factors			Scale				
	Factors	Sub-factors						
		No.		5	4	3	2	1
	2. Delivery System							
1.	Manpower	1	Adequacy of manpower (w.r.t. workload)					
		2	Work load is adequately shared by all					
2.	Capabilities	1	Training at the time of entry in the service					
		2	In-service training					
		3	Training about e-Governance					
		4	Training about management techniques					
		5	Behavioural skills					
3.	Infrastructure	1	Building					
		2	Light					
		3	Water					
		4	Facilities (Canteen, toilets)					
		5	Record room					
4.	Supporting equipments	1	Computer					
		2	Phone					
		3	Other functional equipments available (e.g. medical equipment for 'health', teaching – aids for education)					

3. Internal functioning

S.N.	Internal Factors							
	Factors	Sub-factors						
		No.		Scale				
				5	4	3	2	1
	3. Internal functioning							
1.	Processes	1	Whether easy to understand by citizens					
		2	Whether easy to work by functionaries					
		3	Whether steps taken to simplify, while there is a scope					
		4	Ease of collection of Application Form					
		5	Ease of collection of Delivery Form					
2.	Work culture & Concern for Quality	1	Quality consciousness					
		2	Time consciousness					
		3	Behaviour					
		4	Responsiveness / Sensitivity					
3.	Provision for Participation in decision-making by citizens	1	Feedback about services to departments					
		2	Access to information					
		3	Possibility of participating in planning / decision-making through feedback					

4. Rules and Procedures

S.N.	Internal Factors							
	Factors	Sub-factors		Scale				
		No.		5	4	3	2	1
	4. Rules and Procedures							
1.	Transparency	1	In sharing information					
		2	In informing status of the case					
		3	In decision-making					
2.	Accountability	1	Of head of the office					
		2	Of office staff					
		3	Of field functionaries					
		4	Of service provider					
3.	Rules and legal matters	1	For timely delivery of services					
		2	If rules for timely delivery of services, whether it is followed					
		3	Office manual is followed properly					
		4	Are the forms simple					
		5	In case of inconvenience to citizens, whether there are rules to protect the interest of citizens					
		6	Whether service provider follows rules					

5. Scalability and Revenue

S.N.	Internal Factors							
	Factors	Sub-factors		Scale				
		No.		5	4	3	2	1
	5. Scalability and Revenue							
1.	Revenue generation and BEP	1	Revenue model workable					
		2	Services charges are reasonable					
2.	Scope of services to people	1	Whether most of citizens' services are addressed					
		2	Whether services benefit maximum					
3.	Scalability	1	Sustainability of technology					
		2	Sustainability of revenue model					

Regarding above we need to give the following:

- **Ranking to above factors**
- **Weightage to above factors**

- For Present Status
- For Expected Status

II. External Factors

1. Citizens
2. External Environment
3. Government Policies

Present Status
Factors affecting a System (e-Governance)

External Factors								
S.N.	**Factors**	**Sub-factors**						
		No.		**Scale**				
				5	**4**	**3**	**2**	**1**
	1.Citizens							
1	Citizens needs assessment	1	Assessment made					
		2	Which are the most critical services					
2	Education level of citizens	1	Literacy level					
		2	Computer literacy					
		3	Awareness					
3	Acceptability by citizens	1	Confidence of using e-Kiosk					
		2	Confidence of using e-Kiosk by women					
	2. External Environment							
4	Social and economic environment	1	Support by local people (encouragement					
		2	Community participation					
5	Political environment	1	Support of local political system					
		2	Support of state level political system					
	3. Government Policies							
6	Government polices	1	Policies on incentive for IT and e-Governance					
		2	Rules and regulations for e-Governance					
7	Government support	3	Departments support for providing database					
		4	Inter-department coordination					
	4. Infrastructure							
8	Electricity	1	Availability of electricity					
9	Location of e-Kiosk	2	Distance of e-Kiosk to *Patwaraghar*					

Regarding above we need to give the following:

- **Ranking to above factors**
- **Weightage to above factors**

- For Present Status
- For Expected Status

Definitions of Terms Used in the Book

Definitions of Terms Used in the Book

Accessibility: The extent to which the citizens are able to avail the services when they require it.

Application of Statistical Tools: The changes that occur have to be validated using statistical tools (tests). For example, t-test, chi-square test.

Behavioural / Human Capabilities: These are concerned with ability to deal with other people. These include abilities to lead others, motivate, generate team spirit, resolve conflicts and so on.

Benchmarking: Benchmarks are targets, which define target levels. There can be standards for: what the citizen wants today or wants in the future, what is the best available service, or what is world-class performance. Benchmarks tell us how we are performing today and how good we have to become to be in future.

Benchmarking: It refers to the process of setting standards (existing elsewhere) of performance (in the delivery of services, their quality, cost involved etc.) and then trying to achieve that standard in the best possible manner.

Consistency: By consistency is meant how regularly the service conforms to the expected standard.

Critical to Quality Characteristics (CTQs): The parameters that are vital and impact on the quality of output need to be identified.

Delivery System: The term delivery system refers to agencies or organisations through which development programmes are implemented to ensure availability of inputs and / or services to people for various sectors such as agriculture, marketing of agricultural produce, health, education to children and drinking water and so on.

S. N.	Delivery System / Department	Services delivered (a select list)
1.	Tehsil,	Delivery of certificates, disaster management
2.	Agriculture	Agriculture inputs
3.	Education	Primary education
4.	Health	Health services like immunisation, family planning
5.	PHED	Drinking water

Desired Standards: Targets set about the delivery of services, their quality, timeliness etc.

Dynamic Data: When there is a change in data due to displacement of a citizen or his income or caste, the related data of that citizen needs change, and so accordingly the database has to be changed.

Effectiveness: Effectiveness measures the extent to which the impact of a policy conforms to the objective.

Efficiency: It is a relationship between inputs and output indicating whether the inputs are properly utilised.

E-governance (e-gov.) Services: Services that are availed from the government departments, through e-Kiosk.

E-governance: It is a use of information and communication technologies with the aim of improving information and service delivery (of government sector), encouraging citizen's participation in the decision-making process and making government more accountable, transparent and effective.

Emotional Intelligence: It is the ability to sense, understand and effectively apply the power and acumen of emotions, as source of human energy, information, connection and influence.

Good Governance: It means achieving the desired goals and delivering through a system of adequate capacity to perform with sound norms and values. Good governance is in essence about being able to provide equal socio-economic and political opportunities to people, being responsive to people's needs, being able to provide basic services to people, and being fair and accountable in dealings.

Human Capital: It refers to the level of skills and knowledge to design, construct, operate, and maintain infrastructure.

IT Compatible Process: Processes that can be used efficiently and complementarily together with IT.

Lead Time: It refers to the time the government machinery takes to deliver services or to provide information to the citizens or to redress their grievances.

Organization Development (OD): It refers to the long-range effort to improve an organization's problem-solving capabilities and effectiveness to cope with changes in its external environment with the help of behavioural science technology, research, and theory.

Patwarghar: Office where Patwari works.

Process Mapping: A roadmap that helps to explain how a process functions.

Process: A process is a structured, measured set of activities designed to produce a specified output, or a specific ordering of work activities across time and place, with a beginning, an end, and clearly identified inputs and outputs.

Quality: It reflects how close the output is with respect to the benchmarks / standards fixed.

Reliability: The delivery of services is said to be reliable if the citizens can avail them on time without having to approach the delivering agencies (government departments) again and again.

Responsiveness: The manner and the sensitivity, with which the delivering agencies (government departments) cater to the needs of the citizens.

Timeliness: Timeliness refers to the delivery of services on time.

Value System: It refers to the way people in any organisation think, respond and work. And, in the context of decentralisation, values would include transparency, responsiveness for people's concern, decision-making process, accountability, opportunities for people's participation, working with people, commitment, team-work, and quality and efficiency of work.

Work Culture: It refers to values that are followed in an organisation, and these values determine the work culture.

References

References

Atkinson, Philip E., *Creating Culture Change: The Key to Successful Total Quality Management,* Productivity Press (India) Pvt. Ltd., Madras, 1993.

Barua, Anitesh, S. H. Sophie Lee, and Andrew B. Whinston, *The Calculus of Reengineering,* Department of Management Science, UT Austin, 1995.

Bhatnagar, Subhash and Robert Schware (ed.), *Information and Communication Technology in Development: Cases from India,* Sage Publications, New Delhi, 2002.

Brynjolfsson Erik, Renshaw Amy, and Alstyne Marshall Van, http://ccs.mit.edu/papers/CCSWP189/CCSWP189.html, MIT Sloan School of Management, Cambridge, UK.

Chalapathi R.S., *Developing 6 Sigma Competencies,* Excel Books, New Delhi, 2002.

Collins, Jim, *How to Tame Technology,* Business & Economy, New Delhi, 18 June-2 July, 2005.

Cummings Thomas G. and Worley Christopher G., *Organization Development and Change,* Seventh Edition, Thomson Asia Pvt. Ltd., Singapore, 2002.

DAC, *Evaluation of Programs Promoting Participatory Development and Good Governance,* Synthesis Report (OECD), 1997.

Vijaybaskar M and V Gayathri, *ICT and Indian Development,* Economic and Political Weekly (E&PW), 14th June 2003.

Economic Survey Govt. of India, 2005.

Ernberg, Johan, *Empowering Communities in the Information Society: An International Perspective,* [http://www.fao.org/WAICENT/FAOINFO/SUSTDEV/CDdirect/CDre0042.htm], 2000.

Fenwick, John, *Managing Local Government,* Chapman and Hall, London, 1995.

Firth David, *Smart Change,* Capstone Publishing Limited, USA, 1999.

Forojolla S.B., *Educational planning for development,* Martin's Press INC, New York, 1993.

Girija, Atul, *Institutionalizing And Implementation of India online Modalities and Mechanisms and other Emerging Concepts Practices in E-Governance, 'Conference on IT',* Department of Administrative Reforms, Government of India, 2002.

Gupta M. P, Kumar P, Bhattacharya J, *Government Online, Opportunities and Challenges,* Tata McGraw Hill Publishing Company Limited, New Delhi, 2004a.

Gupta M. P, *Promise of E-governance, Operational Challenges,* Tata McGraw Hill Publishing Company Limited, New Delhi, 2004c.

Gupta M. P, *Towards E-governance, Management Challenges,* Tata McGraw Hill Publishing Company Limited, New Delhi, 2004b.

Gyani, Giridhar J., *Training Manual on IS0 9000:2000 and TQM,* Raj Publishing House, Jaipur, 2001.

Handbook for Change Agents, Centre for Good Governance, Andhra Pradesh, 2003.

Hawley, Steven, *Cyberstars and HELP: Urban Youth Empowerment: Digital Divide Network.* [http://www.diitaldivi-dentwork.org/cyberstars.asp], 2000.

Hollis, Guy, *Transforming Local Government: A Practical Management Guide to Local Government Restructuring and Renewal,* Longman Group Ltd., Essex 1994.

http://ccs.mit.edu/papers

IDRC, *Evaluating Governance Programs,* Report of a workshop, 8 April 1999, Ottawa, 1999.

Jaikumar, R., *Postindustrial Manufacturing,* Harvard Business Review, 1986: 69-76.

Kaufman, Roger A., *Educational System Planning,* Prentice hall INC., New Jersey, 1972.

Liker K. Jeffrey, *The Toyota Way,* Tata McGraw Hill Publishing Company Limited, New Delhi, 2004.

Luthans, Fred, *Organizational Behavior,* Tata McGraw Hill Publishing Company Limited, New Delhi, 1998.

Moetsabi, Titus, *Participatory Approaches for Promoting Rural Connectivity,* [http://www.fao.org/WAICENT/FAOINFO/SUST-DEV/CDdirect/CDre0030.htm], 2000.

Mohanty R.P. and Lakhe R.R., *TQM in the Service Sector,* Jaico Publishing House, Mumbai, 2002.

Norris, Mason & Lefrere, *Transforming e-Knowledge: A Revolution in the Sharing of Knowledge,* Society for College and University Planning, 2003.

OECD, *Citizens as Partners - Information, Consultation and Public Participation in Policy-Making,* 2003.

Osborne, David and Gaebler, Ted, *Reinventing Government,* Addison Wesley Publishing Company Inc., Reading, 1992.

Osterman, Paul, *Impact of IT on Jobs and Skills,* The Corporation of the 1990s – Information Technology and Organizational Transformation. Ed. Michael Scott Morton, Oxford University Press, Oxford, 1991.

Pande Peter S., Neuman Robert P., Gavanagh Roland R., *The Six Sigma Way,* Tata McGraw Hill Publishing Company Limited, New Delhi, 2003.

Pareek, Udai, *Understanding Organizational Behaviour,* Oxford University Press, New York, 2004.

Pearce II Jhon A. and Robinson Richard B. Jr., *Strategic Management,* AITBS, Delhi, 1996.

Peppard Joe and Rowland Philip, *The Essence of Business Process Re-engineering,* Prentice-Hall of India Private Limited, New Delhi, 2002.

Puri Renu and Sharma G. L., *Leveraging Human Potential for Excellence,* Excel Books, New Delhi, 2003.

Richardson, Don, *The Internet and Rural Development: Recommendations for Strategy and Activity,* [http://www.fao.org/WAICENT/FAOINFO/SUSTDEV/CDdirect/CDDO/execsum.htm], November, 2000.

Terry George R. and Franklin Stephen G., *Principles of Management,* AITBS, Delhi, 1994.

The Quality Network Inc., *Business Process Benchmarking,* 1995.

www.development.gateway.org

www.egovdatabase.gov.in

Index

Index

V, W